Secondary
Instructional
Methods

Secondary
Instructional
Methods

Kenneth D. Moore
East Central University

Cheri Quinn
Dickinson College

WCB Brown & Benchmark
PUBLISHERS

Madison, Wisconsin • Dubuque, Iowa

Book Team

Editor *Sue Pulvermacher-Alt*
Production Editor *Gloria G. Schiesl*
Designer *Lu Ann Schrandt*
Art Editor *Joseph P. O'Connell*
Photo Editor *Shirley Lanners*
Visuals/Design Developmental Consultant *Marilyn A. Phelps*
Visuals/Design Freelance Specialist *Mary L. Christianson*
Publishing Services Specialist *Sherry Padden*
Marketing Manager *Steven Yetter*
Advertising Manager *Brett Apold*

WCB Brown & Benchmark

A Division of Wm. C. Brown Communications, Inc.

Executive Vice President/General Manager *Thomas E. Doran*
Vice President/Editor in Chief *Edgar J. Laube*
Vice President/Sales and Marketing *Eric Ziegler*
Director of Production *Vickie Putman Caughron*
Director of Custom and Electronic Publishing *Chris Rogers*

Wm. C. Brown Communications, Inc.

President and Chief Executive Officer *G. Franklin Lewis*
Corporate Senior Vice President and Chief Financial Officer *Robert Chesterman*
Corporate Senior Vice President and President of Manufacturing *Roger Meyer*

Cover Photo © Will & Denise McIntyre/Photo Researchers, Inc.

Part Opener Photos One and Two: © Jean-Claude Lejeune;
Three: © Doug Plummer/Photo Researchers, Inc.;
Four: © Ulrike Welsch/Photo Researchers, Inc.

Copyedited by Mary Davidson Stanton

Interior design by Jeff Storm

Printed in the United States of America by Wm. C. Brown Communications, Inc.,
2460 Kerper Boulevard, Dubuque, IA 52001

10 9 8 7 6 5 4 3 2 1

CONTENTS

PART 2

Preparing for Instruction

Chapter 6

Chapter 7

Chapter 8

Chapter 10

Evaluation and Measurement 258

Chapter 9

Teaching Learning Strategies 234

PREFACE

Secondary Instructional Methods is designed to better prepare students for the complex world of the secondary school classroom. Becoming an effective secondary teacher requires extensive knowledge and skills as well as hard work, commitment, an inquiring mind, and the ability to learn from experiences. The quest for excellence will be difficult, but the satisfaction is worth the effort. This book, therefore, is designed to provide you with the tools for facilitating the quest and the means for achieving excellence.

The first part of the text provides an orientation for teaching in the secondary school. In the first chapter you will find a detailed description of where secondary education is coming from and where it may be going. The second chapter begins with a practical discussion of student development as it relates to the classroom. The final sections of the chapter focus on the art and science of teaching and learning and address the different viewpoints regarding teaching and learning.

The second major part of this book deals with the preparation of instruction for the secondary classroom. It provides comprehensive coverage of planning instruction with a focus on identifying content, writing objectives, writing lesson plans, and selecting instructional strategies. This part includes a pertinent chapter on skills instruction, which stresses the importance of critical thinking and the development of student responsibility as part of the secondary curriculum. Finally, student evaluation and grading are addressed, with various techniques and procedures presented for consideration.

The third part covers the implementation of instruction. The focus is on communication, motivation, reading, and classroom management. The importance of reading and classroom management cannot be overemphasized. Indeed, I view reading ability as central to all instruction in the secondary classroom. Also, a classroom must be well managed if learning is to take place.

The fourth and final part of the text presents an overview of trends in secondary education. It stresses the importance of the continuous upgrading of skills. Finally, teacher preparation and the associated responsibilities of being a professional educator are explored.

I have attempted to describe in detail proven instructional methods, coupled with the best in planning and instructional theory, to prepare preservice secondary teachers for entry into the classroom. I hope the textbook will not only help prospective teachers analyze their own teaching, but provide the means for translating this thinking into effective practice, which will lead to the accomplishment of our society's educational goals. In short, it is my hope that future teachers will find this book valuable as a guide to sound educational practices. This text is intended for use in undergraduate general secondary methods courses, but could be a useful reference for a variety of courses and for inservice teachers.

I have prepared an *Instructor's Manual* (IM) for use with my text. Each chapter of the manual contains: (1) instructional objectives, (2) terms and concepts, (3) outlines, (4) supplementary student activities and discussion questions, (5) supplementary readings, and (6) test items. I hope instructors will find the IM useful in teaching the methods course.

Acknowledgments

I am indeed grateful to the hundreds of students and teachers who provided critical feedback and served as invaluable sources in the preparation of this text. Moreover, I would like to thank the many educators who helped identify the major ideas presented in this textbook. Special gratitude also goes to the school districts who opened their doors to me and offered their support: The Anadarko Public Schools, Anadarko, Oklahoma; The Rush Springs Public Schools, Rush Springs, Oklahoma; The Empire Public Schools, Duncan, Oklahoma; and The Lawton Public Schools, Lawton, Oklahoma.

Many colleagues contributed to this textbook. Chapters 1 and 16 were written in collaboration with Dr. Cheri Quinn; chapter 9, with Susan Bethel; and chapter 12, with Dr. Ruth Loring. Dr. Keith Harrison wrote chapter 6 on instructional media. Finally, I would like to thank Susan Bethel, who is responsible for taking many of the textbook photographs. The textbook is much stronger, due to the innovative ideas and efforts of these talented colleagues.

We wish to acknowledge these reviewers and thank them for their assistance with this edition.

Robert L. Fisher
Illinois State University
Steven K. Million
Winthrop College
Patricia E. Hanley
University of South Florida

Marsha Grace
University of Houston–Victoria
Joseph R. Weaver
Oklahoma Baptist University
Marlene LaCounte
Eastern Montana College
Mack Welford
Roanoke College
Herbert K. Heger
University of Texas–El Paso

I would also like to thank the staff at Brown & Benchmark who helped bring this textbook to life. Linda Harper, who got the project started, deserves special thanks. Paul Tavenner, my editor at Brown & Benchmark, guided the entire process. His leadership and friendship will always be remembered and appreciated.

K.D.M.

PART 1 ▼ ▼ ▼ ▼

Foundations

What is the purpose of secondary education? Careful consideration of this question should be one of the first concerns of a prospective teacher. Part 1 addresses the constantly changing purposes of secondary education. This part also focuses on the general characteristics of adolescence and its associated problems, as well as on the interaction of teaching and learning as it relates to secondary students.

Prospective teachers need to understand teaching and learning in the context of the past and present. Thus, chapter 1 will give some background on where secondary education is coming from and how it has constantly changed its function. On the other hand, because secondary schools are what they teach, prospective teachers need a basic understanding of common secondary programs and the related curriculum. This understanding will often influence the way a subject is taught.

Adolescence can be a period of turmoil, and this turmoil can affect teaching and learning. Chapter 2 will focus on this dynamic. The

different phases of development will be addressed along with related adolescent issues. Finally, chapter 2 will consider the organization for effective teaching, the use of time in the classroom, and the different theories of learning.

1 The Secondary School

✎ **So, you want to teach in the secondary school. But what is a secondary school? What is secondary education? How has the history of secondary schools shaped the organization of secondary schools today? Too little knowledge can be a dangerous thing!**

Overview

The organization of schools varies considerably from community to community. One agreed-upon, "correct" method of organization does not predominate the field of education. From early colonial days, when the Latin grammar school prepared students for entry into the university, to the present system where students pass through several stages of preparation, the nature of the structure of schooling has been one of change. This chapter will explore the development and evolution of the secondary school concept.

An examination of the purposes of secondary education and the competing demands of educators, parents, politicians, students, and the community will set the stage for our study of the methods used in secondary classrooms. Likewise, an investigation of the curriculum and curricular concerns will provide insight into what secondary schools are supposed to do and how competing groups have tried to influence both the process and the products of schooling.

Finally, this textbook schoolhouse is filled with students of varying ages, academic abilities, and developmental levels, to round out a teaching model that will enable you to begin your study of teaching methods for secondary education.

Objectives

After completing your study of chapter 1, you should be able to do the following:

1. Identify the origins of American secondary schools, noting the causes for divergence from European models.

2. Write outlines of four organizational structures of secondary schools in the United States today.

3. Enumerate the competing demands placed on schools and evaluate those demands most likely to be met.

4. Present your view of the control and the purpose(s) of secondary education.

5. Outline the secondary curriculum types and requirements common to typical secondary schools.

6. Explain the purposes of general, exploratory, and career education.

7. Explain the purposes of accreditation agencies and analyze the benefits of accreditation for various constituencies.

8. Propose an alternative to minimum competency testing of students and teachers.

9. Describe the six steps to teaching excellence.

Chapter Terms and Key Concepts

Academies
Accountability
Accreditation
Boston Latin Grammar School
Career Education
Core Curriculum
Curriculum
Dame School
English High School
Exploratory Education
Functionalist
General Education
Junior High School
Latin Grammar School
Magnet School
Massachusetts Act of 1642
Middle School
Minimum Competency Testing
A Nation At Risk
Old Deluder Satan Act
Progressives
Secondary School

T he American public schools are dedicated to the concept of providing an education to all the children and youth of the nation. The **secondary schools**—junior high and senior high—are critical to the achievement of this noble goal. Are they equal to the task? To begin to answer this question, we need a grasp of the evolution and organization of secondary educational structure.

Evolution and Organization

There is no single organizational pattern for secondary schools in the United States. In some communities, the elementary school encompasses kindergarten or first grade through eighth grade, and the secondary school is the high school, which comprises ninth through twelfth grades. In other areas, you will find an elementary school that accommodates students through sixth grade, a junior high school for seventh and eighth grades or for seventh, eighth, and ninth grades, and a high school for ninth or tenth through twelfth grades. Yet other places have an elementary school that ceases at the fourth or fifth grade, a middle school that begins at fifth or sixth grade and ends at seventh or eighth, a junior high that begins at seventh and ends at eighth or ninth grade, and a high school that finishes with whatever grades are left. In still other communities, schools are divided by other means—such as grade-level centers, intermediate high schools (ninth and tenth grades), and magnet schools— embracing a myriad of interests and organizational structures that accommodate a variety of teaching and learning styles.

The organizational structure of our schools appears to be a bit confusing! Is there not one right way to organize secondary education? The answer to this question is a complicated one because the variety of organizational structures for secondary education is as rich as the variety of students served in the secondary schools of this country. Table 1.1 outlines some of the organizational structures found across the United States. This outline is not all-inclusive. Other patterns can also be found.

Early Colonial Education

Colonial American schooling reflected the roots of the colonists with two major societal needs being served: maintenance of Protestant religious beliefs and ensuring social stability. According to Spring (1986), this need to preserve Protestant religious beliefs and maintain the power of established leadership led directly to the public school movement of the nineteenth century.

The early colonial schools were part of the Puritans' efforts to provide a religious community that would serve as a model for the rest of the world. To this end, Massachusetts in 1642 passed the first law intended to address the need for educating children. This statute, called the **Massachusetts Act,** required parents to teach their children to read the Scriptures and the capital laws of the land. The law was a direct result of the Reformation belief that people needed direct access to the Scriptures—access attained only through the ability to read. In effect, it was believed that

TABLE *1.1*   Organizational Structures of Schooling

Grades	Level
K to 8*	Elementary
9 to 12	Secondary (high school)
K to 6*	Elementary
7 to 8 or 7 to 9	Secondary (junior high school)
9 to 12 or 10 to 12	Secondary (high school)
K to 4* or K to 5*	Elementary
5 to 8 or 6 to 8	Transitional (middle school)
9 to 12 or 10 to 12	Secondary (high school)

*For purposes of illustration, consider kindergarten as a regular part of the elementary school. Several states do not require kindergarten.

Satan would prevent people from understanding the Scriptures unless the Scriptures were read directly. The Massachusetts Act was strengthened further in 1647 by passage of the famous **Old Deluder Satan Act.** The law stipulated that every town of 50 or more families pay a person to teach reading and writing. These schools, known as town schools, set a precedent: that the community or government was responsible for educating the children when parents were not capable of doing so (Reed & Bergemann, 1992).

The Massachusetts Act also required that adults to whom children were apprenticed teach the children a trade and reading skills so that a pauper class, so prevalent in England at the time, did not develop. By 1650, Connecticut had adopted a law similar to Massachusetts. Rhode Island's laws in 1655 were similar but made no reference to apprenticeship (Rich, 1992).

The town-school system thrived and met colonial needs as long as people lived close to one another and villages remained compact. As settlers dispersed in search of more and better land, however, the town schools were replaced with the so-called moving-school system. The moving-school system consisted of a schoolmaster who traveled from village to village, holding school at each site for several months before moving on. Understandably, this system proved inadequate, and soon the district school system began to develop. In this scheme, a township was divided into districts, with each district having its own school and schoolmaster. Because each district was independently financed by its own town, this system proved fairly inexpensive and afforded some measure of schooling for all children.

The quality, quantity, and availability of schooling varied greatly during the colonial era. Children attended reading and writing schools, with instruction occurring in homes, churches, and schools. Sons of the elite typically attended a reading and writing school called a **dame school,** often conducted in the teacher's home. These schools were open to boys and girls and were often the only schooling that girls received. Generally, girls could only use the school building and receive schooling when boys were not using the school building. Girls had little access to schooling until after the Revolution.

The teaching materials in the early colonial schools included the Bible and, late in the seventeenth century, *The New England Primer*. Children entered school around the age of 6 or 7 and remained for only three or four years. Religious and moral instruction were the curricular vehicles for teaching religion and moral values in keeping with community expectations. Many children received only enough instruction to ensure that they gained salvation and obeyed the laws of the colony. The learning atmosphere was repressive and grim. Students kept quiet and did their work, which emphasized memorization. Group instruction and recitation were generally nonexistent.

Early Secondary Education

In 1635, the forerunner to the secondary school was established in Boston. This school, the **Boston Latin Grammar School,** was intended to prepare young men to attend college. Indeed, these early secondary institutions came to be known as college preparatory schools—with the term *prep school* still carrying this classical connotation today. These schools were public and open to all social classes. The Old Deluder Satan Act of 1647 also required communities of 100 or more families to establish Latin schools. By 1700, there were 26 such schools throughout New England. However, enrollment was small and often limited to the upper class.

The curriculum of the **Latin grammar school** was quite limited. The courses to be mastered, which comprised Latin and other classical subjects, reflected the post-Renaissance belief that knowledge of the classical Greek and Roman works produced an educated person. Boys entered the Latin grammar school around age 7 or 8 and spent seven years studying Latin. The limited choice of classes posed no problem for young men in the colonial era: The only college in existence at the time was Harvard, and admission was based on the ability to write, read, speak, and understand Latin. Young men from the privileged class were expected to receive a higher education that would prepare them for the ministry or political leadership.

The demand for practical instruction in everything from navigation and engineering to bookkeeping and foreign languages led to the development of private English grammar schools in the 1700s. Classes were offered at various places and times with commercial subjects, rather than religious ones, being taught. The private English grammar schools were more flexible than Latin grammar schools and commonly accepted female students.

Looking back at the notion that one of the purposes of colonial education was to maintain social stability, it is easy to see why the idea of using education as the agent of social change developed. Indeed, the concept of educating all young people to assume productive places in a rapidly changing society began to be a focus of American education.

Changing Focus

In 1751, Benjamin Franklin established an academy in Philadelphia. Franklin's academy was a uniquely American institution. With the fomentation of the American Revolution and the increased emphasis on commerce and trade came the need for a school that prepared better-trained workers. This need was filled by Franklin's academy. The curriculum, far different than that of the Latin grammar schools, introduced practical subjects. In effect, through the creation of separate Latin and English departments, Franklin's academy attempted to combine the ideas behind the Latin and English grammar schools into one school. English, arithmetic, writing, the sciences, commercial subjects, navigation, and surveying were included in the curriculum along with the traditional Latin and Greek. Two important purposes were served by the establishment of Franklin's Academy and the **academies** that were modeled after it: First, they provided a utilitarian education, and second, they promoted the culturization (inculcation of the dominant groups' cultural norms) necessary for entry into mainstream American life. Academies were private and required the payment of tuition; however, unlike the grammar schools, girls and children of the aspiring poor were allowed to attend.

A third type of secondary school, the English Classical School, was established in Boston in 1821. The curriculum was styled after the academies, offering a practical education. The school changed its name to the **English High School** in 1824, and another uniquely American innovation was launched. The English High School is commonly referred to as the first American public high school and was designed to teach boys the knowledge needed to become merchants and mechanics. Parents were pleased that they now had a choice of how their sons would be educated. A separate high school for girls was established in 1826, but it was closed two years later because of the high demand for service—that is, because it was public-supported, the mayor of Boston was afraid it would bankrupt the city if service was provided to all the girls wishing to attend.

Public support for high schools was affirmed with the Massachusetts Law of 1827. This law, an extension of the 1647 Massachusetts law (the Old Deluder Satan Act), required that a high school be established in all communities with 500 or more families and that Latin and Greek be offered in districts of 4,000 or more. Several additional states soon followed the lead of Massachusetts, and by 1860 public high schools had spread to many cities across the nation.

The first **junior high school** to receive national attention was established in Berkeley, California, in 1909. The junior high school in Berkeley received much attention because it embraced a model of strict departmentalization of disciplines in preparation for high school. Intermediate schools that included seventh and eighth grades had been established in New York City in 1905, and by 1915, ninth grade had been added to these schools (Spring, 1986).

Research in the field of developmental psychology suggesting that certain types of environments were better suited for early-adolescent learners prompted the establishment of junior high schools early in the twentieth century. These junior high schools, which served several purposes, provided vocational training, an earlier differentiated curriculum that tended to be gender-specific, preparation for high school, and earlier ability-grouping. Another task of the junior high school was to foster socialization—accomplished primarily through clubs and athletic teams. The early emphasis on tracking and vocational guidance gave way to vocational exploration and prevocational guidance by the 1920s and became the accepted model for junior high schools.

The advent of the **middle school** is a much more recent phenomenon and once again represents a uniquely American innovation. The middle school movement, begun in the 1950s, is a philosophical position rather than simply a grade-level structure. The patterns of grade levels encompassed by the middle schools identified early in this chapter attest to the philosophical nature of the movement. Middle schools are not lower-level junior high schools or high schools. They are student-centered and typically include some form of team teaching and individualized instruction. The rationale behind the growth of middle schools lies not only in the belief that these grade groupings provide a closer developmental match among children, but is coupled with a philosophical underpinning that recognizes the needs of early adolescents.

The focus of middle school teaching is to proceed from mastery of knowledge to utilization of knowledge (Wiles & Bondi, 1993). Subject specialists, who are trained as secondary teachers, are employed alongside subject generalists, or those trained as elementary teachers, on the assumption that a healthy balance will be struck between the structure of the disciplines and the need to teach the whole child.

The middle school is probably best classified as a transitional level of education—neither elementary nor secondary in philosophy, structure, or operation. Wiles and Bondi (1993) report that the middle school movement has moved into the organizational mainstream and likely will continue to dominate intermediate education as we prepare for the twenty-first century. Moreover, some middle school advocates believe that the junior high school as a grade-level entity will disappear completely by the end of the twentieth century.

Middle school organizations focus on the use of teacher-adviser programs, provide transition and articulation activities, use interdisciplinary teaching and block schedules, and provide staff-development activities for refining an extended range of teaching strategies appropriate to middle school–age students (Cawelti, 1988; Jacobs, 1989; Connors and Irvin, 1989). Clearly, commonly used secondary school teaching strategies will need extensive modification to be appropriate for use at the middle school level. Wiles and Bondi suggest that team teaching with an emphasis on activity-oriented interdisciplinary units, rather than traditional secondary teaching, should be the focus of instruction at the middle school level. For this reason, middle school instructional methods will not be the focus of this book.

Current Trends in Secondary Education

Since the early 1980s, several groups have studied the nation's secondary schools and found them wanting. In 1983, with the publication of *A Nation At Risk: The Imperative for Educational Reform* (National Commission on Excellence in Education, 1983), a great national debate began on how to improve the nation's schools. Indeed, education even became a major campaign issue in the presidential election of 1984, and it has remained a salient political issue ever since.

A Nation At Risk was probably the most widely read and best-known report on the state of education in the United States. The report claimed that "if an unfriendly foreign power had attempted to impose on America the mediocre educational performance that exists today, we might well have viewed it as an act of war." The report cited problems with a high rate of illiteracy among 17-year-olds and minority youths, a drop in SAT scores, and the need for colleges and businesses to offer courses in remedial reading, writing, and computation. The report further called for more academic course requirements for all high school students, more stringent college entrance requirements, upgraded and updated textbooks, longer school days and years, and a career-ladder plan for teachers.

High School: A Report on Secondary Education in America, a book written by Ernest L. Boyer and published in 1983, made recommendations for reorganizing the secondary school curriculum, for improving the quality of secondary school teachers, and modifying administrative arrangements. It also addressed the issue of recruitment and retention of talented people in the field of teaching.

In 1984, Theodore R. Sizer's *Horace's Compromise: The Dilemma of American High Schools* was published. Sizer addressed the constraints schools place on teacher behavior and said that teachers should be provided working conditions that allow them to better help individual students. Suggesting that the goal of education should be the development of students' thinking skills, Sizer recommended that educators address *depth* rather than breadth of content. He proposed that schools be organized into small administrative units, with emphasis placed on inquiry and expression, mathematics and science, literature and the arts, and philosophy and history. Moreover, he believed, teachers should be responsible for working with no more than 80 students.

In late 1987, William Bennett, former secretary of the U.S. Department of Education, advocated a high school curriculum—described in his *James Madison High*—in which a student would complete a program in seven core areas:

4 years of English
3 years of science
3 years of mathematics
3 years of social studies
2 years of foreign languages
2 years of physical education/health
1 semester of art
1 semester of music/fine arts

TABLE *1.2* Milestones in Secondary Education

Milestone	Time	Description
Boston Latin Grammar School	1635	Emphasized Latin and classical studies; designed to prepare young men for college
Massachusetts Act of 1642	1642	Required each town to determine whether its young people could read or write
Old Deluder Satan Act	1647	Required that towns of 50 or more families establish town schools and that communities of 100 or more families establish Latin schools
English Grammar Schools	Eighteenth century	Private secondary schools designed to provide practical rather than college-preparatory studies
Academies	Eighteenth and nineteenth centuries	Private secondary schools designed to prepare young people for business and life; emphasized a practical curriculum, but gradually shifted back to college preparation
English Classical or High Schools	1821 to present	Provided public secondary schooling; combined functions of Latin grammar schools and academies (college preparation and preparation for life and business)
Massachusetts Law of 1827	1827	Required communities of 500 or more families to establish a high school
Junior High Schools	1909 to present	Designed to provide students in grades 7 to 9 with better preparation for high school
Middle Schools	1950 to present	Designed to meet the unique needs of preadolescents, usually grades 6 to 8; an alternative to junior high schools
A Nation At Risk	1983	Widely read and best-known report on state of education in the United States
America 2000	1990 to 1991	Goals and an agenda proposed by President George Bush for reforming the nation's schools

Bennett's proposed "Madison High School" focused primarily on academics. Indeed, some people argued that the program was *too* academic and that it was directed toward college-bound students (Voreacas, 1987).

The call to reform schools continues in the 1990s. Indeed, a new educational agenda (see chapter 16) to be achieved by the year 2000 was established by the Bush administration early in the 1990s (Reed and Bergemann, 1992). Movement in the areas of school restructuring and teacher preparation and empowerment is currently underway. These trends more than likely will continue throughout the 1990s.

This concludes our brief look at the evolution of secondary schools to their present-day form. Table 1.2 gives an overview of this evolution.

Modern Secondary Education

Secondary schools today are an amalgam of the various forces and trends that preceded their formation. The vast majority of high schools could be classified as comprehensive—providing courses of study for college-bound, business, or vocational students and for those students with an interest in the fine arts. In rural and other areas, high schools offer home economics, earth science, and agricultural courses along with the traditional core curriculum. In some urban areas, high schools gear instruction to students with particular interests. These **magnet schools** may specialize in the performing arts or in higher mathematics and sciences, or they may adopt a particular philosophy as the guiding principle for course offerings.

As reported earlier, the junior high school—traditionally designed for grades 7 and 8 or for grades 7, 8, and 9—have begun to give way to the middle school, which usually encompasses grades 6, 7, and 8. Junior high schools tend to be organized in much the same way as senior high schools, with students moving from one teacher and one subject to another after each 45- or 50-minute period. The teaching staffs are trained subject-area specialists, and the emphasis—like in the high school—is competitive. Students are often tracked by ability levels, and the curriculum usually parallels the tracking system used in the high school. While tracking does exist at the junior high level, it tends to be less rigid than tracking in the high school. Junior high activities also parallel those of the high school, with special interest clubs and competitive sports serving as the training ground for future high school athletes and student leaders.

Control of Schools

The United States educational systems, both public and nonpublic, are governed by law. Although the Constitution does not provide specifically for public education, the Tenth Amendment has been interpreted as giving individual states power over education. Therefore, education is legally the responsibility and function of each of the 50 states.

State legislatures generally are responsible for creating, operating, managing, and maintaining the state school system. They make decisions regarding tax structure, school financing, pupil conduct and control, certification standards, teacher rights, programs of study, and standards of building construction.

Local school boards attend to the basic day-to-day operation of schools and ensure that pupils are educated within the constraints set by the state. In effect, the local boards obtain revenue for the schools, maintain schools, purchase school sites and build buildings, organize materials and supplies, organize and provide programs of study, admit and assign students to schools, and employ necessary workers and regulate their services.

Of course, the ultimate control of schools lies in the hands of the people. Through the power of their vote, citizens can influence legislatures and boards of education to support—or not support—various bills and issues. These legislatures and boards often are strongly influenced by special interest groups as well.

Expectations and Standards

Secondary schools are organized around a set of expectations regarding the purposes of education. A brief glance at history reveals that notions about what purposes secondary schools should serve have varied along with economic, social, and political realignments. For example, when non-English speaking, non-Protestant immigrants flooded into the country in the nineteenth century, the schools took up the banner of "culturization." When the perception that the Soviet Union was outdistancing the United States in the space race with the launch of Sputnik in 1957, the schools, with the financial support of the federal government, placed renewed emphasis on science and mathematics.

Likewise, standards for performance have changed as expectations about what exactly secondary education should *do* has changed. One unresolved problem of schools, particularly secondary schools, is how to provide equal educational opportunity while assuring the public that a high-quality education is being provided. Since the 1954 *Brown* v. *Topeka Board of Education* ruling, which mandated equal educational opportunities for children of color and dictated that this equity could only be accomplished in integrated schools, there has been an ongoing debate about how the schools can provide both quality and equity to a diverse student population. Factor into this equation legislation of the 1970s that mandated equal opportunities for children with handicapping conditions (again to take place in an integrated setting), and you can begin to appreciate the competing expectations and demands with which schools and teachers must contend. Most recently, state legislatures across the country have begun to mandate some kind of AIDS education—a direct reaction to the spread of AIDS in the United States.

The public has sought, even demanded, that schools focus on the needs of more and more groups of young people. In addition, the public has demanded that schools include coursework that addresses health, economic, and societal issues as well as the "basics." Funding for these needs has been sporadic and inadequate, yet the public has also demanded accountability for student performance, particularly in the area of basic skill acquisition.

The attempt to control quality in the public secondary schools and ensure some form of standardization has resulted in an accrediting process that mandates review at the state level and rewards approval at the regional level. All states require periodic review of programs for accreditation. A few states have used this process to declare some schools "educationally bankrupt" and have assumed control of the schools. Often, students who wish to attend more prestigious institutions of higher education must attend regionally accredited schools. Moreover, school choice plans (where students choose the high school they attend) are likely to increase the demand for careful scrutiny of school programs as parents "shop" for schools for their children.

Purposes of Secondary Education

Like the organization and structure of secondary education, the purposes of secondary education have evolved with the changing social, economic, and political needs of the country. In the colonial era, as stated earlier, the primary purpose of secondary education was to prepare young men of privilege for the ministry or for governmental service. For the masses, the ability to read was considered an adequate education to assure societal continuity and adherence to legal and religious dictates.

The advent of the academies and later the English High School marked the beginning of an educational experience designed to prepare better workers and "Americanize" recent immigrants. Built into these systems was the desire to prepare young people for the marketplace and to produce good citizens for an infant democracy. It was during this period that the educational enterprise and the preservation of the nation became permanently linked.

By 1890, the secondary schools were promoting the notion that an academic emphasis was important for all young people, regardless of their intended career paths. Post–Civil War industrialization, urbanization, access to inexpensive newspapers, the growth of railroads, and a new wave of immigration all contributed to the realization of the potential of public schools as agents of social change. Immigrants from Eastern Europe needed to be Americanized if they were to be included in the social mobility that defined the American dream. The National Education Association's Committee of Ten—chaired by Charles W. Elliot, then president of Harvard University—recommended an academic curriculum for all students and strongly opposed the rigid tracking systems that were widespread in Europe. The secondary schools of Europe segregated academic-oriented students from those who would not go beyond a high school education; the limits to schooling were set relatively early in a student's career. The European rigid tracking systems were believed to be counterproductive in an American society that sought to assimilate large numbers of immigrants and meet the needs of a growing industrial economy. A common educational experience would better provide the opportunity to forge a common social link.

In the period from the beginning of World War I to 1940, yet other ideas about what secondary schools ought to do emerged. Two opposing views of what schooling ought to be about competed for dominance. On one side of the debate was John Dewey and others, known as **Progressives,** who believed that schooling should be child-centered and instruction project-oriented. Opposing this view were critics who argued that the Progressive approach sacrificed important social learning in its quest to promote individual development. These critics, who were called **Functionalists,** believed that the curriculum of the secondary school ought to serve the purposes of the larger society by preparing young people to assume their roles in adult society. In many ways, this debate still rages. The middle school movement embodies many of Dewey's beliefs—for example, emphasizing the education of the whole child in a supportive, exploratory atmosphere that stresses individual learning. On the other hand, the social learning important to Dewey's critics is also incorporated into the middle school concept through team teaching and innovative grouping for instruction. Likewise, the deemphasis on competitive sports and the tendency in the middle school toward a core curriculum that provides equal learning opportunities for all children would also satisfy the functionalist group.

A 1918 report commissioned by the National Education Association set the tone for secondary education goals in this era. This report, *Cardinal Principles of Secondary Education,* was undergirded by the belief that secondary education should be guided by "the needs of the society to be served, the character of the individuals to be educated, and the knowledge of educational theory and practice available" (p. 7). According to this report the major function of secondary schools was to provide a democratic education. The seven cardinal principles were health, command of fundamental processes, worthy home membership, vocation, citizenship, worthy use of leisure time, and ethical character. One example of how the Cardinal Principles guided curriculum in the early twentieth century and how they have continued to exert influence today is the requirment that all students at the secondary level take a course in American government. Today, the expectation that an American government course can promote good citizenship prevails, and it is also possible to trace the inclusion of health and physical education courses to the parameters of the Cardinal Principles.

From the time of the United States' entry into World War II until 1956, education was characterized by society's desire to maintain the status quo. Conformity was the rallying cry of this era. Years of instability, fostered by the two world wars and the Great Depression of the 1930s, made people long for a sense of normalcy. It was during this period that suburban expansion became popular. Adhering to societal norms and maintaining the existing social order was best served by rigidly tracking students and emphasizing functional outcomes. Rather than a concern for how learning is affected by sex roles, socioeconomic status, and minority group membership, the emphasis was on traditional values. The tracking system was largely segregated by gender, socioeconomic status, and race (in the relatively few schools that were racially integrated).

The launch of Sputnik in 1957 convinced the American people that schools, particularly secondary schools, were not doing a good job of preparing young people to contribute to the economic, social, and political well-being of the country. A shift in purpose predictably followed. The federal government funneled large sums of money, primarily through the National Science Foundation, into the effort of improving the quality of secondary education. More emphasis was placed on the academic disciplines, particularly mathematics and science.

By 1968, in the midst of domestic unrest and bitter divisions over American involvement in the Vietnam conflict, the emphasis of secondary schools once again was redefined. At this juncture it was believed by many that the schools had failed to address the individual needs of young people. The response to this criticism was a wave of renewed efforts to create alternatives to the traditional ways of organizing schools. The smorgasbord of curricular offerings reflected the confusion and apprehension of society at large. African-American studies, women's studies, the peace curriculum, and the environmental curriculum were all reactions to societal concerns. Once again student-centered learning was emphasized, and the ideas of John Dewey were revived. The processes of educational delivery were also

examined. Schools emphasized one process over another, with one school taking a humanistic approach, while another chose a more traditional functionalist approach.

Today, most people view academics as the central reason for secondary school existence. As they see it, students go to school to learn subjects—that is, to learn information and develop their intellects. This viewpoint is reflected in how secondary schools are organized. School days are divided by subjects—algebra I, English I, physics, government, Spanish II, music, world history, speech, and computer science.

Academic achievement is not the only function of secondary schools today. They are also expected to train students for jobs. But how this can be accomplished in today's world is a matter of debate. The debate centers around whether students should be prepared for specific jobs rather than for a wide variety of occupations. For example, should a high school student be trained to use computers in his or her senior year, or would class time be better spent on mathematics and computer science? Or, should a person who is weak in reading and writing be provided with vocational training?

For many students, the primary purpose of high school is college preparation. Nationally, approximately 50 percent of high school students pursue further education. Thus, secondary schools must prepare students for more schooling, which in turn will prepare them for jobs.

Finally, secondary school must prepare some students for uncertain futures. These students do not want to focus on career goals in high school but may decide to do so at a later date. Therefore, they must be prepared for possible future study.

Because of the diversity in the kinds of students secondary schools must accommodate, students usually follow discernible subject paths or tracks according to their assessed ability or aspirations. These paths or tracks (with years required for study) commonly include the following:

Vocational Studies
English/language arts (4 years)
General mathematics (1 year)
Science (1 or 2 years)
Social studies (2 or 3 years)
Health/physical education (3 or 4 years)
Data processing
Selective vocational electives

College Preparatory Studies
English/language arts (4 years)
Mathematics (2 or 3 years)
Science (2 or 3 years)
Social studies (2 or 3 years)
Foreign language (2 years)
Health/physical education (3 or 4 years)
Computer science
Electives

General Studies
English/language arts (4 years)
General mathematics (1 or 2 years)
Science (1 or 2 years)
Social studies (2 or 3 years)
Foriegn language (elective)
Computer science (elective)
Health/ physical education (3 or 4 years)
Electives

Schools today are more than just places to learn. Since about 1975 there has been a return to the more traditional view of the mission of secondary schools. Schools once again have assumed responsibility for transmission of the culture as well as for training students to be viable members in a technological workplace. Academic rigor and careful monitoring of outcomes characterize the secondary school experience today. As noted earlier, the National Commission on Excellence in Education warned in *A Nation At Risk: The Imperative for Educational Reform* of the serious peril to national defense and economic prosperity posed by the decline in quality of education. The 1983 report suggested that the public schools, particularly secondary schools, were responsible for jeopardizing U.S. stability and world economic and military position by failing to prepare the nation's youth for future leadership roles. The report was widely publicized and embraced by the nation, and state legislatures and local school districts responded with a spate of reform efforts and subsequent reports. The continuous call was for more rigorous curricula, careful monitoring of progress, and increased admissions standards for college.

TABLE *1.3*   Purposes of Secondary Education

Period	New Schools	Targeted Population	Purposes
Early Colonial	Latin grammar schools	Privileged boys	Educate for the ministry and public service
Late Colonial Early American	Academies English High Schools	All classes of boys and girls Immigrant children	Train better workers and assimilate recent immigrants into a democratic society with free-market economy
1890 to 1916	High schools Junior highs	Adolescents Young adolescents	Academic emphasis Recognition of differing needs of young adolescents Culturalize new immigrants
1917 to 1940	High schools Junior highs	Adolescents Young adolescents	Competing views a. Focus on individuals b. Prepare for adult world
1941 to 1956	High schools Junior highs	Adolescents Young adolescents	Conformity to societal goals
1957 to 1974	Middle schools Magnet schools	Transitional adolescents Children with special interests and talents	Emphasis on academics until 1967 Emphasis on the individual until 1975
1975 to present	Grade centers	Homogeneous age groups	Back to basics, reform, accountability, core curriculum

Once again, the goals of education appear to be to maintain the status quo, ensure economic prosperity, and assimilate the latest wave of immigrants. Getting "back to the basics" and accountability are the concepts currently in vogue in secondary education.

The function and purposes of secondary education continuously change. However, the more they change the more they stay the same. Table 1.3 offers a summary of these changing purposes.

This completes our brief overview of the evolution and organization of secondary schools. Review table 1.3 and the Purposes of Secondary Education Application Guidelines, and complete exercise 1.1, which will test your understanding of the evolution and organization of secondary schools and how exceptions and standards have changed over time.

Curricular Imperatives and Successful Teaching

Secondary schools are similar in many respects, but they also vary in some important ways. The curriculum, student body, and teaching strategies of a secondary school will reflect the values, attitudes, beliefs, and goals of the community in which it exists. If we define the **curriculum** as all the

Application Guidelines ▼

Application of Knowledge

Exercise 1.1   Purposes of Secondary Education

Test yourself on the following secondary education concepts. Appropriate responses can be found in appendix A.

1. Almost all elementary schools encompass grades kindergarten through eighth grade, while secondary schools encompass ninth through twelfth grades. (True/False)

2. The Latin grammar schools were established to prepare young men for _____ and _____ .

3. Academies like the one established by Benjamin Franklin in Philadelphia, junior high schools, and middle schools are all American innovations. (True/False)

4. The most widely read and best-known report on the status of American education was _____ .

5. The two opposing views as to what schools ought to do that emerged from the beginning of World War I to 1940 were _____ and _____ .

6. The present-day view of the four primary purposes of schools appear to be _____ , _____ , _____ , and _____ .

learning—intended and unintended—that takes place under the sponsorship of the school, then we have set the stage for a broad interpretation of curriculum and of schooling.

Program Requirements

Embedded in the curriculum requirements of secondary education are three broad academic components: general education, exploratory education, and education for a career. Their placement within the secondary curriculum will depend on such factors as instructional strategies, psychology of learning, and various administrative arrangements.

Junior high schools give students the opportunity to explore a variety of specialized subjects.

General Education

General education is the broad academic area that focuses on "common learning," or developing basic skills. Its primary purpose is to help students become knowledgeable, participating citizens and well-adjusted individuals. Essentially, students are expected to acquire thinking skills and methods for the application of knowledge.

General education usually encompasses the humanities, social sciences, and natural sciences. Learners are expected to develop those skills that are needed to function as an adult in society. Recent alarm at declining test scores has prompted a renewed emphasis on general education and greater accountability from teachers.

Exploratory Education

Exploratory education is a primary focus of the junior high school. It is organized and structured to introduce students, on a limited basis, to a variety of specialized subjects. Students are encouraged to weigh their exploratory experiences in making career-oriented decisions that can be pursued in high school and beyond.

Junior high students generally take courses organized into blocks and taught by specialists. For example, students may be required to complete language arts blocks or social studies blocks. Through such block programs, junior high students are gradually introduced to the departmentalized, subject-centered senior high school.

Career Education

The senior high school provides the structured program that prepares the student for a career. Essentially, with the **career education,** the high school takes the general education and introductions to exploratory education and integrates them into a program leading to career choices. As noted earlier, the senior high school will prepare many students for advanced or specialized education; however, it will mark the end of formal education for some. Therefore, the senior high school curriculum should be designed to satisfy the needs of all students.

The basic senior high school program generally requires of all students a **core curriculum** of approximately seven to nine units of coursework and about seven to nine units of elective coursework. In light of the national concern regarding the quality of education, however, many states are increasing the core requirements for students. For example, many states now require four units of English instead of three, two or three units of mathematics instead of one, and two or three units of science instead of one.

State and Regional Accreditation

Accreditation of secondary schools by state governmental agencies and independent regional agencies serves three major purposes. First, at the state level, accrediting assures a minimum standard of uniformity. Second, at the regional level, accrediting ensures a uniform standard of quality and **accountability** among similar schools. Third, regional accreditation lends credibility to a secondary school's curricular programs.

Most states require accreditation by a state agency for a school to continue receiving state funding and to remain open. At the state level, the concern is for a program that includes all the state required courses necessary for graduation. Moreover, many states demand certain levels of student performance on standardized tests in order for the school to retain accreditation. Publishing the average scores on standardized tests of achievement for each school district in a state has become common. In fact, as noted earlier, several states have set acceptable district achievement levels: If a school district fails to attain this level, it may be declared "educationally bankrupt" and be taken over by the state or closed.

Regional accrediting agencies examine the programs of both colleges and secondary schools. Regional accreditation of elementary school programs is also becoming increasingly common. Uniformity of quality and accountability are important to the regional agencies, because they are charged with providing the link between secondary school preparation and eligibility for admission to institutions of higher education. Many institutions of higher education require graduation from a regionally accredited high school in order to be eligible for admission. With school-choice plans becoming more prevalent, the issue of accreditation becomes even more important.

Students

Students are the intended audience for the curriculum. Therefore, you must have some general information about the nature of the secondary students that you will be teaching. We will deal with problems associated with adolescence (apathy, delinquency, drug and alcohol use, working adolescents, pregnancy, and emotional disorders) and student development in greater detail in the next chapter; however, this brief glimpse will acquaint you with some of the social and emotional baggage with which your students may arrive in class.

Secondary students do not look like they did twenty or thirty years ago, and the differences are not only the result of changes in dress and hair styles. By the year 2000, one-third of all children in schools will be nonwhite (Carnegie Task Force on Teaching as a Profession, 1986). Birth rates are much higher among minority populations than among whites. Moreover, the need to assimilate newly arrived immigrants into American culture is still an important part of the schooling process. But the faces of immigrant youth are no longer European faces. They are the faces of Asians and Hispanics. A large percentage of the Asians are from Southeast Asia, and a large percentage of the Hispanics are from Latin America. As a result of this new influx of immigrants, more foreign languages are being spoken in schools than ever before—and study of these languages has yet to become a part of the formal curriculum.

The traditional family with father, mother, and two children is almost nonexistent today. In fact, only 4 percent of American families fit this model. One in four children live in poverty, with the vast majority being supported by one parent. Women head 90 percent of these families, and 60 percent have an annual income of less than $10,000. More than half of today's mothers work outside the home. The teenage pregnancy rate is higher than ever before in history, with 14 percent of all births by girls under the age of 20. Minority children are much more likely than white children to live in poverty. The growing drug problem in this country has had a profound effect on the ability of some young people to learn. Moreover, the babies of drug-addicted mothers, many of them teenagers, are beginning to enter the public school systems (Sex and Schools, 1986; Reed & Bergemann, 1992, chapter 12).

Many young people are "at risk" of dropping out of school. The dropout rate in U.S. schools has become a manifest social problem. It is estimated that 25 percent (approximately 700,000) of the high school students drop out of school (Becker, 1989). A 1989 report by The National Center for Education Statistics gave the following breakdown of dropout rates: American Indian and Alaska Natives, 42.0 percent; Hispanic Americans, 39.9 percent; Black Americans, 24.7 percent; Whites, 14.3 percent; and Asians and Pacific Islanders, 9.6 percent. "At risk" students tend to lag behind in basic reading, language arts, and mathematics skills; to have behavior problems; get low grades; perform below grade level; are older than other students at their grade level because of previous retention; and are often children of dropouts. Single-parent families account for a significant number of student dropouts. Males tend to drop out more than females. Males often drop out to get a job, while the major reason females drop out is early pregnancy.

Young people from disadvantaged backgrounds need educational services that rethink the purposes of schooling, because these students are at risk of dropping out of high school and remaining in poverty. Teachers need to watch for early signs of at-risk students and seek help before the students drop out of school. In *Dealing With the Dropout Problem* (1990),

N. L. Gage details programs that combat the dropout trend, such as vocational programs that remove at-risk students from the traditional school settings—placing them in new environments that allow them to apply academic learning to real-life situations. Teachers will be required to plan very carefully to meet the needs of such a diverse student population. Failure to recognize and address the needs of these students could give rise to a large portion of the future adult population that cannot participate successfully in this country's marketplace.

Student Performance

No longer does policy permit students to be promoted solely on the basis of completing a particular grade with acceptable grades—even though some teachers continue to do so. An increasing number of states have instituted programs that call for testing at certain grades to determine whether students should continue to the next grade. One issue that has received considerable attention is the increased use of **minimum competency tests** to award diplomas of graduation. At issue is whether or not such tests are accurate measures of the scope of knowledge and ideas learned in school. For those who fail to pass the tests, there is usually a certificate of attendance awarded. Many believe this practice will have a chilling effect on minority students and students with special needs.

A Model of Teaching

Good teaching requires that you make a constant series of professional decisions that affect the probability that students will learn. Thus, good teaching is a multifaceted quest to help students achieve mastery of a subject. Basically, this quest is a six-step cyclic process. The six sequential steps in a model of effective teaching are listed here:

1. Diagnose the learning situation.

2. Plan the course.

3. Plan the instruction.

4. Guide learning activities.

5. Evaluate learning.

6. Follow-up.

This sequential teaching process is illustrated in figure 1.1.

Step 1 involves selecting the curriculum to be taught. This selection process is based on needs: students, society, and subject. Essentially you must diagnose the situation to find out what students already know. You may want to strengthen some areas and reteach some concepts.

Once the situation has been diagnosed, step 2 is to plan and outline exactly what will be taught in the course. That is, you identify the curriculum areas to be addressed and the amount of time allotted to the areas outlined.

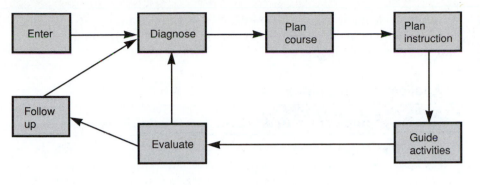

Figure 1.1 *A Model of Teaching. The model is both sequential and cyclic in nature.*

TABLE *1.4*	Curricular Imperatives
Concept	**Description**
General Education	Broad area of school coursework that focuses on developing basic skills and helps students become participating citizens and well-adjusted individuals
Exploratory Education	Primary focus of the junior high schools, where experiences are designed to help students make career-oriented decisions to be pursued in high school
Career Education	Program designed to integrate general education and introductions to exploratory education
Accreditation	Procedures used to verify program and course quality and uniformity as well as to ensure accountability among similar schools

In step 3, unit and daily plans are developed. In other words, you decide exactly what students should know and plan the activities that will bring the desired results. Essentially, objectives are written and the instructional strategy is selected.

Step 4 involves teaching the planned activities. You guide the students through the planned sequence of activities using your knowledge of students, learning theory, and effective teaching techniques.

In step 5, you determine whether you have accomplished the instructional intent; that is, you must evaluate students' mastery of the specifics taught. The results of the evaluation tell you what to do next. If students show mastery, you start the next planning cycle (step 1). If mastery is not demonstrated, follow-up will be needed.

The follow-up (step 6) can be a relatively brief summary of the material covered, while at other times extensive reteaching may be necessary. The extent of your follow-up will depend on the findings of the evaluation analysis.

As you can see, achieving teaching excellence is a major undertaking. The remaining steps in the model of good teaching will be highlighted in subsequent chapters.

Table 1.4 outlines the curricular issues of this section. Review the concepts in table 1.4 and the Curricular Imperatives and Successful Teaching

Application Guidelines, and complete exercise 1.2 to test your understanding of the ideas presented in this section on curriculum, students, and successful teaching.

Application Guidelines ▼

Curricular Imperatives and Successful Teaching

Design the Curriculum to Fit Students

Examples:
1. Examine the background and family life of your students.
2. Critique your curriculum with respect to your aims and goals for students.
3. Analyze the achievement scores of students in detail, noting strengths and weaknesses.

Develop Good Teaching Skills

Examples:
1. Plan well.
2. Follow proven methods of teaching.
3. Always follow up on teaching.

Application of Knowledge

Exercise 1.2   Curricular Imperatives and Successful Teaching

Test yourself on the following curricular imperatives and successful teaching issues. Appropriate responses can be found in appendix A.

1. The primary purpose of general education is the development of common learning. (True/False)

2. Match the definition on the left with the term on the right.
   - *a.* _____ Prepares students for a career
   - *b.* _____ Focus on developing basic skills
   - *c.* _____ Focuses on introduction to a variety of specialized subjects

   1. General education
   2. Exploratory education
   3. Career education

3. Most secondary schools are accredited at the _____ and _____ levels.

4. The traditional family with father, mother, and two children is still common in American society. (True/False)

5. The first step in the effective teaching model is to _____. The last (sixth) step in the model is to _____.

CHAPTER SUMMARY

The system of secondary schooling in the United States has evolved as a result of the social, economic, and political needs of the larger society. Each time societal needs have changed, the purpose of secondary schools has changed.

Secondary schools have not been organized around one widely accepted model, but instead reflect the perceived needs of the community they serve. Some communities have organized schooling into two levels: elementary and secondary. In other communities, you will find elementary, junior high, and senior high schools. In still other communities, schools are divided into elementary, middle, and high schools. Likewise, curricula vary from school to school and community to community. Essentially, the secondary school curriculum will consist of general education, exploratory education, and career education.

Most secondary schools today are accredited at the state and regional levels. State accreditation is often required to maintain quality and continue funding. Regional accreditation is important to achieve uniformity of quality.

Secondary education in the United States continues to be unique: the ultimate control of education rests with the people, who—through legislatures and school boards—effect periodic adjustments according to the needs of changing communities and require that schools be held accountable. This dedication to diversity is in sharp contrast to the value placed on homogeneous groups in other cultures—for example, as it is in the Japanese society. However, European societies are now following the lead of the United States with regard to diversity.

Good teaching is a major undertaking that requires both a sequential and cyclic planning process. Effective teachers must diagnose, plan the course, plan instruction, guide planned activities, evaluate, and, when necessary, follow up.

Discussion Questions and Activities

1. **School visits.** Visit several secondary schools in your area. Collect information about the schools. Are they organized around a particular philosophy? grade level(s)? concentrations of student interest? Is the curriculum readily available to the public? Are the administrators, teachers, and students able to articulate the general education curriculum? exploratory education? career curriculum? Is the school accredited by the regional and the state agency of jurisdiction? Is there evidence of the impact of the changing student population? Are there special programs in place for these students? If so, what are they?

2. **Analysis of school data.** After visiting the schools to collect information, try to imagine what it would be like to teach in each one. What would be the *best* and *worst* aspect of each school for you as a teacher?

3. **The school curriculum.** Examine the documents that outline the curriculum at a nearby secondary school. Interview several students about the school curriculum. Ask them what they are learning in particular courses. What attitudes do the students have about their school experiences? Determine if there is a parallel relationship between what the school teaches and the career aspirations of students.

4. **Designing curricula.** Read Earnest Boyer's *High School.* Do you agree with the recommendations forwarded by Boyer's work? If you could design the ideal high school, what would you include?

5. **School interaction.** Observe and compare the social interactions of junior high and senior high students. How would you characterize the social interactions at each level on formal classroom interaction?

6. **The teaching model.** Visit several secondary school teachers. Discuss their planning. Do they follow the six-step planning model presented in this chapter or a modification of the model? What type of diagnosis does the teachers use? Do they provide follow-up instruction based on evaluation results?

Students, Teaching, and Learning

✎ **Students differ, teachers differ, teaching styles differ, and learning styles differ. It is no wonder effectiveness is such an elusive undertaking.**

Overview

Adolescence is a time of change. It heralds the onset of puberty, with changes taking place in physical, personal, social, and cognitive development. It is a period of patterned growth spurts and sexual maturation, accompanied by an exaggerated concern about appearance and size. Socially, more independence from the family is desired, peer-group influence increases, and activities of interest demand more time. Emotionally, an adolescent's search for purpose and identity can result in moodiness and experimentation. With all these changes, adolescents must learn to cope with the changes while developing a more mature set of behaviors.

Adolescence is also a period when basic skills are being refined, thinking is becoming more complex, life goals are being fashioned, and competencies for life goals are being mastered. Thus, adolescents need teachers who have a good understanding of the teaching-learning process. Adolescents need role models who can help them acquire complex physical, personal, social, and cognitive skills. The teacher must be a mentor, an effective subject-matter expert, a counselor, and a social psychologist.

Although it will be helpful to consider the areas of development in isolation, keep in mind that the adolescent is a complex human being with interdependent systems of mind and body. Physical, personal, social, and cognitive components of development are interwoven to form the total development of the adolescent.

Many factors influence development, teaching, and learning; however, we will focus our attention on those that are relevant to the secondary classroom.

Objectives

After completing your study of chapter 2, you should be able to do the following:

1. Define and describe the adolescent period of growth, as well as the components of development associated with it.

2. Discuss psychobiological, psychosocial, and cognitive development as they relate to adolescence.

3. Identify and discuss issues that have the potential to cause emotional and peer-group conflict for adolescents.

4. Define *teaching*, and explain the concept of teaching as an art and as a science.

5. Describe the characteristics and skills associated with effective teaching.

6. Differentiate among the five categories of time found in classrooms and secondary schools.

7. Define *behavioral* and *cognitive* theories of learning.

8. Describe the information-processing model of memory and learning.

9. Discuss teaching and learning styles as they relate to the learning process.

10. Discuss the importance of and techniques for teaching students how to learn.

Chapter Terms and Key Concepts

Academic Learning Time

Adolescence

Allocated Time

Behavioral Learning Theories

Cognitive Development

Cognitive Learning Theories

Delinquency

Development

Engaged Time

Information-Processing Theory

Instructional Time

Learning

Mandated Time

Personal Development

Physical Development

Psychobiological Development

Psychosocial Development

Punishers

Reinforcers

Social Development

Social Learning Theory

Teaching

Time on Task

Transfer

Adolescence is the bridge between childhood and adulthood. It is a time when young people adjust their behaviors from those acceptable for children to those acceptable for adults. However, you must keep in mind that 12- to 18-year-old students—the age range of the junior and senior high years—are not miniature adults. In fact, they can be described as being neither children nor adults. Adolescents act differently, think differently, and they view the world differently than do children and adults.

Defining just *when* adolescence begins and ends is difficult. However, **adolescence** can be viewed as beginning with the changes preceding the growth spurt and ending with the achievement of adult status. Understanding change is key to adolescent behavior. Consequently, to be an effective teacher of adolescents, you must understand the physical, personal, social, and cognitive developmental factors that influence their behaviors, as well as the principles of teaching and learning as they apply to secondary classrooms.

Adolescent Development

Development refers to the adaptive changes that occur in human beings (or animals) that begin with conception and continue through the entire life span. **Physical development** encompasses the physiological changes of the body as well as changes in motor skills. **Personal development** and **social development** deal with changes in the ways individuals view themselves and relate to others. **Cognitive development** refers to changes in mental activity and thinking ability. This chapter will focus on physical, personal, social, and cognitive development as represented by two widely accepted viewpoints: Erikson's theory of personal and social development and Piaget's theory of cognitive development.

Adolescent development is extremely complex: All aspects of development are intertwined, and each in turn is affected by environmental forces. Therefore, although adolescent physical, personal, social, and cognitive development will be discussed separately, in real life they often can not be separated. Each student will be unique, and the characteristics of any one student will never be exactly duplicated. The discussion will center around generalizations about the nature of adolescents. Exceptions can certainly be found, and interested readers are encouraged to seek out these exceptions.

Psychobiological Development

One of the most important challenges facing adolescents is how to deal positively with psychobiological developmental changes. **Psychobiological development** refers to those psychological factors that are a consequence of biological changes. For example, adolescents must adjust to rapid changes in height, weight, and coordination. This period of rapid change begins with the onset of puberty and signals the move from childhood to young adulthood. It is a period of growing up. For some (usually girls), puberty can come as early as age 9; for others it may not occur until age 18.

Girls generally mature earlier than boys.

Generally, girls will mature earlier and complete the change period in a shorter period of time than will boys. These differences mean that some students will be quite mature by the time others of the same age have just begun to mature. Thus, it is not uncommon to have classes of secondary students who range physically from the quite childish to the very mature.

Adolescents show a great deal of preoccupation with their looks and with grooming. This preoccupation is an important aspect of sexual maturation. As their bodies become more mature sexually, adolescents must make psychological adjustments to their new body image and the associated attractiveness (or unattractiveness) they perceive. Of prime importance during this period is the approval of the peer group. Often the desire for peer approval and a positive image will have repercussions in the classroom. For example, small-group discussions frequently will turn to discussions of clothing, dating, or sexual activities. Therefore, you should not be overly concerned and critical when adolescents give their appearance, social life, and the opposite sex higher priority than class work and your subject. Learn to be reasonably tolerant.

Adolescents are faced with new potentials that often call for experimentation. The physical changes accompanying puberty and the associated maturity leads to expectations from peers, teachers, and parents for more adultlike behaviors from adolescents. Often adolescents have difficulty living up to these expectations. Delayed physical maturation, for example, can have detrimental effects on self-image, which can result in socially induced inferiority. Late-maturing boys often will be less popular, more talkative, and hungry for attention. In general, problems associated with late maturation will be much greater for boys than for girls (Greif and Ulman, 1982). On the other hand, earlier maturers—although they may have a harder time at puberty, experience anxiety, have more temper tantrums, have more conflict with their parents—tend to be more popular and mature in high school and have an academic advantage over later maturers. Generally, early-maturing boys will be more poised and relaxed and suffer fewer psychological problems associated with the physical change of puberty than do those who mature later. Furthermore, this pattern of success often continues into adulthood. For girls, early maturers tend to enjoy a better total adjustment, family adjustment, and personal relations. However, early physical maturing seems to be less important in determining the social status of girls—in fact, it can put them at a definite disadvantage: Girls who are larger than most of their classmates are not valued in our culture. Most researchers have found that early maturation is more of an advantage for boys than for girls (Peterson, Richards, and Boxer, 1983; Simmons, Blythe, and McKinney, 1983). Nonetheless, early-maturing students—who tend to be larger, stronger, and better coordinated—often become class leaders, while late-maturing students tend to not be taken seriously and are often treated as children by peers, teachers, and parents.

Because of recent trends that break down the traditional practice of reserving certain secondary school courses for only one grade level (either for freshman, sophomores, juniors, or seniors), you may have in your classes students as young as 12 with students aged 15 or 16. Indeed, it is not unusual to find ninth-grade classes with juniors and seniors enrolled. These trends cause many secondary classrooms to be widely diverse in the range of maturation of students. Teachers in such classes must be cognizant of the extraordinary range of physiological and psychological development among students and take these differences into account in planning instruction and in teaching. Indeed, use special care in planning activities that require a great deal of concentration and coordination.

Teachers must open the lines of communication with adolescents. Teachers who have a regard for their students, believe in them, and encourage them will achieve open communication. Basically, students will seek not praise or reward or pity, but regard: They want to be acknowledged for their personhood and to be recognized for what they are and what they can become. They often will seek out caring teachers as counselors and mentors. Adolescents want to share with caring teachers in a student-to-teacher (adult) context, not in a child-to-teacher (parent) context or student-to-student (peer) context. The language of acceptance is at the heart of viable communication with adolescents. Adultlike communications calls for listening—active listening (Gordon, 1974). Active listeners carefully attend to what is being said and don't interrupt. The active listener acknowledges remarks by saying "uh huh" or "yes," or by nodding, thus demonstrating attention, interest, and the desire for the adolescent to continue. The adolescent should not be told what he or she should do, but should be given the opportunity to work out his or her own problems with minimum input from the teacher.

TABLE *2.1*   Erikson's Psychosocial Stages

Crisis Stage	Approximate Age	Successful Resolution	Unsuccessful Resolution
Trust vs. Mistrust	0 to 1	Sense of trust and trust in self	Feelings of mistrust and anxiety
Autonomy vs. Doubt	1 to 3	Sense of independence and self-assertiveness	Sense of inadequacy and doubt
Initiative vs. Guilt	3 to 6	Sense of confidence and inventiveness	Sense of fear and low self-worth
Industry vs. Inferiority	6 to 12	Sense of competence and capability	Lack of self-confidence
Identity vs. Role Confusion	Adolescence	Sense of self as person	Fragmented sense of self
Intimacy vs. Isolation	Early adulthood	Closeness and commitment to others	Loneliness and isolation
Generativity vs. Stagnation	Middle adulthood	Expansion of future generations	Concern only for self
Integrity vs. Despair	Later adulthood	Sense of completeness and wisdom	Feelings of hopelessness

Source: Adapted from Erikson, E. H. (1980). *Identity and life cycle* (2nd ed.). New York: W. W. Norton.

Psychosocial Development

Erik Erikson (1980) offers a basic framework for understanding how people grow in relation to the way they interact with others. His theory of **psychosocial development** suggests that personal and social changes are due to cultural factors and that they proceed in stages. According to Erikson, people pass through eight psychosocial stages as they grow and progress through life. Each stage marks a major crisis that must be satisfactorily resolved to proceed normally with life. Each crisis requires that individuals deal successfully with a particular aspect of personality or how they relate to others. If not resolved satisfactorily, a particular crisis must be dealt with later in life. Table 2.1 summarizes Erikson's stages.

Erikson suggests that adolescence is a time when a new sense of self or ego identity is established—when basic drives (ego) are aligned with past crises and with the newly acquired needs, goals, and demands of adolescence and approaching adulthood. Adolescents want to be able to run their own lives and decide for themselves who will be their friends, who to date, what careers they will pursue, and whether they should or should not go to college. In short, adolescents want to free themselves from the restraints imposed by adults and make their own choices. At the same time, however, they look to their peers for support in making decisions. Thus, adolescents need to be involved in classroom decision making, and you need to be aware of the importance of peer support.

Reaffirming their identity and behaving as adults is not easy for adolescents. It requires that they attain independence from parents, teachers, and other authority figures. In effect, they must assume a new role in life. The establishment of this new role represents an ordeal, a crisis that must be resolved to provide a firm basis for adulthood.

TABLE 2.2   Piaget's Stages of Cognitive Development

Stage	Approximate Age	Characteristics
Sensorimotor	0 to 2	Object permanence
		Goal-directed activity
		Use of imitation and thought
Preoperational	2 to 7	Gradual use of symbols and language
		Egocentric thinking
Concrete Operational	7 to 11	Able to solve concrete (hands-on) problems
		Can think logically
		Use of operations and reversibility
Formal Operational	11 to adulthood	Able to think abstractly and logically
		Concern for social issues

Cognitive Development

Adolescence represents a critical period in the intellectual development of the individual. In fact, it is during adolescence that the full capacities of human intellect are realized. The ability to deal with abstract concepts and complex relationships is developed during this period, as is the ability to reason critically. The recognition of an imperfect world dawns during this time, often causing the young person anxiety about seemingly unresolved social ills. A social awareness develops.

One of the most complete theoretical statements about cognitive development is that presented by Jean Piaget (1967), who proposed that our ability to think rationally develops from the interaction of hereditary and environmental forces. According to Piaget, cognitive development unfolds in a stagelike sequence. These stages are presented in table 2.2.

Sensorimotor Stage

The sensorimotor stage extends from birth to about 2 years of age. At this stage, development is based on information obtained through the senses (*sensori*) and from body movement (*motor*). As the child matures, a primitive symbol system unfolds, and the child makes some preliminary association of language labels with concrete objects.

Preoperational Stage

The preoperational stage lasts from about 2 to 7 years of age. During this period, language development occurs at a dramatic rate. The child tends to see things only from the ''self'' point of view. Decisions tend to be made on the basis of intuition, and the child usually cannot explain the rationale for actions.

Concrete Operational Stage

The concrete operational stage spans from about 7 to 11 years of age. This stage marks the beginning of ''hands-on'' thinking. In effect, thinking crystallizes into more of a system: The learner develops the ability to pose and operate mentally in a series of actions. However, the individual must

Younger students functioning at the concrete operational stage need hands-on experiences.

rely on concrete events (past or present) in order to think in this way. Instruction at this level demands a great deal of sensory contact with tangible objects.

Formal Operational Stage

The final stage in Piaget's theory is the formal operational stage, which begins at about 11 years of age. Learners should enter this stage during the adolescent years. This stage is characterized by adult thought with the ability to apply rational logic to problem situations—abstract as well as concrete. The learner begins to think in a more systematic way in solving problems and in forming hypotheses. Many become idealistic at this time and often make suggestions as to the way the world ought to be.

It should be pointed out that not all high school students are capable of formal operational thought—that is, they are not always capable of dealing with abstractions and complex reasoning. In other words, some students in your secondary classrooms will be operating at the concrete operational level of thought. It will be up to you to determine the student's level of abstract thought and to present the subject matter so that they are able to deal with it effectively. Therefore, use care in planning instruction so that you do not underestimate or overestimate the abilities of your students. Students must neither be bored by assigned work that is too simple, nor lost because they are unable to understand the work.

This completes our brief discussion of adolescent development. Those interested in a more detailed discussion of adolescent development should refer to an adolescent development textbook. Table 2.3 summarizes the developmental concepts addressed in this text.

TABLE *2.3*   Adolescent Development

Developmental Component	Description
Physical	Changes in the body and/or changes in motor skills
Psychobiological	Psychological factors that result from biological changes
Personal and Social	Changes in self-view and relations with others
Psychosocial	Erikson's eight stages of personal and social changes individuals experience as they grow and progress through life
Cognitive	Changes in mental activity and thinking ability, which Piaget suggests unfold in four stages

Let's now take a look at some of the issues that teenagers must deal with as they progress through adolescence.

Issues in Adolescence

Adolescence represents a trying and difficult period in a person's life. Many adolescents will experience emotional conflict and peer-group conflict. Indeed, adolescents tend to live stormy lives, with emotions ranging from apathy to emotional disorders.

Apathy

Many secondary students are rather apathetic about school because they find it irrelevant and meaningless. The secondary curriculum has much to do with the level of apathy among students. Several studies (Boyer, 1983; Goodlad, 1984; Sizer, 1984) have shown that the secondary school curriculum is far from challenging and is geared toward lower-order, rote skills. Needless to say, students view these courses as boring, a waste of time, and nothing more than busywork.

The recent reform movement (see chapter 16) has resulted in the call for intensifying the core curriculum and determining success by the results of standardized achievement tests. Many teachers neglect students' analytical, problem-solving, and performance skills in favor of preparing for the achievement tests.

Student apathy can be overcome to some extent by involving students in their own learning. For example, students can be given the opportunity to help plan their own curriculum, create their own products, and engage in analytic discussions. Teachers can contribute by infusing content imperatives in rich lessons designed to engage higher order thinking skills.

Delinquency

Delinquency is a legal term that denotes lawbreaking by those who are not considered adults. There is no simple way of determining factors that lead to delinquency. Indeed, a myriad of factors determine whether or not an adolescent will engage in delinquent behavior.

Peer pressure, poverty, and involvement in questionable peer activities are common causes for socialization into delinquent behaviors. For other adolescents, a poor relationship with parents can lead to delinquent behavior. Whatever the cause, a positive correlation appears to exist between delinquency and self-concept: In general, delinquents have poor self-concepts. It is possible that the poor self-concept leads to delinquency because the individual feels alienated from society.

Generally, delinquents do poorly in school. However, they also often have a problem with school absenteeism. Thus, absenteeism may be the main reason for poor school performance, or, conversely, absenteeism may lead to delinquent behavior.

Gangs have become a major problem in most larger cities (and some small towns) in the United States. Murder, rape, robbery, drug trafficking, extortion, and vandalism are common gang activities. Most gang members are of school age and are often found near school grounds stirring up trouble and vandalizing. Indeed, the fear generated in schools and on school grounds can be intense. As a result, students can be afraid to go to school or, if they do make it to class, find it difficult to concentrate on their studies.

Gangs often come to be because of conflicts between the values of society and those of young people. Gangs can offer people a sense of belonging. Schools and teachers can battle gang influence by encouraging gang members and potential gang members to express their values in school and by giving them a greater voice in developing policies. In effect, young people must be directed into the mainstream of society. They must be given ample opportunity to associate with positive, law-abiding role models within the school system. Moreover, schools should solicit the cooperation and support of parents, community leaders, and relevant agencies in the battle against gang activities and influence.

Almost all adolescents misbehave to some extent. However, some types of adolescent misbehavior are more frequent and more serious than others. Certain misbehavior may yield rewards deemed more valuable than those granted for good behavior. For example, stealing may lead to recognition and prestige from a gang, or disrupting a class may be rewarded with wanted attention.

There are a few general principles that you can follow to prevent and deal with delinquent behaviors when and if they occur. First, make it clear that you will enforce school and classroom rules and report any infractions immediately. For example, report cases of vandalism immediately so that students know it will not be tolerated. Second, deal with absenteeism and truancy by involving parents and by using behavior-modification systems; that is, implement a reward system for classroom attendance. Third, use in-school suspension, detention, and other in-school penalties rather than suspension (and expulsion) for delinquent behaviors. Finally, implement a school curriculum that is relevant to non-college-bound students. For example, vocational programs or work-study options should be available for students not interested in college.

Drug and Alcohol Use

Although drug use in secondary schools varies from district to district, it is viewed as a serious problem nationwide. In fact, in the 1990 Metropolitan Life Survey of American Teachers (Metropolitan Life Insurance Company, 1990), 70 percent of the teachers thought the use of drugs was a serious problem. In addition, in 1990 Lloyd Johnston and associates of the University of Michigan found that 50.9 percent of the 17,000 high school seniors surveyed indicated that they had used an illicit drug at least once. A high percentage of secondary students have tried marijuana, and increasing numbers have alcohol problems. Not surprisingly, drug and alcohol use has a detrimental affect on student academic performance and classroom behavior.

What can you do to help prevent drug and alcohol abuse? First, you can be observant. Be aware that unusual behaviors might suggest drug and alcohol problems. Once a problem is detected, you can direct the student to professional help. If you can earn the respect of students, you can be especially helpful, because students often share personal confidences and problems with teachers they trust and respect.

As a classroom teacher, you should become informed about drugs and their effects on students. Towers (1987) recommends that when confronted with a drug or alcohol problem, teachers should do the following:

1. Explain their concerns to the student.

2. Notify parents of their concerns.

3. Consult with and/or refer to appropriate school staff.

4. Participate as appropriate in the intervention plan.

These suggestions mean, of course, that every school must have a plan for dealing with drug and alcohol problems. Finally, you should find out about the assistance programs and community resources available in your district and discuss and share this information with your students. You can also help curb drug and alcohol problems by working to establish preventive substance abuse programs in your school.

Working Adolescents

Many adolescents hold part-time jobs, which can divert their time, attention, and energy away from school-related activities. In general, you will find that working adolescents tend to be absent more, are less motivated, and will often have lower grades. You may want to take into account employed students when making assignments, and you might consider giving them class time to complete some of their work.

Pregnancy

Teenage pregnancy has become a national problem over the last decade (Children's Defense Fund, 1989). The National Center for Health Statistics (1992) reports that the number of teenage pregnancies is increasing at an epidemic rate. This dramatic problem is significant when we consider the effects on the lives of teenage boys and girls, but is even more alarming when we consider the consequences for the children of these teenagers. Indeed, many adolescent mothers will drop out of school, which limits their future access to a decent, high-paying job. In effect, teenage mothers and their children will be at the bottom of the economic ladder.

Although the problem of teenage pregnancy is serious, there is no easy solution. Sex-education classes and the availability of contraceptives appear to have had little impact on the problem (Alan Guttmacher Institute, 1989).

What can schools do to address the teenage-pregnancy problem? Because information dissemination is still important, most educators feel sex-education classes must be continued. They further feel that strong parent and community support in conjunction with sex education in schools could well produce needed attitude and behavior change. Additionally, sex education combined with health-clinic services can lead to increased birth-control practices (Sex and Schools, 1986). Sex-education classes must address the realities of human sexuality; that is, they must communicate information about emotions, diseases, contraception, abortion, and the consequences of early parenthood. Moreover, pregnant teenagers must be encouraged and assisted so they can stay in school.

Emotional Disorders

During the stormy period of adolescence, emotional disorders may arise, ranging from mild to serious in nature—from depression to anxiety about maturity to suicidal thoughts or attempts. Often drastic changes in behavior (delinquency, self-abusive behavior, etc.) are calls for help during this period. You should be sensitive to such calls and recognize that adolescence is a difficult time for your students. In most cases, you should direct students with identified emotional disorders to get in touch with school counselors, school psychologists, or other trained personnel.

Teenage suicide continues to be a major concern for teachers. The suicide rate among adolescents has been on the rise for the last decade. Indeed, more than 5,000 young people commit suicide each year. Among those that attempt suicide, the vast majority are female. In contrast, those who succeed at suicide are mostly males who use more violent methods. The usual motive for adolescent suicide is extreme depression. You should look for clues that suggest a student or several students may be contemplating suicide: feelings of worthlessness, not getting along with parents, trouble at school, dating problems, giving away personal belongings, social withdrawal, getting angry easily, using drugs and alcohol, and talking or writing about death.

Application Guidelines ▼

Adolescence

Integrate Personal and Social Development in Instruction

Examples:
1. Don't call attention to physical differences and abilities of students.
2. Accept and be tolerant of adolescent concern about appearance and the opposite sex.
3. Delegate class and individual tasks in order to help students develop a sense of independence and responsibility.
4. Be reasonably tolerant of teenage fads.
5. Provide information and models for career choices.

Make Sure Instruction is Appropriate for Cognitive Ability

Examples:
1. Continue to use concrete aids and props when class consists of concrete-level students.
2. Give concrete-level students the opportunity to manipulate and test objects.
3. Whenever possible, teach complex concepts by using examples relevant to students' life experiences.
4. Present problems that require logical and analytical thinking to develop higher-order thinking abilities.

Address Issues of Concern to Adolescents

Examples:
1. Provide information and resources that will help students work out personal problems.
2. Give students accurate feedback on the consequences of their actions, but don't preach.
3. Assist students in examining dilemmas they are or will be facing in the secondary school years.
4. Devote some class time to moral issues and values.

Talk about suicide should be taken seriously. Be sensitive to dramatic mood changes. When you believe suicide is being contemplated, take preventive action immediately. Guide the individual or group to counseling or to psychologists trained in suicide prevention.

This concludes our discussion of the issues facing adolescents. The Adolescence Application Guidelines offer further suggestions related to working with teenagers. Review the summary given in table 2.3 and the Adolescence Application Guidelines, and complete exercise 2.1 to check your understanding of the adolescent period of life.

Teaching

Moore (1989, p. 6) defines **teaching** as "the actions of someone who is trying to assist others to reach their fullest potential in all aspects of development." The personal characteristics and skills needed to accomplish this noble task have been debated for years. Generally, the argument centers around two questions: (1) Is teaching an art or a science? and (2) Exactly what is effective teaching?

Application of Knowledge

Exercise 2.1   Adolescence

Check yourself on the following concepts of adolescent behavior and development. Appropriate responses can be found in appendix A.

1. Define *adolescence:* _____
   _____

2. Match the developmental description on the left with the label on the right.

   a. _____ Factors that are a consequence of biological changes   1. Cognitive development

   b. _____ Changes in thinking and reasoning ability   2. Personal and social development

   c. _____ Changes in the ways individuals view themselves and relate to others   3. Psychobiological development

3. Adolescents are often overly concerned with their appearance. (True/False)

4. According to Erikson, the goal of adolescence is the establishment of a new sense of _____.

5. Students in most secondary classrooms will be at the _____ or _____ level of cognitive thought.

6. Much of the apathy noted on the part of adolescents can be attributed to the content and delivery of the secondary school curriculum. (True/False)

7. Sex education has proven to be an effective deterrent to teenage pregnancy. (True/False)

8. Teenagers are often socialized into delinquent behaviors through their involvement in peer activities. (True/False)

Teaching as an Art and a Science

Do some teachers have better instincts for teaching than others? If so, can these instincts be identified and taught? Some educators argue that teachers are born and not made and that the ability to be an effective teacher cannot be taught. Conversely, other educators argue that teaching is a science with specific laws and principles, which can be taught.

Today, most educators are in agreement with Gage (1985), who argues that there is a scientific basis for the art of teaching. Thus, teaching can be viewed as having both artistic and scientific elements. Essentially, an increasing number of educators accept the viewpoint that individuals who have an interest in teaching will fall somewhere along a continuum like that shown in figure 2.1. Further, many agree that specific artistic and scientific elements can be effectively transmitted.

Effective Teaching

The search for effective teaching is not a new one. Teaching requires a large repertoire of skills and the ability to put these skills to use in different situations. Good teachers improvise: No one approach works equally well all the time and in all situations. In short, effectiveness will depend on the subject, students, and environmental conditions.

Teaching is both an art and a science.

Figure 2.1 *Teaching as an Art and a Science*

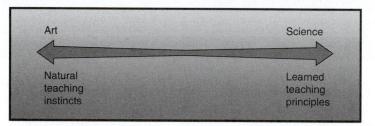

Art   Science

Natural   Learned
teaching   teaching
instincts   principles

Needless to say, effective teaching is complicated. However, the better teachers are proactive—that is, they are active information processors and decision makers. They are strongly committed to the importance of content delivery and tend to be task-oriented. They understand the demands of teaching their content, the characteristics of their students, and the importance of decision making in keeping students on task.

Effective teachers know that good teaching is more than lecturing, discussing, and explaining. To produce the desired classroom results, teachers must be well organized, but above all, they must use time efficiently.

Effective Organization

Classrooms can be organized or disorganized. Better-quality instruction is structured around appropriate content, materials and methods, and interaction patterns. The thoughtfully structured classroom is one in which students engage in meaningful tasks. However, matching instructional tasks with all the interacting variables in a classroom is not easy because of the differences in student ability and potential for learning.

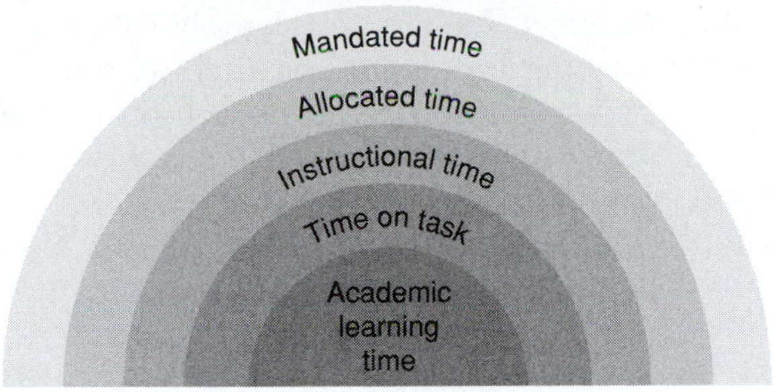

Figure 2.2 *School and Classroom Time*

Mandated time
Allocated time
Instructional time
Time on task
Academic learning time

Well-organized classrooms are businesslike. Classes get started on time, and students know what they are to do with class time. Moreover, students know when it is time to get back to work, and they understand the reason behind and the importance of assignments.

Finally, when a lecture is presented or a group discussion is conducted, it should be well organized with clear, well-illustrated explanations. Lesson content should be constructed and presented in logical order, with ideas that are interrelated and interwoven. In effect, thoughtful lessons are designed so students have meaningful and coherent material to learn. Outlines, schematic diagrams, and hierarchies are effective techniques for organizing and presenting lesson content.

Time in Schools and Classrooms

Time is a valuable and limited classroom resource that must be used wisely. It is often divided into five distinct categories: mandated time, allocated time, instructional time, engaged time, and academic learning time. Figure 2.2 illustrates how the five time categories relate to each other.

The total time available for all activities carried out in the secondary school is established by the state. Typically, secondary schools are in session approximately 7 hours a day for 180 days. This **mandated time** must be used for academic, as well as for nonacademic activities.

State-mandated time must be divided among a variety of subjects that must be taught, with time allotted for transitions between classes, lunch, announcements, and so on. The time appropriated to each of these activities often is called **allocated time.** For example, 45 minutes of each day may be used for homeroom activities, and 50 minutes of the school day may be needed for changing classes. Because secondary schools tend to be subject-oriented, an important goal is to expand the amount of allocated time available for learning.

Teachers must take the available allocated time and translate it into learning through **instructional time.** Despite your best efforts, however, not all students will stay on task or pay attention all the time. For example, some students may be daydreaming when you lecture, some may simply be goofing off, and others may simply be thinking about other things they would rather be doing. As a result, educators refer to another area within instructional time called time on task.

Time on task, or **engaged time,** differs from mandated, allocated, and instructional times in that it is the actual time individual students engage in learning. In effect, students are actively (physically or mentally) participating in the learning process during time on task. This active participation may simply involve listening to a lecture, reading, writing, or solving problems. If students are not actually on task in the learning process, they will not learn. So, another important goal of the instructional process is to improve the quality of time by keeping students on task. Time on task will depend on routine classroom practices, student motivation, and the quality of instruction. Typically, time on task will vary from lows of 50 percent in some classrooms to as high as 90 percent in others (Berliner, 1987).

Time on task isn't always productive. Indeed, students often engage in class activities at a superficial level, with little understanding or retention taking place. For example, they could be watching a film while actually concentrating very little on what is being shown. Thus, you must plan your instruction to make the time on task more productive. In other words, you must maximize **academic learning time.** For some educators (Block, Efthim, and Burns, 1989), academic learning time ideally should reflect student performance on assigned tasks at an 80 percent proficiency level or better.

A lot of instructional time is lost in today's secondary classrooms. In fact, some educators contend that as much as 50 to 60 days may be wasted each year. Some common time wasters are listed below.

1. **Starting Classes**
   Many teachers take 5 to 10 minutes per class to record attendance and make announcements. Systems should be devised for speeding up these housekeeping chores. The use of assigned seats or seating diagrams, for instance, will speed up this duty.

2. **Excessive Use of Films**
   Films are often shown that have little instructional value or are simply used as time fillers—especially on Fridays. Instructional tools such as films and computer activities should be justified in terms of their classroom value.

3. **Discipline Time**
   Disciplinary actions take time and often interrupt instruction. The use of nonverbal actions in curbing misbehavior will allow a lesson to proceed without interruption. The use of nonverbal methods will be discussed at length in chapter 15.

4. **Early Finishes**
   Much instructional time is lost when lessons are finished early. This tendency can often be avoided by planning more instruction than you think you'll need.

5. **Extracurricular Activities**
   Students are often dismissed early for athletic events, plays and rehearsals, music and band activities, and other such activities. Schools should schedule special events on activity days or after school hours.

TABLE *2.4*   Teaching

Concept	Description
Teaching as Art	Effective teachers have natural instincts for teaching
Teaching as Science	Effective teaching comes from learned laws and principles of teaching
Organized Classroom	Classroom structured around businesslike atmosphere and well-planned appropriate lessons
School and Classroom Time	Total time established by the state for schooling

How can you tell when students are off task? Needless to say, this is not easy. Sharpen your observation skills. Watch students' eye contact: Are they watching you during your presentations, or does their eye movement suggest that they are engaged in other interests? Finally, do they ask or answer questions? Be sensitive to the signals that indicate that students are engaged and on task.

Teaching is a complex and challenging process. Table 2.4 summarizes the different teaching concepts, and the Teaching Application Guidelines offer additional suggestions. Review the summary and the guidelines, and complete exercise 2.2.

Learning

Learning can be defined as a change in an individual's capacity for performance as a result of experience. Changes that come about through development (such as sexual maturity or growing taller) are not considered to be learning. We are constantly absorbing information, both intentionally and unintentionally. For example, students may intentionally learn history, but may unintentionally learn to fear the dentist. Of course, your main concern will be with intentional learning. However, don't totally discount unintentional learning, because as you teach, students are determining that the subject is interesting or dull, useful or useless. This learning, although unintentional, is important to the learning process.

There are basically two schools of thought on how individuals learn: behavioral and cognitive. **Behavioral learning theories** tend to emphasize changes in observable behavior—that is, in the way individuals act in particular situations. On the other hand, **cognitive learning theories** tend to emphasize the unobservable mental processes that individuals use in learning and remembering information or skills.

Behavioral Learning Theories

The major principle underscoring behavioral learning theories is that behavior will change according to its immediate consequences. In short, pleasurable consequences will strengthen behaviors, while unpleasant consequences will weaken them. For example, behaviors that earn teacher praise will often be repeated, whereas behaviors prompting teacher reprimands will often be rejected. Those consequences that are found

Application Guidelines ▼

Teaching

Organize and Structure Lessons Carefully

Examples:
1. Make sure you structure lessons to fit student needs.
2. Organize your presentation into clear steps or stages.
3. Plan brief outlines to write on board as lessons are presented.
4. Plan ample time for students' involvement with materials.

Strive for Clear Instruction

Examples:
1. Focus on only one idea at a time.
2. Be flexible: Don't rigidly follow a plan that is not working.
3. Make sure your instructional intent is clear.
4. Keep students on task, and have something productive for students to do if planned instruction is finished early.

Application of Knowledge

Exercise 2.2   Teaching

Check yourself on the following teaching concepts. Appropriate responses can be found in appendix A.

1. Define *teaching:* _____
_____

2. Those educators who argue that teachers are born and not made view teaching as a(n) _____ .

3. Match the time description on the left with its category on the right.

   a. _____ Time students engage in learning | 1. Allocated time

   b. _____ Engaged time that results in at least 80 percent performance | 2. Academic learning time

   c. _____ Time appropriated for each of the school activities | 3. Mandated time

   d. _____ Time appropriated by state for schooling | 4. Time on task

4. It is usually unwise to change your lesson plan during a lesson. (True/False)

5. Teachers can often speed up the beginning of class chores through the use of assigned seating and seating charts. (True/False)

---

pleasurable are generally called **reinforcers,** while those that are found unpleasant are called **punishers.** Reinforcers and punishers will be discussed at length in chapters 13 and 15.

A major outgrowth of the behavioral learning theory has been the **social learning theory.** Developed by Albert Bandura (1969), this theory accepts most of the principles of behavioral learning theory, but places greater emphasis on cues and on internal mental processes. Essentially, social learning stresses the importance of modeling (the imitation of others' behavior) and vicarious experiences (learning from others' successes and failures) in the learning process. For example, students who note that respected peers are interested in science will sometimes develop similar attitudes, or students who observe others receiving teacher praise for good study habits will sometimes follow suit.

Behavioral learning theories are so central to teaching that they are addressed throughout this book. These principles are most directly applied to motivation (see chapter 13) and classroom management (see chapter 15). Indeed, the theories are quite useful in modifying behaviors; however, they are limited in explaining less visible processes such as thinking, learning from a text, or learning through problem solving.

Cognitive Learning Theories

Cognitive psychologists say that learning is an internal process that cannot be observed directly. They suggest that learning produces an internal change, which in turn modifies an individual's ability to respond in a particular situation. Thus, the observed changes that signify that learning has taken place are nothing more than reflections of internal changes.

Cognitive theorists view people as active processors of information—who seek out information in an attempt to make sense of the world around them. In effect, people initiate inquiry that will help them solve problems.

The consequences of actions are also an important component of cognitive learning theories. Instead of proposing the behaviorist view that consequences strengthen actions (act as reinforcers), however, cognitivists maintain that consequences serve as feedback. This feedback reduces the uncertainty of the teacher's reactions to student behaviors that represent learning or repeated actions. In effect, it provides information to individuals regarding the correctness of their understanding and learning as they actively pursue knowledge and practice skills.

Cognitive theorists' conception of how the brain operates so closely parallels the operation of computers that another label for cognitive theory has emerged: **information-processing theory.** Thus, cognitive theorists—like computer programmers—began to think of learning in terms of sensory input, encoding, and retrieval systems.

Information-Processing Theory

One of the principal goals of teaching is to put meaningful information in students' minds so it can be retrieved when needed. Figure 2.3 represents a typical model for accomplishing this task. This first component of the

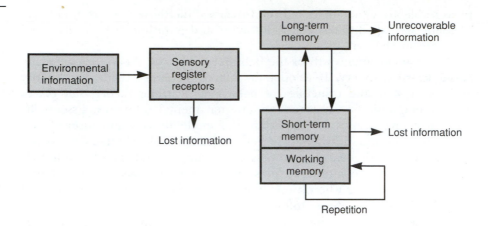

Figure 2.3 *Typical Information-Processing Model*

processing system is the sensory register: Large amounts of information (sights, smells, sounds, tastes, and so on) are constantly received by the sensory register, where it is held for a short time—no more than a second or two. During this time, the individual must decide whether the information is useful and worth remembering. If not, it is quickly lost.

As a teacher, your function will be to direct student attention to what you are teaching and communicate the worth of that information. With all the stimuli bombarding the sensory register, students often must be told what to screen out and what to remember. For example, when students are given a reading assignment, should they read to remember factual information or should they try to understand the abstract concepts related to what is read? Students often reveal the excessive amount of information they must deal with when they ask whether certain information will be on a test. Remember that attention is a limited resource. Avoid asking students to attend to several tasks at once, and, because the selection of what is important takes time, avoid bombarding their senses with too much information at one time. Finally, make clear the importance and usefulness of the information or skills that you teach. This communication is an important aspect of motivation. Communication will be discussed at length in chapter 12, and motivation and motivational techniques will be dealt with in chapter 13.

The second component of the information-processing model is short-term memory: Information perceived as important and useful to a person is transformed into sensory codes and sent to short-term memory, where it remains for only a short period of time (about 20 seconds) before it is forgotten. Information can be rehearsed, however, to prevent its being forgotten. Rehearsal is important to instruction because it gives students time to mentally process the information for storage in long-term memory. This is especially critical when there is a lot of information to process. Thus, lesson pauses and questions give students an opportunity for processing short-term memory information into long-term memory.

Once information has been stored in long-term memory, it is there permanently. However, retrieval often depends on how that information has been organized for storage. You can facilitate information retrieval when you teach by organizing information into meaningful, easily remembered categories and having students practice until they can readily solve problems or recall correct answers. This overpractice strategy, which is referred to as *overlearning,* is an effective way of increasing the likelihood that students will remember what they have learned.

Although much research about learning is yet to be conducted, learning theories based on current understandings help explain how people learn and, therefore, serve as guides for teachers. Indeed, you should try to choose the theory that best fits your own style of teaching.

Learning Theories and Teaching Styles

Just as each teacher has a unique personality, so will each teacher develop a personal philosophy of teaching and a personal teaching style. Usually, teachers' teaching styles are consistent with their own learning styles. Moreover, individual teaching styles will generally be fairly consistent with one of the theories of learning and its practical applications. The learning theory preferences of most secondary teachers are usually influenced by three factors: student characteristics, curriculum materials, and teaching style. You should consider all three factors as you select a learning theory on which to base your instruction.

Because of the unique characteristics of some junior high students, teachers sometimes must select approaches different from those used with older students. For example, junior high teachers often rely on the use and manipulation of concrete materials and turn to behavioral learning theories. Indeed, some students at this age are rather childlike, while others are quite mature. This diversity often requires that reinforcement techniques for motivation and classroom management be employed.

Usually, individual teachers have limited influence on the choice of adopted instructional material they must use in their classes. In many cases, the materials have been developed to reflect a particular learning theory. Therefore, you may be compelled to institute a curriculum that relies extensively on a particular learning process. It is important, then, that you clearly understand the curriculum materials being used in your classroom, as well as the degree to which you support the viewpoint upon which that curriculum is based.

Finally, teachers can maximize effectiveness by understanding their own teaching style, because they tend to rely on the learning theory that complements their personal style. For example, teachers who feel teaching is the passing on of information tend to support the behavioral theory of learning, while teachers who feel it is teaching students to think, analyze, and organize information often prefer a cognitive learning theory or an information-processing approach. Factual information and the management of behaviors are important to the former (behavioral) group, whereas the latter (cognitive) group puts a great deal of emphasis on critical thinking, problem solving, and organizational skills.

Teachers need to develop and rely on a theory of learning that will complement their own personal philosophy of teaching. The adaptation of a theory to the personal style will help the teacher better understand his or her own strengths, weaknesses, and preferences. However, you should not place all your emphasis on one type of learning. For example, teaching factual information is just as important as conveying the ability to think, reason, and analyze. Moreover, it is sometimes necessary to adjust your teaching style to the learning styles represented within your class.

Student Learning Style

Students learn through different channels; that is, they have different learning styles. Some will be visual learners, or those who learn best by seeing or reading; some will be auditory learners, or those who learn best by hearing; and some will be physical learners, or those who learn best through the manipulation of concrete materials. Some students will learn quickly, others rather slowly. Some will require substantial teacher help, others will be able to learn independently. Most of us have taken on each of these learning styles at one time or another, depending on the circumstances; however, we tend to favor one style over another. Differences in learning style are due in part to differences in cognitive style—that is, differences in the way we process and organize information and how we respond to environmental stimuli.

One of the most important differentiations in cognitive styles for teachers to make is between field-dependence and field-independence. Field-dependent people tend to see patterns as a whole and have difficulty separating out specific aspects of a situation or pattern, while field-independent people are better able to see the parts that make up a large pattern. Field-dependent people tend to be more oriented toward people and prefer people-oriented subjects such as history, literature, and the social sciences, and they work well in groups. In contrast, field-independent people are more likely to do well with numbers and with problem-solving tasks, and they often work well on their own. Finally, field-dependent students usually require more structure, need more reinforcement, react more to criticism, and require external cues to enhance learning. Field-independent students, on the other hand, tend to be reinforced internally, are less affected by criticism, are better at analyzing and reorganizing, and, as noted earlier, are better problem solvers.

Another important cognitive-style distinction that teachers should be aware of is that of impulsivity versus reflectivity. Impulsive individuals tend to work and make decisions quickly and tend to concentrate on speed. They are always the first to finish the test or task. In contrast, reflective individuals are more likely to take a long time considering all alternatives on a test or task and tend to concentrate on accuracy.

Impulsive students can be taught to be reflective through self-instructional training. Essentially, these students are taught to pace their work by telling themselves to go slowly and carefully. However, students can also be too reflective. In such cases, they need assistance in learning how to pace their work and in judging when enough analysis has taken place to make a choice.

Although some student differences are easily accommodated, other differences are more problematic. For example, avoiding the overuse of criticism with field-dependent students is not that difficult, whereas teaching field-independent students to better understand social information can be quite difficult. However, flexibility and a willingness to experiment with various techniques will provide opportunities to maximize learning, regardless of student learning style.

Teaching Students to Learn

Even though they already have many years of learning experiences, many secondary students need help in learning how to learn. Basically, you will have three types of students in your classes: students who can learn on their own, students who need some help in learning, and students who need a lot of help in learning. Your job will be to provide training to students who need help with the skills needed in building concepts. You must learn to make information meaningful, help students develop learning and study skills, and teach so knowledge can be applied or transferred to other areas. Too much classroom learning is rote; that is, it is the memorization of facts or associations, such as chemical symbols, rules of grammar, words in foreign languages, or presidents and vice presidents of the United States. Optimal learning takes place when information is made meaningful. Essentially, information must be well organized and tied into an existing cognitive structure. For example, the study of mammals could be tied into an organizational hierarchy of the animal kingdom. The use of advance organizers (an orientation statement about the material to be learned) can also be quite effective in making subject matter meaningful to students. Moreover, advance organizers can help structure new information and relate it to knowledge students already possess. Advance organizers will be discussed further in chapter 7.

Learning for understanding requires that students possess elaboration skills, note-taking skills, summarization skills, and the ability to form questions related to studied information. Elaboration encourages students to think about new material in ways that connect it to information or ideas already in the students' minds. One strategy for accomplishing this goal is to question students about the material as it is taught (see chapter 7). Other commonly used strategies for increasing student understanding of lecture or reading materials are to have students take notes about the main ideas as they are presented or read, have them write brief summary statements about what they have heard or read, or have them generate their own questions about the material.

The ultimate goal of teaching and learning is to develop students' ability to apply classroom-acquired information outside the classroom or in different subjects. For example, students should be able to write a letter outside the classroom, or they should be able to use mathematical skills in their science class. This ability is referred to as **transfer.** With transfer, you are trying to develop the ability to apply knowledge acquired in one

TABLE 2.5   Learning

Concept	Description
Behavioral Learning Theories	Behavioral changes (learning) produced as result of immediate consequences to actions—where behaviors are strengthened by pleasurable consequences and weakened by unpleasant consequences
Cognitive Learning Theories	Changes produced as a result of learning is a reflection of internal changes in an individual's ability to respond in a particular situation
Information Processing	The model that uses a computer analogy to explain memory and learning, or how the human mind takes in, stores, and retrieves information
Teaching Style	The personal teaching preference of teachers, which is usually consistent with a learning theory and its application
Student Learning Style	The channel through which a student learns *best* (visual, hearing, feeling, etc.)
Cognitive Style	The way information is processed and organized and how individuals respond to environmental stimuli
Transfer	The ability to use information acquired in one situation in new situations

Application Guidelines ▼

Learning

Establish Standards and Develop Students' Confidence as Learners

Examples:
1. Recognize accomplishments.
2. Reinforce efforts as well as successes.
3. Use cueing to develop student confidence.
4. Stress the positive.

Organize Instruction for Understanding

Examples:
1. Help students focus on important information.
2. Help students separate supporting and nonsupporting details.
3. Help students see the connection between previously known and new information.
4. Provide practice and repetition of information so overlearning results.
5. Present information in clear, meaningful, and organized way.
6. Use examples and nonexamples as well as similarities and differences in teaching concepts.

Teach Students to Be Learners

Examples:
1. Emphasize the value of lifelong learning.
2. Determine your own and students' learning styles, and use this knowledge to better organize instruction.
3. Be a model for various learning styles.
4. Focus instruction on problem solving.
5. Develop student reasoning, critical thinking, and analytical skills.

situation to new situations. Presumably, students in a Spanish class will be able to communicate with people who speak Spanish. The likelihood of transfer can be enhanced by making the original learning situation as similar as possible to the situation to which information or skill will be applied. For instance, business mathematics should be taught through the use of realistic problems from the field of business. Of course, another means for accomplishing transfer is thorough learning: Students cannot use that which is not thoroughly understood. Finally, similarity and thoroughness make it more likely that students will be able to apply newly acquired information to real-life problem situations.

This completes our study of learning. Table 2.5 summarizes the learning concepts addressed in this section, and the Learning Application Guidelines give some additional suggestions. Review the summary and guidelines, and complete exercise 2.3.

A good understanding of students, teaching, and learning will greatly facilitate one of the major missions of education—literacy. Full realization of this mission will be difficult, but with a greater knowledge of all aspects of education comes success.

Application of Knowledge

Exercise 2.3   Learning

1. Define *learning:* _____
   _____

2. Match the learning concept characteristic on the left with the appropriate term on the right.

   a. _____ Major emphasis placed on unobservable internal mental processes
   1. Behavioral learning theories

   b. _____ Major emphasis placed on memory and retrieval
   2. Cognitive learning theories

   c. _____ Major emphasis placed on observable changes in behavior
   3. Information processing model

3. Generally, individual teaching style will be consistent with one of the theories of learning. (True/False)

4. Most secondary students are good auditory learners. (True/False)

5. Field-dependent students tend to see patterns as a whole, while field-independent students see the various components that make up the whole. (True/False)

6. An important goal of teaching is to maximize student reflectivity. (True/False)

7. Describe four techniques that can be used to help students develop skill in learning for understanding.
   a. _____
   b. _____
   c. _____
   d. _____

CHAPTER SUMMARY

Adolescents come to your classroom with differences in physical, personal, social, and cognitive abilities. During the secondary school years, many changes occur. There will be a physical growth spurt, sexual maturation, and a search for a new identity and independence. Cognitively, adolescents often will be idealistic about what is right and wrong in the world. According to Piaget, they will be developing and testing their ability to deal with abstractions and will be working on complex reasoning skills. In effect, many will be making the transition to formal operational thought. These and other learner characteristics should be taken into account when planning and organizing your instruction.

Adolescence is a period of conflict for teenagers. It is a time of apathy for many, because they find much of their schooling irrelevant and meaningless. Other problems often associated with secondary school youth are delinquency, drugs and alcohol, balancing school and a job, and, for some, emotional disorders.

Effective teaching is an art as well as a science. It calls for organization and the wise use of time.

The time mandated by the state must be allocated both to instructional and noninstructional time. Instructional time must be organized so that time on task is maximized. However, time on task must be turned into academic learning time (performance on assigned tasks at 80 percent or better) for teachers to be truly effective.

Most teachers will develop a teaching style that is in accordance with their own learning style. This style will be linked directly to one of the theories of learning: behavioral or cognitive. Also, an understanding of the information-processing model of learning should prove useful in explaining memory, retrieval of information, and forgetting.

Your duty as a teacher is to maximize learning. You will be more successful in this function if you adapt instruction to students' learning styles and to teaching students how to learn. It is especially important that instruction be aimed at functioning in the real world. Thus, you must pay particular attention to teaching for transfer, so students can use skills developed in classroom situations in solving real-life problem situations.

Discussion Questions and Activities

1. **Classroom observation.** Visit several public school classrooms. Collect and analyze data with regard to the following:

    a. The physical, personal, social, and cognitive development of students.

    b. Student apathy.

    c. Teaching and learning effectiveness.

    d. The use of classroom time.

2. **School and classroom time.** How could you improve academic instructional time and academic time on task? What procedures and/or rules would you implement for starting (and ending) your class to improve instructional time?

3. **Teachers' view of effective teaching and learning.** Interview several teachers at the junior and senior high level. How do they define effective teaching and learning? How do they know when it has occurred in their classrooms? How would they measure effective teaching and learning?

4. **Principals' view of effective teaching and learning.** Interview two junior high and two senior high principals. How do they view effective teaching and learning? Is their view the same as that of the teachers? If not, which view do you tend to support?

5. **Evaluation of effective teaching and learning.** Visit at least two local school districts. Do these school districts evaluate their teachers? If so, who conducts the evaluation? What criteria are used? What do teachers think of the evaluative process? What do you think of the criteria? Would you want to be evaluated using these criteria?

PART 2 ▼ ▼ ▼ ▼

Preparing for Instruction

T he central focus of part 2 is on preparing for teaching. Effective teachers must plan and plan well. They select their content with care, identify lesson learning intent, select appropriate media, select and implement appropriate teaching strategies and methods, and finally they evaluate learning and assign grades.

The key to success as a teacher is a well-designed curriculum and a sound repertoire of instructional practices. Therefore, the program design of a school district is often central to successful instruction. However, it is the teacher who has the final say in what will be taught and what objectives will be pursued. Chapters 3, 4, and 5 will help you determine and organize the curriculum that will lead to the intended goals of a course. In addition, chapter 5 will show you how to design and carry out unit, weekly, and daily plans.

Effective instructional media and teaching methods will often make or break a lesson. Chapters 6, 7, 8, and 9 will focus on helping you choose and use appropriate media and methods for specific learning intent. The strengths and limitations of specific media and various teaching strategies and methods will be addressed.

Eventually teachers must evaluate results and assign grades. To this end, you must have a clear understanding of evaluation, measurement, and testing. Chapters 10 and 11 will address test construction, test scoring, and the conversion of test data into grades. The strengths and limitations associated with various test-item types and grade assignment techniques will be explored.

Identifying and Organizing Content

✎ **Time: You only have so much. It cannot be created, but it can be controlled. So use it wisely and productively. Diagnose and plan!**

Overview

The curriculum is one of the most critical ingredients in a secondary school program. Indeed, the curriculum often makes or breaks a school. Therefore, a school curriculum must be identified and selected with care.

An effective education is achieved when the learning situation is accurately diagnosed as to the appropriateness of the curriculum to be taught. In other words, content must be selected for the appropriate entry level of students. This selection process cannot occur by chance: It must thoughtfully weigh the needs of both the students and of society, and it must be based on the structure of the subject itself.

Diagnosis requires that information be collected. Such information can be obtained from students' cumulative records, from personal contact, and from other concerned parties. Whatever the sources, it is important to seek input from such sources prior to planning a course.

The final decision as to what will be taught in the classroom will be up to you as the classroom teacher. In some cases, assistance in making curriculum decisions will be available from curriculum committees or from curriculum specialists. However, in most cases, you alone will make the curriculum decisions.

Once the students' entry level has been determined, courses must be planned. Specific units must be formed and sequenced, and time allotments made for the units. These plans must remain flexible so adjustments can be made as the year progresses.

Objectives

After completing your study of chapter 3, you should be able to do the following:

1. Define *curriculum* and describe the different kinds of curricula.

2. Differentiate between the initial and continuous phase of diagnosis and the sources of information for each phase.

3. Identify the sources and tools that can be used in supplying diagnostic information for making educational decisions.

4. Outline the needs of society in relation to students as they relate to the curriculum of the secondary school.

5. Explain the influences of the subject structure on the secondary school curriculum.

6. Name and describe the three levels at which the content of a course can be selected.

7. List and explain the areas that must be addressed in planning a course for the year.

Chapter Terms and Key Concepts

Creative-Generative Level

Cumulative Record

Curriculum

Diagnostic Evaluation

Disabled

Explicit Curriculum

Extracurriculum

Handicapped

Hidden Curriculum

Imitative-Maintenance Level

Mastery Curriculum

Mediative Level

Needs

PL 94-142

Self-Fulfilling Prophecy

Student-Centered Curriculum

Subject-Centered Curriculum

This chapter will focus on the selection of curriculum for a course. We will first look at the curriculum and its general structure. The remainder of the chapter will be devoted to selecting the appropriate curriculum and to course planning.

The Curriculum

What is a curriculum? Or, more specifically, what exactly is the curriculum of a typical secondary school? A broad definition and interpretation of curriculum as a systematic plan of instruction was presented in chapter 1. However, specialists have suggested several different definitions for the term *curriculum*. For our purposes, let us define **curriculum** as all the planned and unplanned learning experiences that students undergo while in a school setting.

Eisner (1985) suggests that schools teach more than they intend. Some of what is taught is explicit (planned), while other material conveyed is not. Basically there are three kinds of curriculum that students experience: explicit curriculum, hidden curriculum, and extracurricular programs.

Explicit Curriculum

The **explicit curriculum** (formal curriculum) comprises those learning experiences that are intentional. Instruction has been carefully planned; resources—including money, space, time, and personnel—have been allocated for the accomplishment of curricular goals; curricular plans are written in documents that are readily available; the curriculum is evidenced in the lessons taught in the classroom; and the learning experience is formally evaluated. The formal curriculum encompasses the sequence of courses and objectives mandated by the state, the curriculum guide developed by the school district, the textbooks used in the classrooms, and the schedule of classes available for students. Based on the framework established by the state, the explicit curriculum generally derives from local curriculum-development efforts, with curriculum guides being developed that assist teachers with implementation. Figure 3.1 illustrates the levels of curriculum-planning involvement as it flows from the state to the classroom. As illustrated, the ultimate goal of the curriculum is to bring about learning and growth.

Some of the explicit curriculum is determined at the federal level. Laws like Public Law 94-142 (**PL 94-142**), also known as the Education for All Handicapped Children Act, dictate the degree and nature of service that will be provided for children with special needs. Court cases also have further defined the curriculum. For instance, placement of limited English–speaking students in classes for the mentally retarded on the basis of intelligence tests administered in English has been declared illegal by the Supreme Court.

Local concerns can have a tremendous impact on the explicit curriculum. For example, a rash of teenage suicides led one school district to increase the number and type of counselors available to students. A rural

Figure 3.1 *Levels of Curriculum Planning*

State Curriculum Planning

1. Identify philosophy that guides curriculum implementation
2. Determine progression of essential content taught
3. Outline modifications of curriculum to special populations (e.g., handicapped, gifted, etc.)

District Curriculum Planning

1. Establish content goals keyed to state guidelines
2. Determine appropriate teaching activities and assignment strategies
3. Develop appropriate curriculum guides; set up outline for unit plans; list and sequence major topics

Classroom Units and Lesson Plans

1. Establish how curriculum-guide goals are implemented in the classroom
2. Address topics to be covered, materials needed, activities to be used
3. Identify/develop evaluation strategies
4. Develop/identify adaptations to special populations

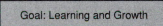

Goal: Learning and Growth

area would likely resist eliminating home economics and agricultural courses in the face of financial cutbacks, but might be willing to sacrifice a vocal-music program. A high school with a nearby vocational school may not choose to offer industrial arts or business classes.

Whatever the curricular imperatives for a given secondary school, they will be formalized in documents available to the patrons of the school. It is the explicit curriculum that the teachers and administrators will spell out when they tell parents exactly what their children are required to know.

Hidden Curriculum

The **hidden curriculum** is sometimes referred to as the "implicit" or "unintended" curriculum. The hidden curriculum consists of those learning experiences—both positive and negative—that produce changes in students' attitudes, beliefs, and values, but are not part of the explicit curriculum. Some students learn negative behaviors and attitudes, such as how to cheat, dislike school, and manipulate adults. Still others may learn positive behaviors and attitudes, such as how to learn effectively, to cooperate with others, and to like science. As you can see, you must guard against communicating and modeling undesirable behaviors and attitudes. Negative behaviors and attitudes are often easily learned by students.

The hidden curriculum often reflects societal values, such as rewarding great success, ignoring average performance, and criticizing or punishing failure. The social "pecking order"—in terms of gender, language, cultural differences, and socioeconomic status—is an inherent part of the hidden curriculum. The control mechanisms within the school and the classroom are part of the hidden curriculum. The distribution of resources that support the school curriculum is part of the hidden curriculum. The decisions about tracking, both for student and teacher assignments, convey messages about relative worth and, as such, are part of the hidden curriculum.

Extracurriculum

The **extracurriculum** is an elective extension of students' regular coursework, which does not carry credit toward graduation. Common examples of extracurricular activities include school clubs (e.g., chess club, French club, student journalism club, etc.), minicourses, heritage clubs, band activities, and pep clubs. Other extracurricular activities, such as the school newspaper or chorus groups, are direct spin-offs of curricular requirements.

Extracurricular activities are generally geared toward students' interests, needs, and aspirations. They serve to add spice and augment a school's formal curriculum. As such, extracurricular activities can be used as reinforcers for the more formal curriculum. The extracurriculum should be given careful consideration and planning.

Curriculum Structure

Generally, a school district will have the flexibility to pattern its curriculum any way it chooses. Typically, these organizational patterns tend to range between the extremes of being subject-centered on one side and student-centered on the other (see figure 3.2). The subject-centered curricular organization tends to be content-oriented; conversely, if a curriculum follows a student-centered pattern, it is learner-oriented. In general, most districts organize their curriculum (1) as an eclectic combination of several patterns, (2) with most programs falling somewhere toward the middle of the continuum, and (3) with a good deal of variety from class to class and

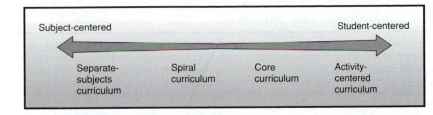

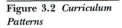

Figure 3.2 *Curriculum Patterns*

teacher to teacher. How the curriculum is organized will be influenced strongly by the philosophical position on the purpose of education taken by the district.

Subject-Centered Curriculum

The **subject-centered curriculum** is still the most widely used curriculum pattern in U.S. secondary schools. It regards learning primarily as cognitive development and the acquisition of knowledge and information. With this approach, all the subjects for instruction are separated. In general, the content areas are taught in isolation, with no attempt at integration.

The subject-centered curriculum places emphasis on oral discourse and extensive explanations. It expects teachers to plan instruction before teaching begins and to organize it around the content, and it assumes that certain content should be taught to all students. The subject-centered curriculum usually consists of a study of specific facts and ideas. The teaching methods usually include the direct strategies: lectures, discussions, and questions (see chapter 7).

The most widely used subject-centered curriculum is the separate-subjects curriculum. The separate-subjects curriculum content is divided into fairly discreet areas of study—algebra, history, composition, chemistry, literature, and so forth. The required subjects (general education) usually make up most of the secondary school program, and students are given little choice in selecting courses. However, some districts are giving students more opportunity to select electives.

Some feel that the subject-centered curriculum does not adequately foster critical or creative thinking, or develop an understanding of societal issues. This approach often places emphasis on the memorization of facts and ideas and, moreover, tends to focus on the past. For example, social-studies instruction often consists of the study of the past and the related facts.

Supporters and defenders of a subject-centered curriculum argue that the approach has stood the test of time and that not all subjects can be studied at once—as other curriculum approaches propose to do. They further argue that study cannot be all-inclusive: There is simply too much information and it must be ordered as well as segmented.

A second type of subject-centered curriculum is referred to as a spiral curriculum. The spiral curriculum is organized around the material to be taught. It is similar to the separate-subjects pattern, but differs in two notable ways. First, the spiral curriculum puts more emphasis on the

TABLE 3.1 Contrasting Curriculum Patterns

Subject-Centered Curriculum	Student-Centered Curriculum
Focus on subject matter	Centered on learner needs
Centered on subjects	Centered on cooperative determination of subject matter
Teacher organizes subject matter before instruction	Emphasis on variability in exposure to learning
Emphasis on facts, knowledge, and information	Emphasis on skills
Generally lower-level learning	Emphasis on immediate meanings of learning
Emphasis on uniformity of exposure	Emphasis on indirect strategies
Emphasis on direct strategies	

concepts and generalizations; in other words, it places the emphasis on the structure of knowledge. Second, it is designed to fit sequentially with students' developmental thinking stages.

Student-Centered Curriculum

A **student-centered curriculum** can be described as an activity curriculum. In effect, a student-centered curriculum focuses on student needs, interests, and activities. In its purest form, a student-centered curriculum operates with students as the center of the learning process. Activities are planned jointly by the teacher and students. The teacher is seen as a stimulator and facilitator of student activity. However, because of the subject-matter emphasis in most secondary schools, student-centered curriculum has never secured a firm foothold at the secondary level.

One kind of student-centered curriculum is the core curriculum. The core curriculum is a student-centered pattern with several subject-centered characteristics. Typically, it combines subjects into broad fields of study. This pattern of organization is found most frequently in junior high schools. The subjects most often combined in core curricula are social studies and language arts, mathematics and science, and social studies and science.

Still another type of student-centered curriculum is the activity-centered curriculum. Like the core curriculum, activity-centered curriculum is patterned around the needs and interests of students. However, the content coverage is more flexible than with the core curriculum. Learning by doing and problem solving are emphasized. As such, particular detailed lessons often are not planned, because the teacher cannot anticipate what student interests will surface or where their inquiry will take them.

The subject-centered curriculum and the student-centered curriculum patterns represent two opposite ends of a curriculum continuum. Table 3.1 contrasts the two curriculum patterns.

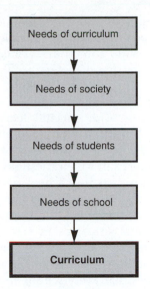

Figure 3.3 *Influences on Curriculum Selection*

Curriculum Selection

Students and, ultimately, society will be the consumers of the secondary school curriculum. As such, both deserve to supply input as to what should be taught. Moreover, the structure of a subject often dictates what and how the subject should be taught—that is, the content as well as the sequence of teaching. The well-planned curriculum, then, will take into account student and societal **needs** as well as the subject itself. However, you must keep in mind that students, society, and the subject structure are influenced by other factors, as depicted in figure 3.3.

Diagnostic information gives curriculum developers valuable data that can be interpreted for a variety of purposes. Most frequently, however, such information is used strictly for establishing and checking standards of achievement. Achievement test scores, for example, are often used for nothing more than making comparisons of district group scores with national norms; renewed instructional emphasis is then placed on those areas found to be below the national norms. Such use of achievement test scores is the narrowest interpretation and use of diagnostic data.

Needs of Students

The more you know about your students, the easier will be your task of bringing about the desired learning. In short, to be an effective educator, you must identify your students' **needs**—their strengths, weaknesses, aspirations, limitations, and deficiencies. These student needs can be academic or social. Some students may be lagging in reading or in mathematics, while others may be gifted, academically talented, or creative. An awareness of these differences is needed so you can devise ways of providing adequate instruction. In addition, you must take into account differences in social and cultural background as well as different student abilities.

Some of your students will be academically able or even bright, while others will be slower, **disabled,** or **handicapped.** *Disabled* has been defined as the inability to do something (Hallahan & Kauffman, 1991). *Handicapped*, on the other hand, refers to those individuals who are mentally retarded, deaf or hard of hearing, speech-impaired, visually handicapped, seriously emotionally disturbed, orthopedically impaired, multihandicapped, or those with specific learning disabilities or other health impairments, and who therefore need special educational services (Turnbull, 1990). A handicapped person may or may not be disabled, depending on the circumstances in which the individual finds himself or herself. For example, an individual in a wheelchair is not disabled unless a situation is encountered that restricts his or her performance. Student differences often require that you adapt your classroom's physical environment and your instructional strategies in ways that better accommodate the unique needs of mainstreamed or special students. In other words, you must learn to modify your instruction to fit the needs of all students.

PL 94-142 requires that every school system in the nation provide a free, appropriate public education for every child between the ages of 3 and 21 (Hallahan & Kauffman, 1991). A major provision of PL 94-142 is the establishment of a written individualized education program (IEP) for each handicapped student. The program must state present levels of functioning, long- and short-term goals, services to be provided, and plans for initiating and evaluating the services. Carrying out IEP goals and objectives may require lesson modifications, such as adapting assigned work, developing special reproduced materials for teaching difficult concepts, planning and writing special study guides, or obtaining and using special equipment.

The use of differentiated assignments is a must when working with mainstreamed special-needs students. This is accomplished by varying the length and difficulty of assignments, or by individualizing the curriculum as much as possible. For example, you might require only half as much writing for a student with motor difficulties. Similarly, you might allow a student with speech difficulties to write a paper instead of giving a speech.

Another prelesson planning task is to identify your students' entry levels: Determine what students already know about your subject and their mastery of necessary prerequisite skills.

How do you go about diagnosing the needs of students, especially when you usually won't meet them until the start of the school year? Diagnosis is a two-phase process, with an initial phase and a continuous phase. The initial phase takes place prior to the arrival of students in your classroom, whereas the continuous phase follows their arrival.

Initial Diagnosis Phase

Initial **diagnostic evaluations** are usually administered prior to the beginning of the school year to determine students' entry level (readiness) in curriculum areas. These diagnoses provide the information needed for the correct placement of students in tracks and courses.

Diagnostic information generally comes from two sources: performance in past coursework and performance on achievement tests. Too frequently students are placed solely on the basis of performance in a completed class or on the basis of grades received in past related courses. Such procedures may lead to incorrect placement if performance information is incorrectly analyzed. For example, a teacher's bias or high expectations may lead to unrealistic placement. Moreover, grades can often give misleading information as to overall ability.

One critical piece of diagnostic information needed by all teachers is their students' reading levels. If your potential students have reading difficulties, you need to secure materials that will aid them with their comprehension and understanding. We will address the special problem of reading in detail in chapter 14.

Sometimes teachers gather diagnostic information with a pretest at the beginning of a unit. The information provided by such tests tells the teacher where to start instruction. At times, it may be necessary to teach or review needed prerequisite skills before beginning a new unit.

As a teacher with five or six different classes or preparations per day, you will often not have much time to determine students' entry level. Indeed, sometimes the only way to obtain diagnostic information on students will be to ask fellow teachers. At other times, you even may have to rely on intuition at the beginning of a unit, until you can obtain more accurate information as the unit is being taught.

Continuous Diagnosis Phase

Diagnosis should be a never-ending process. After you begin a unit of study, the original diagnosis should be revised as more information is gleaned from students' performance on oral and written work. As individual student deficiencies are noted, remedial work should be planned for bringing the student up to the level of his or her peers. Some students may need even more assistance than you can provide. At such time, outside assistance from specialists, if available, should be sought.

No matter what form of diagnostic evaluation takes place during instruction, an evaluation should be administered at the end of each unit. The data obtained from these evaluations should be carefully analyzed when determining the need for follow-up. Follow-up is essential in keeping all students at the same level of mastery.

Diagnostic Tools

Accurate diagnosis requires an ample supply of information about students. Therefore, you need to be familiar with the different sources of diagnostic information. Because diagnostic tools will be addressed in detail in chapter 10, only a brief overview will be presented at this time. Four particularly useful diagnostic tools are described here.

1. **Cumulative Record Folder**
    The **cumulative record** usually comprises a record of all the student's test scores (aptitude, intelligence, achievement, etc.), as well as the student's health records. In addition, this file contains various anecdotal comments made by the student's teachers over the years.

Through personal contact with students, teachers can gain valuable insight into students' strengths and weaknesses.

2. Personal Contact
Working with students on an individual basis will give you the opportunity to gather considerable information. In other words, your direct observations, analyses of students' work, and conversations with students often provide valuable diagnostic information.

3. Conferences
Many times parents, counselors, and other teachers can serve as viable sources of diagnostic information. When problems develop, individual conferences with others who are in a position to supply pertinent information should be planned.

4. Open-Ended Themes and Diaries
Giving students opportunities to write about their feelings and their in-school and out-of-school lives can lead to some valuable diagnostic data. Frequently, such information will provide insight into the reasons for student problems and inadequacies.

Caution should be exercised when referring to cumulative records and conferences, so that expectations are not unduly influenced by information gleaned from these sources. In other words, take care in making sure that your decisions are objective and fair. Your attitudes and expectations may serve as **self-fulfilling prophecy**—that is, your students may behave in the manner consistent with your expectations, rather than in response to other factors.

Needs of Society

Curriculum must be planned not only in terms of student needs, but also in terms of the needs of society in relation to students. In a complex society in which vast and rapid changes are occurring, however, establishing what demands society should make of education is a difficult task. Some curriculum planners take a more simplistic view of what skills are needed to be a fully functioning member of society: Some educators feel that mastery of basic skills, preparation for a vocation or college, the ability to drive, consumer knowledge and skills, and a broad and general knowledge represent the essential curriculum for students.

Other curriculum planners, impressed with the multitude of concerns faced by society, are not sure what role education will play in a future that is increasingly unpredictable and technological. Certainly, education for national citizenship is to a great extent the function of the school. Thus, education needs to embrace not only intellect, but the whole person—with the ability to think, reason, and apply. Indeed, many curriculum planners feel that education must vitalize and address world political freedom, basic humanity, and social and economic problems. What will be required, then, are curricula that foster basic skills and include programs that provide citizenship, consumer, global, health, career, and sex education.

Issues for curricula are constantly changing in step with societal changes and new expectations. However, some educators claim that today's education has failed to probe deeply into the realities of society and, therefore, has essentially failed to address rapidly shifting societal forces (Boyer, 1983; Goodlad, 1984; and Sizer, 1984). These educators further argue that schools too often are loaded with coursework that is irrelevant to the needs of students and society.

The decline in achievement test scores has received widespread attention from the press, legislatures, educators, and the public (Parkay and Stanford, 1992). Some observers have argued, based on these declining scores and other assessment efforts, that schools are failing in their primary function of educating students. Some have gone so far as to suggest that the school curriculum has ceased to be relevant and viable for our present societal needs. Subsequently, as noted in chapter 1, reform and restructuring of education has become a national issue. Reports such as *A Nation At Risk: The Imperative for Educational Reform* (National Commission on Excellence in Education, 1983), *High School: A Report on Secondary Education in America* (Boyer, 1983), *Horace's Compromise: The Dilemma of American High School* (Sizer, 1984), and *America 2000: An Education Strategy* (Reed and Bergemann, 1992) attest to the criticism and national attention that has been directed toward the improvement of education.

Many curriculum reformers of the 1980s and 1990s now realize that schools have been asked to do too much and have attempted to define some unifying major purposes for schools. Some of these reformers have suggested that schools concentrate on students' academic competencies. The College Board (1983) has identified five basic competencies expected for college entrants: reading, writing, mathematics, reasoning, and studying. On the other hand, the report titled *Educating Americans for the 21st Century* (National Science Board Commission on Precollege Education in Mathematics, Science, and Technology, 1983) suggests that schools put more emphasis on scientific and technological literacy. The report recommends that all secondary students be required to take at least three years of mathematics and three years of science and technology.

John Goodlad (1984) and Ernest Boyer (1983) recommend a common core of courses be required of students. Goodlad argues for a better balance of subjects with a broader breadth of study. He recommends a core of requirements within five domains: mathematics and science, literature and language, society and social studies, the arts, and the vocations. In contrast, Boyer recommends that the schools' first priority should be the mastery of language. He believes that the three-track vocational, academic, and general system should be eliminated and that, instead, a core curriculum consisting of literature, arts, foreign language, history, civics, science, mathematics, and technology should be required. In addition, Boyer suggests four goals are appropriate for schools:

1. Develop students' capacity to think critically and communicate effectively.

2. Help students learn about themselves and their heritage.

3. Prepare students for work and further education.

4. Help students fulfill their social and civic obligations.

In 1990, President George Bush outlined six national goals for American education to be reached by the year 2000 (National Goals for Education, 1990):

Goal 1: All children in America will start school ready to learn.

Goal 2: The high school graduation rate will increase to 90 percent.

Goal 3: American students will leave grades 4, 8, and 12 having demonstrated competency in challenging subject matter including English, mathematics, science, history, and geography, and every school in America will ensure that all students learn to use their minds well, so they may be prepared for responsible citizenship, further learning, and productive employment in our modern economy.

Goal 4: U.S. students will be first in the world in mathematics and science achievement.

Goal 5: Every adult American will be literate and will possess the skills necessary to compete in a global economy and exercise the rights and responsibilities of citizenship.

Goal 6: Every school in America will be free of drugs and violence and will offer a disciplined environment conducive to learning.

These six goals were extended by President Bush with his ambitious *America 2000: An Education Strategy* (1991). This plan spelled out these elements:

1. Strategies for attaining the six national goals set in 1990.

2. Funding to create by 1996 a ''New Generation of American Schools'' (at least 535) around the country.

3. A 15-point accountability plan for parents, teachers, schools, and communities to measure and compare results among schools.

4. ''New World Standards'' in five core subjects for what students need to know and be able to do.

5. A voluntary system of national testing, the American Achievement Tests, based on the New World Standards.

6. Incentives to states and local districts to adopt policies for school choice.

7. Governor's Academies for Teachers designed to assist teachers in helping students pass the American Achievement Tests.

8. The creation of the New American Schools Development Corporation, a nonprofit organization to oversee innovative school-reform efforts.

9. The creation of electronic networks to serve the New American Schools.

10. The creation of skill clinics where people can acquire knowledge and skills needed for employment.

Decisions regarding the curriculum to be included in today's secondary schools will not be easily made. Teachers and curriculum specialists must work together in developing and implementing a truly viable curriculum for a modern society. We must not be satisfied with only a good education, but we must require a great one—one that addresses the realities of our age.

Needs Derived from the Subject

Because the curriculum is also defined by the structure of a subject that students should learn and teachers should teach, a school curriculum must be in vital contact with two areas of reality: the growing body of knowledge in the subject field itself and the extent of understanding of the subject needed by the ordinary person. Therefore, current curricula for secondary schools must focus on these two areas.

First and foremost, the curriculum in the school must be valid. But a field of study is never static; it continues to grow. The mainstay of current curriculum, specific facts are educationally the least valuable, and yet they should form the core of the curriculum to be taught in schools. However, it is the basic ideas, concepts, and modes of thought that form the true essence of the curriculum; that is, as Jerome Bruner (1977)

TABLE 3.2   The Curriculum

Concept	Description
Curriculum	Planned and unplanned experiences that students undergo in school settings
Explicit Curriculum	Information, skills, and attitudes that a school intends to teach
Extracurriculum	Learning experiences that are an elective extension of students' regular coursework
Hidden Curriculum	Behaviors, attitudes, and knowledge that a school unintentionally teaches
Subject-Centered Curriculum	Curriculum patterns wherein subjects are separated into separate courses of study
Student-Centered Curriculum	An activity curriculum that focuses on student needs, interests, and activities
Needs	Academic and societal areas in which students have weaknesses, limitations, or deficiencies
Initial Diagnosis	Collection of information on students' needs prior to the beginning of instruction
Continuous Diagnosis	Collection of information on students' needs after instruction begins
Diagnostic Tools	Devices used to collect information about students

suggests, the "structure of the subject," the "basic ideas," and the "fundamental principles" permit understanding and make a subject meaningful. Therefore, the secondary school curriculum should focus on carefully selected principles, which constitute the basic core of a subject. To learn the structure of a subject, in short, is to learn a body of knowledge.

Too often a textbook is the sole source of content for a course, with discipline scholars being the determiners of what is included in the textbook. From the subject-matter perspective, it is believed that discipline scholars know best how subjects should be structured and organized in a text, as well as the relative emphasis that various topics should be given in the curriculum area. However, most students do not share the scholars' aspirations for becoming scientists, mathematicians, musicians, or historians. This fact should be kept in mind as a relevant curriculum is developed for implementation in the classroom. In selecting the content, you must watch out for the tendency of discipline scholars to "protect their turf" by extolling its importance.

Recently, the structure of a subject has been dictated in terms of competencies to be demonstrated by learners. For example, the state of Oklahoma has established learning outcomes for students completing all grades and subjects. These standards relate to the basic principles that undergird the different curriculum areas. Basically, the competencies represent the minimum knowledge and skills needed by individual students at the respective grade level.

In short, schools must pay particular attention to their curricula, and curriculum developers need to direct their attention to three major areas of need: the learner, the society, and the subject. Table 3.2 summarizes the concepts related to school curriculum and areas of curriculum need. The Curriculum Application Guidelines offer further suggestions related to needs. Keep in mind that curricula, student needs, and societies

Application Guidelines ▼

change over time—and no curriculum has reached a state of perfection. Therefore, you need to decide the appropriate content to be taught in your classroom. Before you continue with the next section, review table 3.2 and The Curriculum Application Guidelines, and complete exercise 3.1.

Selection of Content

Historically, teachers and schools have selected their content based on a wide variety of reasons and criteria. However, according to Tanner and Tanner (1980), teachers and schools tend to select content essentially at one of three distinct levels: (1) imitative-maintenance, (2) mediative, and (3) generative-creative.

Imitative-Maintenance Level

Imitative-maintenance level teachers "rely on textbooks, workbooks, and routine activities, subject by subject" (Tanner & Tanner, 1980, p. 636). Essentially, teachers at this level are turning the entire process of content selection over to the author of the adopted textbook. They begin with the first chapter and follow the sequence of chapters until the year ends. If all goes well, the last chapter is finished on the last day of the year. If not,

Application of Knowledge

Exercise 3.1 The Curriculum

Test yourself on the following diagnosis concepts. Appropriate responses can be found in appendix A.

1. Match the description on the left with the proper curriculum term on the right.
   - a. _____ Curriculum based on needs and interests of students
   - b. _____ The intended material to be taught
   - c. _____ The unintended teachings

   1. Explicit curriculum
   2. Hidden curriculum
   3. Activity-centered curriculum

2. Factors beyond the teacher's control often influence the starting point of instruction. (True/False)

3. Diagnosis has an initial as well as a continuous phase. (True/False)

4. The only reason school districts give achievement tests is to provide diagnostic information. (True/False)

5. Student instructional entry level and topic selection and sequence are determined by these factors:
   - a. _____
   - b. _____
   - c. _____

instruction either stops at whatever chapter the class happens to be on at the end of the year, or is rushed through the remaining chapters so the textbook is completed.

At the imitative-maintenance level, the curriculum is used without critical evaluation. The unique needs and skill levels of students are not addressed. Sadly, change comes only when a new textbook is adopted. Often the resultant curriculum is dead-ended and segmented.

Some teachers feel that a textbook is sacred and must be finished at all cost. Indeed, these teachers often rush through the last few chapters during the last couple of weeks of school just to finish the textbook. This practice is indefensible and shows a lack of advanced planning.

Mediative Level

Teachers at the **mediative level** follow the basic adopted textbook, but are aware of, and integrate, emergent societal conditions into the classroom content (Tanner & Tanner, 1980, p. 638). The teacher uses multimedia materials, segmental curriculum packages, and other available resources to address societal concerns (e.g., the environment, AIDS, the energy crisis, and so on). Although teachers at this level supplement the basic textbook, the content remains segmented and still isolated from the relevant needed skills of students.

Teachers at this second level do not blindly follow a textbook sequence. They realize that textbooks are not all-inclusive, and they augment the textbook to a limited degree. Put simply, these teachers are not rigid; they are aware; they plan; and finally, they tap external resources to enhance instruction.

Creative-Generative Level

Finally, **creative-generative level** teachers take an aggregate approach to content selection (Tanner & Tanner, 1980, p. 638). At this level, the selection of content is districtwide or schoolwide. Some districts have curriculum committees or districtwide curriculum specialists who work with teachers in the selection of course content. This approach to curriculum development requires much cooperative planning on a districtwide basis.

Frequently, detailed curriculum guides are produced by school districts to assist teachers in planning their courses. These guides often suggest possible content sequences, identify learning outcomes, indicate alternative assignment levels, suggest alternative instructional techniques, recommend evaluation procedures, and list supplementary instructional resources.

At the creative-generative level, course content is based on an analysis of the needs of students, society, and the subject. Problems are identified, and instruction is planned in an attempt to find solutions. To this end, research and independent judgment is used in selecting content and resources and in adapting them to the classroom situation. Sadly, few teachers function at this level. Indeed, most teachers operate at the imitative-maintenance or the mediative levels in the selection of course content.

TABLE 3.3   Content Selection Levels

Level	Description
Imitative-Maintenance	An adopted textbook is used to determine content
	Selection determined by author of textbook
	Usually no assistance is available from district in selecting content
Mediative	An adopted textbook determines content, but is supplemented somewhat with societal issues
	There is an awareness that textbooks aren't all-inclusive and need some supplementing
Creative-Generative	Content selection is districtwide
	Assistance is given to teachers by committee or specialists
	Teachers serve on selection committee and have a central role in selecting content

Table 3.3 gives a summary of the levels of content selection. However, most school districts offer at most only limited curriculum assistance to teachers. As such, teachers are often obliged to undertake course planning on their own. We will look at procedures for accomplishing this task in the next section.

Planning the Course

All teachers are responsible for the instructional emphasis within their classrooms. They are responsible for organizing instruction in such a way that students receive instruction in, and achieve mastery of, the state-mandated curricula. But state-mandated curricula do not complete the picture of those things deemed important for students to learn. There are "generic" lessons that take place in the classroom that are rarely found in the curricular documents of the state or the district. There also are worthy "enrichment" activities deemed important by the teacher and by the students. Decisions must be made about the time, personnel, energy, and resources allocated to each of these important components of the curriculum.

Glatthorn (1987) suggests that 60 to 75 percent of instructional time should be allocated to the state-mandated curriculum. Glatthorn calls this the **mastery curriculum** and defines it as those learnings considered essential for all students to know. He further states that the teaching of the mastery curriculum requires highly structured, well-planned, sequenced units and lessons that produce measurable results. The generic curriculum comprises the interpersonal and intrapersonal attitudes, beliefs, skills, and knowledge that do not tend to lend themselves to a highly structured plan of instruction. Enrichment involves those things that are nice to know, but are not essential for all students. A graphic model of curricular allocation as suggested by Glatthorn is shown in figure 3.4.

The procedures for identifying the content for a complete school program (K–12) can be quite sophisticated. Essentially, such procedures should be left to textbook writers in deciding what to include in a textbook

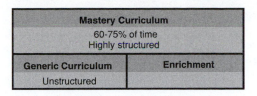

Figure 3.4 *Allocating Curricular Time*

series or to developers of curriculum programs for a school district. Only rarely will the classroom teacher be expected to develop the scope and sequence of a program. As noted earlier, however, teachers should plan their courses in terms of student needs, district goals, and societal needs.

Frequently, your first task as a teacher will be to plan your course(s) for the school year. Basically you must lay out your instruction for the year for each subject you teach. To do so, you must address certain questions.

1. What major topics (chapters) will be covered? Can you justify your selection?

2. Should the class textbook content (chapters) be supplemented?

3. How should the topics (chapters) be grouped to form units of study? Why?

4. In what sequence should the planned units be taught? Why?

5. How much emphasis should each unit receive? In a 35-week course, how much time should each unit receive (in weeks and fractions of weeks)?

Your answers to such questions should result in a systematic layout of your course for the year. You will need to consult the curriculum guidelines of your state and school district and any required standardized tests your students must take. Most teachers use an adopted course textbook as the core for planning. Such a procedure could, for example, yield a unit sequence of study and time allotments for a course as follows:

Unit 1
    The Universe (3 weeks)
    Chapter 1   Stars
    Chapter 2   Galaxies

Unit 2
    The Solar System (4 weeks)
    Chapter 4   The Earth
    Chapter 5   The Moon

Unit 3
    The Earth's Atmosphere (4½ weeks)
    Chapter 6   Atmosphere
    Chapter 8   Sun, Water, and Wind
    Chapter 9   Weather

Unit 4
    The Earth's Crust (5 weeks)
    Chapter 11   Rocks
    Chapter 12   Volcanoes
    Chapter 13   Earthquakes

Unit 5
    The Changing Crust (4 weeks)
    Chapter 14   Weathering
    Chapter 15   Erosion
    Chapter 10   Mountain Building

Unit 6
    The Earth's History (4 weeks)
    Chapter 16   Geologic Time
    Chapter 17   Stories in Stone

Unit 7
    Animal Life (4 weeks)
    Chapter 3   Place and Time
    Chapter 18   Development of Life

Unit 8
    Human Life (4½ weeks)
    Chapter 20   Human Life Begins
    Chapter 19   The Human Environment

Your course plan should be flexible, so changes can be made during the year. As you analyze the textbook and select chapters to be covered, recognize that not all chapters need to be covered, that the textbook chapters may not include all the content areas you want to teach, that the text sequence is not always the best sequence for every class, and that all chapters are not of equal importance. Also make time allotments based on your intended methods and procedures and on the importance you place on the topic.

Finally, leave a couple of weeks at the end of the year open, in case more time is required than originally planned to finish some of your units. The extra time can always be used for review or enrichment if it is not needed for unit instruction.

One of the chief values of course planning is that it permits you to better plan for desirable media and instructional materials (e.g., films, special equipment, computer programs, special books, and so on). In fact, some school districts even require that all special materials be requested at the beginning of the year. In such districts, course planning will be essential.

This concludes our discussion of content selection. Review the Content Selection Application Guidelines, and complete exercise 3.2, which will check your understanding of this section.

Application Guidelines ▼

Content Selection

Organize for Effective Teaching

Examples:
1. Seek assistance in planning from school district specialists and/or from fellow teachers.
2. Supplement the basic, adopted course textbook. Add content and societal issues that you believe are important and should have been included in the textbook.
3. Organize your course according to your knowledge of the needs of students and society and of district goals.
4. Select and sequence your content according to your knowledge of your subject.
5. Base your unit's time allotments on the importance you want placed on the specific unit as well as on the instructional methods to be used and the activities to be completed.

Application of Knowledge

Exercise 3.2   Content Selection

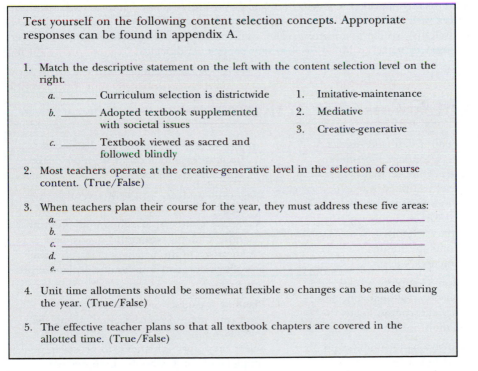

Test yourself on the following content selection concepts. Appropriate responses can be found in appendix A.

1. Match the descriptive statement on the left with the content selection level on the right.

   a. _____ Curriculum selection is districtwide

   b. _____ Adopted textbook supplemented with societal issues

   c. _____ Textbook viewed as sacred and followed blindly

   1. Imitative-maintenance
   2. Mediative
   3. Creative-generative

2. Most teachers operate at the creative-generative level in the selection of course content. (True/False)

3. When teachers plan their course for the year, they must address these five areas:
   a. _____
   b. _____
   c. _____
   d. _____
   e. _____

4. Unit time allotments should be somewhat flexible so changes can be made during the year. (True/False)

5. The effective teacher plans so that all textbook chapters are covered in the allotted time. (True/False)

CHAPTER SUMMARY

School districts and teachers must make practical decisions about curricula. The curriculum of a school consists of all the planned and unplanned experiences students undergo in the school setting. The three categories of secondary school curricula are the explicit curriculum, hidden curriculum, and extracurriculum.

Curriculum decisions often are based on the philosophy of the district. The curriculum pattern can be subject-centered or student-centered, or an integrated combination of both forms.

Curriculum decisions should not be made blindly. In essence, the decisions regarding what to teach should be based on an analysis of the situation; that is, content selection should be planned so that instruction fulfills the needs of students and society. Moreover, classroom instruction must be selected and sequenced so that the instruction is based on the structure of the subject.

Many devices are available for diagnosing the learning situation. Among those commonly referred to are students' cumulative records, personal contact with students, conferences with parents and other school personnel, and students' written comments. Such devices should be used to make an initial di-agnosis of the learning situation as well as to carry out continuous diagnosis after school starts.

Once the learning situation has been diagnosed, class content must be selected. This selection process can take place at three distinct levels: (1) imitative-maintenance, (2) mediative, and (3) generative-creative. At the first and second levels, the teacher bases the content on an adopted textbook. Ordinarily teachers at the imitative-maintenance level follow the textbook blindly, without supplementals; whereas at the mediative level, teachers integrate societal issues into the curriculum to a limited degree. When operating at the generative-creative level, the selection of classroom content is carried out by a curriculum committee or with districtwide curriculum specialists. Frequently, this assistance comes in the form of curriculum guides.

Often teachers must plan their course for the year with little assistance. In such cases, the usual procedure is to use the adopted textbook as a source for the selection of course topics. These topics (chapters) are combined into units, and a unit sequence with time allotments is then established. The course plan should remain flexible, however, so any needed modifications can be made during the year.

Discussion Questions and Activities

1. **The curriculum.** Obtain a state and district curriculum guide for secondary education. How would you improve the secondary curriculum at the level you plan to teach? Should teachers be free to determine what they will teach? What forces commonly influence the secondary school curriculum? the explicit curriculum? the hidden curriculum? the extracurriculum?

2. **Classroom observation.** Complete several classroom interaction observational activities in different secondary classrooms. Focus the collection of information on the following:

   a. Actions that help you better understand students and their behaviors.

   b. Information gained from conversations within the classroom environment that help you understand students' needs, likes, and dislikes.

   c. The weaknesses and strengths gained from an examination of students' class work and homework.

3. **Diagnostic devices.** Visit with several secondary school teachers. Make a list of diagnostic tools that are commonly used to diagnose students' strengths, needs, and weaknesses. Do the teachers make effective use of achievement test results in planning instruction?

4. **Planning a course.** Select a basic textbook from your area of specialization. Using the selected textbook, plan a 35-week course. Select the topics (chapters) to be covered, supplement the textbook where needed, combine the topics (chapters) into appropriate units of study, and make unit time allotments.

Goals and Objectives

✎ **Oh, what to teach—content, processes, attitudes, values, morals? The possibilities are inexhaustible! Decisions, Decisions!**

Overview

Selecting the curriculum is only the beginning in planning for instruction. You must now clarify your purpose and instructional intent: You must decide exactly what you want students to learn, how they will learn it, and how you will know they have learned it. Generally these three steps occur simultaneously with the setting of priorities regarding time, objectives, materials, and methods of instruction.

This chapter will address the establishment of goals and objectives, while chapters 5, 10, and 11 will be devoted to lesson planning, evaluation of student learning, and testing and grading, respectively.

Objectives

After completing your study of chapter 4, you should be able to do the following:

1. State valid rationales for stating instructional goals and objectives.

2. Contrast the terms *educational goals, informational objectives,* and *instructional objectives.*

3. Prepare (write) educational goals.

4. Describe the four components that make up a properly written instructional objective.

5. Describe the three domains of learning.

6. Classify objectives into cognitive, affective, and psychomotor domains, and rate them as higher- or lower-level within each domain.

7. Prepare (write) informational objectives and instructional objectives at different levels of cognitive, affective, and psychomotor sophistication.

Chapter Terms and Key Concepts

Affective Domain

Cognitive Domain

Goal

Informational Objective

Instructional Objective

Objective

Psychomotor Domain

Almost anything you try in the classroom will result in some type of learning, but not always desirable learning. To be effective, learning must have direction, it must have purpose. For example, your school might want to direct instruction toward the Seven Cardinal Principles of Secondary Education (see chapter 1). Your task would then be to decide on the specific learning techniques that will lead to the attainment of these principles. Thus, even though they are broad and abstract, the Seven Cardinal Principles would be used to generate course content and related specific objectives. Viewed in this context, an objective can be interpreted as a clear and unambiguous description of instructional intent. It is finite and measurable. Its accomplishment can be verified.

An **objective** is not a statement of what you plan to do; instead, it is a statement of what students should be able to do after instruction. For example, if the purpose of instruction is to foster student understanding of the conditions that led to World War II, the objective would *not* be, "The *teacher will present* information about World War II." It doesn't matter at all what the teacher does if students do not learn. Remember the purpose of instruction is to get students to learn. Therefore, the objective might be, "The *students will discuss* economic conditions in Europe prior to the beginning of World War II." Objectives, then, should place the emphasis on student outcome or performance.

Rationale for Objectives

Teaching, as noted in chapter 1, can be envisioned as a six-phase process (see figure 1.1). Once the content to be taught has been selected, objectives must be written related to the selected content. The written objectives will then set the framework for the instructional approach and the student evaluation.

Instructional Framework

Objectives establish the framework for instruction: They compel you to provide the environment and sequence of activities that will allow students to reach the stated intent. For example, if your objective is the instant recall of specific information (such as the elements in the periodic table), your activities must apply to the recall of the information. If, on the other hand, the objective is related to the use of information in problem solving, then practice in problem-solving procedures must be provided. Thus, objectives spell out general strategies and specific activities for their attainment.

Objectives also prescribe exactly what skills or knowledge students must manifest as a result of instruction. In other words, your objectives will set the framework for the evaluation process.

Communication of Intent

Objectives also serve an important communication function. Today, clear and measurable objectives need to be stated for the benefit of students, parents, and program accountability. Through the use of properly written objectives, educators can show where students are, as a group or as

individuals, with respect to the stated objectives. Administrators can communicate similar information to school boards or the community at large. Objectives will make it clear to students your expectations prior to instruction. This communication will eliminate guesswork related to students' learning (e.g., "Will this be on the test?"). Thus, when you communicate your objectives, students know exactly what is expected of them, and they no longer have to guess what is important. They know whether it will be on the test!

Objectives are widely used in education today. Public Law 94-142, for example, requires that an Individual Education Plan (IEP) be written for every handicapped student in your class. And for each of these plans, specific objectives must be written for the students. Furthermore, individualized program and mastery learning techniques, as well as some state and district regulations, require the specification of objectives. Thus, as a prospective teacher, you must understand and develop the skills for prescribing and writing your instructional intent (objectives).

Teacher Accountability

Finally, the movement for teacher accountability has become a simple extension of objectives, testing, and evaluation. Teacher accountability means that teachers are responsible for the quality of their instruction and the progress of their students. Generally, teacher performance related to planning and instruction is measured through classroom-based observation and evaluation by administrators. Typically, student progress is measured by performance on nationally normed standardized tests.

Figure 4.1
*A Three-Stage
Accountability Model*

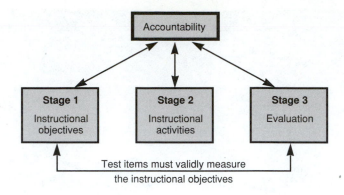

A three-stage accountability model is depicted in figure 4.1. The first stage in the model is the establishment of objectives—that is, learning intent. In stage 2, instructional activities designed to develop student mastery are implemented. The final stage is the determination of whether the intent was accomplished. In other words, did you do the intended job? You must show that the intended learning outcome has taken place. You are being held accountable for the student's acquisition of the desired learning as stated in the objectives.

As shown in figure 4.1, objectives drive the entire instructional process. Therefore, it is essential that objectives be clear and measurable, because the evaluation will be determined by the objectives. That is, the evaluation must measure the outcome that is specified in the objective. The following examples illustrate incorrect and correct evaluations of intended learning outcomes.

Objective: The student will use geometric formulas.

Wrong outcome evaluation: Derive geometric formulas.

Better outcome evaluation: Please find the area and volume.

Objective: The student will swim 100 yards in boiling oil.

Wrong outcome evaluation: Explain the theory and philosophy of oil swimming.

Better outcome evaluation: Please swim.

Note that the first objective does not call for the ability to derive geometric formulas, but for using them. Likewise, the second objective does not require that students explain the theory and philosophy of oil swimming, but rather that they actually swim. Obviously, your evaluation must assess what was specifically stated in your objectives. These specifics were the learning intent.

Instructional intent can be stated at varying levels of specificity. At the general level, statements of instructional intent are presentations of the broad goals of instruction. At a more specific level, instructional intent tells what students will be able to do following instruction. When writing

TABLE *4.1*	Examples of Educational Goal and Objective Specificity
Type	**Example**
Educational Goal	The student will develop computer literacy
Informational Objective	The student will be able to write a simple program in BASIC
Instructional Objective	Given a set of specific requirements, the student will be able to write a simple error-free program in BASIC

instructional intent, you begin by identifying your goals at a broad level and follow these with the more specific objectives. Thus, movement is from a general frame of reference to a more specific frame. Let's now look at this process in greater detail.

Objective Specificity

There is a difference in the levels of specificity at which instructional intent should be written. While **goals** are usually broad statements used to describe the purposes of schooling or the purposes of a course, objectives are narrower statements of the intended learning of a unit or specific lesson. A nomenclature that makes a distinction between goals and objectives has been developed; however, there is little agreement about terminology. The terms *educational aims, educational goals,* and *general objectives* are often used to denote broad instructional intent, whereas the terms *performance objectives, informational objectives, behavioral objectives,* and *instructional objectives* are often used to denote the more specific instructional intent.

This text will address three levels of specificity: educational goals, informational objectives, and instructional objectives. Educational goals and the more specific instructional objectives can be thought of as forming a continuum from general to specific, with goals being written for a school course or unit, followed by (in descending order) informational and instructional objectives written for specific lessons and exercises. Examples of these three levels of specificity are shown in table 4.1. Note that the level of specificity increases as you move down through the examples, with the informational objective being subordinate to the educational goal and the instructional objective being subordinate to the informational objective.

Educational goals are broad and may take an extended period of time to be accomplished. Note how the goal in table 4.1 is the actual intent of the course: It is what the teacher wishes to accomplish in the broadest sense—in this case, computer literacy. The informative and instructional objectives then support the educational goal: They tell what the student will do to show that they are computer literate. Following are other examples of what some secondary school educational goals might be.

1. The students will develop a command of the fundamental processes of science.

2. The students will expand their leisure time activities.

TABLE *4.2*	Illustrative Verbs for Writing Goals		
A apply appreciate **B** believe **C** comprehend cope **D** demonstrate develop	**E** enjoy **F** familiarize fully appreciate **G** grasp **I** imagine **K** know	**L** like **R** realize recognize **T** think **U** understand **V** value

3. The students will develop good ethical character.

4. The students will formulate an appreciation for all vocations.

5. The students will develop good health habits.

Note that these statements are so general and broad that they appear to give us little help in instruction. Yet on closer examination, they do give us general direction and, therefore, represent the first step in deciding what to teach. They set the general direction we wish to take with our instruction. To this end, educational goals are usually concerned with covert (nonobservable), internal changes, which are less clearly measurable than are the behaviors associated with the more specific objectives. Some handy verbs that should prove helpful in writing educational goals are listed in table 4.2. Notice that the verbs used in writing educational goals are often rather vague, ambiguous, and open to interpretation. They lack the specification of exactly what, in observable terms, the student is to do to show that the intended learning has taken place.

Our next step in the planning process is to decide the specifics related to our goals. That is, we must now decide in a more precise manner exactly what students should know and, consequently, do to demonstrate that these goals have been accomplished. These decisions are stated in our more specific objectives: informational and instructional.

Stating Objectives

The primary purposes of secondary schools is to cause students to learn. Thus, as a result of your instruction, there should be a change in state within your students. This change in state must be overt (observable), with students acting differently than they did before being involved in the learning process.

Objectives must lay out everything you intend to accomplish, but must not imply things you do not want to say. Consequently, informational and instructional objectives must be unambiguous as well as testable and measurable. Table 4.3 suggests some verbs that are appropriate for informational and instructional objectives. Note the difference in clarity of language between the verbs listed in tables 4.2 and 4.3.

TABLE 4.3   Illustrative Verbs for Writing Informational and Instructional Objectives

A	E	P
add	explain	pick
adjust	G	point
analyze	graph	pronounce
arrange	I	R
B	identify	read
build	L	recite
C	label	run
calculate	list	S
choose	locate	select
circle	M	sing
classify	measure	sort
compare	N	state
construct	name	U
contrast	O	underline
D	operate	W
define	order	write
describe		
draw		

Instructional Objectives

Instructional objectives precisely communicate learning intent. Mager (1984) and Kibler, Barker, and Miles (1970) recommend that an expression of instructional intent comprise these four elements:

> First, the terminal behavior or *performance* should be spelled out; you should detail the actions that will be accepted as evidence that the intent has been achieved.

> Second, specify the *product* or what is to be produced by the student actions.

> Third, describe the *conditions* under which the student action is to be expected.

> Fourth, state the *criteria* of acceptable performance; you are describing how well you want the students to perform.

At times not all of these elements may be necessary. The object is to clearly communicate your intent. Thus, sometimes informational objectives (addressed later in this chapter) will suffice, and sometimes not.

Element One: Performance

The first element of an instructional objective is the specification of what students are expected to do after they receive instruction. This action is clarified in your selection of a word, usually a verb, which indicates what students are to do or produce. Because the purpose of instruction is to elicit a predetermined action, instructional objectives should always be written in terms of observable student performance. Special care must be taken in selecting the proper verb, so that you achieve clarity of language with no ambiguity in meaning. You and your interested colleagues and your principal must interpret the same meaning from each verb used in your objectives. Subjective terms such as *know, realize,* and *understand* should not be used as performance verbs in writing your objectives. These terms are open to interpretation and often have different meanings to different individuals. In a word, you should use terms which denote observable (overt) actions or behaviors. Verbs, for example—such as *list, name, state, bisect,* and *graph*—prompt observable behaviors that in turn will help you evaluate your instructional intent. Table 4.3 gives further examples of appropriate verbs for writing instructional objectives.

Element Two: Product

The second element of an instructional objective is to specify what is to be the result of the students' performance. It is this product of students' actions that you will evaluate in determining whether the objective has been mastered. This product can be a written sentence, a written sum, listed names, a demonstrated skill, or a constructed object. Students, for example, could be asked to produce a 300-word essay, a list of nouns, an analysis of the characters in a play, or the solutions to a set of quadratic equations.

The product is the outcome that you've planned to result from the instructional process. In other words, it is what you want students to be able to do after your instruction that they (supposedly) couldn't do prior to instruction.

Element Three: Conditions

The third element in the statement of an instructional objective is to establish the conditions under which the learner is to perform the prescribed action. Conditional elements can refer to the materials, information, or special equipment that will or will not be available to students; any special limitations or restrictions as to time and space; and any other requirements that may be applicable. Consider this example: "Given the formula, the student will be able to calculate the attractive force between two masses." This objective tells students that they need not memorize the formula—that they will be given the formula and they should simply know how to use it. Note the use of "Given the formula" for the conditional statement. Terms and phrases such as "Given" and "With (Without) the aid of" are commonly used in conditional statements.

Conditions must be realistic and clearly communicate expectations to students. They should make your desires more explicit. Following are other examples of conditions that might be included in an instructional objective:

Given a list of chemical elements . . .

After reading chapter 10 . . .

Using class notes . . .

With a ruler, protractor, and compass . . .

Within a 10-minute time interval and from memory . . .

On an essay test . . .

Given the necessary materials . . .

During a 5-minute interval . . .

From a list of compound sentences . . .

Without the aid of references . . .

These are a few examples of how conditions can be included as elements in instructional objectives. Essentially you should attempt to visualize under what conditions you want students to show mastery and prescribe these conditions in your objectives. As shown in the examples, conditions are usually written as the first component in the objective, but their placement can be anywhere in the objective. For example, the objective "The student will identify, on a multiple-choice test, Newton's laws of motion with 100 percent accuracy" has the conditional component ("on a multiple-choice test") toward the middle of the objective.

Element Four: Criteria

The fourth, and last, element of an instructional objective is the level of acceptable student performance. This is where you state the lowest level of performance that you will accept as showing mastery. This component can be established in terms of time limits, percentage of correct answers, minimum number of correct answers, ratios of correct to incorrect responses permitted, an acceptable tolerance, and other observable operations. These standards, or criteria, should be stated clearly so that students know in advance exactly what the standards are by which their performance will be judged. In other words, criterion levels should be stated as in the following specific examples:

. . . at least three reasons . . .

. . . 9 of the 10 cases . . .

. . . with no spelling errors

. . . with 80 percent accuracy

. . . 90 percent of the 20 problems

. . . within ± 10 percent

. . . to the nearest hundredth

. . . correct to the nearest percent

. . . within 10 minutes

. . . in less than 5 minutes

. . . at least two problems within a 5-minute period

. . . within 20 minutes with 80 percent accuracy

Each of these criterion levels represent well-defined standards toward which students can strive. Usually such standards are selected rather arbitrarily on the basis of past experiences and class expectations.

Carefully defined levels of desired performance are essential for effective instruction. However, you should take care not to set standards that are too high or out of reach. You should know your students so you can set reasonable levels of performance.

Now that you know the four elements of an instructional objective, you are ready to differentiate between informational and instructional objectives.

Informational Objectives

Frequently you will want 100 percent of the class to attain 100 percent of the objective—that is, 100 percent mastery. Furthermore, objectives often will have no special conditions. In these cases, informational objectives will usually meet your instructional needs.

Informational objectives are abbreviated instructional objectives. While instructional objectives contain the four elements noted earlier, informational objectives specify only the student performance and product. Consider, for example, the following instructional and informational objectives written for the same instructional intent.

Instructional objective: Given the voltage and resistance, the student will be able to calculate the current in a series or parallel circuit with 100 percent accuracy.

Informational objective: The student will be able to compute the current in a series or parallel circuit.

Notice that the informational objective is an abbreviation of the instructional objective in that it omits the conditions ("given the voltage and resistance") and the criterion for judging minimum mastery ("100 percent accuracy"). The informational objective contains only the performance ("to compute") and the product ("the current in a series or parallel circuit"). Frequently the conditions are such that they are understood. In the cited example of informational objective, it is understood that the necessary information must be provided in order to calculate the current. Moreover, it should be understood that only 100 percent accuracy would be desired.

Informational objectives will often be adequate when you share your instructional intent with students. However, if you feel more information is needed to communicate the exact intent, you should write instructional objectives, or perhaps informational objectives with the conditions or the criteria added. Let's now look at the communication of objectives.

Communication of Objectives

As noted earlier in the chapter, objectives should be spelled out for students if you are to get maximum value from them. At the secondary level, this communication is usually presented at the beginning of a unit of study in written form. One useful format that is recommended for stating multiple objectives is to use an introductory statement to communicate common needed conditions and/or a criterion level. The remainder of each individual objective is then listed with the performance verb, the product, and additional desired conditions. For example:

Upon completion of the "Earth in the Universe" unit, you should be able, on an end-of-unit exam, to perform the following objectives with 70 percent proficiency:

1. Identify the various stars discussed in class.

2. Use constellations to locate stars.

3. Identify three current ideas about how the universe originated and developed.

4. Describe nebulas, where they occur, and how they may form.

5. Find latitude and longitude of places from globes or maps, and locate places on globes or maps from latitude and longitude.

6. Name the planets in their order from the sun.

7. Identify some of the physical characteristics of each of the planets.

8. Describe the actual and relative sizes of earth and moon, and the paths they follow around the sun.

TABLE *4.4* Instructional Intent

Concept	Description
Educational Goal	Broad statement of instructional intent used to describe general purpose of instruction
Instructional Objective	Narrow statement of learning intent comprising four components: performance, product, conditions, and the criteria
Informational Objective	Abbreviation of instructional objective with only the performance and product specified

Application Guidelines ▼

Instructional Intent

Clearly Communicate Your Instructional Intent

Examples:
1. Write educational goals to set the framework for writing the more specific instructional intent.
2. Let instructional objectives act as guides to student learning and as advanced organizers (discussed further in chapter 5).
3. Use objectives to better design appropriate learning experiences.
4. Use objectives as an aid in designing evaluation procedures.

Write Appropriate Objectives

Examples:
1. Make sure objectives are relevant and don't just require the recall of trivia.
2. Make sure objectives clarify the intent of instruction for students.
3. Don't let objectives promote a narrow range of student performance: Learning other than that specified in lesson objectives can and should take place during a lesson.
4. Be sure objectives include one and only one learning product, and be sure the product accurately indicates the learning desired.

The exact format used in communicating objectives to students is not critical, but they should be spelled out in precise terms. You should tailor your communication of objectives to the specific needs of your students.

This concludes our formal discussion of goals and objectives. Table 4.4 summarizes the key concepts covered to this point, and the Instructional Intent Application Guidelines give some additional pointers. Review the summary and guidelines, and complete exercise 4.1 to check your understanding of goals and objectives.

Exercise 4.1   Instructional Intent

Test yourself on the following concepts. Appropriate responses can be found in appendix A.

1. Learning can be defined as a change in behavior. It must be observable and measurable. (True/False)

2. Objectives represent descriptive statements as to what the teacher will do during the instructional process. (True/False)

3. Which one or more of the following represent valid rationale(s) for writing objectives?
   a. Objectives set the framework for student evaluation.
   b. Objectives detail *all* the learning that should take place in the classroom.
   c. Objectives can be used to communicate the instructional intent to parents.
   d. Objectives should be used to directly influence the selection of the instructional approach for a lesson.

4. The different levels of specificity of instructional intent, in descending order, are _____ , _____ , and _____ .

5. The four elements that should be included in an instructional objective are _____ , _____ , _____ , and _____ .

6. The word, usually an action verb, used to describe student performance in an objective should be observable, countable, and testable. (True/False)

7. An informational objective can have more than one product. (True/False)

8. Informational objectives are abbreviated versions of instructional objectives in that they include only the _____ and _____ elements.

Taxonomies of Objectives

Objectives can be classified into three primary categories on the basis of their instructional focus: thinking, attitudes, and physical skills. These areas of focus represent the three domains of learning: cognitive, affective, and psychomotor. However, in reality, the domains do not occur in isolation. While some behaviors are easily classifiable into one of the three domains, others will overlap a great deal. This overlap is diagrammed in figure 4.2. A good example of this overlap is seen when students are required to complete an assignment that involves a written response. In so doing, they must recall information and think (cognitive); they will have some emotional response to the task (affective); and they must use fine motor skills to make the necessary writing movements (psychomotor).

The three domains for objectives were designed to form hierarchical taxonomies of student learning—from simple to complex—with each level making use of and building on the behaviors addressed in the preceding level. However, the levels do not imply that behaviors must be mastered sequentially from the lowest level to the highest level. Indeed, instruction can be directed toward any level of complexity.

Figure 4.2 *The Three Domains of Learning*

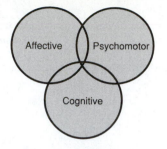

Don't write objectives at specific taxonomy levels just to have objectives at all levels. Although it is possible to write objectives at any of the taxonomy levels of the three domains of learning, Mager (1984) suggests that once you have made a suitable analysis of your instructional intent, you will know what you want your students to learn and will write your objectives at the intended levels automatically. Furthermore, you must guard against falling into the habit of writing objectives only for the lower levels of learning within a particular domain because writing higher-level learning objectives is more difficult. A working knowledge of the taxonomy, or levels, of the domains can prevent this pitfall to some extent. In other words, you can use your knowledge of the taxonomies to formulate the best possible objectives for your teaching intent, to not write objectives at a particular level, and to ensure that your teaching is not totally focused on the lower levels.

Although an overview of the three domains of learning and the associated major categories of each taxonomy follows, a more detailed description of the domains can be found by referring to one of the objective references. The information presented about cognitive taxonomy levels is adapted from the work of Bloom (1956); the material on affective taxonomy levels, from the work of Krathwohl (1964); and the coverage of the psychomotor taxonomy, from the works of Harrow (1972) and Jewett and Mullan (1977).

Cognitive Domain

Objectives in the **cognitive domain** are concerned with the thinking and reasoning ability of students. Because the ability to think can range from simple recall of information to more complex thinking behaviors, Benjamin Bloom (1956) and his associates developed a hierarchical classificational system, or taxonomy, to help teachers gain a better perspective on the behaviors to be emphasized in instructional planning.

Bloom's taxonomy classifies cognitive-thinking ability into six categories, ranging from the fairly simple recall of information to the complex assimilation of information and evaluation. These categories, along with verbs commonly used to express the required behaviors, are listed in table 4.5. Let's now briefly examine the six levels of Bloom's taxonomy.

TABLE 4.5   Bloom's Taxonomy and Illustrative Action Verbs

Level	Student Action
Knowledge	Identify, define, list, match, state, name, label, describe, select
Comprehension	Translate, convert, generalize, paraphrase, rewrite, summarize, distinguish, infer, alter, explain
Application	Use, operate, produce change, solve, show, compute, prepare, determine
Analysis	Discriminate, select, distinguish, separate, subdivide, identify, break down, analyze, compare
Synthesis	Design, plan, compile, compose, organize, conclude, arrange, construct, devise
Evaluation	Appraise, compare, justify, criticize, explain, interpret, conclude, summarize, evaluate

Level One: Knowledge

The term *knowledge* refers to the simple recall or recognition of previously learned materials. This may involve the recall of terminology, basic principles, generalizations, and specific facts such as dates, events, persons, and places. For the most part, no manipulation or interpretation of the learned material is required of students. The information is usually retrieved in the same form that it was stored. Students, for example, could be required to remember the names of major scientists, or to memorize a poem, or to recognize chemical symbols, or to recall mathematical proofs.

Knowledge-level objectives usually focus on the storage and retrieval of information in memory. In other words, the thinking ability required is in tapping the appropriate signals, cues, and clues to find and bring knowledge from memory. In a sense, the knowledge-level category lays a foundation for the higher-thinking ability categories in that it provides the basic information needed for thinking at the higher levels. However, teachers at times tend to overuse the knowledge category. An example of an informational knowledge-level objective might be as follows:

The student will be able to identify the present governmental officials in the state government.

Level Two: Comprehension

Comprehension represents the first level of understanding. The handling of information extends beyond the memorization of previously learned material to changing its form or making simple interpretations. Comprehension activities could require that students translate material to new forms, explain and summarize material, or estimate future trends. For example, you could ask students to interpret given information, or translate information from one medium to another, or simply describe something in their own words. An example of an informational comprehension-level objective might be as follows:

Given a graph of economic data, the student will be able to interpret the information in his or her own words.

Level Three: Application

Application entails putting learned information to use in reaching a solution or accomplishing a task. Students are asked to use remembered principles or generalizations to solve concrete problems. The process may require the application of rules, general ideas, concepts, laws, principles, or theories. For example, students apply the rules of grammar when writing a term paper, or they apply geometrical theorems when solving geometry problems. To be categorized as an application activity, a problem must be unique—that is, it must not be one that was addressed in class or in the textbook. An example of an instructional application-level objective might be as follows:

Given a quadratic equation, the student will be able to determine its two roots.

Level Four: Analysis

Analysis can be defined as breaking down complex material into its component parts so it can be better explained. This may involve subdividing something to explain how it works, or the analysis of relationships between parts, or the recognition of motives or organizational structures. A science teacher, for example, might ask how the circulatory system works, or a communication teacher might ask that a speech be analyzed, or a social studies teacher might ask for the national attitude toward war. An example of an informational analysis-level objective might be as follows:

Given a chemical compound, the student will be able to correctly break it down into its simplest elements.

Level Five: Synthesis

Synthesis occurs when components are combined to form a new whole. With synthesis, a new and unique form must be produced from available elements. This may involve the creation of a unique composition, communication, plan, proposal, or scheme for classifying information. The unique creation may be in verbal form or physical form. Students, for example, could be asked to use the British and American form of government to create a completely unique governmental system. The key to synthesis-level activities is the incorporation of known ideas to form unique patterns or to create new ideas. A possible instructional synthesis-level objective might be as follows:

Given a societal problem, the student will be able to propose at least two possible solutions to the problem.

Level Six: Evaluation

Evaluation means that a judgment is required as to the value of materials or ideas. Students are called upon to make quantitative and qualitative judgments on the extent to which internal or external criteria are satisfied. To accomplish this end, students must (1) set up or be given appropriate criteria or standards and (2) determine to what extent an idea or object meets the standards. For example, students could be asked to decide who was the greatest president, or they could be asked to determine the best

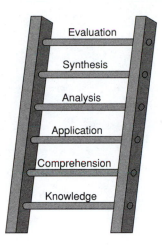

Figure 4.3 *Traditional Model of Cognitive Taxonomy as Ladder*

Evaluation

Synthesis

Analysis

Application

Comprehension

Knowledge

source of energy for the United States. Indeed, most questions that ask students to decide the best/worst or identify the least/most important will require thinking and reasoning at the evaluation level. An example of an informational evaluation-level objective might be as follows:

> **Given a video of a tennis match, the students will rate the match in terms of the tennis tactics and skills outlined in class.**

The advantage of the Bloom taxonomy is its utility in different subjects. However, the body of work by Orlich and associates (1990), Arons (1988), Haller, Child, and Walberg (1988), Wittrock (1986), Nickerson (1985), and Beyer (1984) has lead to a novel interpretation of how the cognitive taxonomy may operate. Instead of the six major categories viewed as a ladder (figure 4.3) that must be climbed one level at a time, a three-dimensional model (figure 4.4) can be offered. This model is analogous to an apple. The outward peel represents knowledge, the first level. The meat of the apple is analogous to the comprehension (understanding) level, and the higher levels of thinking represent the core of all understanding. This model views the cognitive categories as interactive, with the comprehension level being the key to unlocking the other levels. That is, once you truly understand (comprehend) the knowledge, then you can branch into any of the remaining four categories—application, analysis, synthesis, or evaluation. There is no need for one to move through the categories one step at a time. Students can move from understanding to evaluation, from understanding to analytic thinking, from understanding to creativity, or from understanding to application.

Affective Domain

Objectives in the **affective domain** are concerned with the development of students' attitudes, feelings, and emotions. They can vary according to the degree of internalization of the attitude, feeling, or emotion.

Clearly, because teachers must be concerned with the total development of students—not just development in the cognitive domain—the writing of objectives for the affective domain should be an integral part of

Figure 4.4
Three-Dimensional Model of the Cognitive Taxonomy

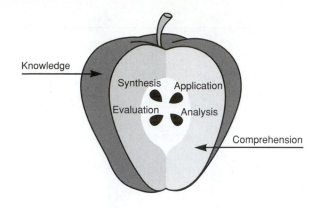

the planning process. Yet, because of the difficulty of writing objectives for the affective domain, this has not been the case. Affective-domain objectives are difficult to write because attitudes, feelings, and emotions are hard to translate into overt, observable behaviors. For example, the affective objective "The student will value freedom" is not properly written. The behavior "value" is not observable or measurable. The verb *value* must be replaced with an action that shows observable behavior: "The student will support the Constitution of the United States during class discussions on the Constitution." This objective would provide one, and only one, of many possible indicators that the student "values" freedom.

Behaviors related to the affective domain must take place in a "free choice" situation if they are to give a true indication of student attitudes, likes and dislikes, and feelings. If not free choice students may exhibit the desired behaviors for a reward of some type or because they want to please you. Students, for example, who attend class every day may not be doing so because they like coming to your class or because they like the subject, but may be doing so because of the grade. However, the objective "The student will eagerly participate in class discussions" would specify one possible indicator that the student liked the class.

Another free-choice technique sometimes used to reveal attitudes, feelings, emotions, and interests is the administration of various affective-domain inventories. These instruments will be discussed at length in chapter 10.

David Krathwohl and associates (1964) developed a classification system, or taxonomy, for categorizing affective responses into five levels according to the degree of internalization. That is, it is organized as to the degree to which an attitude, feeling, value, or emotion has become part of the individual. The taxonomy levels and some illustrative verbs commonly used for revealing the extent of internalization are given in table 4.6. In a sense, the taxonomy forms a hierarchical continuum of internalization—ranging from a person's mere passive awareness to an individual's being characterized by certain values and attitudes. Let's now take a brief look at the taxonomy levels.

TABLE 4.6   Affective Domain Taxonomy and Illustrative Action Verbs

Level	Student Action
Receiving	Follow, select, rely, choose, point to, ask, hold, give, locate, attend
Responding	Read, conform, help, answer, practice, present, report, greet, tell, perform, assist, recite
Valuing	Initiate, ask, invite, share, join, follow, propose, read, study, work, accept, do, argue
Organization	Defend, alter, integrate, synthesize, listen, influence, adhere, modify, relate, combine
Characterization by a Value or Value Complex	Adhere, relate, act, serve, use, verify, question, confirm, propose, solve, influence, display

Level One: Receiving

Receiving can be defined as being aware and willing to attend freely to stimuli and messages in the environment (listen and look). All teachers want their students to listen and be aware of classroom stimuli. At this level, students are attending to what the teacher is presenting, but the attention is not active involvement. An example of an informational receiving-level objective might be as follows:

> **The student will follow given directions, without their needing to be repeated because of student inattentiveness.**

Note that the student must be attentive and make a conscious effort to pay attention to the classroom environment rather than to other stimuli. However, the attention can be rather passive.

Level Two: Responding

Responding requires active participation: A person is not only freely attending to stimuli, but also voluntarily reacting to that stimuli. This involves physical, active behavior, where students make choices about issues. An example of an informational responding-level objective might be as follows:

> **The student will willingly assist other students with their homework when they encounter problems.**

At this level, students have developed an interest and make a choice to participate. Further, they are satisfied with this participation.

Level Three: Valuing

Valuing refers to voluntarily giving worth to an idea, phenomenon, or stimulus. Behaviors at this level are selected even when there are alternatives. Students not only accept the worth of a value; but that "worth" is internalized. An example of an instructional value-level objective might be as follows:

> **When given alternatives, the student will share concerns about the need for clean air and water on at least two occasions.**

Note that students are given alternatives and the opportunity to repeat the choice. Also notice that the choice must be made freely.

Level Four: Organization

The term *organization* refers to building an internally consistent value system. At this level, a set of criteria is established and applied in choice making. The individual takes on value positions and is willing to defend them. An example of an informational organization-level objective might be as follows:

> **The student will voluntarily seek information related to career opportunities and prepare for selected career goals.**

Organization means one has made a commitment. In a sense, a "philosophy of life" has been internalized.

Level Five: Characterization by a Value or Value Complex

If behaviors reveal that an individual has developed a value system and acts consistently with the internalized values, then *characterization* by a value or value complex has been established. At this level the individual displays individuality and self-reliance. An example of an informational objective at the level of characterization by a value or value complex might be as follows:

> **In a class discussion, the student will defend the rights of *all* individuals to express their ideas and opinions.**

Demonstration of this objective would reveal that an individual is acting consistently with an established value system.

Psychomotor Domain

Objectives in the **psychomotor domain** relate to the development of muscular abilities that range from simple reflex movement to precision and creativity in performing a skill. The psychomotor domain is especially relevant in physical education, music, drama, art, and vocational courses, but all subjects will relate to this domain to some degree.

Although the psychomotor domain was the last to have a taxonomy developed for it, several systems have now been developed. The four-level system presented here is based on and adapted from the work of Harrow (1972) and Jewett and Mullan (1977). As you read through the levels and illustrative verbs presented in table 4.7, notice how the processes can be applied to such areas as physical education, music, art, and vocational education.

Level One: Fundamental Movement

Fundamental movements are those that form the basic building blocks for the higher-level movements—for example, the ability to track objects, grasp objects, or crawl and walk. A sample informational objective for the fundamental-movement level might be as follows:

> **The student will be able to properly hold a tennis racket for the backhand.**

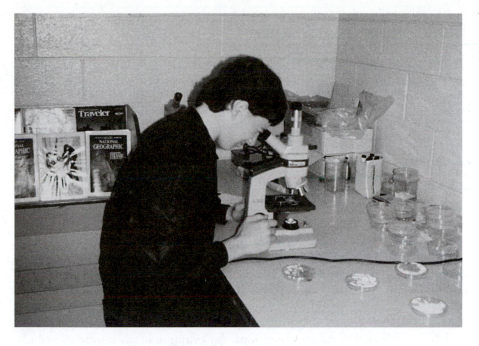

TABLE *4.7*   Psychomotor Domain Taxonomy and Illustrative Action Verbs

Level	Student Action
Fundamental Movement	Track, crawl, hear, react, move, grasp, walk, climb, jump, grip, stand, run
Generic Movement	Drill, construct, dismantle, change, hop, clean, manipulate, follow, use, march
Ordinative Movement	Play, connect, fasten, make, sketch, weigh, wrap, manipulate, play, swim, repair, write
Creative Movement	Create, invent, construct, manipulate, play, build, pantomime, perform, make, compose

Notice this objective deals with the fundamental movement of the proper grasp of a tennis racket. Indeed, it is basic to the higher-level tennis movements.

Level Two: Generic Movement

Generic movement refers to the ability to carry out the basic rudiments of a skill when given directions and under supervision. At this level, efficient motor patterns, timing, and coordination are being developed and refined. Awareness of the body in motion and of the arrangement and use of the body parts is learned. However, the total act is not performed with skill. An example of an instructional objective for the generic-movement level might be as follows:

> **Under supervision, the student will be able to perform a required musical score with no more than five errors.**

TABLE 4.8	Objective Domains
Domain	**Description**
Cognitive	Category of learning that focuses on the ability to think and reason, comprising these six cognitive taxonomy levels: knowledge, comprehension, application, analysis, synthesis, and evaluation
Affective	Category of learning concerned with emotional development, encompassing these five affective domain taxonomy levels: receiving, responding, valuing, organization, and characterization by a value or value complex
Psychomotor	Category of learning related to muscular and motor-skill development, consisting of these four psychomotor domain taxonomy levels: fundamental movement, generic movement, ordinative movement, and creative movement

This level of motor skill requires supervision in that it represents the initial learning of a series of movements.

Level Three: Ordinative Movement

Ordinative movement marks the competence in performing a skill ably and independently. The entire skill has been organized and can be performed in sequence. Conscious effort is no longer needed: The skill has been mastered, and there is precision of performance. At this level, the skill can be carried out by habit under complex conditions. An example of an informational objective at the ordinative-movement level might be as follows:

Given a dive to perform, the student will be able to carry out the step-by-step technique without pausing to think.

Level Four: Creative Movement

Creative movement, which calls for the ability to produce and compose, will serve the personal purposes of the performer. That is, the individual should be able to invent unique motor options, or improvise originality into a movement, or combine several movements into a personal unique motor design, or invent a new movement pattern. An example of an informational objective at the creative-movement level might be as follows:

Given a dance routine, the student will be able to make appropriate changes to incorporate personal dance strengths.

Instruction and learning in the classroom frequently will contain elements of all three domains. Nevertheless, your objectives usually will place primary emphasis on either the cognitive, affective, or psychomotor domain. Furthermore, remember that the three domain taxonomies can be valuable tools for upgrading your writing of objectives. However, don't become a slave to the taxonomies; instead, base your objectives on the needs of your class, and use the taxonomies as a guide. Finally, strive to incorporate the higher levels of each taxonomy in your learning experiences.

This concludes our discussion of the three learning domains and their respective taxonomies. Take a few minutes to complete exercise 4.2, which will check your understanding of the concepts presented in this section. However, before doing so, review the concepts presented in table 4.8 and the Objective Domains Application Guidelines.

Application Guidelines ▼

Objective Domains

Write Objectives for Instructional Intent

Examples: 1. Analyze your instructional intent prior to writing your objectives; then focus your objective on the appropriate domain and taxonomy level.
2. Consider your instructional approach and your evaluation when writing your objectives. Make sure your objectives are reasonable and can be accomplished and evaluated with available resources.
3. Address all three domains in the writing of your objectives. Too often, emphasis is placed only on the cognitive domain.

Application of Knowledge

Exercise 4.2   Objective Domains

Test yourself on the following objective domain concepts. Appropriate responses can be found in appendix A.

1. The three primary domains of learning for which objectives can be written are
_____ , _____ and _____ .

2. Most teachers find it easier to write objectives for the affective domain than the psychomotor domain. (True/False)

3. The creation of a unique communication would fall into one of the higher levels of cognitive domain learning. (True/False)

4. Classify each of the following objectives according to its most prominent behavior: cognitive (C), affective (A), or psychomotor (P).
   a. _____ Given an interest inventory, the student will rate English on the high end of the scale.
   b. _____ The student will be able to correctly adjust a microscope.
   c. _____ The student will voluntarily attend the school play for no extra credit.
   d. _____ The student will be able to solve rational algebraic expressions.
   e. _____ Given the required information, the student will be able to establish a monthly budget for a family of four.

5. Most objectives can be easily classified into one of the three domains of learning. (True/False)

CHAPTER SUMMARY

Objectives specify your instructional intent for your students; that is, they specify what your students should be able to do following instruction. Moreover, objectives set the framework for your instructional approach and the evaluation of student learning.

The specificity of instructional intent varies from broad educational goals to very narrow specific objectives. The term *educational goals* denotes broad instructional intent, followed by—in order of specificity—informational objectives and instructional objectives, with the more specific objectives being subordinate to educational goals. The actions called for by educational goals are overt, nonmeasurable behaviors used to give your instruction general direction, whereas the actions called for by informational and instructional objectives are overt and measurable. Instructional objectives consist of four components: performance, product, conditions, and criteria. On the other hand, informa-

tional objectives specify only the performance and the product; the conditions and criteria are usually not specified.

Your objectives should always be spelled out for students. This communication is usually provided in written form at the beginning of a unit of study. In most cases, informational objectives will suffice for laying out your learning intent. However, it should be kept in mind that objectives are intended to specify a minimum level of learning. Other incidental learning should be encouraged and expected as students progress through the objectives.

Objectives can be written for any one of three domains of learning: cognitive, affective, and psychomotor. These domains generally do not occur in isolation; they overlap a great deal. A hierarchial taxonomy of learning levels has been established to assist teachers in writing their objectives for each of the three domains of learning.

Discussion Questions and Activities

1. **Analysis of secondary textbook objectives.** Review the teacher's edition of a secondary school textbook in your subject that lists the unit and/or chapter objectives. Address the following questions in your review.

   a. Are informational objectives given for the chapters? Are instructional objectives?

   b. Are objectives written for all three domains of learning?

   c. Are the objectives written at the different taxonomy levels within each of the learning domains?

2. **Writing goals and objectives.** Consider your subject, and write a broad educational goal that you feel should be addressed in the

secondary school. Now write at least three different informational and instructional objectives that tell what students should do to show you that they have accomplished the goal.

3. **Writing objectives for cognitive, affective, and psychomotor domains.** Write ten cognitive- and psychomotor-domain objectives for a topic from your area. Make sure the objectives span the various taxonomy levels of sophistication. Now write five affective-domain objectives at various taxonomy levels for the same class. Let your classmates review and critique your objectives.

Unit and Daily Planning

5

✎ **Instinct is not the key to effective lesson presentation. In reality, the easy "ebb and flow" of the good delivery is a well-planned event.**

Overview

Why do teachers plan? This chapter will focus on this question and on techniques for effective planning. We will explore some of what is known about the processes of planning and decision making.

Because planning is essential to achieve excellence in instruction, the planning processes that result in the successful delivery of knowledge, attitudes, values, and skills will be explored. We will consider the different levels of planning, as well as the personnel associated with the planning processes. Finally, we will focus our attention on the basic components of unit and daily lesson planning. This examination will include a rather detailed explanation of specific planning procedures and several different formats.

Objectives

After completing your study of chapter 5, you should be able to do the following:

1. Describe the four levels of planning.

2. Identify and describe the key components of a unit and daily lesson plan.

3. Differentiate between teacher-centered and student-centered instruction, and name various methods associated with each.

4. Explain the importance of daily lesson planning in the learning process.

5. Operationally define *set induction* and *lesson closure,* and explain their importance to teaching.

6. Operationally define *instructional strategy*, and name its two components.

7. Describe the four variables that should be considered in the selection of an appropriate instructional method.

8. Develop a unit plan for a given area within your area of specialization.

9. Develop daily lesson plans for a unit or series of units.

Chapter Terms and Key Concepts

Advance Organizer

Closure

Course Planning

Daily Lesson Plan

Instructional Strategy

Lesson Procedure

Methodology

Reflective Teaching

Set Induction

Teacher-Student Planning

Team Planning

Unit Plan

Weekly Plan

No two teachers teach in the same way; similarly, no two teachers plan in exactly the same way. Planning serves two practical functions: It allows you to anticipate instructional needs in advance so materials can be gathered and organized, and it provides a plan that directs classroom interactions. The excellent lesson delivery of effective teachers often appears spontaneous. However, these teachers have—formally or informally—planned each daily lesson with care. They have mastered the lesson content and the related teaching skills to the extent that their delivery is poised and automatic.

Planning for instruction is one of the most important things a teacher or group of teachers can do. Even experienced teachers spend time planning. They replan the presentation of lessons that they have taught many times to avoid becoming stale and routine.

Planning Instruction

As shown in figure 5.1, teachers should engage in four levels of planning. Course and unit planning are broader in scope than weekly and daily planning. Course and unit plans determine the direction you will take and what the general impact of the entire curriculum will be.

No matter what the level of planning, decisions must be made with respect to the coordination of course content, instructional materials, and the special needs of students. Therefore, before we look at the levels of planning in greater detail, let us focus our discussion on team planning, teacher-student planning, selecting instructional materials, and making provisions for students who have special needs.

Team Planning

Team planning can have tremendous value. For example, if all the social studies teachers were to coordinate their course plans, then the possibility of duplicating efforts or of leaving out important lessons would be reduced. Careful planning as a team can increase the time for enrichment activities. Team planning also facilitates coordination efforts among disciplines. The American literature teacher and the American history teacher, for example, could design their courses so that they were covering the same time frames simultaneously. Students would have the opportunity to see the connectedness of the two disciplines. Moreover, reading and writing assignments could be planned to enhance student understanding of how the milieu influenced the writers of a particular era.

Figure 5.1 *Levels of Planning*

Course planning — General
Unit planning
Weekly planning
Daily lesson planning — Specific

Opportunities for teachers to engage in critical thinking and analysis are greatly enhanced through team planning. A team approach calls upon teachers to critically analyze the content of their respective courses so the concepts can be merged into one unified, workable whole. Teaming demands careful attention to details so each member of the team knows what to do, how to do it, and when to do it. In addition, it requires that evaluation be carefully thought out, to ensure that plans are executed properly and accomplishing their intended function.

Teacher-Student Planning

Students as well as teachers can be engaged in the planning process. The extent to which students participate in the planning of their own learning activities varies greatly from classroom to classroom. In many classrooms, the only involvement students have is in the selection of class projects, reports, and outside readings. However, by engaging students, the teacher gains insights into student interests and areas of weakness and strength. A **teacher-student planning** process promotes ''ownership'' of the curriculum. If students communicate that they already possess an understanding of intended instructional material, they could be tested on the material. If, in fact, they do have a good understanding of the material in question, then valuable time and resources could be reallocated to other areas. How many times have each of us studied the colonial period of American history but failed to spend any time on the period following World War II?

Instructional Materials

Essential to effective planning is the survey and preparation of available media and materials for instruction. Textbooks, audiovisual materials, supplementary reading materials, and supplies and equipment for group and individual projects should be examined and coordinated with your lesson. Time spent on reviewing what is available in the district will be time well spent. You should preview films and computer software, review printed materials, and learn to use the latest instructional technology.

The incorporation of a wide variety of instructional materials will improve your lessons and heighten students' attention and interest. The use of videotapes and computer software in presenting examples and non-examples of concepts, for instance, will serve as a lesson stimulus. We will address instructional media in detail in chapter 6, and the effective use of various motivational techniques will be covered in chapter 13.

Students with Special Needs

Some of your students will be slower academically, while others will be bright; some will be skilled socially, while others will be less poised. However, you must plan your instruction to fit the individual needs and interests of all students. Examples of lesson modifications might include developing special worksheets to help teach difficult concepts, modifying assigned work, developing special study guides, giving oral exams, and obtaining and using special equipment with the physically handicapped or gifted.

Teachers with special students or mainstreamed students (handicapped students placed in regular classes) must learn to modify their plans and give differentiated assignments. You can do this by modifying or varying the length or difficulty of assignments. For example, in a science class, you might assign two experiments to your slower students, three experiments to the average students, and four—or perhaps more demanding— experiments to high-achieving or exceptional students. Similarly, you might require only half as much writing from English students who experience motor difficulties.

Another approach for differentiating assignments is to vary the type of work students do. For example, some students can be allowed to complete and submit their written assignments on a word processor. Creative students may occasionally be allowed to submit a creative project instead of a written report. Students occasionally might be allowed to assist each other or work together in groups.

Some planning guidelines for working with students who have special needs follow:

1. Gathering information about the nature of the exceptional student's difference and how that difference might affect the learning process.

2. Getting help from district special-education or resource experts.

3. Gathering the equipment needs of exceptional students to allow them to function at an optimal level.

4. Adapting the curriculum and your teaching strategies to better serve the needs of the exceptional student.

5. Individualizing the curriculum as much as possible in your classroom.

6. Providing for the removal of barriers, both physical and psychological, that limit the full functioning of exceptional students in your classroom.

Having looked at the general planning of instruction, let us look next at the four planning levels in greater detail.

Course Planning

The broadest and most general type of planning you will perform as a classroom teacher is **course planning**. Although in most cases the textbook forms the basic structure for most course plans, it should not be the main premise of instruction. Beginning teachers should use their textbooks and state-curriculum suggestions as instructional guides and should integrate supplementary materials into the basic text structure. Experienced teachers, however, often structure their courses on the basis of experience and use the textbook and state-curriculum suggestions to supplement the experience base.

Unit Planning

Courses are usually divided into a sequence of manageable units of study that represent discrete segments of the year's work in a given subject. Each unit is organized around a specific theme or a cluster of related concepts. For example, a unit in earth science might be titled "Plants," or a unit in English literature might be titled "The Short Story." Units provide a structure or framework for the design of a course. In effect, a unit is a series of many intended learning activities and experiences unified around the theme or cluster of related concepts.

Unit planning can be deemed more critical than other levels of planning. The **unit plan** links the goals, objectives, content, activities, and evaluation you have in mind. These plans should be shared with students to provide the overall road map that explains where you are going. Such communication expresses to students what they are expected to learn.

The unit plan has several components. The plan is titled by the topic that represents the unifying theme for the unit. These topics may follow the chapter headings in your textbook or the areas within your subject that the various curriculum guides direct you to cover. These topics could be derived through team planning or through teacher-student planning. As discussed in chapter 3, unit topics generally are taken from the headings of course plans. The plan should spell out your goals and specific instructional objectives. A somewhat detailed outline of the content should be included, as should learning activities appropriate to the content and to the learners. A list of needed instructional materials and resources should be provided. Finally, the methods you intend to use for evaluating student learning needs to be specified. More specifically, a well-constructed unit should include the following components:

1. **Topic**
   Presumably a subject suggested by a course outline, textbook, or state-curriculum guide.

2. **Goals and Objectives**
   A list of your learning intent in broad and specific terms.

3. **Content Outline**
   An outline of the material to be covered—with as much detail as you feel is needed—which should help clarify the subject and help you with the sequence and organization.

4. **Learning Activities**
   Teacher and student activities—comprising introductory, developmental, and culminating activities—that, when arranged into a series of daily lessons, will lead to the desired learning outcome.

5. **Resources and Materials**
   A list of materials to be selected and prepared for the unit.

6. **Evaluation**
   An outline of your evaluation procedure—including homework, tests, or special projects—which should be planned and prepared prior to instruction.

Units will vary greatly in scope and duration depending on the grade level and subject. Generally they range in duration from a few days to a few weeks. Other examples of typical units are the court system in government, astronomy in the tenth grade, and photosynthesis in high school biology.

There are several sources available for assisting teachers with their unit plans. In some states the curriculum is quite explicit, and the goals and topics that must be covered are mandated. When this is the case, the prescribed goals and topics are usually presented in terms of minimum requirements, so there is still plenty of justification for the careful planning of additional learning units. Even when a good deal of the content of courses has been predetermined, it is still necessary to plan the sequence, present the content, and test the outcomes. Many school districts also have a mandated curriculum that must be included in any course plan. These demands for covering specific content do not preclude the need for planning.

The course textbook offers clues for unit planning. However, content must be selected and organized with regard to your goals and learners. You must recognize that a particular author's view of sequence, for instance, may not serve your needs or the needs of your students. Textbooks are written for a wide audience and should be viewed as one of the tools for teaching a course, not as the course itself.

The information to be presented will form the bulk of a unit. This material generally should extend beyond the concepts contained in the textbook and should be correlated with the unit objectives. Once the topics, sequence, and time for each topic has been determined, you must develop unit objectives that relate to the selected content. The goals should be your guide in determining unit objectives. You must now designate the specific student outcomes desired, as well as the level of behavioral complexity. Of course, keep in mind that the level of complexity will set the framework for your lesson activities and the evaluative process. Because chapter 4 was devoted to the writing of goals and objectives, we will not discuss them further here.

Learning activities must now be identified that will support the unit. The learning activities need to be chosen carefully to ensure that the objectives can be met. In addition, your unit objectives and activities should be grouped into daily lessons for implementation. The selection of activities and the grouping of your unit objectives and activities require that decisions be made about how best to accomplish your planned goals. If you intend to illuminate the court system at work, you might plan a variety of activities, such as having students read about the court system in their textbooks, holding a mock trial, showing a film about a court case, or taking a trip to a nearby courtroom to observe a trial in session. Indeed, you might decide that a visit from a district attorney or a judge may be in order. These are all decisions that need to be made early in the planning process to allow time for arranging these activities.

Always keep in mind that a unit consists of a series of daily lessons. The unit can be viewed as the whole, with the individual lessons as its parts. Thus, the individual lessons must be selected so they are interrelated and address the learner outcomes that are specified in the objectives of the unit as a whole.

Planning for instructional materials is an important part of the entire planning process. You need to familiarize yourself with the materials available in your school building and school district. You also need to investigate your community for possible sources of learning materials. A field trip to a courtroom may be problematic if the nearest court is several miles away and you have failed to contact the court or to arrange for permissions and transportation. Beginning teachers need to establish contact with veterans in their building who are willing to share information with them about how to accomplish these kinds of tasks. As you plan for instructional materials, it is a good idea to keep a notebook or journal of available materials and resources.

Finally, how will you know if the students have learned what you intended in your carefully planned unit? The answer lies in carefully planning for evaluation. Will you give paper-and-pencil tests? If so, how often? Will student participation enter into the evaluation process, and how will you determine the value of each student's participation? These questions and others must be answered in the planning phase. We will address the evaluation process in detail in chapters 10 and 11.

Figure 5.2 *Abridged Daily Lesson Format*

	Monday	Tuesday	Wednesday	Thursday	Friday
Period 1	Pages 126–134	Activities 1 and 2	Activity 3	Pages 141–155	Exercises 1–4
Period 2	Pages 126–134	Activities 1 and 2	Activity 4	Pages 135–140	Exercises 2 and 5
Period 3	Planning	Planning	Planning	Planning	Planning
Period 4	Pages 126–134	Activities 1 and 2	Activity 3	Pages 141–155	Exercises 1–4
Period 5	Experiment 10	Field Trip	Pages 203–210	Activity 11	Pages 211–225
Period 6	Pages 126–134	Activities 1 and 2	Activity 4	Pages 135–140	Exercises 2 and 5
Period 7	Experiment 10	Field Trip	Pages 203–210	Activity 11	Pages 211–225

Weekly Plans

Most school districts ask that teachers submit a short-form weekly lesson plan so that, in the event the teacher is absent, the substitute teacher will have some idea of what was to be covered that day. A typical short-form **weekly plan,** as shown in figure 5.2, outlines each day's lesson for one week on a single sheet of paper. These weekly lesson plans vary greatly in detail from school to school. They essentially are short, watered-down copies of the week's daily lesson plans, written on special forms provided by the school.

Daily Lesson Plans

The most detailed and specific type of plan is a **daily lesson plan,** which simply defines the objectives and class activities for a single day. Thus, unit planning does not eliminate daily planning; rather, because the objectives, activities, experiences, and necessary materials have been specified in the unit plan, the daily lesson plan flows naturally out of the unit plan. However, the exact structure of the daily lesson plan will depend on the type of lesson being designed. Lesson plans should reflect the individual needs, strengths, and interests of the teacher and the students. Lesson planning should never be dictated by rigid standards that prevent and stifle creativity. Indeed, you will rarely carry out a lesson entirely as planned. You must anticipate what is likely to happen as you teach your planned lessons and make modifications as needed. Good teachers expect to adjust their plans as they move along, and they have alternatives in mind in case they are needed. Needless to say, the fact that most plans must be modified as they are taught does not justify the avoidance of thorough initial planning. Few teachers can ''wing it.'' However, planning does not ensure success. The delivery counts for a great deal.

Postlesson Evaluation

Student evaluation should be an integral part of every lesson taught. As described here, evaluation entails postinstructional assessment of student performance. During evaluation, you determine the degree to which learners have attained the anticipated outcomes of the lesson.

Once a lesson has ended, a clear picture of how well students have mastered the stated objectives must be in your grasp. If there is a discrepancy between the intent and the mastery achieved, then you must decide whether reteaching is necessary.

The postlesson assessment that emerges from a lesson can vary widely in specificity and level of formality. Sometimes it will come from information gained during question-and-answer sequences. Sometimes it will consist of information gleaned from student-group work, individual seat work, or completion of class activities. And at other times, the assessment may be formal (quiz or test).

Postlesson assessments help ensure that students are not pushed on to new content before they have mastered needed prerequisite skills. In effect, they help you identify learning problems prior to the end of a unit, when a unit evaluation is usually administered. You can often avoid many classroom problems if you will conduct and use information obtained in postlesson assessments. It is generally wiser to plan reteaching for students who are having difficulty with lesson concepts and to design enrichment activities for those having no difficulty, than to proceed to the next lesson.

Lesson Formats

Planning establishes a proposed course of action that serves as your guide, from which appropriate deviations can be made. Following are some sample daily lesson plans. These formats differ somewhat in style, but each focuses on the type of learning desired.

Lesson Plan Format 1 A lesson plan should provide needed structure to a lesson, but be general enough to allow for flexibility. Writers in the area of planning (Orlich et al., 1990; Jacobson et al., 1989) suggest the following basic lesson plan format:

1. **Objectives**
   The specific learning intent for the day, selected from the unit plan.

2. **Introduction (set induction)**
   An activity used at the beginning of the lesson to attract student attention and interest.

3. **Content**
   A brief outline of the content to be covered in the lesson.

4. **Methods and Procedure**
   A sequential listing of developmental activities for the day, selected from the unit plan.

5. **Closure**
   The lesson wrap-up activity.

6. Resources and Materials

A list of instructional materials needed for the lesson.

7. Evaluation Procedure

An activity or technique that will determine how well students have mastered the intended learning outcomes of the lesson.

8. Assignment

The in-class or homework assignment to be completed for the next class period.

Lesson Plan Format 2 The second format has been suggested by advocates of the Madeline Hunter instructional design. It is a detailed and prescriptive seven-component plan with a highly structured format that emphasizes student involvement and success (Hunter, 1980). It is appropriate for skill learning and many forms of teacher-centered instruction, such as lecturing, lecture recitation, and socratic questioning. The more student-centered lessons such as discussions and problem solving would not fit into this format (Shulman, 1987). The seven components of this format follow:

1. Anticipatory Set

A teacher activity designed to prompt students to focus on the lesson before the lesson begins.

2. Objectives and Purpose

Teacher statements that explicitly inform students as to what will be learned in the coming lesson and how it will be useful.

3. Input

The new knowledge, processes, or skills students are to learn.

4. Modeling

The examples used in developing an understanding of the knowledge, processes, or skills being taught—including the techniques used to illustrate the new knowledge, processes, or skills.

5. Checking for Understanding

A method for determining whether students understand the learning intent, which may occur before or during the teacher-directed activity (modeling) or during the student-guided activity.

6. Guided Practice

Student practice of new knowledge, processes, or skills under teacher supervision (in-class).

7. Independent Practice

Unsupervised practice of new knowledge, process, or skill (assigned seat work or homework).

Lesson Plan Format 3 This format is suggested for use with the small-group learning strategy. Small-group strategies generally require that students be prepared for their task and be debriefed once the assigned task has been addressed. Therefore, the planning process will be a student-centered format with the following components:

1. **Objectives**

   Statements of the specific learning intents or of what students should be able to do upon completion of the lesson.

2. **Initial Focus (set induction)**

   Teacher-directed activity to get student attention and interest focused on the required assigned task.

3. **Major Task**

   Teacher-directed presentation of required assigned group task, directions for group work, and options available to students.

4. **Group Activity**

   Student task assigned by teacher, who can offer strategy options or require that students develop their own.

5. **Debriefing**

   Student analysis and presentation of the product of the assigned task, as well as of the strategies that were and were not effective.

6. **Resources and Materials**

   Listing of the materials needed for groups to work on and complete assigned task.

7. **Evaluation**

   Formal and informal techniques that will be used to check whether students have achieved task and objectives.

The plans presented above are intended to be illustrative, not all-inclusive. Some alternate lesson plan formats are shown in figures 5.3 and 5.4. Each alternate format has been logically structured for a specific type of lesson. You should select the format that will lend direction to your lesson, but not be a manuscript from which to read verbatim statements.

As the lesson formats presented in this section suggest, teachers vary widely in their approaches to daily planning. Some develop detailed daily plans, whereas others merely write out a few notes as reminders. The sample lesson plans presented in figures 5.5 through 5.8 illustrate how the various components are constructed.

Table 5.1 offers a summary of the planning concepts covered in this section. Before you move on to the next section, review table 5.1 and the Planning Application Guidelines, and complete exercise 5.1.

TABLE *5.1*

Planning

Type	Description
Team Planning	Group or team of teachers organizing instruction so that each supplements the other
Teacher-Student Planning	Involving students in planning process and basing learning activities on students' interests, which promotes student ownership of curriculum
Course Planning	Broad planning of instruction for year or term
Unit Planning	Discrete segment of a year's work organized around a specific theme or cluster of related concepts
Weekly Planning	Short-form outline (on a single sheet of paper) of instruction for one week
Daily Lesson Planning	Detailed description of objectives and activities for one instructional period, which should flow naturally out of the unit plan

Application Guidelines ▼

Planning

Organize Lessons Well

Examples:
1. Adapt your teaching to student needs and interests.
2. Match teaching strategies to objectives.
3. Be flexible: Try different strategies.
4. Develop unit plans with a particular class in mind.
5. Plan interesting ways of introducing your units.
6. Design parts of your units for low-ability, average-ability, and high-ability students.
7. Duplicate the unit plan for the students so they can follow it.

Be Aware of Time Constraints

Examples:
1. Estimate how much time the class will spend on each activity.
2. Make your procedure too long at first. Overplan so you don't run out of material before the class ends.
3. Leave enough time at the end of your lesson to make an adequate homework assignment.
4. Allow a few minutes at the beginning of the period for taking attendance and making announcements.

Lesson Plan Structure

As a teacher, you will probably imitate a favorite teacher in your initial planning; later you will modify the initial structure to fit your individual style. Regardless of the amount of detail or general format, an examination of the various lesson plan formats reveals that each contains three common elements: the set induction (cognitive set), the lesson itself (instructional strategies), and the lesson closure.

Application of Knowledge

Exercise 5.1 Planning

Check yourself on the following planning concepts. Appropriate responses can be found in appendix A.

1. Name the two practical functions of planning.
   a. _____
   _____
   b. _____
   _____

2. Match the planning level on the left with the appropriate description on the right.
   a. _____ Discrete segments of a year's work   1. Course plans
   b. _____ Instructional activities for one class period   2. Unit plans
   c. _____ Broadest type of planning   3. Weekly plans
   d. _____ Short-form outline of plans on single page   4. Daily plans

3. List and briefly describe the six components of a well-constructed unit plan.
   a. _____
   _____
   b. _____
   _____
   c. _____
   _____
   d. _____
   _____
   e. _____
   _____
   f. _____
   _____

4. A textbook is probably the most reliable source of assistance in planning. (True/False)

5. Daily lesson plans should vary according to the focus of the desired learning. (True/False)

Set Induction

The **set induction** is what you do at the outset of a lesson to get students' undivided attention, arouse their interest, and establish a conceptual framework for the information that follows.

Until your students are attentive and prepared to listen (until they have a *cognitive set*), it is usually unwise to begin a lesson. Your opening activity—frequently related to the homework assignment or some recent lesson—will have to be repeated if you have not gained their attention.

You must plan some strategies for getting the students' undivided attention. Keep in mind that you will be competing with a host of other attention-getters: student-body elections, an assembly, the "big game," a change in weather, a recent or pending holiday, the breakup of *the* campus romance. Whatever the distractions, it is pointless to proceed without the attention of the students.

One way to get attention is to do nothing. Stand quietly. Students will soon focus their attention on you. Students are accustomed to teachers' frequent talk. Absence of teacher talk will attract their attention. This is particularly useful if only a few students are inattentive.

1. Unit topic: _____

2. Objectives: _____
   _____

3. Set induction: _____
   _____

4. Procedure for discussion: _____
   _____

5. Key questions
   a. _____

      Possible answers: _____
      _____

      Summary: _____
      _____

   b. _____

      Possible answers: _____
      _____

      Summary: _____
      _____

   c. _____

      Possible answers: _____
      _____

      Summary: _____
      _____

6. Conclusions: _____
   _____

7. Closure: _____
   _____

8. Evaluation: _____
   _____

9. Assignment: _____

Another technique is to begin talking in a very low tone, gradually increasing volume. Most of us want to hear what we cannot hear. The low tone of the teacher's voice will attract attention.

Some teachers turn the lights on and off. This is generally done in elementary schools, but can sometimes be effective at the secondary level.

If you use one of these techniques on a regular basis to cue the students to attention, chances are the students will begin to look for your cue even before you start. The lesson is guaranteed to be more successful if everyone is ready to learn.

While getting student attention is important for cognitive set, it is also instrumental in sparking student interest and involvement in the lesson. Provide a tickler. Pose a perplexing problem. Share a story. These are all possibilities for setting the stage for teaching.

1. Lesson topic: _____

2. Objectives: _____
   _____

3. Set induction: _____
   _____

4. Procedures or steps
   a. Problem identification: _____
      _____

   b. Data collection: _____
      _____

   c. Formulation of hypotheses or assumptions: _____
      _____

   d. Analysis of data or materials: _____
      _____

   e. Testing hypotheses or assumptions: _____
      _____

   f. Conclusion or judgment: _____
      _____

5. Closure: _____
   _____

6. Evaluation: _____
   _____

7. Assignment: _____
   _____

Figure 5.4 *Outline of Inquiry and Problem-Solving Lesson Plan Format*

Motivating students is not always an easy task. Be ready and willing to be creative. Let your topic and known student interests provide clues for creating lesson motivators. If the hottest rap group around is doing a concert nearby, use that news to spark a discussion of freedom of expression as you study the Bill of Rights. A recent oil spill could serve as a catalyst for a lesson on pollution problems. A plastic sack filled with a styrofoam cup, a disposable diaper, a lipstick in three layers of packaging, a can of motor oil, a can of aerosol hairspray, and a bottle of toxic weed killer could serve as an introduction to a lesson on the role of big business in environmental pollution. Several magazine advertisements could provide a springboard for a persuasive-writing lesson.

Suspense can generate excitement, interest, and involvement. Begin the class with a discrepant event or an interesting demonstration. For example, build a working model of a volcano in earth science, show pictures of the Old West in social studies, or mix paints to create various paint colors in art. Make the discrepant event or demonstration as surprising or novel as possible. Even better, involve the students directly in showing the discrepant events or in conducting demonstrations.

Models, diagrams, or pictures situated in visible spots will capture attention and interest. You might begin the lesson by soliciting student

Figure 5.5 *Creativity Lesson Plan*

Topic:	Creating a school
Objectives:	The students will be able to do the following:
	1. Give examples of the special features of different secondary schools.
	2. Apply terms associated with secondary schools to an original student project.
Introduction (set induction):	Spend 10 minutes using pictures to review various secondary school terms. Students create a glossary of important secondary school terms in the form of a three-column chart giving terms (e.g., curriculum, hidden curriculum, extra-curricular activities, administration, scheduling, minicourses, flexible scheduling, modules, learning centers, staff, discipline, and school district), definitions, and examples (e.g., the principal is an administrator).
Content:	None
Procedure:	1. Divide class into groups of four (five). Group members are to work cooperatively on planning and drawing an imaginary secondary school.
	2. Students are to give their school a name and decide on its main function (prepare students for work force, college, or vocational school).
	3. Each school should feature a curriculum, disciplinary process, class time schedule, administration setup, and so forth.
	4. Students are to decide on other special features of their school (music programs, sports, busing of students, clubs, etc.).
Closure:	Each group presents its proposed secondary school. The class will discuss the drawbacks and advantages of each group's presented proposal.
Materials:	School pictures, textbooks, glossary, large pieces of drawing paper or poster paper, felt pens or markers.
Evaluation:	Observe student participation as they work on assigned project. Check each group's imaginary secondary school and its main function.
Assignment:	Outline problems that must be overcome to implement the secondary school that your group created. Be prepared to discuss the identified problems in class.

comments. For example, you might ask the class to guess what a diagram or picture represents or how a model functions.

Posing a provocative question and presenting a hypothetical problem are also effective lesson starters. Be careful to use truly thought-provoking questions and hypothetical situations that present interesting dilemmas. Superficial use of these techniques provide little motivation for students to become engaged in the learning process. Questions like "What would happen if . . . ?" and "How do you account for . . . ?" have the potential to spark student interest and participation; whereas questions like "What was the date of . . . ?" or "Who was the author of . . . ?" are likely to bring any interest to a halt after the one "right" answer is given. A hypothetical situation is best used when it can pose a dilemma: "Given

Figure 5.6 *A Sample Language Arts Lesson*

Topic:	The elements of story writing

Objectives: Given a picture stimulus, students will be able to write a short fiction story that contains the needed elements for a short story.

Introduction (set induction): Read aloud a short fiction story that will be of interest to the class. (*Jumping Mouse*, a short myth, demonstrates the elements in an interesting but condensed form.)

Content: The elements of a short story

I. Short story beginning
   A. Describes the setting
   B. Introduces the main character
   C. Introduces the plot (problem or goal the main character attempts to solve or achieve)

II. Middle story elements
   A. First roadblock (character's attempt to reach goal)
   B. Second roadblock
   C. Climax of story (character reaches goal)

III. Story ending
   A. Make conclusions
   B. Wrap up any loose ends

Procedure:
1. After the oral reading, ask students to explain when and how the author introduced the main character.
2. Discuss the promptness with which authors introduce the main character, setting, and plot in short stories. Record responses on the chalkboard using the bell-shaped curve to portray the elements of short stories.
3. At this point, ask students to summarize the elements needed in a short story's beginning. (They should be able to identify; introduction of the main character, description of the story setting, and introduction of the story plot.) It is important to convey to students that the order in which the elements are introduced is not important; but rather, that the inclusion of these elements is a crucial feature of the short story.
4. Next, ask students to recall the first roadblock (or difficulty the main character had in attempting to reach the intended goal). Record responses on bell curve and stress that the middle of a story includes the majority of the story— including the story's climax.
5. As students recall the roadblocks presented in the short book, continue to record these on the bell-shaped curve to demonstrate the rising tension presented in the story.
6. Ask students to describe how the main character finally confronted and solved the problem presented in the introduction of the story. Explain that this element is called the climax of the story. The climax should be placed at the top of the bell-shaped curve to isolate it as the peak of the story.
7. Ask students to summarize the elements that constitute the middle parts of a short story. (The bell-shaped curve on the chalkboard should reveal that the middle story elements are composed of roadblocks in the main character's attempt to reach a goal, and the climax or the reaching of that goal.)
8. Finally, ask students to talk about the brevity the author uses to end the story quickly once the main character has reached his or her goal.

Figure 5.6 *Continued.*

(continued)

Closure:	Ask students to make an outline of the elements of a short story using the information presented on the bell-shaped curve.
Evaluation:	Consider students' answers to questions during class discussions. Check students' short-story outlines as work is being completed.
Assignment:	Let each student choose a picture from a magazine and instruct them to use the outlines as a guide in writing a short story about the picture selected.

Figure 5.7 *Sample Samll-Group Strategy Lesson Plan*

Topic:	Classifying information
Objective:	At the completion of this lesson, the student will be able to classify information into groups on the basis of similar or common attributes.
Initial focus:	Why should we learn to classify information into categories or groups? Discuss at least three reasons for classifying information.
Major task:	Skim text (pages 107–121) for important ideas or items that might be classified. Agree on categories (groups or labels) that could be used to classify text information. Choose three unused practice items in the text and have individual students label the items accordingly. Ask individual students to share their labels with the class to ensure understanding. Form groups of three. Instruct the groups to classify the items below in at least two ways.
	Items: Wichita, chair, Dallas, Denver, mule, Boston, horse, New York, house, Chicago, deer, bed, picture, Lincoln, elephant, and Oklahoma City.
Group:	Students work on classification activity. Each group will produce two schemes. Schemes are to be recorded on transparency film.
Debriefing:	Each group will present their two classification schemes to the class. The class will react and make recommendations.
Resources and materials:	Textbook, transparency film (two sheets per group), transparency pen (one per group), and classification item list.
Evaluation:	Check for students' ability to classify practice items during the major task phase of the lesson, participation in group activity, and appropriateness of the two classification schemes by each group.

the power and the money, how would you solve the problem of . . . ?'' is such an example. Used strategically, both of these techniques are promising in their potential for promoting student interest and involvement.

Students generally learn more from a lesson when they know what is expected of them. Thus, to maximize learning, you should plan introductory remarks that will provide students with what Ausubel (1963) calls an **advance organizer:** Plan remarks that will give students a "what to look for" frame of reference. Basically, the concept of the advance organizer is related

Figure 5.8 *Sample Key Questions/Discussion Lesson Plan*

Topic:	A cashless society
Objectives:	The students will be able to do the following:
	1. Explain his or her feelings about the effects of Electronic Funds Transfer systems (EFT) on society.
	2. Participate in group discussion and decision making.
Set induction:	Money isn't going to be needed in the future. You will have no use for cash in everyday life.
Procedure for discussion:	A question will be presented to the class for discussion. Responses will be recorded on the board. A summary of the responses will be made.
Key question 1:	What effect will a cashless society have on daily life?
Possible answers:	Computers will deal with money. Everyone will use checks and/or credit cards. Vending machines will change. Some types of crime will decrease while other types will increase.
Summary:	We will have to change surprisingly little to become a cashless society.
Key question 2:	How do you think Electronic Funds Transfer systems (EFT) will change consumer behavior?
Possible answers:	Problems with budgeting money may result. Buying by television, catalog, and telephone will increase. People will be concerned less about prices and money.
Summary:	Electronic Funds Transfer system (EFT) will create many problems in society.
Key question 3:	Where do you think Electronic Funds Transfer systems (EFT) will have the greatest impact?
Possible answers:	More checking accounts will be opened. Banks will issue more credit cards. All stores will take checks and credit cards. Prices will increase because of bad checks and fraud.
Summary:	Bank and consumer interaction will increase, as will the incidence of some types of crime.
Conclusions:	A cashless society would have a positive and negative effect on society. An Electronic Funds Transfer system likely would lead to less individual privacy and more control over people and their daily life.
Closure:	Review responses recorded on board. Ask pertinent questions regarding recorded responses.
Evaluation:	Consider student's participation in discussion and decision making. Also evaluate question-and-answer sequences.
Assignment:	Keep track of the number of times and types of transactions in which cash is needed in a 24-hour period. What effect would an Electronic Funds Transfer system (EFT) have on your life?

closely to the establishment of student interest, but it is usually more specific in nature. Advance organizers can be generalizations, definitions, or analogies (Orlich et al., 1990). For example, a science teacher might start a lesson about light with a generalization about the major characteristics of light. A social studies teacher might start a lesson on war by relating it to a football game. No matter what form it takes, an advance organizer serves the purpose of giving students needed background information for the upcoming lesson or of helping them remember and apply old information to the lesson. Thus, the advance organizer acts as a kind of conceptual bridge between the new and old information.

Some teachers use a verbal statement of lesson objectives as the advance organizer. However, you must take care to translate the written objectives into a form that is both understandable and interesting to students. For example:

Objective. The students will be able to correctly calculate the force of gravity on an object.

Translation. [*Teacher holds a light and heavy object overhead.*] When I drop these objects, watch them closely. [*Teacher drops objects.*] There was a continuous increase in their speed as they fell, which requires that a force act on them. What is this force and how strong is it? Why do both objects impact at the same time? [Silence.] Today, we are going to answer these questions.

You must set the stage for the learning process. If you fail to arouse student attention and interest and establish a framework for your lesson, the remainder of the lesson often is wasted. Listen to the conversations of your students for topics that you can use to start your lessons. A simple remark related to the topic is all that will be needed to get the discussion started.

Strategies and Procedures

How will you teach the objectives you have targeted? What will the students read? Is a short lecture the best method for presenting the information, or would an inquiry lesson better suit your purposes? Should the students work individually or in groups? Would a guest speaker be beneficial, or would a field trip serve your objectives better? These are the kinds of questions you must ask as you prepare daily lessons. Once again, the unit plan and the nature of the material, as well as the resources available, will guide these decisions.

A well-planned lesson consists of the content to be taught as well as the **instructional strategy** to be employed in teaching it. The instructional strategy consists of two components: the methodology and the lesson procedure. The instructional strategy is the global plan for teaching a particular lesson. It can be viewed as analogous to the overall plan for winning a tennis match or basketball game.

The **methodology** acts as the student motivator and sets the tone for the lesson. It consists of planned patterned behaviors that are definite steps by which the teacher influences learning. The methodology should be designed and organized so that it captures and holds the attention of students and involves them as much as possible in the learning situation.

The **lesson procedure** is the sequence of steps that has been designed for leading students to the acquisition of the learning objectives. For example, you may decide on the following sequence for a lesson on atomic energy.

1. Present a short introductory lecture on atomic energy.

2. Show a film on splitting the atom.

3. Conduct a summary discussion on the content of the film.

4. Conduct a question-and-answer session on major points covered in the lecture and in the film.

As you see, the procedure consists of sequenced teacher and student activities used for achieving the lesson objectives.

When you plan, don't overlook student practice. Students must have the opportunity to test themselves on the content. Providing these opportunities must be a regular part of the daily lesson plan. Two types of practice are important: *Guided practice*—or practice with the help and encouragement of the teacher—and *independent practice*—or practice without the help and encouragement of the teacher—should take place during the course of each lesson.

Practice opportunities need not be meaningless worksheets. Guided practice can be oral. Guided practice can be geared for group participation or for group creation of a product or a set of ideas. The important thing is to furnish a "safety net." It is through guided practice that the teacher can observe whether or not the students understand the concepts to be learned. Concepts that have not been fully understood can be retaught immediately. Reteaching could be accomplished by allowing the peer group to restate the concepts in the language of the students. Immediate reteaching is more effective than trying to return to a previous topic several days later. If the unit requires that learning be cumulative, one misunderstood lesson can have serious consequences for later learning. Once the teacher is confident that students can proceed without the safety net, it is time to provide for independent practice.

Independent practice generally is homework. However, homework need not be meaningless worksheets either. The exploration of one concept in depth; the interview of one appropriate expert; the building of one model, one drawing, one map, one idea—all these avenues for discovery can be more valuable than copying definitions from the textbook.

Finally, you may want to evaluate your daily lesson objectives. You have set the stage, identified the objectives, developed the strategies and planned for practice. Now you may want to include in your plan a daily evaluation of student learning. There are several techniques for assessing student learning. These will be discussed in detail in chapters 10 and 11. Always refer to the lesson objectives when determining how you will evaluate student progress. If the objectives are well written, the methods for evaluation are more easily determined.

Your instructional strategy is the actual presentation of the lesson content. It comprises your techniques for giving students information. Deciding on a methodology requires that you choose—from a wide variety of methods, activities, and learning experiences—those techniques you feel will best lead to the desired learning outcomes.

Methodology Selection

Instructional methods can influence students directly through focused, teacher-directed instruction or influence them indirectly by involving them actively in their own learning. Most instruction can be categorized into two basic types: teacher-centered and student-centered. Comparisons of these two methods of instruction are given in table 5.2. The teacher-centered instructional approaches are more "traditional" or didactic, with students acquiring knowledge by listening to the teacher, by reading a textbook, or both. In the teacher-centered instructional approach, students are passive recipients of information. In contrast, student-centered approaches to instruction invite students to participate actively in their own learning experiences. The two instructional approaches are equally effective in bringing about learning. Concepts in math, for example, can be taught through a teacher-centered approach such as the lecture method or through a student-centered approach such as cooperative learning.

TABLE 5.2   Comparison of Teacher-Centered and Student-Centered Methodologies

Method	Amount of Teacher Control	Intent and Unique Features
Teacher-Centered Instructional Approaches		
Lecture	High	Telling technique. Teacher presents information without student interaction.
Lecture-Recitation	High to moderate	Telling technique. Teacher presents information and follows up with question/answer sessions.
Socratic	Moderate	Interaction technique. Teacher uses question-driven dialogues to draw out information from students.
Demonstration	High to moderate	Showing technique. Individual stands before class, shows something, and talks about it.
Modeling	High	Showing technique. Teacher or individual behaves/acts in way desired of students, and students learn by copying actions of model.
Student-Centered Instructional Approaches		
Discussion	Low to moderate	Interaction technique. Whole-class or small-group interact on topic.
Panel	Low	Telling technique. Group of students present and/or discuss information.
Debate	Low	Telling technique. Competitive discussion of topic between teams of students.
Role Playing	Low	Doing technique. Acting out of roles or situations.
Cooperative Learning	Low	Doing technique. Students work together in mixed-ability group on task(s).
Discovery	Low to moderate	Doing technique. Students follow established procedure for solving problems through direct experiences.
Inquiry	Low	Doing technique. Students establish own procedure for solving problems through direct experiences.
Simulations/Games	Low	Doing technique. Involvement in an artificial but representative situation or event.
Individualized Instruction	Low to moderate	Telling/doing technique. Students engage in learning designed to fit their needs and abilities.
Independent Study	Low	Telling/doing technique. Learning carried out with little guidance.

Source: Moore, K. D. (1991). *Classroom teaching skills* (2nd ed.). New York: McGraw-Hill. Used with permission.

With all these possible methods, which method should be selected for a particular lesson? Suffice it to say that the best choice is often based on experience. However, the lesson procedure, as well as other factors, often must be considered in your selection of methods. Indeed, some writers (Orlich et al., 1990) suggest there are four factors that affect the selection of the appropriate instructional method for a particular lesson: content and objectives of the lesson, teacher characteristics, learner characteristics, and learning environment.

Your lesson must have a purpose. Are you trying to teach in the cognitive, affective, or psychomotor domains? The selection of a methodology and related experiences will depend on the teaching domain. In addition, your selection should be related to such factors as goals, specific learning objectives, and content. For example, if you are trying to teach a psycho-motor skill or develop an attitude, the lecture method is not a desirable approach.

You—as well as all teachers—have unique sets of personal experiences, background knowledge, teaching skills, and personality traits that make you more comfortable and effective with certain methodologies than with others. Obviously, you will select those methods that have proven most successful in the past. Because teachers are inclined to select the methodology that makes them feel most comfortable, it is easy to get into a teaching rut. Therefore, you should be prepared to experiment with different methods. You cannot become comfortable or even familiar with methods you have not tried.

Your selected methodology must also match the maturity level and experiences of your students. You would not use the lecture method with slower students or with students who have trouble paying attention to verbal messages. Just as teachers often prefer one teaching style, students will feel comfortable and learn better when the method fits their abilities, needs, and interests. Keep in mind that when your method is mismatched with students' preferred style, learning will not take place at the maximum level. Thus, you should select the best method for a particular class.

Obviously, your selected method may not always be the best one for all students in a single class, but it should be the best method for the class as a whole. Indeed, in order to fit the abilities, needs, and interests of every student in a class, you must individualize the instruction. However, individualizing instruction does not mean that you leave students on their own at all times. Some direct instruction (active teacher-centered instruction) should be used even when individualizing. After all, you will be responsible for organizing the content and directing the learning process.

The environment and related environmental factors also must be taken into account when you select your methodology. Factors such as the space available, time of day, and weather can influence a lesson greatly. For example, one should not select a method such as the discovery method, which requires a great deal of space, when little space is available and when you have a large class.

Finally, how much time should you devote to each of the two approaches to instruction? This is a complex question. This decision will vary depending on the subject, the grade level, the amount of time that students have available for the lesson, the materials available, and the philosophy of the teacher and school. Indeed, whenever possible, try to vary your method and become skilled in combining a variety of methods into a total lesson strategy.

Procedure Selection

As noted earlier, the lesson procedure is your outline, or model, of instruction for the implementation of the lesson, and it generally takes one of two basic forms: the teacher-centered or student-centered model. These approaches differ on the amount of structure offered students. The traditional model (teacher-centered), involves all students in all activities at the same time, while the interactive model (student-centered)—through its diagnostic-corrective-enrichment activities—provides a high degree of individualization, because it enables students to learn at different paces and to use different materials. We will address the teacher- and student-centered models at length in chapters 7 and 8, respectively.

No matter whether you are an experienced teacher or a novice or how much detail is included in a written lesson plan, the lesson must be well structured to be successful. The structure should incorporate instructional strategies and techniques that will keep students interested and motivated. Henson (1981) suggests several such techniques:

1. Make your activities meaningful through active involvement of students.

2. Make the content as relevant as possible.

3. Keep the instructional atmosphere as safe and informal as possible.

4. Be enthusiastic about the material you are teaching.

5. Challenge students by pointing out problems, inconsistencies, and contradictions throughout your lessons.

6. Share your lesson goals, objectives, and procedures with students so that they will know where they are going and how they are going to get there.

7. Whenever feasible, use the ideas, suggestions, and opinions expressed by students so that they will feel you value their input.

Attention to the above suggestions and to the factors that should be considered in selecting an instructional strategy will lead to more effective instruction.

Closure

How will the lesson end? Will the bell ring and the students file out to begin another lesson in a different subject area? This is not a satisfactory way for the lesson to end. A **closure** activity should provide a logical conclusion; it should pull together and organize the concepts learned. Once your lesson has been concluded, the lesson closure consolidates main concepts and ideas and integrates them within the students' existing cognitive structure.

Closure should be more than a quick review of the ideas covered in the lesson. It should be designed to enable students to organize the new material in relation to itself and to other lessons. It should show the relationship among the major ideas and tie together the parts of the lesson. Closure is a vital, and often overlooked, component in the teaching-learning process. Indeed, it is as vital as your set induction and your lesson itself.

Closure isn't something that takes place only at the conclusion of a lesson: Sometimes you may want to achieve closure during the course of a particular lesson. Shostak (1982) suggests that closure can be appropriate in the following situations:

1. For following up a film, record, play, or television program.

2. For summarizing the presentation of a guest speaker.

3. For closing a group discussion.

4. For summarizing experiences of a field trip.

5. For consolidating the learning of a new concept.

6. For ending a science experiment.

7. For ending a long unit of study.

Many methods of providing closure are available. Having students relate the material learned back to the general theme is one way to achieve closure. Examples of how this method is implemented include such statements as "The characteristics of this play make it an excellent example of a comedy," "These proofs tend to support our original generalization that a negative number times a positive number results in a negative number," and "This form of government fits our model of a dictatorship."

Cueing is another technique for reaching closure. Have students fill in an outline you have provided that includes the main points of the lesson. Use cueing questions or statements. Examples of cueing questions are "What are the major concepts derived from our study of environmental problems?" and "Which governmental agencies can we credit with primary involvement in environmental issues?" Cueing statements might include "There are four major environmental issues that society must address, and they are . . ." and "You learned the following things about waste disposal: one . . ." Cueing is an important skill to develop. In a courtroom, cueing is called "leading the witness." In the classroom, cueing is a necessary tool for organizing conceptual learning.

You can also draw attention to the completion of the lesson through the use of summary questions. A question such as "What were the four major ideas covered in today's lesson?" or "Joe, can you summarize today's lesson?" or "Let's see if we can draw any conclusions from our discussion?" can effectively close a lesson.

Connecting new and previously learned material can help students reach closure. A structured statement can be used, such as "Let's relate this to yesterday's study of the nervous system," "This form of art is similar to the other forms of art we have studied," and "Can we relate this example to examples we have studied in the past?"

Another common way for achieving closure is to have students demonstrate or apply what they have learned. If they cannot demonstrate or apply the new concept or skill, then learning is questionable. Examples of this technique include teacher questions such as "Can you give me other examples of verbs and adverbs?" or statements such as "Let's diagram the two sentences at the top of page 123 as the textbook did in its examples" and "Let's do the oral exercises on page 97 together." Demonstrating or applying new information at the conclusion of a lesson has the added advantage of providing needed immediate feedback to the students. Many teachers have students do in-class assignments to achieve closure by application and to provide the needed feedback.

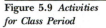

Monday

| Period 1 | Review homework
Introduce film
Show film
Discuss film
Give assignment |

Figure 5.9 *Activities for Class Period*

Every student in your class must achieve closure on a lesson. One student's achievement of closure does not indicate that all students have achieved it. Just because one student is able to answer closure questions correctly, it does not mean that all can. Therefore, you must take care to ensure that all students have achieved closure.

Lesson Planning for Everyday Use

The formats we have described in this chapter are probably more detailed than the formats you will use in the schools. Experienced teachers use an abridged format—commonly found in planning books—like that shown in figure 5.2.

Planning-book formats that are blocked out in terms of days and periods are useful for keeping track of a week's class activities. However, because of the limited space available in these books, teachers usually list only major activities or topics for a class period, as is shown in figure 5.9. A quick glance tells the teacher the major activities for the period of the day. This is often helpful in keeping track of where a unit is going.

The use of a planning book does not mean that thorough planning is unnecessary. Every lesson should be thoughtfully designed in detail. The shortened plan can be helpful for communication with school administration; in fact, some teachers submit a copy of the completed planning-book format for the required weekly lesson plan.

Reflective Teaching

A rather new model that is presently receiving much attention is the concept of the teacher as a reflective decision maker. Donald Cruickshank (1987), the primary architect of **reflective teaching,** suggests that reflective teachers consider their teaching carefully and, as a result, are more thoughtful and alert students of teaching. Essentially, according to Cruickshank, careful reflections on past experiences will result in teacher growth and lead to more effective planning and teaching.

Teaching practices tend to become routine with time and are repeated with very little or no forethought. Through reflective teaching, however, a teacher might examine student satisfaction with a lesson or examine whether all students were actively involved in a lesson. Reflective teachers learn to formulate their own rules, principles, and philosophies that can guide them to better practices. In other words, teachers who reflect on their practices—who submit them to examination—become better decision makers and, consequently, better planners and successful teachers.

TABLE 5.3 Lesson Plan Structure

Component	Description
Set Induction	Activity at outset of a lesson to get students' undivided attention, arouse interest, and establish a conceptual framework
Instructional Strategy	The methodology and procedure, or the global plan of a lesson
Methodology	Planned patterned behaviors that are definite steps by which the teacher influences learning
Procedure	Sequence of steps designed to lead students to the acquisition of the desired learning
Closure	An activity designed to pull a lesson together and bring it to a logical conclusion

Application Guidelines ▼

Lesson Plan Structure

Implement Lessons Carefully

Examples:
1. Focus your lesson at the beginning so students see your purposes. Communicate your objectives.
2. Break your lessons into clear steps or stages.
3. Review periodically.
4. Ask questions to check for understanding.
5. Outline the lesson on the chalkboard in an easy-to-follow sequence.
6. Drive your objectives home with a summary, review, drill, student-led summation, or short quiz at the end of the lesson.
7. Provide concrete examples that explain and reinforce information.
8. Use appropriate vocabulary.
9. Provide adequate practice of objectives to be mastered.

Follow the Plan

Examples:
1. Follow your plan fairly closely, but don't let it handcuff you.
2. Stick to the topic.
3. Leave a plan when it is going so badly that something must be done to save it.

This concludes our discussion of lesson plan structure. Table 5.3 gives a summary of section concepts. Review table 5.3 and the Lesson Plan Structure Application Guidelines, and complete exercise 5.2 to check your understanding of the concepts presented in this section.

Application of Knowledge

Exercise 5.2 Lesson Plan Structure

Test yourself on the following concepts of lesson plan structure. Appropriate responses can be found in appendix A.

1. Name and briefly describe the three major components of the daily lesson plan.
   a. _____

      _____

   b. _____

      _____

   c. _____

      _____

2. Advance organizers can be used effectively for achieving lesson closure. (True/False)

3. Label each of the following methods of instruction as teacher-centered (T) or student-centered (S).
   a. _____ Discussion
   b. _____ Socratic
   c. _____ Lecture
   d. _____ Inquiry

4. The "outline" for the implementation of a lesson.
   a. Methodology
   b. Set induction
   c. Procedure
   d. Closure

5. Why is it necessary to provide closure for a lesson?

   _____

   _____

   _____

6. Define *reflective teaching:* _____

   _____

CHAPTER SUMMARY

Successful teachers are effective planners. Therefore, novice and experienced teachers alike must plan and plan well. Courses must be organized, units must be developed, and weekly plans must be written. Finally, daily lesson plans must be developed and implemented.

Several people can be involved in the planning process. Both team planning and student-teacher planning are valuable in some situations. You will have to make decisions about when these methods of planning are appropriate for the content and students to be taught.

Comprehensive unit plans—which comprise a title, goals and instructional objectives, an outline of content, learning activities, resources and materials, and evaluation strategies—are necessary for coherent instruction. The increased demands on public schools—to teach things traditionally taught in the home, the church, or the community—make it essential to plan carefully for instruction.

The planning of your daily lesson presentation should be viewed as one of the most important components of effective teaching. If your daily lessons are not leading to high-quality learning, perhaps you should review and pay more attention to the opening or closing of your lesson activities or the strategy used.

First, a strong set induction (or cognitive set) is crucial for a lesson. It sets the tone and establishes a conceptual framework for the coming activities. It should be planned so that you have captured the attention of every student present. When lessons are started before a cognitive set is established, students may miss the important beginning of your lesson.

Second, the methodology and procedure form the lesson's instructional strategy. The method used forms the heart of a lesson; it is here that you decide whether a teacher-centered or a student-centered mode of delivery will be most appropriate. In making this decision, you must keep in mind that the prime purpose of your method is to accomplish the students' acquisition of the intended learning. You must take into account your objective, your abilities, the intended learners, and the environ-

ment. A maxim to remember in selecting the method is this: "The student should participate." Students should respond actively in some manner, or they at least should be mentally alert.

Third and finally, your lesson also should have a well-planned ending, or closure. This can be done with a recapitulation of what was covered, a summary, a series of open-ended questions, or student application of the covered concepts. This ending should be carried out before the closing bell rings.

Recently, attention has been directed toward teachers as reflective decision makers—educators who reflect on past experiences in planning their instruction. In other words, reflective teachers examine their practices before they implement them.

Attention to the three basic components of a daily lesson will lead to stronger lessons. A good rule to keep in mind is that you should spend adequate time on each component.

Discussion Questions and Activities

1. **Classroom observation.** Be an observer in several classrooms. Note the structure of the lessons being presented. Can you identify the elements that make up the lesson plan? How is set induction achieved? How is closure achieved? Can you draw any conclusions as a result of your observations?

2. **Set induction techniques on television.** Watch the beginnings of several television programs, and notice how the concept of cognitive set is used to get viewers interested in the upcoming program. Can you use the same techniques in the classroom environment?

3. **Closure techniques on television.** Watch the endings of several television programs, and notice whether closure is achieved. If so, how?

4. **Textbook.** Examine the teacher's guide for a textbook in your field at the grade level you would like to teach. Are the units and lessons organized as you would like to teach them? How would you change the sequence if you had to use this text for teaching? Are there things you would like to leave out or add?

5. **Research.** Go to the library and collect as many examples of unit and lesson plan models as you can find. Try to think of one lesson in your field that is particularly suited to each model you discover. Develop a few lesson plans using the models you have collected.

6. **Planning a lesson.** Plan a lesson presentation for the topic of your choice from your subject area. Include in the plan the three key ingredients that make up a well-written lesson plan.

6 Instructional-Media Learning Tools

✎ **True learning is doing! Direct experiences enlighten us. The senses become engaged, and the brain is engaged.**

Overview

Successful teachers are aware of what exists in the way of instructional tools and activities—what beneficial characteristics they offer and how they may best be incorporated into the teaching-learning process. If nothing else, this body of information and know-how will help stifle classroom boredom for both teacher and students.

This chapter is designed to make the reader more aware of the variety of instructional-media learning tools available to teachers when they plan, teach, and eventually evaluate a lesson. More specifically, it offers practical information about a select number of these tools—what they are, what advantages they offer, what limitations they may have, and how best to use them. Described in this chapter are textbooks, chalkboards, bulletin boards, flat pictures, transparencies, slides, filmstrips, motion pictures, video programs, interactive video, and computers.

Objectives

After completing your study of chapter 6, you should be able to do the following:

1. Supply practical information about a select number of instructional-media learning tools, which enable teachers to make more informed choices when planning, teaching, and evaluating instruction.

2. Identify instructional advantages and limitations associated with textbooks and programmed texts as instructional tools.

3. Describe characteristics, advantages, limitations, and uses of chalkboards and bulletin boards as instructional tools.

4. Describe formats for and the characteristics, advantages, limitations, and uses of still pictures as instructional tools.

5. Describe characteristics, advantages, limitations, and uses of motion pictures, video technology, and computers as instructional tools.

Chapter Terms and Key Concepts

Bulletin Board

Chalkboard

Computer

Computer-Assisted Instruction

Computer-Managed Instruction

Filmstrip

Flat Pictures

Interactive Video

Motion Picture

Programmed Textbooks

Slides

Transparencies

Videodisc

Video Programming

P ause for a moment to consider the notion of *variety*—how variety itself permeates a school system and the teaching-learning process. Students enter a classroom with a variety of temperaments, backgrounds, and ways in which they learn. Among the many problems facing a teacher is the task of coping with this variety in order to promote learning. As you plan student learning experiences, a major task will be to choose from a vast array of audiovisual aids and resource materials.

Because the selection of instructional tools is central to the planning process, it is important that you be aware of certain "givens" when planning, using, and evaluating the success of one or a combination of instructional-media learning tools. Awareness of these givens tends to put things into a more professional, systematic perspective when the tools are used. Consider these givens:

1. The nature of the teaching-learning situation has been assessed, and learner characteristics have been determined. With this information, the motivational value of the instructional media should be assessed.

2. Learner objectives have been determined and/or modified accordingly. Media should then be selected to maximize the teaching of these objectives; media use should not be an afterthought.

3. The use of any instructional tools has been purposefully planned as an integral part of the lesson. The media will be of little value if there is insufficient time for its proper use or if other lesson components make it inappropriate.

4. The media tools are of good quality in content and physical characteristics. In effect, be sure to select the most appropriate and effective form of instructional media.

5. The user knows how to correctly use the tool and associated hardware: The user should view it, read it, handle it, and otherwise employ or review it prior to exposing students to it.

The unique value and possible selection and implementation of the variety of instructional tools will depend on the above cited criteria. However, there are certain general guidelines that should be followed in the selection of instructional aids and resources.

General Instructional–Media Selection Guidelines

If instruction is to achieve maximum effectiveness, learning experiences should be as direct as possible (for instance, through manipulation of objects, writing, and real-life situations). That is, students should be involved in "learning by doing." They should utilize as many of their senses as possible; and when all the senses are engaged, learning will usually be most effective and the longest lasting (Dale, 1969).

Conversely, instruction can be provided through abstract experiences, where students are exposed to symbolizations (words, numbers, and symbols). Abstract learning usually involves only one or two of the senses. However, verbal and visual symbolic experiences cannot be completely

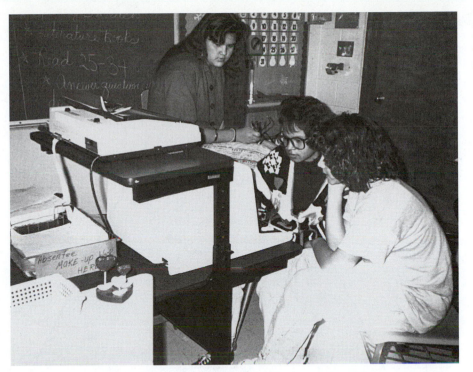

avoided when teaching. So, when planning instructional experiences, you should select those activities that involve students in the most direct experiences. Figure 6.1 depicts the range of such experiences, from concrete to abstract.

As shown in figure 6.1, instructional experiences form a type of continuum: from direct, concrete experiences that involve all the senses to verbal, abstract experiences that involve only one sense. Of course, various reasons—time, student characteristics, subject—may impede you in offering direct experiences. Thus, sometimes you must settle for experiences higher on the continuum. Verbal experiences may be necessary, but the most effective learning experiences are those that involve the most senses.

Printed Materials

Printed materials remain the most used type of learning tool used in secondary classrooms. Indeed, a tremendous amount of reading material suited for most secondary curriculum areas is available to secondary school classroom teachers. These materials include pamphlets, brochures, workbooks, paperback books, newspapers, and magazines. Most of these materials are provided free of charge or for a small fee. However, the textbook remains the major source of printed information used in teaching.

Figure 6.1 *Levels of Experiences*

Source: Adapted from Dale, E. (1969). **Audio visual methods in teaching.** *New York: Holt, Reinhart & Winston, 108.*

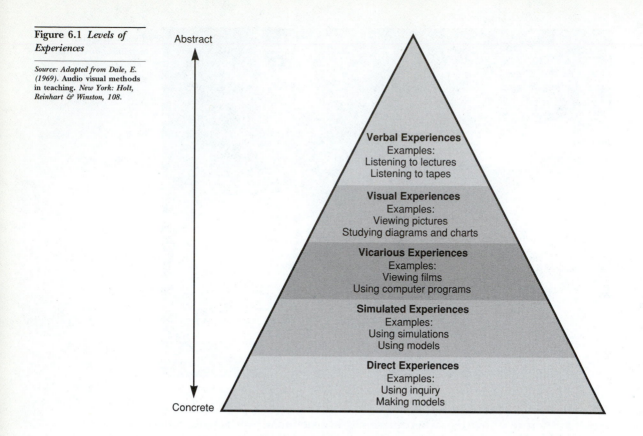

Abstract

Verbal Experiences
Examples:
Listening to lectures
Listening to tapes

Visual Experiences
Examples:
Viewing pictures
Studying diagrams and charts

Vicarious Experiences
Examples:
Viewing films
Using computer programs

Simulated Experiences
Examples:
Using simulations
Using models

Direct Experiences
Examples:
Using inquiry
Making models

Concrete

Textbooks

Textbooks traditionally are the most common aid to instruction available to teachers and are one of the most powerful (Lorber & Pierce, 1983). They are versatile and convenient, and they permit random access to information and messages they contain. They may be used alone, with other texts, and as a source of enrichment and supplemental material. Additionally, they are easily obtained, maintained, and portable, and they contain not only verbal material and explanation, but also provide excellent visualization of concepts and information (Brown, Lewis, & Harcleroad, 1983).

Callahan and Clark (1988, p. 25) state, "The most ubiquitous of the resources for course, unit, and lesson planning is the textbook." Such a statement underscores what seems to be one major advantage of textbooks: They aid a teacher in planning. Textbooks are cited as helpful in planning in that they provide a unifying factor to classroom instruction and a means for organizing and structuring a course. They offer a selection of common subject matter and readings—arranged in some logical order—and they can be used in determining and emphasizing content. Textbooks, especially teachers' editions, are also helpful in planning because they supply a selection of teaching-learning tactics, strategies, activities and questions, and a wealth of information, reading, and study. They also frequently provide information relative to other sources of teaching materials and tools. Some observers—like Brown, Lewis, & Harcleroad (1983)—submit that characteristics such as these help in the improvement of teaching.

Textbooks also offer an economic advantage in that they are relatively inexpensive, last a long time, and can be used repeatedly. The fact that they offer, in a single volume and in a variety of ways (verbal, pictorial, graphic), a variety of information is further evidence of the economy of textbooks.

On a more specific instructional level, textbooks can be adapted to independent study, tutorial endeavors, and individualized instruction because they lend themselves to self-pacing. Textbooks can allow students without reading problems to acquire information quickly and efficiently, serve as a basis for discussion of commonly available information, and help learners grasp the relationship between cause and effect (Lorber & Pierce, 1983). Additionally, Callahan and Clark (1988, p. 447) suggest that "textbooks can make an excellent base for building interesting, high-order learning activities (discussion, inquiry, research activities) that call forth critical thinking and other higher mental processes."

It must be pointed out that most of the disadvantages associated with textbooks stem from their misuses. Indeed, Lorber and Pierce (1983, p. 109) write, "Perhaps the greatest single misuse of texts is allowing them to dictate what will be taught." Still other teachers let the textbook assume too great a role in classroom teaching and in curriculum making. Textbooks can give rise to "textbook teaching," during which principal teaching and learning activities become characteristically a deadly routine of assigned readings and recitations (Brown, Lewis, & Harcleroad, 1983, p. 385), which are often accompanied by sets of written answers to questions. Teachers sometimes use a "chapter a week" approach, which places undue emphasis on how fast and how many pages are being covered, rather than on what content, skills, behaviors, attitudes, and understandings are being fostered. As for the readers themselves, textbooks can lead them to put emphasis on "reading to remember," which may tend to stifle critical thinking, problem solving, and student interaction and creativity. Thus, textbooks may "relieve the learners of the need to do their own organizing and prevent them from thinking and drawing conclusions independently" (Brown, Lewis, & Harcleroad, 1983, p. 385).

Contentwise, textbooks may also provide sketchy treatment of often minimal content and do little to prompt learners to pursue further study. This tendency is illustrated by the text's failure to cover all important principles and concepts and by the fact that textbooks generally are an incomplete source of content written at the bottom levels of the cognitive domain (Henson, 1988). Often they contain outdated material, as well as sexual, racial, and other biases. Textbook limitations also result from the fact that their authors are not likely to be familiar with the instructional objectives and the group of students with which a teacher is working (Lorber & Pierce, 1983).

Another factor associated with the limitations inherent in textbooks is that those who select them may not know how to select one adequately. We will address textbook selection, as well as the effective use and

TABLE *6.1*   Classroom Printed Materials

Concept	Description
Textbook	Common aid used by teachers in planning and presenting subject matter to students
Programmed Text	Content presented in a series of carefully planned sequential steps followed by immediate feedback

evaluation of textbooks, in greater detail in chapter 14. However, remember that a high-quality textbook helps students learn when it is used appropriately. At the minimum, you should check to see that the text is organized in a manner that enables curricular goals and objectives to be reached. This entails checking to see that the content—both verbal and visual—is appropriate, suitably sequenced, and at the desired reading level. Also involved in textbook selection is checking on whether the text is physically attractive, what it costs, and the availability and quality of teachers' guides, teachers' editions, and other supplemental materials, as well as on the reputation, reliability, and service record of the publishing company.

Programmed Textbooks

Programmed textbooks or programmed workbooks present content information in a series of carefully planned sequential steps. These steps are followed by immediate feedback related to learning progress, and in some programs remediation is provided as problem areas are identified.

The major advantage associated with programmed text is the active involvement of students in the learning process (students are required to construct or select a response). A second advantage is that the learning of misconceptions is reduced because of the immediate feedback related to the correctness of students' responses.

Conversely, there are certain limitations associated with the use of programmed text. Because programmed text requires that students be able to read and comprehend what is being read, it is limited to students who exhibit these skills with a competence commensurate with the level of the text. Also, because programmed text usually deals with basic, factual information, it has limited value in developing critical thinking and creativity. In effect, divergent thinking of any kind is discouraged and is incorrect thinking.

This completes our brief look at printed materials. Table 6.1 summarizes the different types of printed materials presented in this section, and the Classroom Printed Materials Application Guidelines offer some further suggestions. Review the summary and guidelines, and complete exercise 6.1.

Application Guidelines ▼

Classroom Printed Materials

Select Printed Materials Carefully

Examples:
1. Select a variety of printed materials so that the needs of all students are addressed.
2. Use paperback books to supplement or replace textbook sets.
3. Gather newspapers and magazines for use in your classroom.
4. Be aware of what constitutes a good textbook in your field.
5. Select programmed materials to fit the needs of individual students.

Use Printed Materials Efficiently

Examples:
1. Plan wisely so duplicated materials and supplementary materials can be reused.
2. Supplement and enrich your subject content with newspapers and magazines.
3. Monitor all programmed materials with care, and collect information regarding its effectiveness.

Application of Knowledge

Exercise 6.1   Classroom Printed Materials

Check yourself on the following section concepts. Appropriate responses can be found in appendix A.

1. On the continuum of instruction experiences, printed materials tend to be at the _____ (concrete/abstract) end.

2. Printed materials in most secondary classrooms are usually limited to a textbook. (True/False)

3. Textbook teaching can represent a problem when the textbook is given too great a role in classroom-curriculum decision making. (True/False)

4. It is usually unwise to use a textbook when putting your instructional emphasis on independent study. (True/False)

5. Programmed text differs from the regular classroom textbook in the following way:
   _____
   _____

Nonprojection Verbal and Visual Experiences

Most secondary students' learning experiences will be related to non-projection verbal and visual experiences—that is, their teachers will rely heavily on the use of words, symbols, and sounds. Chief among the nonprojection media commonly used in the secondary classrooms are display materials and flat pictures.

Display Materials

Perhaps the most commonplace of all teaching tools are the display materials: chalkboards and bulletin boards. These devices can be found in almost any secondary classroom, and most of us fail to think of them as media.

Chalkboards

Chalkboards are found in practically every classroom in the nation and probably constitute the most widely used of all media tools—except possibly the textbook (Bullough, 1988). Some point to the **chalkboard** as the teaching tool that "is about the *most useful and versatile*" of the visual aids teachers have available (Callahan & Clark, 1988, p. 453).

The advantages of the chalkboard are numerous and varied. Perhaps its most important advantages center around the fact that it is always there and ready for use, that it can be used with a high degree of flexibility, and that the material placed on it can be easily erased, replaced, or modified (Wittich & Schuller, 1973). Teachers can use chalkboards to present preplanned subject matter and associated verbal and visual materials— such as key words, outlines, lists, instructions, examples, diagrams, sketches, and graphs. Chalkboards can reinforce oral explanations and presentations and clarify difficult concepts. Material placed on them can be easily covered until the time comes to refer to it. Teachers can use chalkboards for building lesson elements that proceed from simple to complex ideas and for developing explanations step by step and point by point.

Additionally, unplanned material and information that comes into play as a lesson unfolds may be placed on chalkboards as big, bold, and colorful as desired. A teacher may place long-term notices and announcements and examples of student work on them as well. Furthermore, "down time" is not a concern, because chalkboards require little maintenance and no electricity or operating instructions, and the cost for materials is very low (Simonson & Volker, 1984, p. 11). Chalkboards offer advantages to students by allowing them to demonstrate abilities and more actively participate during class (Lorber & Pierce, 1983). Students can do practice work on chalkboards, and you can provide immediate feedback on the accuracy of their work, on knowledge of procedures, and on content being studied. Truly, as Wittich and Schuller (1979, p. 125) maintain, the chalkboard can be a medium for two-way communication; it becomes the property of the whole class, and "the more aware we become of the chalkboard's many possibilities, the more we will get from using it."

Chalkboards are a simple medium but are sometimes misused. Their flexibility can be a disadvantage for the user. Indeed, as Callahan and Clark contend, "Chalkboard work is impermanent and transitory. The swipe of the eraser . . . destroys the old material. One cannot save material placed on the chalkboard without rendering the chalkboard useless for anything else" (1988, pp. 453–454). Some teachers may write and erase too quickly and not allow enough time for students to take notes. Often teachers place material on the chalkboard that is too difficult to read because it is messy or written in letters too small to be read, or because the surface of the chalkboard has not been kept clean, or because the teachers have not planned in advance how it will be used in a given lesson. Indeed, students frequently complain or lose interest in a lesson because of their inability to read material presented on a chalkboard. These practices are not insurmountable, however, and when eliminated, you can make maximum use of the chalkboard's potential as an instructional tool.

Better Chalkboard Practices and Procedures A sound practice for any teacher who works with a chalkboard to follow is to plan ahead how it will be used. Such preplanning is emphasized by Brown, Lewis, and Harcleroad with this suggestion: "Think before you write or draw—to consider what you want to show and how best to arrange it" (1983, p. 99). Generally, it is advised that the teacher maintain eye contact with the students, not with the chalkboard. Talk to the students, not to the chalkboard. When you are writing on the board, stop talking so you can better concentrate on what you are writing, then turn and talk. When possible, place material on the board before class starts. Avoid cluttering: Leave plenty of empty, blank space to ensure proper contrast between what is written or drawn and the surface of the chalkboard itself. Plan on preventing distraction by covering material already on the board until it is used and by erasing or removing it when you have finished with it. Keep writing brief, to the point, and large enough to be seen—and avoid abbreviations. Some suggest that you should print neatly, rather than using script, and make letters 2 to $2\frac{1}{2}$ inches high and $\frac{1}{4}$-inch thick for a 32-foot room (Heinich, Molenda, & Russell, 1989). Others suggest using a single-stroke Gothic letter or an uncomplicated cursive style, with an arbitrary letter height of about 3 inches (Bullough, 1988). Whatever the case, make sure letters can be seen easily and are legible from as far as students will sit. The best test is to walk to the maximum expected viewing distance and check. Further, one should plan on using not only proper chalk, but also chalk in varied colors for emphasizing special material. Consider this excellent suggestion the next time you write with chalk: "Hold the chalk like a knife and pretend you are slicing tomatoes on the kitchen counter. Use firm downward strokes, and rotate the chalk as you use it so that lines will be uniform as the chalk wears" (Simonson & Volker, 1984, p. 10). Additionally, placing a few dots across the chalkboard before class will help lines of writing appear level to viewers.

Practices and procedures are readily available for chalkboard users. For example, with the help of the overhead projector or the opaque projector, you can place drawings on the chalkboard: Simply project an image on the chalkboard and trace it. Also, teachers may purchase or construct their own devices to aid them in drawing and in placing information on a chalkboard. Some examples are compasses, protractors, line templates, and multiple-chalk holders. Templates made of a variety of hard materials (wood, masonite, plastic, metal, cardboard) in varying shapes and sizes also are examples of such devices or tools. The teacher simply places the template on the chalkboard in the desired location and traces around its edge. Bullough (1988) advises gluing a soft material, such as Styrofoam or foam rubber, to the back of templates to muffle noise and prevent slipping when they are placed on the chalkboard.

Another device for drawing on chalkboards is the use of "pounce patterns" to produce "pounce drawings." These drawings are best created by taking a picture (a black-and-white line drawing is preferable) and punching clean holes in it, so that when punched, the holes indicate the outline and desired features in the drawing. The punched picture is then placed on the chalkboard, and a chalk eraser is patted (pounced) over it; when the picture is removed, a series of chalk dots remain. The teacher then merely connects the dots with a chalk line, and the desired figure is drawn.

Bulletin Boards

Another type of display tool is the **bulletin board.** Bulletin boards rank among the least expensive and most extensively available instructional tools. Most classrooms are likely to contain one, although the size, shape, and color may vary considerably among classrooms. Bulletin boards, when used effectively, are an excellent means for instructional communications.

However, as Kemp and Dayton (1985) emphasize, communication must take place quickly and efficiently. Even though they are cited as among the most productive instructional resources and are useful at all levels and in all fields (Brown, Lewis, & Harcleroad, 1983), they are also described as an example of a less alterable display format (Locatis & Atkinson, 1984).

Bulletin boards are advantageous in that they tend to serve a variety of functions. Indeed, bulletin boards can motivate, inform, stimulate, and even decorate. They may be used for interpreting, supplementing, or reviewing material being studied and for reinforcing skills, understandings, and behaviors learned. Bulletin boards allow students to learn how to communicate visually and provide a medium for reporting individual and group activities and data. They may be portable, either teacher- or student-made, and they can turn a classroom into an exciting, attractive place— causing a subject or unit of study to come alive as they promote or inform. Additionally, bulletin boards can serve in contributing to learners' aesthetic growth and facilitate study of single-copy material.

Most of the limitations associated with the use of bulletin boards are often the result of teachers' inabilities to effectively design and use them. If they are to succeed as an effective instructional tool, they ought to be created and employed with specific characteristics and practices in mind. When designing a bulletin board, a teacher must decide whether it is to be used for informal or formal purposes. Informal use generally involves the display and presentation of prepared materials—such as notices, pictures, and news clippings, as well as information resulting from meetings or discussions—and can be accomplished without tremendous amounts of planning (Simonson & Volker, 1984). Formal use implies that more deliberate, careful, prior planning must occur when a bulletin board is designed, and it involves a more complex use of production techniques, titles, captions, and information to help meet specific instructional objectives (Simonson & Volker, 1984). Formal bulletin boards ought to focus on a single topic or idea and be taken down when they no longer hold students' attention.

It is suggested that all bulletin boards be kept up-to-date, uncluttered, and more pictorial than verbal, and that they demonstrate a wise use of design and layout tools such as space, line, shape, form, color, and texture. They should appear balanced and pleasing to the eye, grasp and retain students' attention, and present information in an organized, attractive manner. Kemp and Dayton (1985, p. 171) seem to get to the heart of all techniques for designing, producing, and using bulletin boards by posing the following questions:

How will attention be captured so that interest is stimulated?

How will attention be held until the message has been read completely?

Can the message be easily understood in one reading?

Teachers who successfully design, produce, and use bulletin boards as instructional tools are those who wisely attend to the task of answering these questions.

Flat Pictures

Every flat picture may not be worth the proverbial thousand words, but those that are *wisely* chosen and used as instructional tools certainly move a considerable distance in that direction. Their instructional availability and potential are often limited only by a teacher's lack of vigor and creativity when using them. Generally, **flat pictures** are considered to be a type of opaque, two-dimensional, still picture that represents something real or imagined. (Other types of still pictures, including overhead transparencies, filmstrips, and slides, will be considered later.) Flat pictures also may be described as "illustrations in magazines and books, photographs, study prints, and the like—pictures that can be examined without benefit of a projector or viewer" (Heinich, Molenda, & Russell, 1989, p. 33).

Most decidedly included among the advantages of flat pictures are their low cost and availability. Found throughout newspapers, calendars, magazines, or advertisements, flat pictures literally exist almost everywhere—in an astounding variety of sources, on a variety of subjects, and at various levels of sophistication. They can be made with ease, tailored to meet specific instructional needs, and used in a self-paced manner.

Flat pictures can be manipulated in order to bring a desired effect: An entire lesson may center on one or a series of flat pictures; and they can be used to illustrate common experiences and to motivate. They also help communicate and focus attention on issues and information in order to introduce and clarify. Flat pictures tend to serve as springboards for stimulating further inquiry, reading, and study. They help convey abstractions and make side-by-side comparisons as well as develop critical judgment and visual interpretation skills. They present messages to our most highly developed sense—the visual, and they can even be used in evaluating learner progress and achievement. Truly, the advantages provided by flat pictures as instructional tools are perhaps as numerous as their sources.

Like most instructional tools, flat pictures do have some limitations. Because most are relatively small in size, their detail cannot be seen when used with a large group. Those who attempt to use an opaque projector to overcome this problem may rid themselves of one limitation, but often encounter other problems associated with this type of projection. Flat pictures are further limited by their two-dimensional nature and lack of depth. Their lack of motion may also make it difficult to locate examples that will depict exactly what is desired. Many may not be instructionally suitable, either because they contain too little information to do the job or because they contain material that is irrelevant. Likewise, a lack of accuracy may be evident. Sizes, distances, and colors may be distorted, thereby prohibiting a student from properly interpreting the materials and information presented. Often students lack the visual literacy skills necessary to interpret or "read" flat pictures.

Those who work with flat pictures can compensate for the medium's shortcomings and use them to their maximum potential by paying attention to several fruitful practices. Heinich, Molenda, and Russell (1989) suggest that when selecting flat pictures, make sure they characteristically

TABLE *6.2*	Nonprojection-Media Tools
Media Tool	**Description**
Chalkboard	Permanent display fixture, which comes in variety of colors, used to present written information
Bulletin Board	Two-dimensional display surface made of cork or cardboard
Flat Picture	An opaque, two-dimensional, still picture

make use of good composition practices, present a clear message, use color effectively, and offer good contrast and sharpness. One also must remember that when used as instructional tools, flat pictures should be suited to a purpose, make specific contributions to the lesson, be accurate, authentic, interesting, easily understood by and visible to viewers, and never be passed around during class (Henson, 1988). As Lorber and Pierce (1983, p. 114) suggest, one should be cautioned that "very complex pictures are not well suited for younger students regardless of how attractive they may be otherwise." Further, they maintain that colored pictures are usually going to grasp and hold student attention better than those that are black and white.

Table 6.2 gives a summary of nonprojection-media tools, and the Application Guidelines offer some helpful suggestions. Review the summary and guidelines, and complete exercise 6.2.

Projected Verbal and Visual Experiences

The chalkboard and overhead projector have outlived most other teaching aids. While the chalkboard represents a nonprojection instructional tool, the overhead projector represents one of several projection devices available to secondary classroom teachers.

Still Projected Materials

As indicated earlier, overhead transparencies, filmstrips, and slides are examples of still pictures, as are flat pictures. Unlike flat pictures, however, these three types of still pictures require special projection to be used as instructional tools. Even though all three consist of images or words placed on some kind of special transparent film, they remain examples of pictures, and it must be remembered they exhibit some of the same advantages as flat pictures. Still, they each will be treated as separate instructional tools in this section.

Overhead Transparencies

Overhead transparencies, generally referred to as **transparencies,** are a popular, widely used instructional tool with acclaimed versatility. This very positive image is considered by some (Kemp & Dayton, 1985) to have been prompted by improvements in the development of more efficient, lightweight overhead projection systems, by the availability of simple

Application Guidelines ▼

Nonprojection-Media Tools

Using the Chalkboard

Examples:
1. Practice your board writing so that it is neat and legible.
2. Start each class with a clean board.
3. Use colored chalk as a visual highlight.
4. Record student contributions on the chalkboard.
5. Avoid cluttering board; once item on board has served its purpose, erase it.
6. Print instruction on the board.

Using Bulletin Boards

Examples:
1. Display a single idea or topic on each bulletin board.
2. Make bulletin board displays neat and uncluttered.
3. Whenever possible, build participation devices into your bulletin boards.
4. Change bulletin boards periodically; in some cases, they should be changed after a few days.
5. Give students the opportunity to plan and put up displays.

Using Flat Pictures

Examples:
1. Make sure pictures are appropriate for students who will be seeing them.
2. Whenever possible, use colored pictures.
3. Make sure pictures are large enough to be seen easily.
4. Ensure pictures are relevant to information being studied.

Application of Knowledge

Exercise 6.2   Nonprojection-Media Tools

Check your understanding of the following nonprojection-media tools. Appropriate responses can be found in appendix A.

1. Chalkboards can be a medium for two-way communication; that is, teachers can use them to communicate with students and vice versa. (True/False)

2. When the chalkboard is used as the medium for communication, no preplanning is necessary. (True/False)

3. List some of the functions that can be accomplished with bulletin boards:

   _____

   _____

4. A major advantage associated with flat pictures is their diversity. (True/False)

5. The maximum potential of flat pictures can be enhanced by selecting pictures with the following characteristics:

   _____

   _____

techniques for producing them, and by their dramatic effectiveness. Transparencies are a very simple and effective means of instructional communication and can be quickly and easily made by classroom teachers.

A teacher's success with transparencies usually depends on the quality of the content and physical characteristics of the finished product and on how proficient a teacher is in operating the appropriate projector. Physically, transparencies are made by placing images and words on clear sheets of acetate or plastic film, of about an 8½-by-10-inch size and of varied thickness. The images or words may be placed on the film by hand or by using special techniques and machines.

It seems evident from varied sources that overhead transparencies are a beneficial instructional tool in several ways. For one thing, they allow the teacher to remain at the front of the classroom and have face-to-face contact with students. This characteristic provides a high degree of control. When the projector is turned on, student attention goes to the content on the screen. When the projector is turned off, attention centers once more on the teacher. Additionally, because transparencies do not require a darkened room, the teacher is able to retain a brightly projected, colored image with the classroom lights on. The fact that the lights can remain turned on enables the teacher to see what is going on—a control factor. The availability of small, lightweight, easy-to-maintain, and easy-to-use overhead projectors and the existence of a myriad of materials and techniques for producing transparencies at the local and teacher levels have been instrumental in the development and use of transparencies as instructional tools. Further, they can be prepared in advance and may even serve as a viable substitute for chalkboards. If a teacher would rather purchase transparencies than produce them locally, they are commercially available in a variety of subjects and at varied levels of sophistication and understanding.

When used creatively, transparencies can be an exciting instructional medium for presenting both verbal and visual ideas to large groups—for example, special, advantageous techniques such as overlays or masking allow the teacher to demonstrate progressive disclosure and presentation of information in developmental sequences. Heinich, Molenda, and Russell (1989) cite a study by James Cabeceiras (1972) that suggests that those who use overhead transparencies tend to be more organized and have more student participation in discussions. Interestingly, even the hint of the existence of these two qualities makes it wise for a teacher to consider using transparencies as an instructional tool.

Many of the limitations associated with transparencies seem to stem from poor production techniques or from a teacher's inability to use them properly. Some kinds of transparencies require special equipment, materials, and skills to produce, whereas others are so easily produced with thermal machines and thermal film that it may cause some teachers to make transparencies of poor quality because they misuse the process. These teachers may make transparencies from master copies on which the words are printed too small. Indeed, as pointed out by Bullough (1988), an original typed or printed page is seldom good for making a transparency. Moreover, teachers often crowd too many words onto transparencies, making them look too cluttered.

Other factors can limit the optimum use of transparencies: They are not intended for use in independent or individualized study; some teachers may present information so quickly that students do not have adequate time for taking notes; and often the teacher and parts of the projector block viewers' lines of sight.

So, it would seem that the limitations encountered when using transparencies as an instructional tool are likely to be of little consequence if a teacher learns the proper techniques for producing them and for operating the associated equipment. Limitations do not have to interfere with using transparencies to their fullest potential.

Filmstrips

General agreement indicates that a **filmstrip** is a series of related still pictures strung together on a length of 35-mm film intended to be shown in a fixed sequence, one at a time. Special equipment traditionally is required for filmstrip production and use. Filmstrips generally are perforated along the edges so they can be pulled through the projector by specially designed sprockets. They are extremely popular and one of the more commonly used projected instructional tools. Further, they are relatively inexpensive and widely available on a commercial basis, and they may be effectively combined with audio to form sound filmstrips. However, they are not very easily produced locally in school.

Filmstrips' most obvious advantages are that they are small, compact, and easily stored; easily handled and used; presented in a set, fixed sequence that cannot be gotten out of order; and relatively inexpensive to purchase. Furthermore, filmstrips have the versatility suitable for conventional group instruction and for independent or individualized study. They also may be used in a partially darkened room at a pace controlled by the user. Another advantage of filmstrips is their easy availability in a wide range of subjects at varied developmental levels from a wide range of sources. Because they are a photographic medium, they portray a realistic replication of the colors and images they capture, and they can effectively supplement or be combined with other instructional tools. For example, they often are found as a component of multimedia instructional kits, or as stated earlier, they may be accompanied by sound recordings to form sound-filmstrip presentations. Also, because many filmstrips have numbered frames, these numbers can serve as reference points for easy placement in a lesson plan.

There are three more notable limitations associated with the use of filmstrips. First, they come as a permanently fixed sequence of information and visuals; as such, they do not allow a teacher the flexibility to easily update, revise, or change the order of content. It is possible to cut filmstrips into separate frames and make them into slides; however, one should consult present copyright laws for restrictions on such practices.

A second limitation is that filmstrips are not easily produced locally by a teacher. Producing a filmstrip locally requires the use of specialized camera equipment and techniques as well as the knowledge and use of special chemical processes. Additionally, one must take care not to violate current copyright regulations if copyrighted material is included in a produced filmstrip. Consult a local city or school library or media center for information about copyright laws.

A third, more notable, limitation is that filmstrips can be damaged when being pulled through the projector. Sprocket holes—the perforated holes along both edges of a filmstrip—may be torn out, or the teacher may not place the filmstrip into the projector correctly, causing the sprockets to cut unwanted holes. Further, if the projector fan goes out, the heat from the projection lamp may melt or burn the filmstrip.

In spite of their limitations, filmstrips can be an exciting and fun instructional tool. You should take advantage of their potential.

Slides

Typically, **slides** are small, photographic film transparencies that are individually mounted—generally in 2-by-2-inch frames—and designed to be projected, one at a time. The frames or mounts may be cardboard, plastic, or glass. Slides require specific projection equipment for proper viewing and most often can be easily produced by using any one of a variety of common camera and film formats, including the common 35-mm and the instant-loading 126 or 110 cameras. The 35-mm format is recommended and probably the format preferred by most. Slides, like filmstrips, are a commonly used and inexpensive projected instructional tool and, likewise, are readily available from a variety of commercial sources in varied levels and subjects.

Slides offer a number of decided advantages. Because they are a relatively inexpensive, abundantly available instructional tool, it is easy to build up a sizable collection. The slide medium is also a versatile, flexible one: Slides can be easily revised, updated, and resequenced. Further, they lend themselves to easy local production and can be created with simple cameras and equipment using simple techniques. Teachers need only take the pictures and leave the processing and mounting to a laboratory. It is that simple. Bullough (1988) points out an even simpler, perhaps less known way, of making slides by using slide mounts, thermal transparency film, and a thermal transparency maker or a photocopier.

Additionally, slides, like filmstrips, are actual photographs and thus offer the advantages of more realistic replication of colors and images. They are easily stored, easily used, versatile instructional tools, which permit easy pacing by the user not only for group instruction, but for independent or individualized study programs. Further, as with filmstrips, slides can be combined with other media and materials—such as making them a part of a multimedia instructional kit or combining them with sound recordings to form sound-slide programs. Finally, the equipment used to project slides is easy to operate, comes with trays capable of holding multiple slide sets, and permits the use of remote control devices, which allow a teacher to move around.

Slides do have some, though few, limitations. One is that, because they are separately mounted, they can be easily gotten out of order, placed upside down, or turned backwards. However, you can overcome this limitation simply by establishing a standard way of marking them before they are to be used: First, hold the slide so that the images appear right side up and any words read correctly. Next, rotate the slide until the images and words are upside down. Finally, place a heavy, easily seen mark in the upper right-hand corner as the slide now appears. Now, simply organize the slides so that the mark always appears in the upper right-hand corner; they will always be ready for quick, correct, easy placement into the projector or projector tray.

Because slide mounts are made of cardboard, plastic, or glass, the lack of the standardized materials for mounting slides is also cited as a problem (Heinich, Molenda, & Russell, 1989). Additionally, slides—with the exception of those placed in glass mounts—can be damaged as a result of dirt, dust, or fingerprints. They even may be accidentally scratched with fingernails. Cardboard mounts often begin to separate or fray along the edges and corners, causing them to catch in the tray or projector when being used. When this begins to happen, the mounts usually must be replaced. Even though the mounts are easy to obtain and replace, some view this as an added expense associated with slides. Others consider the costs not only for purchasing projection equipment and film, but also those for developing and processing the film to be a limitation of slides.

Motion Pictures and Video/Television

It has been implied (Kemp & Dayton, 1985) that motion pictures and video are similar in that they each portray moving images along with sounds and that these sounds may be those occurring naturally or contrived and tailored to fit specifically desired situations. Additionally, as instructional tools they both provide a teacher opportunities for presenting, describing, and clarifying information, ideas, and concepts; for teaching a skill; for condensing or expanding time; and for affecting attitudes. And they give viewers a "you are there" experience.

Although both motion pictures and video generally are used as multisensory instructional tools that present messages through both sight and sound channels, motion pictures sometimes come without sound. Both are popular instructional tools. Motion pictures have been around longer; however, some observers such as Bullough (1988) suggest that video will replace motion pictures—except for large-screen projection purposes. According to Knirk and Gustafson (1986), film will become obsolete because of the advantages offered by video as a record/playback instructional tool. Further adding to this likelihood is the fact that present electronic-distribution systems allow motion pictures to be shown via television.

Gerlach and Ely (1980, p. 333) state that a "**motion picture** (sometimes called a movie or film) is a series of still pictures (frames) usually 8-mm or 16-mm in size, taken in rapid succession," and that "when projected by a motion picture projector, they give the illusion of motion." The images are presented one at a time, but so quickly it "fools" the eye into believing it is seeing motion. Motion pictures also are a highly available, frequently used instructional tool. Some educators credit motion pictures with being "the most widely applicable, the most powerful among the resources for teaching and learning" (Brown, Lewis, & Harcleroad, 1983, p. 233).

Video programming (television) is an immediate, widely available, and frequently used instructional tool, and some even refer to it as "perhaps the most pervasive medium in our society" (Locatis & Atkinson, 1984, p. 214). Programs may be purchased, rented, or produced and used locally in a school, or they may be received from a remote, commercial, or public television station.

Programs may be received from remote stations by broadcast or closed-circuit means. While broadcast programs are sent through the air and received by antennae or microwave systems, closed-circuit programs are sent and received through varied lengths of wires. A videotape playback unit is a simple example of a closed-circuit means.

A distinction is also made between "educational" and "instructional" television. *Educational television* is designed for a broader purpose and serves to inform or educate in general, whereas *instructional television* is aimed at specific classroom instruction and at meeting specific instructional objectives. Both broadcast and closed-circuit programming may serve as sources for educational and instructional television.

Whatever the case, both motion pictures and video have potential as instructional tools and have certain common advantages. The fact that they are both forms of motion media and that each may be used to capture the other only underscores these commonalities.

As has been implied, both motion pictures and video allow a teacher to communicate by using the two most direct channels for learning: sight and sound. They depict motion; permit the capture, retrieval, and manipulation of information; promote the building of a common base for experiencing and understanding the world in general; and impact the emotions. More specifically, they both are flexible media: They enable step-by-step demonstrations and observations to be shown and repeated in critical sequences, and they allow observation of items and events that are too dangerous or too difficult to view because of time, distance, and size limitations. Both may be used to dramatize or depict historical events and personalities, present problem-solving situations, promote critical thinking, and both may serve as springboards for further study, research, and learning. Finally, they mutually provide the teacher an alternate avenue for enriching and supplementing instruction.

Even though motion pictures and video programs share certain common characteristics and advantages, motion pictures offer several specific advantages that video programs presently do not. Because they are a film medium—rather than an electronic one, as is the case with video—motion pictures tend to provide brighter, more intense, and more realistic colors and images. Additionally, motion pictures may be obtained from a wider range of sources and are available in a greater number of subjects and titles than are video programs. However, this imbalance could quickly change in the near future because of the increasing popularity of video instruction brought about by the availability of more efficient, inexpensive video equipment and the rising costs of motion pictures and associated equipment. Perhaps it is also worth pointing out that certain special techniques are better suited for motion-picture technology than for video—techniques such as animation, long-range photography, microphotography, and time-lapse photography, as well as slow-motion photography and slow-motion projection.

All the above-mentioned specific advantages have helped motion pictures maintain their popularity and potential as instructional tools; however, motion pictures are limited in some respects. For one thing, they do not permit flexible pacing of the material presented. Some may present material too slow for some viewers and too fast for others. Motion pictures may also distort reality, present incorrect information, promote misconceptions, and cause misinterpretations of intended messages. They may contain irrelevant information, emphasize the wrong points, or contain unacceptable material. Other limitations associated with motion pictures center around the subject of related equipment. Equipment for motion-picture production is expensive and usually not readily available in schools. Even if available, the equipment does not yield a finished product for immediate classroom use: The film must first be processed. Such factors limit local production. Likewise, motion picture–projection equipment is expensive, and it is cumbersome and confusing to operate. Finally, the use of motion pictures presents certain logistical problems. Motion pictures usually are not readily available in a school. They must be ordered in advance, and they require special facilities for viewing. It often may be difficult to get them when they are needed, and motion-picture catalogs may contain poor descriptions of their contents (Gerlach & Ely, 1980).

A more significant advantage of video is that it can be produced easily on a local-school basis. Only a minimal amount of equipment is necessary, and it is easy to use and is becoming more portable. Videotapes come in cassette format and are inexpensive, especially the ½-inch format. Further, they are reusable, can be edited with the use of special equipment, and are easily duplicated.

Video is immediate. It allows the quick capture of information and, if desired, immediate feedback. Recorded programs may be played back instantly. Whatever the source—local production or commercial venture or even broadcast programs—special programs, demonstrations, techniques, experiments, and materials may be easily and quickly transmitted live to special audiences or delayed/stored and used later. Such an advantage enables many schools to offer subjects that, for whatever reason, they otherwise may not be able to offer. In cases where programs are taped for later use, however, remember to be careful not to violate copyright laws.

Easy production and flexibility benefit students as well—inviting them to get involved in their learning. For example, as suggested by Brown, Lewis, and Harcleroad (1983), students may be permitted to record field trips, prepare programs dealing with careers and community problems, record guest speakers, make movies, or make their own shows and programs.

Just as video programs and motion pictures have some qualities and advantages in common, they also share certain limitations. In fact, all the limitations cited earlier for motion pictures may also apply to video programs—with the exception of some of those relating to immediacy and production ease. Still, the implementation of video as an instructional tool may present other specific problems. For one thing, students come to school as users of television; however, the fact that they see so much of it—with its rapid-paced, canned, general-entertainment format—means teachers may not be able to hold students' attentions very long. Even when video programs are produced locally by the school, their level of sophistication may not match that of the programming to which learners are accustomed and, likewise, cause inattention.

Because video generally is viewed in small-screen format, many students may not be able to see what is presented very well. Even though large video projection capabilities exist, they are expensive, and too often the video images tend to become poorer in quality when enlarged. To some, video programs seem to be depersonalized or tend to take over the job of the teacher (Gerlach & Ely, 1980). Others, like Knirk and Gustafson (1986), maintain that the capabilities for providing feedback to learners are lacking with video, especially with respect to instructional television programming. Many hope to minimize or remedy these and other limitations of video as its popularity and use as an instructional tool increases and as improvements are made in its technology and its distribution and utilization systems.

Finally, as a teacher, you need to consider the powerful role that motion pictures and videos will play in your classroom. They should be used with a specific purpose in mind. In other words, you must make certain that the content of media presentations is directly congruent with your lesson objectives. To this end, you should preview all programs before they are viewed by students to be certain that the content matches your objectives. Students should then watch the presentation with the knowledge that they will be held accountable for the content and objectives portrayed. In this way, students will be alerted to what they should look for, a technique that enhances the likelihood that they will be attentive to media presentations in a meaningful way.

Videodisc and Interactive Video Technology

Two advantages concerning video technology that have not been singled out are the availability of videodisc technology and the capability of forming interactive video systems, some of which can be formed by linking video components with computer components.

Although both videotapes and videodiscs may serve as storage media for interactive video systems, the latter seems to have more potential. Some view **videodiscs** as "a development of great promise" (Brown, Lewis, & Harcleroad, 1983, p. 237), and others allude to its "promise to revolutionize TV instruction" (Bullough, 1988, p. 305). A videodisc, like a phonograph record, is a video recording and storage system in which audiovisual signals are recorded on a plastic disc. Videodisc technology permits very high levels of user interaction, random access, and quick retrieval of any one piece of the tremendous quantity of information and materials that can be stored on a disc.

The instructional uses of videodisc technology are still being explored, and the technology is expensive in several ways, but it does offer advantages. One of the most obvious is its capacity to store great amounts of information and material. It is reported, for example, that one disc can store up to 54,000 separate frames of still images, up to 50 hours of digitized stereo music, or 330 minutes of motion images with sound (Heinich, Molenda, & Russell, 1989). Put another way, one disc will store the capacity of more than 600 carousel slide trays. Further, any frame may be quickly accessed without causing wear.

Knirk and Gustafson (1986) point out other advantages of the videodisc technology: They can store material in full-color, full-motion format, or as still visuals with sound; they can be used for distributing almost any set of instructional materials; and they are small in size, which permits easy storage and minimizes costs when distributed by mail. Additionally, Brown, Lewis, and Harcleroad (1983) maintain that standard video receivers reproduce excellent-quality images from videodiscs.

Advantages notwithstanding, videodisc technology does have limitations. Because videodisc players are expensive and most do not permit local school recording, original copies of programs must be made at remote sites, and they are expensive. And only a limited number of companies produce these master discs. Such limitations may discourage widespread use of videodisc technology for a while in public schools. Further research and study seems to be called for concerning the potential of videodisc technology as a viable instructional tool. Also needed are more concentrated efforts at lowering associated costs, which would permit wider instructional availability.

As implied earlier, video-system components may be linked to computer-system components to form an **interactive video** system. As such, interactive video as an instructional tool taps the benefits of both video and the computer: The user can individually access, sequence, and pace both images and sound. Heinich, Molenda, and Russell, in referring to this capacity for creating a multimedia learning environment, suggest, "Interactive video is a powerful, practical method for individualizing and personalizing instruction" (1989, p. 200). Interactive video systems allow learners to become more involved in their learning.

The most primitive level of interactive video simply may be a video playback unit consisting of a monitor and a videotape or videodisc player. Users "interact" with the tool by manipulating, as desired, such controls as PLAY, FREEZE/PAUSE, FORWARD, or REVERSE. Videodiscs and videodisc players are preferable in a unit like this because of their tremendous storage capabilities. The more sophisticated interactive video systems have the video player connected to a computer, which more fully provides the feature of "interactivity" for the user. The computer thus serves as a means through which the user controls access to and the management of the verbal and visual information that provides the directions and activities for any given lesson. And, as commanded by the computer, the video equipment, whether tape or disc format, simply permits viewing and hearing of the associated audiovisual material.

In the more sophisticated levels of interactive video, the computer and video systems function together as a synergistic unit, rather than independently. Such a relationship combines the advantages of both video technology and computer technology to provide an excellent instructional tool with tremendous potential. This is especially true for those interactive video systems using videodisc technology. Upon reviewing the previously stated advantages offered by videodisc technology, one can easily see why.

Despite their advantages, however, the more sophisticated interactive video systems, especially those that use videodisc players, are costly; and presently, there seems to be a void in the number of suitable instructional programs available. Consequently, it may be a while before they are widely used in public school instruction.

Computers

Computers can be a powerful tool in a teacher's repertoire. Wittich and Schuller (1979, p. 276) describe a **computer** as "a glorified calculator that can store, or 'memorize' large amounts of information and produce, or retrieve, it on demand." With the advent of microcomputers, computers have become commonplace and a major technology in modern society. Their popularity in education has resulted in an irreversible impact on schools. Indeed, with their word-processing and recordkeeping capabilities, and their quick and easy spreadsheets and high-quality graphic programs, computers have established their effectiveness as instructional tools.

Additionally, according to Henson (1988, p. 245), a computer can expand the types of instruction received by students, improve on current teaching modes, and free teachers to increase their personal attention to students. He further maintains that "positive experiences can come from meaningful interactions with computers in professional methods courses, especially when students learn concepts concurrently with the application of those concepts—that is, with 'hands-on' experiences.'' An example of this would be when computer training exercises are integrated into computer programs that actually call for students to do word processing while using the training programs.

Computers have become less expensive and more versatile, and if teachers know their potential and have the proper software, the capabilities are limitless. However, widespread interest in adapting computers to serve as instructional tools is rather recent.

Computers characteristically offer many advantages as instructional tools. Their success has flourished with the advent of the microcomputer, with its increased availability at less cost. As Brown, Lewis, and Harcleroad (1983) point out, microcomputers are compact in size and relatively portable; permit the use of flexible, practical, and effective self-contained units of instruction; allow vast amounts of data and information to be quickly stored and used for reference, manipulation, and problem solving; and provide several sources of output, including by screen, printout, and signals passing over wires to remote places. They also may be used for controlling other instructional tools, such as slides, filmstrips, motion pictures, and video programs.

Generally, computers encourage students to become actively involved in the learning process and thus can serve as motivational tools. Further, they do not get tired, angry, distracted, impatient, forget, and they can function with more speed and less error than a teacher. Indeed, computers have become so sophisticated that they can interpret the English language and mimic human instructors in response to students. According to Lillie, Hunnun, and Stuck (1989), computers also benefit students by helping them improve self-confidence, develop a sense of accomplishment, and overcome computer anxiety. Additionally, computers can serve the unique needs of a variety of students from diverse backgrounds, including the advanced, the below-average, the learning disabled, those from low-income families, and those with limited English skills. Another major advantage of computers is that, with the appropriate software, they can be used by both teachers and students for word processing and desktop publishing. Accordingly, they permit the user to produce, save, retrieve, edit, and print both text and visuals for term papers, letters, pamphlets, newsletters, brochures, or books.

Utility programs are available specifically for teachers that facilitate such functions as keeping records of appointments and grades, test writing and analysis, or puzzle generation. Computers' capabilities in areas such as these are extensive, and educators have taken advantage of them. The instructional role computers have assumed in the classroom basically has taken two forms: computer-managed instruction (CMI) and computer-assisted instruction (CAI), which is sometimes referred to as computer-based instruction. Most of the classroom instructional use of computers is microcomputer-based rather than mainframe computer-based.

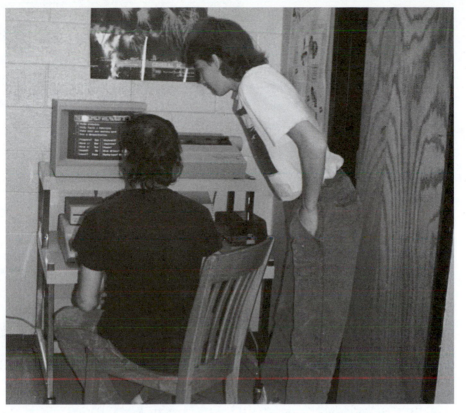

Computer-Managed Instruction

The primary purpose of **computer-managed instruction** (CMI) is, as the name implies, the management of records. Specifically, teachers use it for handling student records, diagnosing and prescribing materials, monitoring progress, and testing. Computer-managed instruction does not provide instruction, but it may contain instructional programs; that is, the programs contain activities that focus on identified student needs.

Some computer-managed instruction packages will include instructional objectives, corresponding test items, and instructional support. In such systems, computers often are used for testing students' mastery of objectives and for recording each student's progress; for diagnosing weaknesses, recommending remedial work if necessary, and indicating when the student is ready to move on to the next step; and for providing needed additional practice.

Teachers who have become computer-literate and have microcomputers available for their use can manage instruction with these computers and maintain sophisticated records on students. Indeed, as teachers develop test items for the units they teach, these items can be programmed into the computer for random selection when the time comes for testing. Moreover, computer-literate teachers will find word-processing programs useful in producing reading materials, course outlines, handouts, and tests; database-information systems useful in collecting and recording information; and spreadsheet information useful in recording grades and calculating end-of-term grades.

Computer-Assisted Instruction

Computer-assisted instruction (CAI) usually serves one individual student at a time, compared with mainframe-based instruction, which is capable of serving several users simultaneously. The major strength of computer-assisted instruction is that it is interactive: Information, questions, and other stimuli flow from computers to students, but then the students can provide input that shapes the next computer output.

With computer-assisted instruction, acquisition of information and skills is accomplished through the use of a computer system and a computer program. The computer system usually consists of a computer, either a microcomputer or a mainframe terminal; a display unit called a *cathode ray tube;* and a data-storage system, such as a disk drive. Programs may be designed to fit individual needs at any desired ability level, pace, or degree of complexity. These programs are sometimes referred to as "canned software." The four main types of programs for computer-assisted instruction are those for drill and practice, tutorial activities, simulation, and games.

Drill and practice programs fall at the lowest level of computer use and are the most common of the computer-assisted instruction programs. They contain exercises that repeatedly put the learner into contact with quantities of information, facts, problems, and relationships for the purpose of learning and mastering concepts and skills or committing material to memory.

Tutorial programs are designed to emulate a human tutor: Unlike drill and practice programs, they initially present new information; and depending on learner responses, they may present additional or supplemental information. Such presentation may take the form of written explanation and descriptions, questions and problems, or graphics and visual illustrations. Tutorials seem to be more sophisticated than drill and practice programs.

Simulation programs call on the students to role-play and model reality. With these programs, learners make decisions while emulating or interacting with "real life" or "close to life" situations and processes in order to learn from their responses. They are especially helpful and thought-provoking when they ask students to make decisions concerning situations or processes involving danger.

Gaming programs engage learners in activities where they must follow specific rules in order to reach a specific goal. They are supplied activities that help build skills, usually cognitive or psychomotor. Students follow rules, compete, think through situations, manipulate objects, or even solve puzzles. Whatever the form such programs take—drill and practice, tutorial, simulation, or game—they invite learners to become more actively involved in their own learning, and they allow teachers greater control over the learning process as coordinators and facilitators rather than merely information givers.

Even though many people look on computers as established, effective instructional tools, still others criticize them because of what they consider characteristic limitations. For one thing, notwithstanding the fact that costs have decreased in recent years, computers are still expensive. Many think that dollars spent on hardware, software, and maintenance are better spent for more teachers, higher salaries, or for other instructional materials. Some consider the role of the teacher too uncertain in computerized instruction, or some think computers may replace teachers. Others fear they stifle creativity, limit the imagination, emphasize narrow facts at the expense of broad generalizations, disallow socialization, dehumanize instruction, and lack the human capacity to appreciate and attend to learner human needs.

The use of computers is also criticized because of perceived instructional limitations and problems, such as the tendency to overuse drill and practice programs while ignoring higher-level applications. Other objections are that programs often are unrelated to instructional goals, teach a very narrow range of objectives, or disallow oral and written responses from students. The easy, illegal duplication of software programs, the poor quality of some software programs, and the incompatibility among software programs also can limit their effectiveness. Further, some teachers resist using computers simply because they believe they are too complex or they do not like the mechanical control they have over the learning process. A limiting factor to some is the fear that the computer may be perceived as a magical panacea or cure-all for solving all the world's instructional problems.

Additionally, logistical concerns may limit the use of computers. For example, having to deal with issues like placement of the computers, user priority, supervision of users, and acquisition of software, paper, and ribbons may cause some teachers not to bother using computers as instructional tools.

One must remember, however, computers are "dumb" machines until a person tells them what to do. They can do nothing until software programs are placed in them. When this is done, depending on the quality of the software, then and only then can they begin to serve as useful instructional tools. People have to make them work! Yet, according to Lillie, Hunnun, and Stuck (1989, p. 174), the future of the computer is still unclear:

> **The extent to which computers and computer-based instruction will be integrated into the mainstream of American education in tomorrow's schools will depend on the flexibility and acceptance of many different groups of people—teachers, teacher trainers, school administrators, parents, and policy makers. It will not be easy for computer technology to live up to its potential and become a tool for shaping significant new approaches to instruction.**

This concludes our discussion of various projection-media tools. Table 6.3 summarizes the projection-media tools addressed in this section. Also, teacher-tested suggestions are offered in the Projection-Media Tools Application Guidelines. Review the table and guidelines, and complete exercise 6.3.

TABLE *6.3* Projection-Media Tools

Media Tool	Description
Overhead Transparencies	Images and/or words placed on clear sheets of acetate and shown by projecting light through the film onto a screen
Filmstrips	A series of related still pictures strung together, pulled through a projector, and projected onto a screen for viewing
Slides	Small, film transparencies individually mounted and projected onto a screen one at a time
Motion Pictures	A series of still pictures projected onto a screen in rapid succession
Video/Television	The transmitting of still or moving images with accompanying sound over wire or through space
Computers	Device that can store and manipulate information, as well as interact with user

Application Guidelines ▼

Projection-Media Tools

Preparing to Use Projection Media

Examples:
1. Set up your equipment, and have it ready to go before class.
2. Practice writing on transparencies, and also practice making overlays.
3. Try preparing your lecture outline on transparencies.
4. Prepare students for filmstrips, slides, motion pictures, and videos; establish a cognitive set.
5. Peruse catalogs and periodicals that review computer software in your teaching field.
6. Teachers should learn to use computers: Enroll in a course or workshop to learn about computers.

Using Projection Media

Examples:
1. Whenever possible, use color on transparencies. Color adds interest and emphasis.
2. Switch the projector off when you want student attention to shift back to you, or when changing transparencies.
3. Face the class when using projectors.
4. Accept comments and discussion while filmstrips and slides are being shown.
5. Stop film or videos periodically to discuss content.
6. Follow up on motion pictures and videos with discussion.

Application of Knowledge

Check your understanding of the following projection-media tools. Appropriate responses can be found in appendix A.

1. Because of the difficulty in preparing good transparencies, teachers should have them prepared by media-production professionals. (True/False)

2. Most of the problems associated with transparencies come from poor production techniques or from improper use. (True/False)

3. Filmstrips are not easy to produce locally by teachers. (True/False)

4. Filmstrips and slides are useful for group instruction and for independent or individualized study. (True/False)

5. A major classroom benefit derived from motion pictures and videos is the "you are there" feeling it communicates to students. (True/False)

6. A major problem associated with the videodisc is the lack of space to store data. (True/False)

7. Explain what is meant by an *interactive video system:* _____

    _____

8. Describe the four main types of programs used in computer-assisted instruction (CAI):
    a. _____
    b. _____
    c. _____
    d. _____

CHAPTER SUMMARY

Many forms of media-learning tools are available to teachers, including the common textbook and various other nonprojection and projection tools. The nonprojection media include such forms as chalkboards, bulletin boards, and flat pictures, while the projection forms comprise overhead transparencies, filmstrips, slides, motion pictures, video, and computers. Each of these forms has advantages and limitations. The best media to use in any given situation will depend on: (1) the teaching-learning situation, (2) the learner objective, (3) the value of the media to the lesson, (4) the quality of the media in content and physical characteristics, and (5) the ability of the user to use the media correctly.

Interactive video and computers are relatively new media forms. Despite their respective advantages and limitations, they are the only media tools that are two-way communicators. It is the ability to respond to the user's input that makes interactive video and computers among the most powerful media available to teachers.

Regardless of the instructional tools chosen, it is important to remember that no one tool or combination of tools is going to be *the* means to accomplish all ends in the teaching-learning process. However, the sheer variety of instructional tools in existence gives teachers a number of ways for dealing with the wide range of student temperaments, backgrounds, and learning styles encountered on a daily basis.

Discussion Questions and Activities

1. **Classroom visitations.** Visit several classroom teachers and discuss with them how they use the textbook. See how this compares with what you have learned about textbooks in this chapter.

2. **Bulletin boards.** Plan a bulletin board that will help introduce, summarize, or cover the content of a lesson about a subject or concept in your major field. Be sure to consider the advantages offered by flat pictures and include them in your display.

3. **Transparencies.** Consult several of the chapter references for tips on producing transparencies, and use the tips to produce a handmade and thermal transparency.

4. **Multimedia.** Develop a 45-minute, multimedia lesson that incorporates the bulletin board, chalkboard, transparency, and motion picture or filmstrip and then microteach it.

5. **Technology stores.** Visit a local computer store and, if possible, view a demonstration of a word-processing unit. Do the same for a video store, and view how a videodisc player and interactive video system operates.

Direct Teaching Methods

✎ The lecture is alive and well! We may criticize it, judge it inferior, and question its merit. However, we continue to speak; students continue to listen. But do they *hear?*

Overview

We will now engage in a study of specific actions and skills that elicit learning. In this chapter, we will study three direct approaches for organizing and presenting integrated bodies of knowledge for instruction: exposition, exposition with interaction, and demonstration.

Effective questioning patterns have long been associated with good teaching. As such, it is important that prospective teachers learn to recognize behavior patterns related to the productive use of the different levels of questions, as well as the different kinds of questions and proven questioning techniques. Thus, in this chapter, we will focus special attention on questioning in the classroom.

▼   ▼   ▼   ▼

Objectives

After completing your study of chapter 7, you should be able to do the following:

1. Discuss factors that should be considered in selecting teaching techniques and strategies.

2. Define *exposition teaching* and discuss the strengths and weaknesses of the various methods within this teaching strategy.

3. Explain the importance of and techniques for improving the lecture method.

4. Define *exposition with interaction teaching*, and describe the various methods within this teaching strategy as well as their appropriate uses.

5. Explain the importance of incorporating different levels and types of questions.

6. Identify and differentiate between the different categories of questions as well as the levels within these categories.

7. Identify and differentiate between focusing, prompting, and probing questions.

8. Define *wait-time 1, wait-time 2, halting time,* and *silent time.*

9. Define and explain the benefits derived from the use of the redirecting technique, wait-times, and halting time.

10. Identify guidelines that should be followed in effective questioning.

11. Differentiate between questioning and the Socratic method.

12. Describe the two demonstration methods, valid reasons for their use, and techniques for their effective implementation.

Chapter Terms and Key Concepts

Convergent Questions

Demonstration

Divergent Questions

Empirical Questions

Evaluative Questions

Exposition Teaching

Exposition with Interaction Teaching

Factual Questions

Focusing Questions

Halting Time

Inquiry Demonstration

Lecture

Lecture Recitation

Mental Operation System

Probing Questions

Productive Questions

Prompting Questions

Redirecting

Reinforcement

Socratic Method

Telelecture

Textbook Recitation

Wait-Time

S uccessful secondary teachers draw from a variety of strategies (methods and procedures) in accomplishing their instructional purposes. Strategies should be selected that best serve the delivery of content and achievement of the purposes and objectives. If strategies are just arbitrarily chosen, then their emphases are on themselves, rather than content, purposes, or objectives.

Strategies, then, should be viewed as utilitarian: they serve to achieve the instructional intent. For example, if the intent of a social studies lesson is to share views on some controversial issue, it is obvious that the discussion method and applicable procedures should assist in achieving this objective. The lecture method, or simply showing a film, would not support the intent of the lesson.

With all the possible strategies, how do you decide which is best? Experience often can be the best basis for selection; however, other factors often must be considered in your selection of strategies:

What are students' needs?

What is age of students?

What is intellectual ability of students?

What are the students' physical and mental characteristics?

What are the students' attention spans?

What is the lesson purpose?

What content is to be taught?

You should take such factors into account when you consider teaching strategies, and, above all, select those strategies that should best serve your given teaching situation.

Some strategies influence students directly, while others influence students indirectly; that is, some strategies emphasize focused, teacher-directed instruction, while others involve students actively in their own learning. Thus, there are two major ways of delivering instruction: directly or indirectly. The direct delivery of instruction (''telling'') is the ''traditional'' or didactic mode, where knowledge is passed on through the teacher or the textbook, or through both. The indirect avenue of instruction (''showing'') provides students with access to information and experiences, whereby they develop knowledge and skills.

How much time should be devoted to each of the two modes of instruction? This is a complex question. At this point, suffice it to say that the amount of time spent varies, depending on the subject, grade level, students, time and materials available, and the philosophy of the teacher and the school. However, experience suggests a compelling relationship between method of instruction and student retention, depicted in table 7.1, where a blend of ''telling'' and ''showing'' techniques results in greater retention. Furthermore, varying the strategy can positively affect student motivation to learn. It is a fortunate situation when you have a choice of equally effective strategies for achieving your instructional intent.

TABLE *7.1*   Relationship between Method of Instruction and Retention

Methods of Instruction	Recall 3 Hours Later	Recall 3 Days Later
Telling When Used Alone	70%	10%
Showing When Used Alone	72%	20%
Blend of Telling and Showing	85%	65%

In such instances, it is possible to choose a method and procedure (strategy) that will foster motivation, improve classroom control, or cost less to implement. Indeed, you should become skilled in combining various strategies into a total lesson package.

The remainder of this chapter will elaborate on the direct modes of instruction: exposition teaching, exposition with interaction teaching, and demonstration teaching. These are modes of instruction with which you have had much experience. We will look at the more indirect modes and procedures in the next chapter.

Exposition Teaching

Exposition teaching is considered to be the best way to communicate large amounts of information in a short period of time. Exposition techniques comprise those methods in which some authority—teacher, textbook, film, or microcomputer—presents information without overt interaction taking place between the authority and the students.

Lecture

The **lecture** is probably the most widely used exposition teaching method. Virtually every secondary school teacher employs it to some degree, and some use it almost exclusively. Although much criticized by current educators, the lecture does possess some unique strengths.

Strengths of the Lecture

The lecture is an excellent way of presenting background information when building a unit frame of reference or when introducing a unit. Indeed, it often can be just the tool for setting the atmosphere or focusing student activities. Moreover, a short lecture can effectively wrap up a unit, activity, or lesson. Finally, the lecture is time-efficient; that is, planning time is devoted to organizing content, rather than on instructional procedure. Thus, the lecture affords the teacher ample opportunity to collect related material, assemble it into a meaningful framework, and present it to students in a relatively short period of time. The teacher simply plans a lecture for the entire instructional period.

Weaknesses of the Lecture

The lecture has several serious flaws, however. First, it fosters passive learning with very low student involvement. Students are expected, and even encouraged, to sit quietly, listen, and perhaps take notes. Thus, it is not a good approach for helping students develop skills in thinking, problem solving, and creativity.

Second, lectures frequently are boring and do not motivate. For this reason—except in unusual cases—very little of a lecture is retained by students. Indeed, because lectures tend to focus on the lowest level of cognition, understanding and transfer is often limited.

Finally, the lecture method may lead to the development of discipline problems. Most lectures generate little interest, and student attention soon wanes and turns to more stimulating and often undesirable activities. Thus, not only does the lecture lose the attention of those involved in these unwanted activities, but the lecture itself is disrupted. The wise secondary school teacher should always remember this: Adolescents are easily bored and usually have a low tolerance for boredom.

TABLE 7.2	Sample Table of Contents Used in Textbook Lecturing
Chapter 1	The Science of Biology
Chapter 2	The Nature of Living Matter
Chapter 3	The Beginning of Life on the Earth
Chapter 4	Units of Living Matter
Chapter 5	The Classification of Living Things
Chapter 6	The Bacteria
Chapter 7	Microbes and Disease
Chapter 8	The Seed Plants
Chapter 9	The Higher Plant Body
Chapter 10	One-Celled Animals—The Protozoa
Chapter 11	The Mammals
Chapter 12	Muscles and Their Actions
Chapter 13	Life of the Past
Chapter 14	Human Life of the Past

Variants of the Lecture

Let's now examine some of the variants of the lecture commonly used in secondary schools. Three such variants are the telelecture, textbook lecture, and prerecorded lecture.

Telelecture

Normally, the lecturer and students are in the same room. In some rural areas, however, an insufficient number of students needing or desiring a specific course in one district may not warrant the hiring of a teacher for that course. Luckily, with the marvels of modern technology, it is possible for several districts to "hire" a needed teacher and transmit lectures from a studio classroom to other locations by means of telephone, cable, or microwaves. This **telelecture** enables students who are not in the immediate classroom to hear the lectures. Often, the remote students may talk to the lecturer and ask questions by means of a telephone link. Special science, mathematics, and language courses are now being taught in this manner across the nation.

Textbook Lecture

Lecturing from the textbook could well be the most common teaching method used in secondary schools. The content of such lectures usually is structured directly from the course textbook, progressing from chapter 1 to the end of the book without deviation, as illustrated in table 7.2.

Textbook teaching requires very little preparation on the part of the teacher when the structure of the textbook is strictly followed. Indeed, when one is teaching in a content area without adequate academic preparation in that content area and does not wish to spend the time to become content-competent, textbook lecturing becomes an ideal technique. Thus, the lack of time needed for preparing lesson plans and lack of content mastery are reasons for the popularity of this method of instruction.

Textbook teaching suffers from all the problems of lecturing, but it has a couple of unique flaws. First, the content of the course often becomes rigid: Normally, no new content is added to the lecture, and the course content is determined entirely by an external author who is not in complete harmony with the needs of students, school, and community. Second, the lectures can get extremely boring, because the teacher usually is lecturing about the material students were assigned to read. If no new content is added to the lesson, students tend to either read the text or listen to the lectures—seldom both.

Prerecorded Lecture

A lecture is easily captured on tape or film. Such tapes or films can be and often are prepared by local school districts and by commercial publishers. Prerecorded lectures, however, have several disadvantages when compared to live lectures. First, and perhaps most importantly, there is *no* direct contact between students and lecturer; no minute-by-minute adjustments can be made based on feedback and questions. Additionally, student attention becomes a major problem when the lecture is on tape or film; attention lags more quickly than when a person is actually present. Finally, tapes and films quickly become obsolete as new information is gleaned regarding content and teaching techniques.

Despite the flaws, prerecorded lectures have some merits. Most important is their capacity for individualized instruction, because a tape or film can be played as many times as desirable. We will address individualization of instruction in greater detail in the next chapter.

Planning the Lecture

Preplanning is essential for a good lecture. Lectures must be well crafted to be clear and persuasive. The lecture must be designed to gain—and maintain—student attention throughout the lesson, instill motivation, and accomplish lesson objectives. Let's now look at some techniques that can help achieve these ends.

The most successful secondary school lectures are relatively short. Even older, brighter high school students probably won't listen to a lecture for more than about 20 minutes. Therefore, limit your lectures to short periods of time, and periodically change to other activities (preferably to those that require active student involvement). For example, the subdivisions of a lesson (with time allotted for each activity) might be as follows:

1. Overview of topic (10 minutes).*

2. Show a film (20 minutes).

3. Discussion of film (10 minutes).

4. Demonstration (5 minutes).

5. Wrap-up and review (5 minutes).*

*Denotes activities where the teacher is lecturing.

Although this plan uses lecturing where appropriate, it relies on other techniques to augment the learning—namely, discussion and demonstration. Only three-tenths of the time is devoted to lecturing; most of the time allows for more student involvement.

In preplanning, give careful attention to the start of your lecture. Determine the specific objectives of the lecture, and share them with your students at the beginning of your lecture. Research (Wulf & Schane, 1984) shows that when objectives are shared, intentional learning tends to increase. Moreover, your lecture introduction should arouse student interest, be motivational, and it should establish a framework for the lesson. (See chapter 5 for a review of these topics.)

In preparing the lecture, you must decide what students are to do while you lecture. Will students be asked to take notes? Will students be involved in some assigned seat work? If yes, instructions and guidelines must be planned accordingly. Using the chalkboard or passing out written instructions are often the best ways for establishing these guidelines.

A lecture must have closure (see chapter 5). Once given, the lecture theme should be related to the course and/or to what has already been taught. This can be accomplished through a review of the major points of the lecture.

In summary, a good lecture must be well planned if it is to be clear and persuasive. Try following this good planning formula:

Tell students what you are going to tell them.

Tell them.

Tell them what you have told them.

The proper application of this formula will result in a logical, well-organized lecture with a firm introduction and a well-planned wrap-up.

Presenting the Lecture

An effective lecture must maintain student interest and attention from beginning to end. Factors such as the tempo, audiovisual aids, stimulus variation, and language can exert major influence on student interest and attention.

Tempo

The tempo or pacing of your lecture should be moderate (not too slow or too fast). If the pace is too fast, students become discouraged with their inability to understand and keep up; if too slow, they become bored and look elsewhere for stimulation. Use feedback checks to ascertain whether students are understanding your material, and adjust your pace according to the feedback you obtain.

Audiovisual Aids

Visual aids should accompany all lectures. The use of the chalkboard, models, pictures, transparencies, and diagrams can greatly enhance a lecture. Use any media that can help convey your message; they should

stimulate student interest and keep them attentive. Indeed, make your lectures as multisensory as is feasible. Multisensory input will usually result in better learning.

Teach students to take notes. A good lecturer, for example, will outline the major points on the chalkboard or on an overhead projector. Such outlines provide students with the structure and time needed for developing their note-taking skills. Once students have become skilled note takers, the practice of supplying an outline can be discontinued.

Stimulus Variation

As you plan your lecture, create an introduction that will grab students' attention, and augment your lecture with actions that will maintain this attention. Stimulus-variation techniques, such as gestures, pauses, and teacher movement, can help keep student attention directed toward your lecture. As student attention wanders, a tap on the board, a hand gesture, sudden silence (a pause), or physical movement often will refocus attention back on your lecture.

Enthusiasm is contagious. If you express a high level of interest and sense of importance about your topic, students often become spellbound, anxious to find out what is so interesting. But be a bit careful: Too much enthusiasm can direct attention toward you, the teacher—and away from the lecture topic.

Table 7.3	Exposition Teaching
Method	**Description**
Lecture	Teacher presents information with no overt interaction with students
Telelecture	Lecture transmitted from central-studio classroom to distant classrooms
Textbook Lecture	Lecturing directly about material presented in the textbook
Prerecorded Lecture	Lecture that has been recorded on videotape or film

Humor and rhetorical questions can also attract and keep student attention. Humor can help reduce anxiety, while rhetorical questions, used in conjunction with pauses, give students the opportunity to consider and think about the information presented.

Finally, eye contact can help maintain attention. Eye contact gives students the feeling that you are addressing them personally. Indeed, eye contact can provide a teacher valuable feedback on how well a lecture is being received. So look at your students; glance around and move about the room based on what you see.

Voice and Language

Delivery can make the difference between a boring and stimulating lecture. Keep your voice low-pitched, be expressive, and make sure all students can hear. Your voice can bring words to life. Voice volume, rate, tone, inflection, and pitch can all communicate valuable information.

Deliver your lectures in Standard English, and use vocabulary that students will understand. That is, don't talk over their heads. Also, avoid using slang expressions and street language in your lectures. Such language will only confuse your students.

Balancing the Lecture

Lecturing to secondary school students is inevitable for most teachers; however, it should be used sparingly and mixed with other appropriate methods. For example, a teacher could follow up a 5-minute lecture by having students complete a worksheet, by conducting a small-group discussion, or by asking students to conduct an investigation.

Indeed, a 50-minute class period often can be divided into a number of short lectures, with a distinct change in modality between lectures. These changes will serve to retain students' attention and hold their interest for the complete period. Above all, adjust your lecture time and style to students' attention span. Break up your lecture with other methods and activities. Devise a questioning sequence, give students a problem to solve, or give students a short break.

Table 7.3 summarizes the different exposition-teaching methods, and the Exposition Teaching Application Guidelines give some suggestions for using these techniques. Review the summary and guidelines, and complete exercise 7.1.

Application Guidelines ▼

Exposition Teaching

Preplan Well

Examples:
1. Plan an attention-getting introduction.
2. Share your objectives with students.
3. Keep lectures short; plan a variety of activities.
4. Plan a closure activity—that is, plan a review or application-ending activity.

Delivery

Examples:
1. Try techniques that keep student attention: Vary your tempo, incorporate audiovisual aids, use stimulus variation, and let your voice enliven your message.
2. Mix your lectures with other in-class activities.

Application of Knowledge

Exercise 7.1   Exposition Teaching

Test yourself on the following section concepts. Appropriate responses can be found in appendix A.

1. The lecture method is employed correctly by most secondary teachers. (True/False)

2. Which of the following characteristics represent strengths of exposition teaching?
   a. It is highly motivational.
   b. It promotes high retention.
   c. It is time-efficient.
   d. It offers rigid structure.

3. The most widely used exposition teaching method is _____.

4. Which of the following statements are true with regard to effective lecturing?
   a. Effective lectures should be kept to about 30 minutes.
   b. A good attention-getting introduction is essential to an effective lecture.
   c. Planning a lecture should include deciding what students are to do while you lecture.
   d. You can never be too enthusiastic when lecturing.
   e. Audiovisual aids can help make lectures more effective.
   f. It is often good practice to use student-slang expressions in your lectures.
   g. Lectures should be used sparingly, and, whenever possible, mix your lectures with other strategies.

Exposition with Interaction Teaching

Exposition with interaction teaching is a method of teaching in which some authority presents information and follows it up with questioning that determines whether the information has been understood. Essentially, this method is a two-phase technique: First, information is disseminated by the teacher or through students' study of written material. Second, the teacher checks for comprehension by asking questions to assess student understanding of the material explained or studied.

The comprehension-monitoring phase of this teaching technique requires that the teacher be knowledgeable and an effective questioner. Because questioning is so essential to the overall success of exposition with interaction, let's first analyze this important skill in some detail.

The Art of Questioning

Proper questioning is a sophisticated art at which many of us are less than proficient, even though we have asked thousands of questions in our life. Good questioners must be skilled in formulating good questions: Questions must be asked at the appropriate level, they must be of the appropriate type, and, above all, they must be worded properly. Moreover, the art of questioning requires mastery of techniques for follow-up to students' responses—or lack of response—to questioning. Let's now look at the different levels at which questions may be asked.

Levels of Questions

Questions may be categorized as "narrow" or "broad." Narrow questions usually ask for only factual recall or specific correct answers, while broad questions seldom can be answered with a single word. Moreover, broad questions often do not have one correct answer and call on students to reach beyond simple memory. Broad questions usually prompt students to use the thinking process in formulating answers. Both narrow and broad questions contribute to the learning process. However, too often teachers rely too heavily on narrow questions when learning would be greatly enhanced through both types of questions.

You must adapt the level of your questions to the purpose for which they are being asked. Consequently, ask questions that reveal whether students have gained specific knowledge as well as questions that stimulate the thinking process. Because thinking can take place at several levels of sophistication, it is important that you as a teacher be able to classify—and ask—questions at these different levels.

Many effective classificational systems have been developed for describing the different levels of questions. Most of these systems are useful only to the extent that they can provide a framework for formulating questions at the desired level within a classroom environment. Consequently, some teachers may only want to use a two-level classification system, while others may want to use a more detailed system.

We will focus our attention on two systems that will be of most benefit to you as a classroom teacher: The first widely used system classifies questions as either *convergent* or *divergent;* the second categorizes questions according to the mental operation students use in answering them. These two classification systems are only two of the many systems to which you can refer in your classroom. However, when you prepare your questions, evaluate them according to some classification system. By so doing, you will significantly improve the quality of your questions.

Convergent and Divergent Questions

One of the simplest and easiest ways of classifying questions is to determine whether they are convergent or divergent. **Convergent questions** are those that allow for only a few right responses, while divergent questions allow for many right responses.

Questions regarding concrete facts that have been learned and committed to memory are convergent. Most Who, What, and Where questions are classified as convergent. For example:

"Who was the twenty-fifth president of the United States?"

"What type of equation is $x^2 + 3x + 3 = 0$?"

"Where is Stratford-on-Avon located?"

"What was the major cause of the Great Depression?"

Convergent questions may also require that students recall and integrate or analyze information for determining *one expected* correct answer. Thus, the following questions would also be classified as convergent:

"Based on our discussion, what was the major cause of the Vietnam War?"

"By combining the formulas for a triangle and a rectangle, what would be the formula for finding the area of a trapezoid?"

"Based on our definition of a noun, can you name three different nouns?"

Most alternate response questions, such as yes/no and true/false questions, would also be classified as convergent, because the responses available to students are limited.

Conversely, questions calling for opinions, hypotheses, or evaluations are divergent in that many possible correct responses may be given. For example:

"Why do you suppose we entered World War II?"

"What would be a good name for this painting?"

"Can you give me a sentence in which this word is correctly used?"

"Why is it important that we continue with our space program?"

TABLE 7.4   Categories of Questions

Mental Operation Questions	Guilford's Structure of Intellect	Bloom's Taxonomy
1. Factual	Cognitive/memory	Knowledge/comprehension
2. Empirical	Convergent thinking	Application/analysis
3. Productive	Divergent thinking	Synthesis
4. Evaluative	Evaluative thinking	Evaluation

Divergent questions should be used frequently because they encourage broader responses and, therefore, are more likely to engage students in the learning process. They prompt students to think! Convergent questions, however, are equally important in that they deal with the necessary background information needed in dealing with divergent questions. In the classroom, it is generally desirable to initially use convergent questions and move toward divergent questions.

Mental Operation Questions

J. P. Guilford (1956) in his Structure of Intellect model classified all performed mental operations into five major groups: cognitive, memory, convergent thinking, divergent thinking, and evaluative thinking. Based on this model and Bloom's Taxonomy of six cognitive levels, the Mental Operation system for classifying questions was developed (Moore, 1991). Table 7.4 shows the relationship between the Mental Operation system, Guilford's Structure of Intellect model, and Bloom's Taxonomy. The **Mental Operation system** is basically a four-category system that combines the cognitive and memory categories of the Guilford model into a single factual category. In addition, it combines four of Bloom's categories into two categories. The categories of questions that make up the Mental Operation model are factual, empirical, productive, and evaluative.

Factual questions test the student's recall from memory information learned by rote or through the mental processes of recognition. Factual questions are the narrowest and lowest level of questions. Some examples of factual questions are listed here:

"Who drilled the first oil well?"

"Joe, can you define the short story?"

"Which of these is the chemical formula for salt?"

"What is the formula for the volume of a cylinder?"

Empirical questions require that students integrate or analyze remembered or given information and supply a single, correct *predictable* answer. Indeed, the question may call for quite a lot of thinking, but once thought out, the answer is usually a single, correct response. Empirical questions are also narrow questions. Some examples of empirical questions include the following:

"Based on our study of California, what conditions led to it becoming a state?"

"Given that this circle has a radius of 5 centimeters, what is its area?"

"According to the information provided in the text, what is the most economical source of energy presently being used in the United States?"

"Which of these two forms of government is most like the British?"

Note that when solving these questions, students must recall learned information and carry out some type of mental activity with that information in order to arrive at the correct answer. However, there is only one correct predictable answer.

Productive questions do not have a single correct answer, and it may be impossible to predict what the answer will be. Productive questions are open-ended and call for students to use their imagination and think creatively. As such, these questions ask students to develop a unique idea. Although the broad nature of productive questions prompts students to go beyond the simple recall of remembered information, students still need the basic related information in order to answer these questions. Following are some examples of productive questions:

"How can we improve our understanding and use of English?"

"What changes would we see in society if we were to eliminate unemployment in the world?"

"What are some possible solutions to the problem of world hunger?"

"What do you suppose the painter's intent was in this painting?"

Finally, **evaluative questions** require that students put a value on something or make some kind of judgment. Evaluative questions are special cases of productive questions in that they too are often open-ended. However, they can be more difficult to answer than are productive questions in that some internal or external criteria must be used; that is, some criteria must be established for making the judgment. The responses to evaluative questions can often be predicted or limited by the number of choices. For example, the question "Which of these two short stories is the best?" limits the responses to two, whereas the question "What is the best automobile made today?" allows for a variety of responses. Other examples of evaluative questions are these:

"Who was our greatest scientist?"

TABLE 7.5   Levels of Classroom Questions

Category	Type of Thinking	Examples
Factual	Student simply recalls information	"Define . . ." "Who was . . ." "What did the text say . . ."
Empirical	Student integrates and analyzes given or recalled information	"Compare . . ." "Explain in your own words . . ." "Calculate the . . ."
Productive	Student thinks creatively and imaginatively and produces unique idea or response	"What will life be like . . ." "What's a good name for . . ." "How could we . . ."
Evaluative	Student makes judgments or expresses values	"Which painting is best?" "Why do you favor this . . ." "Who is the best . . ."

> "How would you rate our success in controlling government spending in this nation?"

> "Do you think the author of the play developed the characters sufficiently?"

> "Are Native Americans portrayed accurately in the movies?"

These questions call on students to make judgments based on internal criteria. However, when student responses will be formally evaluated and bear directly on grades, you must establish evaluative criteria. The alternative is to rely on students' internalized criteria, which you can neither evaluate, confirm, nor refute. You can establish evaluative criteria for your evaluative questions by following them up with an empirical or productive question that asks for the reasons behind the stated judgment or value, or by making sure your evaluative questions are developed and asked in a way that includes external criteria.

Utilization of the Mental Operation system of classifying questions (table 7.5) should give you the needed framework for improving your questioning skill. You should be asking questions at all four levels of the system, instead of at the factual level only, as many teachers tend to do. To this end, you should plan and ask more productive and evaluative questions than is commonly done by teachers. These questions will give your students the opportunity to think and reason.

Types of Questions

As an effective teacher, you must ask the right type of questions. That is, you must adapt the type of question to the specific purpose for which you are asking the question. For example, you may want to ask questions to determine the level of your students' study, to increase student involvement and interaction, to increase clarification, or to stimulate student awareness. These purposes would call for different types of questions.

Focusing Questions

Focusing questions, which may be factual, empirical, productive, or evaluative, are used to direct student attention. Focusing questions can determine what has been learned by students, motivate and arouse student interest at the start of a lesson or during the lesson, stimulate involvement and check understanding during a lesson, or check students' understanding of lesson material at the close of a lesson.

Was the assigned chapter read by students? No use discussing the material if it wasn't read! Did the students learn and understand the material assigned? Can students apply the information? Focusing questions can provide valuable information regarding these concerns. Ask factual questions to check on basic knowledge at the beginning of a lesson or during a lesson. Use empirical questions to have students figure out correct solutions for problems related to assignments or issues being discussed. Pose productive and evaluative questions for motivating and stimulating thinking and interest in the topic.

When opening a lesson or a discussion with a question, it is good practice to use a productive or evaluative question that focuses on the upcoming topic. The question should be such that it arouses students' interest and thinking. For example:

"What do you suppose would happen if I were to drop these two objects at the same time?"

"How could we test the hypothesis suggested by the results?"

"Should we do away with the income tax in the United States?"

These questions should then be followed with questions at all levels to develop understanding and to maintain interest.

Prompting Questions

What should you do when a student fails to answer a question? Most teachers will answer the question themselves or move on to another student. This technique will get your question answered, but it fails to involve the original student in the discussion. Rather, it leaves that student with a sense of failure, which, more than likely, will result in even less participation in the future. A better way to address this problem is to use a prompting question as a follow-up to the unanswered question.

Prompting questions use hints and clues that aid students in answering questions or assist them in correcting an initial inaccurate response. Thus, a prompting question is usually a rewording of the original question—with clues or hints added. Consider this example of a prompting questioning sequence:

TEACHER: What is x^2 times x^3? Pat.

PAT: I don't know.

TEACHER: Well, let's see if we can figure it out. What do we do with the exponents when we multiply variables?

PAT: Multiply?

TEACHER: No.

PAT: Add!

TEACHER: Right! So, if we add 2 plus 3, what will our answer be?

PAT: [Pause.] 5.

TEACHER: So what would x^2 times x^3 be?

PAT: x^5.

TEACHER: Very good, Pat.

Your use of prompting questions with students should lead to a sense of success when they finally answer correctly. Indeed, the successes could even act as reinforcers to students, which hopefully will result in even greater participation.

Probing Questions

Up to this point we have discussed focusing questions and prompting questions. The former can be used for determining the level of learning and understanding and for increasing student participation, whereas the latter can be used when no response to a question is forthcoming. Another situation with which a teacher must contend occurs when the student's response is incorrect or correct, yet insufficient because it lacks depth. In such cases, you should have the student correct the mistake or ask that they supply the additional needed information. This is accomplished through the use of probing questions.

Probing questions aim at correcting, improving, or expanding a student's initial response. They compel the student to think more thoroughly about the initial response. Probing questions can be used for correcting an initial response, eliciting clarification, developing critical awareness, or refocusing a response.

You may want to ask a probing question for the purpose of clarification. Students sometimes give flimsily thought-out answers or give only half-answers to questions. These responses should be followed up with probing questions that force the student to think more thoroughly and urge him or her to firm up the response. Here are examples of such probing questions:

"What are you saying?"

"What do you mean by the terms . . . ?"

"Would you say that in another way?"

"Could you elaborate on those two points?"

"Can you explain that point more fully? It lacks clarity."

You sometimes may want students to justify their answers; that is, you may want to foster their critical awareness. This also can be accomplished with probing questions. Probing questions that could be used to develop critical awareness include these:

"What is your factual basis for these beliefs?"

"Why do you believe that?"

"What are you assuming when you make that statement?"

"What are your reasons for those assumptions?"

"Are you sure there isn't more evidence to support that issue?"

Finally, you may want to probe for the purpose of refocusing a correct, satisfactory student response to a related issue. Examples of questions that could serve this function follow:

"Let's look at your answer with respect to this new information."

"Can you relate your answer to yesterday's discussion?"

"What implications does this conclusion have for . . . ?"

"Apply these solutions to . . ."

"Can you relate Mary's earlier answer to this issue?"

The different types of questions will be invaluable to you as teaching tools. When used effectively, they can increase student participation and involve students in their own learning. You should practice these different questions and become proficient in their use.

Questioning Techniques

Certain techniques associated with asking questions will tend to increase the quantity and enhance the quality of the students' responses. Let's now look at four such techniques.

Redirecting

Redirecting is a technique that is useful for increasing the amount of student participation. It allows you to draw students into a discussion by asking them to respond to a question in light of a previous response from another student. Because this technique requires several correct responses to a single question, the question asked must be divergent, productive, or evaluative. The following is an example of how you might redirect a question:

TEACHER: We have now studied the administration of several presidents. Which president do you think made the greatest contribution? [*Pause. Several hands go up.*] Cindi?

CINDI: Lincoln.

TEACHER: Jeff?

JEFF: Washington.

TEACHER: Mary, what is your opinion?

MARY: John Kennedy.

You should note that with redirecting, if you are using it correctly, you do not react to the student responses. You simply redirect the question to another student. Thus, it is hoped that this technique will lead to greater student participation and involvement and, consequently, to greater learning and increased interest.

The redirecting technique can also be used effectively with students who are nonvolunteers. You should try to involve these nonvolunteers as much as possible because, as noted earlier, participation enhances learning and stimulates interest.

It is important to remember, however, that nonvolunteers should never be forced to answer; rather, they should be given the opportunity to contribute to the discussion. In addition, you should give nonvolunteers ample time to consider a response. The time needed for students in considering their responses to questions is referred to as **wait-time.** Let's now look at the appropriate use of wait-time in questioning.

Wait-Time

Students need time for thinking over and pondering the responses they will give to your questions. Research by Rowe (1974a, 1974b, 1978), however, has shown that teachers on the average wait only about *one* second for students to give an answer. Rowe's research also revealed that when teachers learn to increase wait-time from three to five seconds, the following results occurred:

1. Student response time increased.

2. Failure to respond tended to decrease.

3. Students asked more questions.

4. Unsolicited responses tended to increase.

5. Student confidence increased.

Basically, there are two types of wait-time. *Wait-time 1* is the time provided for the first student response to a question. *Wait-time 2* is the total time a teacher waits for all students to respond to the same question or for students to respond to each other's response to a question. Wait-time 2 may involve several minutes. If you are to engage students more in your lessons, you must learn to increase your wait-time tolerance, so students have more opportunities to think and ponder their answers.

The typical pattern of questioning in the average classroom can be depicted as follows:

Teacher ⟶ Student A

Teacher ⟶ Student B

Teacher ⟶ Student C

This pattern represents nothing more than a question-and-answer period. The teacher asks a question of an individual student, the student answers, the teacher moves to the next student, asks a question, the student answers, the teacher moves to the next student, and so on. Students often receive little time for thinking and expressing themselves and usually no time for reacting to each others' comments. In fact, most of the questions are typically at the lower level. Appropriate use of questioning techniques, higher-level questions, and wait-time can and should change this sequence to one that could be portrayed like this:

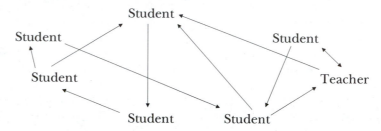

This pattern facilitates student discussion, welcomes extended responses, and provides opportunities for commenting on other students' questions and for asking questions. There is real involvement! Indeed, you will find that extending the time you wait after a question from three to five seconds—and giving students time to react to your questions and other students' responses—is well worth the added effort.

Halting Time

When presenting complex material, you need to learn to halt in what you are saying and give students time to think. This pause is referred to as **halting time.** No questions are asked, and no student comments are elicited. In using the halting-time technique, you would present some complex material or complicated directions and then stop momentarily, so students have time to consider the information or carry out the directions. During this pause, you would visually check with the class to see whether they are with you and understand what you are trying to communicate. If your observations are positive, you continue. If students appear to be confused, you may want to redo the explanation or directions.

Reinforcement

Once you have asked a question and an acceptable response has been given, you must react to the response. Should you merely accept the response without comment and continue with the lesson, or should you offer praise for a job well done? Your **reinforcement**—that is, your pattern of reaction—will have a powerful effect on the direction of the interaction in the classroom.

Rewards and praise often work in encouraging students to participate. Phrases like "Fine answer," "Great," "What an outstanding idea!" and "Super" may be used when rewarding students' correct answers.

Reinforcement is often a good idea, but the too-frequent application of reinforcement can negate the benefits derived from the use of wait-time. If reinforcement is given too early in an answering sequence, other students may decide not to respond because they fear their answer could not match an earlier response. After all, didn't you say the earlier response was "Great!" Rather than give reinforcement early in the questioning-answering sequence, you should allow as many students as possible to respond to the question, then reinforce all of them for their contributions. You can always return to the best answer for further comment.

Tips on Questioning

Asking good questions is an art. However, it is an art that can be mastered with practice. Let's now look at some questioning tips that may prove helpful.

Questions should be clear, and you should ask the question before designating who is to answer. Ask the question, wait for the class to think about it, and then specify an individual to answer. As usual, there are exceptions to this rule. When you call on an inattentive student, it is often wise to designate the individual first so that the student is sure to hear the question. Similarly, you should call the name first of slow or shy students so that they can prepare themselves.

Distribute your questions around the class fairly. Avoid directing all questions to a selective few bright students. However, avoid some mechanical system for asking questions, because students soon catch on to systems—such as going by alphabetical order or going row by row—and will pay attention only when it is their turn.

Do not ask more than one question at a time. Asking too many questions at once often confuses students. Simultaneous questions permit no time to think, and when several questions are asked, students are not sure which question to answer first.

Do not ask too many questions. Often there will be a need to establish a knowledge base before initiating a questioning sequence. This is especially true when the questions to be asked require thinking and reasoning.

Ask questions at all ability levels in the class. Some questions should be easy, while others should be more difficult. Also, use questions to help students modify their inaccurate responses. Use prompting and probing questions to help students think more thoroughly about their responses. This approach will increase involvement, develop better thinking skills, and reinforce student successes.

Finally, listen carefully to student responses. Wait at least three seconds following a student response. This allows the student time for making further comments and gives other students time to react to the initial student's response.

One last point about exposition with interaction: The key to the effective use of these teaching methods is good questioning. Therefore, you must work on and refine your ability to think, plan, and ask questions throughout your lessons. Let's now look at three teaching methods for exposition with interaction: lecture recitation, textbook recitation, and the Socratic method.

Lecture Recitation

Lecture recitation is an instructional method in which the teacher presents information by telling and explaining, and follows up with question-and-answer sessions at periodic intervals. Thus, questions are used for summarizing the content of the lecture and for helping students consolidate and organize the presented information.

The lecture-recitation method is often efficient in terms of time, flexibility, and learning, while actively involving students in the lesson. Its basic structure of teacher talk–teacher question–student response–teacher talk makes questioning the key component to the method. Moreover, this method is highly adaptable to a large variety of topics and frequently is employed as a companion to the lecture method or as a companion to the study of a textbook. Indeed, it is a form of recitation.

A hybrid form of the lecture-recitation method in which questions are interspersed throughout the lecture has proven to be most popular among classroom teachers (Goodlad, 1984). When proper lecturing is executed and when questions are strategically used, this method is an effective and efficient way of teaching content. That is, the questions can and should be designed to provide feedback on understanding, add variety to the lecture, and maintain the students' attention. Moreover, questions from students can also help clarify the content and shed light on how well the lecture is being understood.

Textbook Recitation

The **textbook recitation** method is relatively simple: You assign students content to read and study in their textbook and then question them on what they have read and studied. Textbook recitation is an effective technique for teaching basic information simply because students are often motivated to read and study the assignment in anticipation of being called on to recite the information. However, this method does not foster true understanding and the application of the assigned content.

Textbook recitation, on the other hand, has the added advantages of giving students feedback on the accuracy of the content learned and providing them with the opportunity to learn from the replies of fellow students. Indeed, these ends can be accomplished by planning higher-level questions in advance, with an emphasis placed on questioning sequences that will develop thinking and reasoning skills.

The Socratic Method

The **Socratic method** derives its name from its ascribed adherent: Socrates. It is a technique of using a questioning-and-interaction sequence that is designed to draw information out of students, rather than pouring it into them. This method is purely verbal and interactive. Most teachers use the Socratic method to develop content information.

The Socratic method, in general, involves teaching by asking questions and, in so doing, leading students into a logical contradiction. Essentially, the Socratic method follows a general pattern:

TABLE 7.6   Exposition with Interaction Teaching

Method	Description
Lecture Recitation	Teacher presents information and follows up with questions
Textbook Recitation	Students are assigned content to read and study and are later questioned over information
Socratic Method	Questioning-and-interaction sequence designed to draw information out of students

1. A broad, open-ended question that most students can answer is asked first.

2. A second questioning sequence begins to narrow the range of responses and focuses the students' thinking onto the topic of the questioning strategy.

3. Review lectures and/or statements are interspersed among the questions in order to keep the salient points in the forefront.

4. A final concluding question then brings students to the desired end point.

The technique as originally developed by Socrates must be adapted to the reality of the classroom. The method conceived by Socrates requires a one-to-one relationship between the student and teacher, with the teacher posing a series of questions that gradually tangle the student up to the point where ideas and thinking must be carefully scrutinized. In the classroom, the teacher generally does not focus the questioning sequence on one student, but, rather, questions one student first, then another, and then another—moving slowly throughout the class. Although this technique usually works well, the pure essence of the Socratic technique is often difficult to capture. Still, the Socratic method can be quite effective, and it works best in small-group sessions and in tutorial sessions.

Table 7.6 reviews the teaching methods of exposition with interaction, and the Exposition with Interaction Teaching Application Guidelines offer some helpful suggestions for utilization. Review the table and guidelines, and complete exercise 7.2.

The Demonstration Method

The **demonstration** is the method in which the teacher or some other designated individual stands before the class, shows something, and tells what is happening or what has happened, or asks students to discuss what has happened. A demonstration, then, is a process of teaching by means of using materials and displays, but the only person directly involved with materials is the teacher or individual conducting the demonstration. However, it is often good procedure to have a student conduct the demonstration. This arouses more interest and, although somewhat limited, does involve the students.

Application Guidelines ▼

The demonstration can be effective in many different subject fields. For example, a teacher could demonstrate the steps in writing a business letter, the steps in solving a mathematics problem, or how to adjust a microscope. Essentially, the technique deals mostly, but not totally, with showing how something works or with skill development. The demonstration may be by the teacher, by a student, by film or videotape, or even by a sequence of pictures. Whatever technique is chosen, a demonstration should be accompanied by a verbal explanation or follow-up discussion. In an ordinary demonstration, the explanation accompanies the demonstration. One type of demonstration, however, asks students only to observe in silence. This method is referred to as the **inquiry demonstration.**

The inquiry demonstration is similar to the Socratic method in that students observe the demonstration in silence. These observations are then followed up with teacher questioning or with a discussion of what was observed. Students are asked to think logically, make inferences, and reach conclusions.

There are at least five major reasons for teachers to use the demonstration in conveying a concept or the content in a subject: Among other things, demonstrations are useful when there is danger involved in students using equipment or materials, they save time when absolutely

Application of Knowledge

Exercise 7.2   Exposition with Interaction Teaching

Test yourself on the following section concepts. Appropriate responses can be found in appendix A.

1. For each of the following question types, indicate whether it requires lower (L) or higher (H) levels of student thinking.
   - *a.* Empirical
   - *b.* Factual
   - *c.* Productive
   - *d.* Divergent
   - *e.* Evaluative
   - *f.* Convergent

2. Match each of the types of questions with their appropriate use.
   - *a.* _____ Used for getting students to correct errors or supply more information
   - *b.* _____ Used for directing attention on the lesson
   - *c.* _____ Use of hints and clues that help student answer a question

   1. Focusing question
   2. Prompting question
   3. Probing question

3. The time given the initial respondent for thinking over and pondering a question's answer is called _____ .

4. Reinforcement should follow any student response. (True/False)

5. You should always establish a knowledge base prior to questioning. (True/False)

6. Always designate who is to answer prior to asking a question. (True/False)

7. The strategy in which information is presented to students and students are then questioned over the information is called which of the following:
   - *a.* Lecture recitation.
   - *b.* Textbook recitation.
   - *c.* Both of these.

8. Because it is a purely verbal and interactive technique, the Socratic method relies heavily on questioning. (True/False)

---

necessary, they can show proper use of equipment, they can detail the steps in a particular procedure, or they can get a point across that is not easily expressed in words.

A good demonstration begins with an introduction (cognitive set) that indicates what students are to learn and/or are to look for and, perhaps, defines terms you will use in the demonstration. It is essential that you establish a strong cognitive set prior to conducting an inquiry demonstration. Your introduction should result in a focus of attention on what is to follow, but it should not give the details on what is to take place.

Following the introduction, the demonstration should be completed as simply and as much to the point as possible. If equipment or a procedure is being demonstrated, you should follow the desired action step by step, with pauses and explanations offered as needed in clarifying the actions. Occasionally, when the mere process of listening could interfere with students' observations, you might want to hold comments to a minimum or conduct an inquiry demonstration. In fact, in such cases, you

Students should be directly involved in classroom demonstrations and, whenever possible, should perform the actual demonstration.

might even want to proceed through the demonstration silently the first time and repeat it a second time with explanations. Finally, in conducting classroom demonstrations, the following guidelines should be followed:

1. Go slowly so students can follow.

2. When procedures are complex, break the demonstration down into small components and demonstrate them separately; once students understand the components, conduct the demonstration in its entirety.

3. Repeat steps of the demonstration until students understand.

4. Remember, left and right are reversed, so set up the demonstration from the students' perspective.

After the demonstration, you should do a follow-up to check for understanding. It may be advantageous to have the students walk through the steps with you to test their competency at using equipment or in using a demonstrated procedure. In fact, you might wish to use the Socratic method to determine the effectiveness of your demonstration.

Plan your demonstration for success. Practice your demonstrations before trying them in class to be certain that they will work and that they take a reasonable amount of time. Set up demonstrations so that they are

TABLE 7.7　　　The Demonstration

Method	Description
Ordinary Demonstration	Individual shows and explains something to class
Inquiry Demonstration	Individual shows class something without explanation, and students observe, make inferences, and reach conclusions

visible to all students; seating students in a semicircle around the demonstration often works best. Plan techniques for keeping students attentive. In most cases, presenting demonstrations that are exciting will keep students' interest and attention. But, if needed, questions often are effective at regaining wandering attention.

Table 7.7 summarizes the two types of demonstrations, and the Demonstration Application Guidelines give some planning suggestions. Review the summary and guidelines, and check your knowledge of this section by completing exercise 7.3.

CHAPTER SUMMARY

There are two basic approaches to teaching— direct and indirect—and today's teachers need to enter the profession with a thorough understanding of both approaches. This chapter has detailed some of the direct approaches.

Although often severely criticized, exposition teaching offers an effective way to convey a great deal of information in a short period of time. Therefore, at times, exposition teaching will be the only appropriate technique. In such situations, make it short, lively, and to the point. Tell them what you are going to tell them, tell them, and tell them what they have been told.

For most purposes, exposition with interaction teaching will be more effective than exposition teaching, because the approach tends to achieve a better balance of student and teacher involvement in the learning process. The key to this strategy is questioning. Unfortunately, many teachers are unskilled as questioners.

Asking good questions is an art that is essential to the lecture-recitation and textbook recitation methods. You must adapt your questions to your instructional intent. The recall of information requires the use of narrow (convergent) questions, while the desire to stimulate thinking and reasoning calls for broad (divergent) questions. If a more complex classification system for questions is needed, the Mental Operation model categorizes questions at the factual, empirical, productive, and evaluative levels. You can arouse interest and increase student involvement with focusing, prompting, and probing questions. Also, you will enhance your skill as a questioner if you redirect your questions, use wait-time and halting time, and offer reinforcement.

Socratic teaching is designed to draw information from students through the use of questions. Essentially, the questioning sequences begin with a broad, open-ended question and flow into a series of narrow, probing questions. In the classroom, the questioning sequence should not focus on a single student, but should proceed from one student, to another, and then another.

Demonstrations can be effective when used appropriately. In fact, in some cases, they may be the only way of developing an idea, concept, or point. In conducting a demonstration, you should practice before trying it in class, have all materials at hand, go slowly, often repeat components, and above all make it simple and to the point.

As a teacher, you should experiment with the many direct approaches. Your task should be the practice and modification of these methods so that you may improve student learning and the social-emotional atmosphere of your classroom.

Application Guidelines ▼

The Demonstration

Planning Is Essential to a Successful Demonstration

Examples:
1. Examine your purpose for conducting the demonstration. Make sure a demonstration is the best means to that end.
2. Make sure all material and equipment is available for the demonstration.
3. Try the demonstration yourself prior to trying it in class. Make it simple and to the point.
4. Plan thought-provoking questions to be asked during or after the demonstration.
5. Be prepared to repeat the demonstration as needed to develop your concept.

Application of Knowledge

Exercise 7.3   The Demonstration

Test yourself on the following concepts. Appropriate responses can be found in appendix A.

1. A silent demonstration is called ____.

2. Demonstrations should only be done by the teacher. (True/False)

3. List five valid reasons a teacher might conduct a demonstration:
   a. _____
   b. _____
   c. _____
   d. _____
   e. _____

4. There should always be a follow-up to a demonstration. (True/False)

5. It is good policy to plan questions for use with a demonstration. (True/False)

6. The establishment of good cognitive set is needed only when doing an inquiry demonstration. (True/False)

Discussion Questions and Activities

1. **Strategy selection.** You have been assigned a tenth-grade social studies class. This class consists largely of slow learners. The class is restless, not interested, and hard to manage. What teaching strategies and methods would be best for this class? Give a valid rationale for your selection.

2. **The lecture method.** When would it be appropriate to use the lecture method? Consider objectives and purpose. How would one plan an effective lecture? Consider motivation, length, aids, clarity, and interest. How could you tell whether a lecture has been successful?

3. **Preparing questions.** Prepare examples for each level within the following question categories:

    a. Convergent and divergent.

    b. Mental Operation system.

4. **Questioning in the classroom.** Attend a class in a public school or college classroom. Keep a tally of the levels and types of questions used by the instructor. Did you see any patterns? What other questioning techniques did you observe? Were they successful? Why, or why not?

5. **Teaching.** Prepare and teach a minilesson using a direct-methods approach. Use the miniteaching guidelines and forms in appendix B in planning and analyzing your minilesson.

6. **Teaching analysis.** Make a videotape of your miniteaching lesson, then critically analyze it with your peers.

Indirect Teaching Methods

✎ **To experience is to learn. Indeed, to experience is to grow, to develop—to know!**

Overview

Many theorists argue that learning is an active process. Indeed, they suggest that your function as a teacher is to act as a facilitator, a guide. They view your function as provider of participatory experiences that will result in the desired learning. In this chapter we will study indirect approaches to instruction. Discussions, discovery, inquiry, simulations, individualized instruction, independent study, and mastery learning are indirect participatory alternatives.

Objectives

After completing your study of chapter 8, you should be able to do the following:

1. Discuss reasons for using various participatory-teaching techniques as well as advantages and disadvantages associated with their use.

2. Describe the primary roles associated with various discussion techniques and the respective responsibilities.

3. Explain the four areas that must be addressed in effective discussion planning.

4. Identify strengths and limitations associated with various small-group discussion structures.

5. Compare and contrast the small-group structures of brainstorming, buzz groups, and task groups.

6. Describe the purpose, structure, and function of panels, debates, role-playing, and cooperative learning.

7. Describe the major purpose, characteristics, teacher role, and desired environment associated with heuristic modes of instruction: discovery, inquiry, and simulation.

8. Differentiate between discovery and inquiry learning.

9. Define *problem solving,* and distinguish between the three levels of problem solving.

10. Outline and explain the five-step discovery model, or general scientific method, of investigation and the three-step inquiry approach.

11. Identify strengths and weaknesses associated with various heuristic methods.

Chapter Terms and Key Concepts

Brainstorming

Buzz Group

Cooperative Learning

Debate

Discovery Learning

Discussion

Drill

Heuristic Approach

Independent Study

Individualized Instruction

Inquiry

Mastery Learning

Panels

Practice

Problem Solving

Role-Playing

Simulation

Suchman Inquiry

Task Group

12. Explain the basic features of Suchman's inquiry learning and the procedures associated with its use.

13. Explain the purposes of simulations and games and the benefits and limitations associated with their use.

14. Describe the teacher's function and the appropriate environment conducive to effective implementation of the heuristic methods.

15. Differentiate between human and person-to-computer simulations as well as between simulations and games.

16. Describe the three fundamental individualization strategies: individualized instruction, independent study, and mastery learning.

17. Identify benefits and limitations associated with individualization of instruction.

18. Describe the purpose of drill and practice as well as techniques for their effective use.

Two major functions of education are the development of students' ability to think critically and their ability to perform independent inquiry. This is often difficult, if not impossible, with the more direct teaching strategies. Fortunately, as a teacher you have at your disposal a wide range of methods of more participatory nature. These indirect methods typically are less teacher-directed, but they are more time-consuming.

The Discussion Method

An important, but infrequently employed, indirect teaching method is the classroom **discussion.** What all too frequently passes for a classroom discussion is really nothing more than a lecture with periodic questioning-answering sequences. In a true discussion, students should talk more than the teacher. However, a discussion is not a "bull" session, but a carefully structured exchange of ideas directed toward a specific goal.

Two kinds of classroom goals are conducive to the discussion method. First, many subjects pose questions that have no simple answers. For example, is there a simple answer to the cause of war? What can be done about the rising cost of medical care? How was the work of Hemingway influenced by the politics of that period? Questions of this type are open to interpretation. Through discussion of issues from history, government, economics, literature, and science, students develop understanding of the issues, rather than simply receiving and rehearsing factual information. Thus, discussing controversial issues often will increase knowledge about the issues as well as encourage deeper understanding of the various sides of an issue (Johnson & Johnson, 1985).

The second type of goal that lends itself to the discussion method involves situations where issues from the affective domain are being addressed. Indeed, the discussion method usually is far more effective at changing attitudes, values, and behaviors than is the lecture method. A discussion about drug use, for example, would likely tap into students' attitudes more than a lecture would. Similarly, discussions on issues such as voting, AIDS, poverty, types of music, and art can lead to the establishment of such attitudes as civic duty, patriotism, public-health concerns, and a commitment to the arts.

Open communication and a supportive atmosphere are keys to successful discussions. The classroom should serve as an open forum in which students can feel free to express their opinions as well as review factual material. However, certain roles and procedures are essential to the success of the discussion procedure.

First, the role of the teacher becomes less a director of learning and more a facilitator or guide to learning. However, an active, purposeful leader is needed in guiding the discussion. This individual can be the teacher or, even better, a student. Leaders should not dominate the discussion, but instead should see that the discussion starts smoothly by making sure that everyone understands the purpose and topic of the discussion. Once introduced, the discussion must be kept moving and on track. Thus, discussion leaders occasionally must pose questions to the group and to individuals. These questions should be designed for keeping the discussion on track, preventing individuals from dominating the discussion, getting various individuals involved if they are not participating, and making sure alternative viewpoints are addressed. Finally, the discussion leader should be prepared to summarize periodically the major point of the discussion.

Second, discussions need a recorder (or secretary), who will keep notes on the key points made, create a summary of results, and record the group's conclusions. Occasionally, the teacher may want to assume the recorder role and designate a student group leader. The record can even be displayed on the chalkboard or on an overhead, which makes it possible for the participants to see and use the record for reference purposes.

Third, the participants are expected to be prepared, and they should peruse the materials provided for the discussion. They should be ready to listen, give each other the opportunity for expressing differing opinions, and ask questions.

Finally, in a discussion, the teacher can assume the role of leader, recorder, or a consultant—ready to provide needed resources or advice. Whatever role you assume, you must plan the discussion and make sure the plan is executed. Let's now look at the planning phase of the discussion method.

Planning the Discussion

While few actual materials are usually required in implementing the discussion method, lessons that emphasize the technique must be well organized. If not, most discussions will disintegrate into a sharing of ignorance or into chaos. Basically, four areas must be addressed when planning a discussion activity.

First, you must carefully consider your goals and student preparation needed for achieving these goals. Your goals most likely will be the acquisition of content knowledge or the exploration of attitudes or values. However, unlike other methods where the content or background information is an integral part of the lesson, discussions will require that students be thoroughly conversant with the related information prior to the discussion. That is, students must have something to discuss if the discussion method is to work. Thus, it is essential that you direct your students to be prepared with regard to content knowledge or background information prior to the discussion. This preparation may require that they read an assigned chapter, conduct research, or, in the case of attitudes and value-issue discussions, form a personal position to support.

Second, you must decide whether the discussion should be a large-group (whole-class) or small-group activity. Small-group activities might take such forms as buzz groups, brainstorming, or task groups. The particular type of group used is related to the lesson goals. If the goal is the development of better content understanding or of the ability to analyze, synthesize, or evaluate, a large-group activity would be most appropriate. However, the development of leadership skills, social skills, listening skills, or other related skills probably would call for a small-group activity. Whole-class discussions have some definite advantages—the primary one being the ability to keep the discussion focused on the topic. In addition, it is often much easier to maintain control with whole-class discussions. Unlike small-group techniques, however, whole-class discussions do not give students the opportunity for practicing active listening, editing of ideas, idea building, communication, and turn taking. Thus, if such skills are your goals, small-group work might help you accomplish these goals.

Third, seating must be considered. A productive discussion requires interaction, which often is directly related to the seating arrangement. Seating should be arranged so that students can look directly at each other when they interact. Figure 8.1 shows two possible whole-class arrangements. Note that any student can make eye contact with any other student without turning. Similarly, figure 8.2 shows three possible small-group arrangements which should maximize interaction.

Finally, you must consider the time allotted for the activity. Plan for about 45-minute discussion periods with older students, and shorter periods with younger students. In general, the time given for small-group discussions depends on the type of small group and its function. Small-group discussion time, however, generally is relatively short. Indeed, a good format to follow is to give students very explicit directions as to what is to be accomplished and a time limit for the discussion.

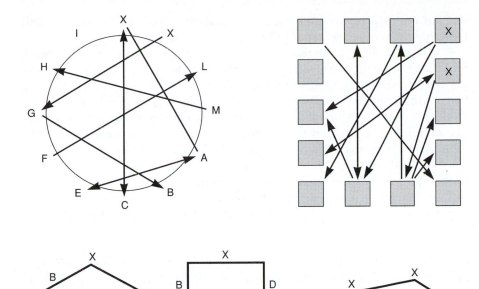

Figure 8.1 *Large-Class Discussion-Group Seating. In order to maximize interaction, students should be seated in a circular or hollow-square arrangement. Arrows pointing through the center indicate that the individual was speaking to the entire group (leader and recorder positions are marked with an **X**).*

Figure 8.2 *Small-Group Discussion Seating Arrangements. Leader and recorder positions are marked with an **X**.*

Only careful planning will result in a successful discussion activity. This planning requires that you have a thorough understanding of the characteristics and function of the two basic discussion forms: whole-class and small-group.

Whole-Class Discussions

Whole-class discussions are similar in some respects to the class-recitation method. You or a designated discussion leader pose questions, listen to student answers, react, and probe for more information. In the true whole-class discussion, however, you try to assume a less dominant role. Rather, you should assume the role of passive moderator and create a pleasant atmosphere conducive to free interaction. Neither you nor any class member should dominate the discussion. Your major task is to make the total class session more interactive.

When carrying out a whole-class discussion, you first should make sure your topic is appropriate for whole-class discussion and that the class has an adequate knowledge base. Next, make up a plan for the discussion that lays out a procedure (agenda), time limits, and discussion ground rules. For example, your procedure might include a teacher introduction session, followed by a 30-minute discussion, followed by a teacher-directed wrap-up. In addition to your 30-minute discussion time limit, you also might set a 2-minute time limit for each student to speak. You also could lay down ground rules such as these: (1) Give a summary of the last student's comments before making your own; (2) Sarcasm is not allowed;

(3) No one will make fun of another student's ideas or comments; and (4) Only the discussion topic will be addressed in making comments.

Plan a lively springboard or set that will get the discussion started. For example, you might start the discussion with a short film, a role-playing incident, an open-ended question, or some contrived situation. Once the discussion has begun, it is the leader's function to keep it on track, summarize as needed, and involve all class members through the use of questions, the redirecting technique, and reinforcement. Finally, the discussion points must be brought to a logical conclusion.

Textbooks are an essential part of most secondary school classrooms, but their value usually suffers through a lack of integration into various teaching strategies. Indeed, in most classrooms, the textbook is integrated into the lecture method only. An effective way of improving student learning, however, is through whole-class discussions built around textbook content. One such strategy, called *listen-read-and-discuss,* begins with a teacher's short overview lecture of the textbook material, which is to be read by students (Alvermann et al., 1987). This short introductory lecture should serve as an advance organizer and should set the framework for the material consequently read by the class. A discussion of the content material follows. This procedure allows students to compare their understanding of the reading with the teacher's presentation. Further, it gives the teacher the opportunity for evaluating and getting feedback on students' understanding of the concepts covered.

Small-Group Discussions

As with any discussion, *small-group discussions* should follow the presentation of information through teacher-directed lessons, assignments, books, or films. When students are adequately prepared, they should form their groups and start to work.

Successful small-group learning requires very careful planning. The different groups will probably gather and work in different parts of the classroom. Under such conditions, it is impossible for you to be with each group. Therefore, you must provide students with clear guidelines regarding their tasks and responsibilities. You should appoint a responsible, well-organized student as leader for each group. The leader's function is to keep the group on task and guide them toward completion of that task, and to ensure that all group members participate. An appointed group recorder should also write down the group's ideas and conclusions. Upon completion of the group activity, each group should be required to report to the rest of the class.

What is the optimal size for small-group learning? There is no easy answer to this question. But some literature suggests that groups of five to seven work best (Dillion, 1987). Our experience indicates that five is the optimal size. In larger groups it is too easy for students to hide and not participate in the interaction, and smaller groups lack the diversity of opinions needed in the interaction.

Small-group instruction has several strengths, chief among which are the development of communication skills, leadership abilities,

Leadership can often be developed through involvement in small-group activities.

open-mindedness, persuasive arguing, and other interpersonal skills. In addition, group work often leads to a stronger sense of personal commitment to decisions made by the group than those made by the whole class or by individuals. Finally, students involved in small-group work are usually given more opportunity for active verbal participation and, in some cases, for physical movement.

Small-group instruction has its limitations as well as strengths. One of the primary problems is the tendency for students to drift off task very quickly, and the activity often disintegrates into bickering and becomes a waste of time. Another danger of small groups concerns the group composition. It is possible—and often quite likely—that some groups cannot work together cooperatively, or that they include students with very similar (or very different) points of view or interests. Such groups often have difficulty reaching conclusions. Careful teacher planning and supervision, however, can combat the limitations associated with small groups.

Groups are often formed and structured for achieving specific purposes. The kinds of groups and functions that can be formed in your classroom are limited in scope only by your own creative design capabilities. Let's now look at three such small group types.

Brainstorming

Brainstorming is a small-group activity designed to generate ideas. The brainstorming session is started by the leader, who introduces a topic or problem and asks each small group to generate ideas, solutions, or comments. The topic can be as simple as "What topics should the class study for enrichment?" or as complex as "What can we do about the low class test scores?" All answers, no matter how wrong, should be accepted as possible solutions. No comments about or reactions to contributions should be allowed until all groups have reported their ideas.

Brainstorming sometimes results in a mood of delightful quest. Therefore, you should emphasize the need for decency and decorum. At the same time, participants need to realize that quantity of suggestions is paramount.

Brainstorming is an excellent initiating process for further activity, such as another discussion, research, problem solving, or small-group activities. For example, the brainstorming suggestions can be evaluated, and those deemed worthy of further study can be addressed in follow-up activities.

Buzz Group

A **buzz group** is a work group of relative short duration. Such a group is established quickly to share opinions, viewpoints, or reactions. The group can be formed easily by counting off or by having those in proximity form a group.

Buzz groups usually consist of from four to seven members and rarely meet for more than 15 minutes. They can be established for a brief discussion of certain ideas or course content. The buzz session then should be followed up with a whole-class discussion of the conclusions or findings.

Task Group

A **task group** sets out to solve a problem or complete a project. Unlike other types of discussion, however, task groups involve students in some kind of work or activity, and each group member has a role or assignment that is clearly defined for all group members. In size, it usually ranges from four to eight members, depending on the problem or project.

Task groups tend to be teacher-directed. The teacher selects the tasks and assigns the group members specific responsibilities. The teacher may also find it beneficial to establish a work schedule and monitoring system. In addition, the teacher should make available any resources needed in accomplishing the identified tasks.

Task groups are best suited for a small number of students who are, or can be, fairly self-directed. The students should be able to create an uninhibited, but productive, environment where discussion can be free and open.

Variants of the Discussion

There are several variants to the discussion method that immerse students in self-directed learning to a limited degree. Four such variants are common to the classroom: panels, debates, role-playing, and cooperative learning.

Panels

Panels, which also are referred to as *round tables,* are a special form of the small-group approach. A group of students—usually five to eight in number—prepare in advance an informal discussion about an assigned issue among themselves in front of the class. One student usually serves as panel chair and directs the discussion. Each panel member makes an informal opening statement; however, no speeches as such are made. A give-and-take session with the class follows the opening statement and discussion.

The topics for panel discussions can evolve from ongoing class activities, or they can be anticipated and preplanned by the teacher. Identification of controversial areas within a given unit is often a relatively simple matter; however, the best panel discussions come from issues that are really important and meaningful to the students.

Most students will need teacher assistance in preparing for their panels. For most panel issues, the group should be given about a week of preparation time. Part of this preparation time should be given in class, so you can oversee the development of their presentations.

You should brief students carefully on the panel procedure to be followed. The initial-panelist presentation should be limited, for example, to about 15 minutes. After this more formal portion of the panel presentation, the discussion should be opened up for a class discussion of the topic or for a question-and-answer session from the audience. This open-ended session then should be followed by a summary of the important points by the panel chairperson.

Debates

The **debate** is a competitive discussion that takes place between two teams; that is, two teams of two or three debaters present opposing sides of an issue. One team presents arguments favoring the issue, while the other presents arguments opposing the issue.

You should begin a debate by teaching the procedure, which comprises these general steps:

1. A moderator introduces the topic and debaters.

2. Each debater makes a brief, formal presentation. A timekeeper times the presentations, warns the debater when time is growing short, and stops the speakers when time runs out. The time allotted is a fixed number of minutes that is established prior to the debate.

3. Each team debater makes a rebuttal that counters the arguments presented by the opposing team. Again, the time allotted is fixed and arranged prior to the debate.

4. The general order of the presentations and rebuttals are:

   First affirmative speaker

   First negative speaker

   Second affirmative speaker

   Second negative speaker

   First affirmative rebuttal

   First negative rebuttal

   Second affirmative rebuttal

   Second negative rebuttal

5. After the formal debate, the moderator can open a general discussion session.

Once students have learned the formal debate format, students who are to be debaters should be given time for planning and researching the topic. Only after sufficient research has been completed should students present their debate.

A less formal approach to the conventional debate—and one that is more useful in the classroom—is the British-type debate. This procedure opens the debate to more participants. The class is divided into two teams, one team favoring the issue and one team against the issue. Two debaters are then selected from each team. The debate steps are as follows:

1. The first speakers, affirmative and negative, present 5-minute presentations.

2. The second speakers, affirmative and negative, present 3-minute presentations.

3. The topic is thrown open to comments, questions, and answers from the teams. These comments, questions, and answers are alternated between the affirmative and negative teams.

4. One member from each team summarizes its case.

5. The debate can be followed up with a general class discussion.

Debates offer students opportunities for presenting supporting evidence for or against an issue, encourage research, and increase awareness of problem issues. On the other hand, they can foster dichotomous thinking and encourage winning at the expense of truth.

Role-Playing

Role-playing is the acting out of roles in recreating historical or future events, significant current events, or imaginary situations (Gilstrap & Martin, 1975, p. 87). The role-playing student tries to "become" another individual and, by assuming the role, gain a better understanding of the person as well as the actions and motivations that prompted certain behaviors.

Role-playing is a group technique that may include almost any number of participants, depending on the purpose. Role-playing commonly consists of these three components: the situation, the role-playing, and the follow-up discussion.

The role-playing episode should be a spontaneous acting out of a situation or incident, which in the process fosters a deeper understanding of the associated actions, motives, and behaviors. You should give students a thorough briefing or detailed preparation regarding the situation prior to the episode. For example, students can assume the role of Einstein and reenact his theories, or they can reenact the writing of the Declaration of Independence, or they can assume the role of Shakespeare in the Globe Theatre. Indeed, students can bring to life scenes from science discoveries, scenes from short stories or plays, events from the lives of different people, courtroom dramatization, legal-ethical situations, mock town meetings, or United Nations sessions. Whatever the episode, describe the situation in detail to your students and set clear guidelines.

A debriefing session should follow any role-playing episode. The class should analyze the episode with respect to the values and behaviors of the participants, as well as the consequences of the actions.

Cooperative Learning

Cooperative learning has emerged only recently as a promising instructional approach in secondary schools. Advantages associated with cooperative learning include (1) higher academic achievement than with competitive or individualistic approaches, (2) development of better interpersonal relationships among students, (3) increased time on task, (4) development of a more positive attitude toward the subject and, (5) a positive attitude toward the classroom experience (Johnson & Johnson, 1985). Several approaches to cooperative learning have been developed (Kagan, 1990; Davidson & O'Leary, 1990); however, most of them share common characteristics.

Cooperative learning generally requires that students work together in mixed-ability groups in accomplishing a set of tasks. Students are placed in groups that are composed of high-, middle-, and lower-level learners. The percentage of high, middle, and low learners in each group should represent the appropriate population of each group in the whole class. Rewards to individual students are often based on the performance and accomplishment of the team. Accountability of individual students for the whole group builds an incentive for students to work productively together.

The size of the cooperative-learning group will vary depending on the task to be accomplished. However, the common group size is four, with individual members typically being assigned specific tasks. In general, cooperative-learning groups are given considerable autonomy. Team members are allowed a great deal of freedom as they decide how to deal with the assigned task.

Cooperative learning is appropriate in many situations. It can be an effective technique for test review, for completing laboratory work, or for practicing skills. However, remember that you are rewarding cooperative learning. All students are involved in their group grade, and the better students are expected to help pull up the team grade.

This concludes our discussion of the various discussion techniques. Table 8.1 summarizes the different discussion methods, and the Discussion Methods Application Guidelines offers some suggestions for using these techniques. Review the summary and guidelines, and complete exercise 8.1.

Heuristic Methods

Teaching can be organized so that it is active, somewhat self-directed, inquiring, and reflective. Such modes of instruction are referred to as *heuristic* teaching methods. In this section, we will address some modes that are designated as heuristic approaches: discovery, inquiry, Suchman inquiry, and simulation and game methods of instruction.

Confusion often is expressed when the discovery and inquiry methods are discussed. Some educators use the terms interchangeably, while others feel they represent subcategories of each other. For

TABLE *8.1*   Discussion Methods

Method	Description
Whole-Class Discussion	All students in class exchange and share ideas regarding an assigned topic
Small-Class Discussion	Five to eight students interact and/or work together in reaching conclusions, generating ideas, or completing a task
Panels	Five to eight students prepare and discuss topics in front of class
Debate	Two competitive teams of two or three debaters discuss topic issue
Role Playing	Students assume the role(s) of individuals in a recreation of an event or situation
Cooperative Learning	Students work together as a team on assigned tasks

Application Guidelines ▼

Discussion Methods

Plan Effectively

Examples:
1. Decide whether a whole-class or small-group discussion would be most appropriate for intent.
2. Make sure students are aware of and well prepared for the desired discussion activity.
3. Arrange seating and time for maximum effectiveness.

Implementation

Examples:
1. Assign discussion leaders and recorders. Make sure leaders and recorders know their responsibilities.
2. Set discussion time limits.
3. Carry out an attention-getting introduction activity to get discussion started.
4. Carry out summary discussion of conclusions or findings of discussions.

the purposes of this textbook, we will consider discovery and inquiry methods as unique, yet somewhat related, techniques. Because the **heuristic approach** actively involves students in problem solving, let's begin our study of the heuristic modes by looking at the problem-solving process.

Problem Solving

A problem exists whenever something gives rise to doubt or uncertainty. The literature generated by John Dewey from 1884 to 1948 advocated a curriculum that was based on problems. Some contemporary curricula and a large number of textbooks rely heavily on Dewey's problem-solving approach along with direct experiences. That is, students are required to solve problems through direct experiences provided by the teacher. Therefore, a good working definition of **problem solving** is the intentional elimination of uncertainty or doubt through direct experiences and under supervision.

Application of Knowledge

Exercise 8.1   Discussion Method

Test yourself on the following section concepts. Appropriate responses can be found in appendix A.

1. Which of the following statements represents a major reason for using discussion techniques?
   a. The development of critical-thinking skills.
   b. To more effectively deal with issues related to the affective domain.
   c. The development of a better understanding of complex issues and situations.
   d. All of these are major reasons for using discussion techniques.

2. Which of the following roles can be assumed by the teacher in a discussion episode?
   a. The discussion leader.
   b. A facilitator of learning.
   c. The discussion recorder.
   d. A planner, organizer, and resource person.

3. The four areas that must be addressed in planning a discussion are these:
   a. _____
   b. _____
   c. _____
   d. _____

4. Unlike lectures, discussions usually don't require the use of a cognitive set (introduction) to be effective. (True/False)

5. The small-group technique that is used for generating unevaluated comments, ideas, and solutions is _____ .
   a. the buzz group   c. brainstorming
   b. the task group   d a textbook group

6. A competitive discussion is called _____ .
   a. role-playing   c. a panel
   b. a debate   d. a competitive group

7. A team approach to learning is _____ .
   a. a debate   c. a competitive group
   b. a panel   d. cooperative learning

Because preparing students for solving everyday problems is an important function of schools, curricular specialists who advocate a problem-solving instructional approach suggest that schools should function to develop traits (or behaviors) that will enable individuals to be effective problem solvers. Furthermore, the experiences provided by the school should articulate the content and processes needed for producing successful problem solvers.

Levels of Problem Solving

Problem solving actively involves students in their own learning. The amount of decision making performed by students, however, can be classified according to three levels of involvement (see table 8.2). As depicted in table 8.2, level I is the traditional teacher-directed method, where the problem as well as the processes and procedures leading to an intended conclusion is provided for students. This level of problem solving can also be referred to as guided problem solving. Level I problem solving is highly

TABLE 8.2	Levels of Problem Solving		
	I	II	III
Problem Identification	Generated by teacher or textbook	Generated by teacher or textbook	Generated by students
Processes for Solving Problem	Decided by teacher or textbook	Decided by students	Decided by students
Establishment of Tentative Solution to Problem	Determined by students	Determined by students	Determined by students

manageable and predictable. It is probably best for students without the ability to engage in higher mental operations and best for teaching basic concepts.

In level II, problems are usually defined by the teacher or the textbook, while the processes for solving the problems are left for students to develop. Level II problem solving gives the learners the opportunity, often for the first time, to find out something by themselves through their own independent skills.

Level III represents almost total self-direction. Students generate the problems and then design ways of solving these problems. This level is often referred to as open problem solving.

Ideally, you should have students independently identify some of their class problems and the procedures for solving them. Student-identified national problems, for example, are an excellent source of issues for supplemental inclusion in a social studies, civics, or government class. However, care should be taken in the amount of independence given students: Some students will be unable to benefit from such freedom, and therefore it should be delayed until a later date.

Discovery Learning

Discovery learning is a means by which students engage in problem solving in developing knowledge or skills. As noted earlier, discovery learning is frequently confused with inquiry.

Actually, either discovery learning or inquiry is or can be a specific kind of problem solving. Whereas discovery follows an established pattern of investigation, inquiry has no such established set pattern: Discovery learning follows the general scientific method for conducting an investigation, as shown in figure 8.3. There is no such method for inquiry learning.

A good working definition of **discovery learning** is intentional learning through supervised problem solving following the scientific method of investigation. Thus, with discovery, the learning must be planned, it must be supervised, and it must follow the scientific method of investigation (see figure 8.3).

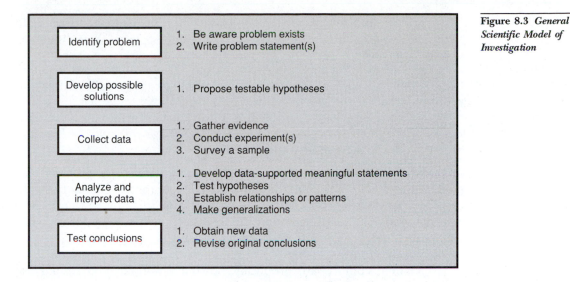

Figure 8.3 *General Scientific Model of Investigation*

Discovery learning can take place at three different levels, depending on the level of problem solving (see table 8.2). At level I, discovery learning is carefully guided (*guided discovery*); at level II, a moderate amount of guidance is administered (*modified discovery*); at level III, it is very casually supervised (*open discovery*).

Discovery Learning Strategies

The degree of success of discovery learning will depend in large part on your ability to plan and execute the problem-solving process effectively. Your role is to provide a situation that lets students identify a contradiction or uncertainty and then to guide and assist them in finding a relationship between what they already know and the newly discovered knowledge. Essentially, you direct the planning, organization, and execution of the general scientific method of investigation (see figure 8.3).

Selecting the Problem Although problem solving is emphasized in discovery learning, students often lack the sophistication to identify their own problems (open discovery); that is, students usually lack the expertise for involvement in level III problem solving (see table 8.2). Therefore, you must be prepared to suggest problems or areas in which students may seek problems. For example, in a science class, you might suggest an examination of pollution in the local river; or in a social studies class, you could suggest an investigation of voter apathy; or in a mathematics class, a discussion of societal mathematics needs might suggest an examination of the mathematics skills needed by individuals in various occupations.

Suitable problems should not be left to chance. Left alone, students often flounder or select problems that are not suitable for your course, or they may select problems whose solutions require materials and equipment that are not available, or problems that are too large and unyielding.

Once students have a general grasp of the problem, you must help them clarify and state the problem in clear, precise terms. You should be prepared to make suggestions or ask questions that will assist students in knowing exactly what they want to find out. These suggestions or questions should be such that students are forced to think and analyze the problem situation for clarity.

Clarification of the problem is a crucial step in finding a solution. If this crucial step is neglected, students often have difficulty in knowing exactly where to start in attempting to find a solution.

Proposing Possible Solutions Once students clearly define the problem, hypotheses and solutions must be generated. Accomplishment of this task requires that data be collected and analyzed. Your function will be to provide materials or make suggestions about where data can be located and to provide resources where information related to the problem area can be obtained.

When students are proposing possible solutions, you should encourage guessing and intuitive thought. Also, encourage healthy skepticism and practice in suspending judgment. Ideally, you want to give students the opportunity for expressing all their ideas in a nonthreatening environment.

Collecting of Data Proposed solutions must be tested; that is, each of the generated hypotheses must be checked for validity. Thus, additional data must be amassed. Data collection sometimes requires that experiments be set up and carried out. At other times, surveys must be conducted. Students often will need guidance and assistance with their data-collection tools and techniques. Experiments must yield valid results, and/or surveys must provide usable data, which often calls for planning and the development of appropriate instrumentation. Students may need your assistance with such planning and instrumentation.

Data Analysis and Interpretation Once collected, data must be analyzed and interpreted. Criteria must be established, and the validity of hypotheses must be judged against these criteria. You might need to guide students in making such judgments and in determining their validity. Students often think they have proven a hypothesis true, when in fact they have not.

Based on the interpretation of data, conclusions must be established. Thus, the data must be carefully examined and evaluated so that conclusions are supported by the data. Although you should not establish conclusions for students, you can help in this process by pointing out patterns, showing relationships, and asking questions. With your help, students hopefully will develop skills in reaching plausible conclusions to their identified problems.

Testing Conclusions Once established, conclusions must be tested and revised. Consequently, the final step in the problem-solving component of discovery is the generation of data that will lend support to the identified conclusions or that will lead to revisions of the conclusions.

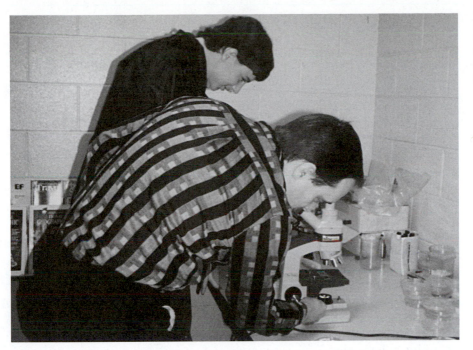

Benefits of Discovery Learning

Discovery learning is active rather than passive learning, which tends to result in a higher degree of intrinsic motivation. With verbal teaching methods, motivation comes only from your comments following class contributions, or following correctly answered questions, or from grades received on assignments. In discovery learning, motivation comes from the activity itself and the excitement of direct involvement. This activity and excitement has the added advantage of increased learning and better retention. Students tend to learn more and retain information longer when they are actively involved in the learning process.

Discovery learning also fosters the development of positive social skills. Obviously, discovery learning requires that students work cooperatively. They must develop skills in planning, following established procedures, and working together toward the successful completion of common tasks.

Limitations of Discovery Learning

The greatest limitation associated with discovery learning probably is the demand it places on you and your students. Because discovery learning is a cooperative process rather than a competitive one, it calls for an adjustment—by students and teacher alike—to the very nature of discovery. With the lack of competition, there is little feedback as to how well students are doing and on how much learning is taking place. This lack of feedback often leads to uncertainty for you and for students.

Discovery learning can also be an inefficient system for covering large amounts of material. This limitation is a major concern to teachers who feel they are expected to cover all the material in the textbook.

Inquiry Learning

Like discovery, **inquiry** basically is a problem-solving technique. Unlike discovery, however, the emphasis is placed on the process of investigating the problem, rather than on reaching a correct solution. In fact, although inquiry is concerned with problem solving, it does not require solutions to the problems being investigated. Thus, where a set pattern is followed in reaching a solution with discovery learning, no established pattern exists with inquiry learning. Indeed, different students may use different strategies in obtaining information related to a problem. Students may even take intuitive approaches to problems.

As with discovery learning, there are three levels to inquiry learning: guided inquiry, modified inquiry, and open inquiry. Thus, you may want to identify the problem and then decide how to investigate it (guided inquiry), or you may want to identify the problem and then have students decide how to go about finding out about it (modified inquiry), or you may want the students to identify the problem and then design ways for obtaining information (open inquiry).

Inquiry Learning Strategies

The inquiry approach is flexible yet systematic. It is systematic in that a basic three-step problem-solving procedure is followed (see table 8.2), yet flexible in that the activities employed in addressing the problem may vary. Let's now look at this three-step procedure.

Identifying the Problem Inquiry learning is closely related to discovery learning. Thus, the problem-selection processes are essentially identical, with either the teacher deciding (as in guided or modified inquiry) or the students deciding (as in open inquiry) the problems or issues to be addressed. This decision, of course, will depend on the sophistication of the students. In short, you must decide whether students are ready and have the skill to identify suitable problems for study. In most cases, however, you must continually monitor the problem-identification process and provide guidance or suitable alternatives for consideration.

Working toward Solutions The second task in an inquiry lesson is of working on a solution to the problem. Again, there should be no set prescription or rules governing the procedure for finding a solution. In fact, decisions regarding strategies directed toward a solution can be teacher-orchestrated (guided inquiry) or student-orchestrated (modified and open inquiry).

The emphasis in inquiry learning should be placed on the process of finding a *problem's* solution, not on the solution itself. Whenever appropriate and within limits, students should be given the opportunity for devising their own strategies for addressing problem situations. Some may want to attack a problem through the literature and a search of textbooks, while others may want to interview experts in the problem area, while others may want to design and carry out experiments of some kind. In a word, freedom should be provided to enable students to develop creative approaches to problem solving. These opportunities will show students how inquiry works in the real world.

Establishing Solutions The success of inquiry learning is not necessarily dependent on reaching a predetermined conclusion. Even when directed by the teacher, inquiry learning should be a highly personal experience for each individual involved. Individuals should be given opportunities for applying themselves totally—so they may put their fullest talents, ideas, skills, and judgments to work in reaching their own unique conclusions.

Suchman Inquiry Learning

J. Richard Suchman (1961, 1966) developed a junior high school–oriented program designed entirely around the concept of inquiry. This program, the Inquiry Development Program (IDP), placed emphasis on physical science and was designed for developing the basic processes associated with inquiry. These processes varied, with some associated with data generation, some with data organization, and some with idea building.

The basic feature of the **Suchman inquiry** is the concept of the "discrepant event." These discrepant events were filmed physics demonstrations—originally presented in short, silent, color, loop cartridges—whose outcomes were contradictory to what was expected. A common example shows a teacher filling a collecting bottle to the brim with water and placing a 3-by-5-inch piece of cardboard over the mouth of the bottle. The bottle is then inverted, with the cardboard held firmly over the mouth. The hand supporting the cardboard is then taken away. The water remains in the bottle—and the cardboard firmly attached—even though the cardboard isn't supported in any way. The title of each of these filmed demonstrations asked why the outcome of the demonstration occurred. The teacher's role was to develop an environment where inquiry could take place.

The original Suchman inquiry approach has changed in two ways. First, the episodes to be considered are usually shown directly through materials by the teacher rather than through films. Second, students receive more guidance from the teacher than did the students in the original program. However, the basic purposes of the inquiry program, which were the development of skills in searching and data processing and the development of concepts through analysis of concrete problems, have not changed.

Suchman Sessions

The Suchman inquiry approach focuses on the process by which information is acquired, rather than on the final information. The problem-solving process associated with this approach occurs in three steps: episode analysis, gathering of information, and reaching conclusions.

Episode Analysis A Suchman session is initiated by having students view a discrepant event. The event can be presented by the teacher or by playing one of the Suchman film loops. After the discrepant event has been presented, the teacher asks the class for ideas, guesses, or hypotheses as to what has transpired. Students are allowed to ask the teacher as many questions as they wish in their attempt to develop these explanations. However, there are three rules that must be followed.

1. All questions to the teacher must be worded so that they can be answered with a yes or no.

2. One student has the floor at a time and can ask as many questions as he or she wants without being interrupted by the class.

3. The teacher will not respond to a question that asks for support of a student-originated theory or hypothesis.

These rules give students the freedom of establishing a sequence and pattern of questions that, in turn, will help lead them to possible hypotheses.

Gathering of Information Once a hypothesis has been presented, it is the class's responsibility to gather data that supports or refutes this hypothesis. Thus, students formulate their own hypothesis and then collect their own supporting or refuting data. The questions asked during this phase have to be phrased in such a way that allows tests to be set up that can verify an answer. "Would the object sink in a different kind of liquid?" and "Would a heavier object sink in the liquid?" are examples of such questions. Also, during this phase, students attempt to determine what conditions were necessary for the final outcome to occur.

The Suchman inquiry approach requires a supportive atmosphere. Students must be given the opportunity for conducting any reasonable tests or experiments to check on the validity of their proposed hypotheses. Although the teacher does provide some information for assistance to students, the class is encouraged to seek data individually or in small groups without help from the teacher. Thus, in the typical Suchman inquiry session, you will find students working independently, working on experiments, reexamining the discrepant event, engaging in questioning sessions with the teacher, and involving themselves in an evaluation of data.

Reaching Conclusions Based on the data obtained, students draw their own conclusions and attempt to explain the cause of the observed phenomenon. In addition, they try to determine why the conditions identified were necessary for the final outcome.

The Suchman inquiry technique can be a valuable tool in a teacher's repertoire. By seeing how problems are solved in the classroom, models are provided that can be followed in solving problems in other areas of their lives.

Benefits of Inquiry Learning

The inquiry method of teaching has several unique benefits. First, it encourages students to develop creative solutions to problems: There are no rigid guidelines, so the imagination can be used without penalty. In fact, students sometimes can go off on tangents and address problems that have little to do with the original problem. Thus, investigations can be as original and limitless as students' imaginations. They are allowed to solve a problem any way they can.

Inquiry often stimulates interest and urges students to solve problems to the very limits of their abilities. They are not penalized for lack of content knowledge. Students are free to use those skills that they do possess in reaching their own solutions.

Lastly, because of the individuality possible in carrying out the problem-solving procedure, it is impossible to fail in inquiry learning. Students carry out the approach to the best of their abilities, then stop without being penalized for not reaching a predetermined solution. Thus, students' self-confidence is enhanced greatly.

Limitations of Inquiry Learning

Inquiry tends to appear, and sometimes tends to be, chaotic. It is possible in a class of 30 students to have as many as 30 different activities that address a single problem. Although the students involved generally cause few problems, inquiry can seem to be an undisciplined process in which little learning is taking place. Anticipating and locating materials can be a major problem. It is impossible to anticipate all the resources that students will require in one inquiry lesson. Indeed, some students may want to conduct experiments, while others may want special reference books in carrying out a literature search. Whatever the need, you must try to anticipate students' needs and make the materials available. This isn't an easy task.

As with discovery learning, a problem associated with inquiry learning is time: Giving students the freedom to engage in problem solving is time-consuming. Moreover, because students investigate to their own limits, some will finish quickly, while others will not want to stop their investigations.

A problem unique to inquiry is evaluation. Because you must provide grades, you need some criteria on which to base your evaluation. This problem can be overcome to some extent by having students keep records of their activities. From such reports you can determine your students' progress.

Simulations and Games

Simulations and game activities can be most useful as teaching tools. Indeed, they provide a variety of learning opportunities in the classroom. Such activities can create interest and relieve tension in difficult curricular areas. Furthermore, students often find simulations and games fun.

Simulation is the presentation of an artificial situation or event that represents reality, but which removes risk to the individual involved in the activity. They can be viewed as models of what exists or might exist under manageable and controlled conditions.

There are two basic types of simulations that can be used in the classroom: human simulations and person-to-computer simulations. Human simulations are usually conducted in the form of role-playing and sociodramas, while person-to-computer simulations often take the form of simulation games.

What is the distinction between a *simulation* and a *game?* There is no clear-cut answer to this question. Usually games are played to win, while simulations need not have a winner. In fact, in some simulations it is

Simulations in which students interact directly with computers are becoming quite common in the classroom.

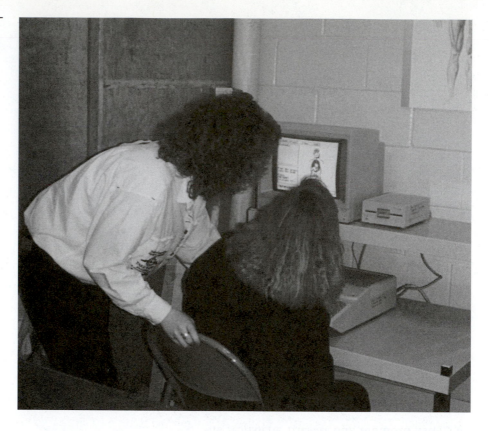

difficult to determine whether there are winners or losers. Regardless of the label, simulations and games are similar in that there are roles that must be assumed and specific types of activities for the participants. In addition, the purpose of a simulation is to encourage students to act out the behaviors and express in their own words the actions and arguments behind an issue. Thus, whether an activity is a simulation or a game is often a matter of semantics.

As stated earlier, **role-playing** involves the acting out of roles, for example, in recreating historical scenes of the past, possible events of the future, or significant current events. Role-playing usually involves some structure, a stated issue to be resolved, and in some cases a winner or loser. Essentially, the idea is to become the individual being played as much as possible, and by recreating the person's actions, gain a better understanding of the person and the related motivations. A role-playing simulation may involve a limited number of individuals in one-to-one interactions or several students in small-group interactions.

The *sociodrama* is a form of role-playing. However, it differs in that it focuses on how the group solves a problem; that is, alternative solutions to problems of concern to the total group are explored. For example, the problem may be related to an issue before a town meeting, or a problem to a family, or a United Nations problem.

Simulation or **educational** *games* involve students in decision-making roles where they compete for certain objectives according to specified rules. Thus, educational games should reflect society; they should offer students the opportunity for experiencing roles that are common in life. However, the competitive nature of games should be kept in perspective. One of the best-known educational games is Monopoly, a simulation board game of the real-estate business.

The use of computer simulations and games is slowly increasing. Computer games are now familiar to everyone; they are often played on home computers and in many classrooms. They now come in a myriad of formats, with the majority of those appropriate for the secondary school classroom involving hand-eye coordination (like Pacman) or problem-solving abilities (like chess or Dungeons and Dragons). Indeed, computer games can function as an excellent motivational device when the chance of playing a game is contingent on doing one's work.

The use of simulations and games offers many benefits:

1. They actively involve students in their own learning.

2. They provide immediate feedback to students.

3. They enable students to practice communication skills.

4. They create a high degree of interest and enthusiasm.

5. They allow teachers to work with a wide range of student capabilities at the same time.

6. They promote and reward analytical and critical thinking.

7. They allow experimentation with a model of the real environment.

Basic to any teaching strategy is its motivational value. Simulations and games appear to be quite effective as motivational tools. Students think they are fun, and they even learn.

Several limitations have also been voiced regarding the use of simulations and games:

1. They demand a great deal of imagination on the part of the teacher and students.

2. They often screen out critical elements; for example, the driver-education simulator often does not include traffic, noise, and the presence of others.

3. The expense involved in obtaining commercially produced simulations and games can be great.

4. Relationships often develop between the teacher and students that are too informal, which can lead to management problems.

These limitations can be overcome with proper planning. The use of simulations and games offers too many special opportunities to be ignored.

Some of the better simulations and games are those designed by teachers who develop and adjust the activities according to their own students. Even better, have your students develop their own simulations and games.

The Teacher's Role

When using heuristic methods, you should function as a facilitator. Accomplishment of your goals usually will call for continuous monitoring of your students.

Problem solving often requires special attention. You must help students constantly in their systematic investigation of problems. You must make sure that you or the students define the problem precisely, and then you must make sure problem-solving methodologies focus on and are appropriately applied to the various aspects of the problem. Indeed, the problem must be established, related issues must be clarified, ways of obtaining information must be proposed, and conclusions or discoveries must be formed. In fact, you would be wise in demanding that students submit periodic progress reports related to their investigative progress.

In using simulations and games, you must be familiar with the desired roles, rules, and conflicts to be followed. In the case of games, you would be wise to play the game yourself first. In addition, it is a good idea to prepare handouts, materials, and/or guides for students.

Heuristic methods require a close working relationship between you and your students. You must constantly be alert for hang-ups and stumbling blocks. Students must not simply be turned loose and allowed to flounder around or follow their own whims.

Classroom Environment

Now that we have addressed the basic tenets of the various heuristic methods and the respective teachers' roles, let's look at the kind of classroom environment that promotes such methods. First, the heuristic methods imply a certain amount of freedom for exploring problems and arriving at possible solutions. Such freedom takes time—with a corresponding reduction in the amount of material that can be covered. Indeed, problem-solving episodes may last for a period of days or even weeks. At times, you may opt to conduct both ongoing problem-solving episodes and regular, more teacher-directed lessons.

Active, self-directed, inquiring learning requires that students be directly involved in the quest for their own knowledge. To this end, the classroom must contain the necessary materials and equipment needed by students in testing their ideas and hypotheses. In fact, as noted earlier, the classroom may even appear somewhat chaotic at times, what with all the different activities that can be taking place simultaneously.

Heuristic methods require openness. Encouragement must be readily available when mistakes are made, and diversity must be encouraged at all times. Permissiveness and sloppy work, however, must not be tolerated. Heuristic methods are most effective in classrooms where there

TABLE 8.3   Heuristic Methods

Method	Description
Discovery	Intentional learning through supervised problem solving following the scientific method
Inquiry	Flexible yet systematic process of problem solving
Suchman Inquiry	Inquiry approach whereby students are presented and asked to explain discrepant events
Simulations and Games	Models of artificial situations and events designed to provide no-risk experiences for students

Application Guidelines ▼

Heuristic Methods

Establish the Problem

Examples:
1. Decide whether guided, modified, or open problem solving is most appropriate for your intent.
2. Make sure class problems are appropriate and solvable.
3. Try to anticipate and have available all materials students will need in their problem solving.
4. Make sure students are aware of and understand all procedures and rules.
5. Establish an open, supportive, nonthreatening atmosphere for students.

Function as Facilitator

Examples:
1. Continuously monitor and assist students so that roadblocks to successful experiences are eliminated.
2. Don't rush students. Heuristic methods often take time and patience.
3. Deemphasize the importance of obtaining a single, correct solution to a problem situation; rather, emphasize the problem-solving process itself.
4. Encourage students to be creative and reflective in their various approaches to problems encountered.
5. Deemphasize the competition and winning or losing in the heuristic modes of instruction.

---

is cooperation, trust, self-control, and conviction. This will require that you plan carefully and emphasize systematic skill building.

This completes our discussion of the various heuristic teaching methods. Table 8.3 summarizes these different methods, and the Heuristic Methods Application Guidelines offer some suggestions for their implementation. Review the summary and the guidelines, and complete exercise 8.2.

Application of Knowledge

Exercise 8.2   Heuristic Methods

Test yourself on the following section concepts. Appropriate responses can be found in appendix A.

1. Discovery and inquiry learning are essentially identical methods. (True/False)

2. Define *problem solving*.
   _____
   _____

3. At what level(s) of problem solving does an authority (teacher or textbook) generate the problem?
   a. Level I   *d.* *a* and *b*
   b. Level II   *e.* *b* and *c*
   c. Level III   *f.* *a*, *b*, and *c*

4. Discovery and inquiry learning are passive forms of learning with a high degree of extrinsic motivation. (True/False)

5. List and describe the *five* steps of the discovery model of investigation.
   a. _____   _____
   b. _____   _____
   c. _____   _____
   d. _____   _____
   e. _____   _____

6. List and describe the *three* steps in the inquiry model of learning.
   a. _____   _____
   b. _____   _____
   c. _____   _____

7. Which of the following are true statements?
   a. Discovery and inquiry learning are efficient ways of teaching content.
   b. The students decide how to solve the problem in the modified and open inquiry methods.
   c. Students often develop a sense of failure when involved in inquiry learning.
   d. An important feature of Suchman inquiry is the use of discrepant events.
   e. Emphasis should be placed on winning with simulations.
   f. An important feature of simulations and games is student involvement in decision making.

8. The acting out of roles to better understand actions and motives is an important feature of _____ .
   a. discovery learning   *c.* simulations
   b. inquiry learning   *d.* educational games

9. The use of heuristic methods requires a highly structured environment along with much teacher direction. (True/False)

Individualized Strategies

Students do not learn or master skills uniformly. Therefore, some sort of individualization is often required in maximizing the potential of each student; this is especially important when students come from different backgrounds and have varying abilities. In this section, we will address three fundamental techniques for individualization: individualized instruction, independent study, and mastery learning. Furthermore, we will take a brief look at the somewhat related topic of drill and practice.

Individualized Instruction

Individualized instruction can take several forms. Ideally, **individualized instruction** engages students in learning plans tailored to meet their interests, needs, and abilities. Accordingly, you might vary one or more of the following: (1) the learning pace, (2) the instructional objectives, (3) the learning method, or (4) the learning materials. Students do not learn at the same pace. Some need more time to attain understanding. Thus, one—and perhaps the simplest—method of individualizing instruction is that of permitting students to work on the same assignments at their own pace. This is accomplished by breaking down the instructional materials into a series of short and related activities or lessons. The faster students or high achievers can move through the lessons rapidly without having to wait for classmates to catch up. Students experiencing difficulty can move through the materials at a slower pace, reworking troublesome areas, and seeking assistance when unable to master the material.

Another technique that can be used for individualizing instruction is varying your objective. If you pretest your class on the intended instructional outcomes (objectives), you may find that some have already mastered these outcomes. Thus, instead of insisting that each student work on the same outcomes, you tailor the activities to the needs and abilities of different students or groups of students. Low-ability students might need to work on all your objectives, while better students might need to work on a small number. Clearly, you will need to break your instruction down into a variety of objectives and related activities to accommodate this type of individualization.

A third individualization technique is of varying the method used in accomplishing the desired outcome. Even when students are working on the same outcome, they can use different means of achieving mastery. One student may rely on a textbook, while another may work with tutors. Still other students with learning difficulties may need to work with special teachers. Self-instructional packages, learning centers, and computer-assisted instruction (CAI) are other possible methods (see chapter 6) that could provide individualized instruction.

The final technique of varying the materials used in accomplishing your objectives can also lead to individualized instruction. As just noted, textbooks can be employed in individualizing instruction. However, some students may read at lower reading levels than their classmates. In fact, some may have severe reading problems, which would hamper the use of any textbook. If reading is a problem, textbooks at different levels can be

One effective teaching technique is to assign students to work in pairs.

made available, as well as other modes—such as films, audiotapes and videotapes, overheads, and models.

Essays and research projects are also excellent ways of individualizing instruction. They allow students or small groups of students to pursue areas of interest. For example, essays can be assigned on broad topics such as the space program, teenage suicide, or the national debt; whereas research projects can be given in such areas as creating an air car, building classroom models, or writing and performing a play. Research projects usually are more challenging than essays; however, students involved in research often gain needed practice in finding and developing materials.

Although the classroom is normally viewed as a place for housing and teaching a class of students, you often can introduce a certain amount of individualization by forming learning groups or through the use of mastery learning. Group organizational structures—sometimes referred to as cooperative or team learning (see cooperative learning section of this chapter), enable and encourage students to learn and assist each other, while mastery learning can be achieved through individual learning or group learning (see mastery learning section of this chapter). Students will often learn and retain more when taught by peers. Thus, groups can be formed so that a range of ability levels and skills is represented within the groups. Also, student assistants can be assigned to work with specific groups on problems, or to lead seminars, or to demonstrate equipment or direct discussions.

```
┌─────────────────┐      ┌─────────────────┐      ┌─────────────────┐
│  Unit objectives │ ───> │    Primary      │ ───> │   Summative     │
│                 │      │   instruction   │      │   evaluation    │
└─────────────────┘      └─────────────────┘      └─────────────────┘
```

Figure 8.4 *The Traditional Model of Instruction*

Independent Study

There is no reason for you to do what students can do for themselves. Older students can often be involved in independent study. **Independent study** can be defined as any educational activity carried out by an individual with little or no guidance. Essentially, independent study is self-directed learning.

Teachers often need time for working with individual students or with small groups. Independent study can provide this time. One way of allowing for this time is by structuring the time students will engage in interesting, creative tasks of their own choosing. For example, students can be allowed to research a topic of personal interest. Other possibilities include reading and reviewing books of interest, or acting as tutor to other students, or working on classroom models. Such activities should be available for students who finish their seat work quickly. They should not be punished indirectly for their rapid completion of an assignment with more of the same work. You might also want to carefully structure long periods of independent study. Self-directed library-research studies on topics of personal interest, for example, often make excellent learning experiences. Most students enjoy working independently on gathering facts on concrete problems. These topics need not always be traditional content-centered topics. Attitude and awareness sometimes may be stimulated by combining factual knowledge with student interests and values.

Mastery Learning

Before we focus on the mastery learning model, we will look at the traditional model of instruction. This traditional model of instruction is shown in figure 8.4. When you use this model, all of your students are involved in all activities at the same time. The instruction begins with an identification of the unit objectives, and then you present the primary instruction to the entire class. The primary instruction comes in the form of lectures, discussions, reading, media presentations, seat work, or some combination of these techniques. After the primary instruction, you evaluate student achievement relative to your objectives.

Like the traditional model, the **mastery learning** model takes a group approach to teaching. This model, through its diagnostic-corrective-enrichment activities, provides a high degree of individualization, because students often learn at different paces and use different materials. As depicted in figure 8.5, the mastery learning model essentially represents a six-step pattern.

As with the traditional model, your first step in using the mastery model is identification of your objectives. Before the primary instruction is delivered, however, a preassessment step is carried out. The purpose of this second step is to determine where students are with respect to the objectives. Some students may lack unit prerequisite skills and need to

Figure 8.5 *The*
Mastery Model of
Instruction

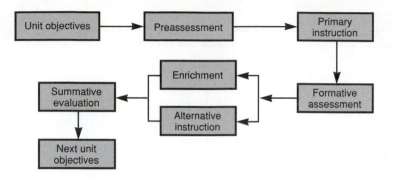

work on these skills prior to receiving the primary instruction. Other students may have already mastered the unit objectives and should be directed to enrichment activities or to the next unit.

The third step in the mastery learning model is the delivery of the primary instruction. This instruction, as with the traditional model, involves all students except those who demonstrated mastery in the activities, and is presented through lectures, discussions, reading, and so on.

At this point—the fourth step—the mastery model parts from the traditional model: A formative assessment (progress check or diagnostic test) takes place. The purpose of this evaluation is to determine which students have achieved the desired mastery level and which students are in need of further instruction. Those at the mastery level are directed to enrichment activities, while those below the mastery level are involved in further objective-related activities. These fifth-step enrichments and alternatives can be structured as group or individual activities. Further formative evaluations should be an integral part of the alternative instructional sequence.

Once the initial alternative activities have been completed, student progress should be checked once again; this cycle is repeated until mastery is achieved. During this sixth and final phase, all students are given a final or summative evaluation.

The basic structure of the mastery learning model can take two forms. In the first, the enrichments and alternatives parallel each other, with the summative evaluation providing closure for the unit. As students achieve mastery, they are routed to the enrichment component until the class is ready for the formal evaluation. The sixth step, the summative evaluation, also may be administered to students at different times. In such situations, students can be tested when the formative evaluation indicates mastery has been achieved. Those students who test early can be involved in other types of individualized strategies, or they can work on the next set of unit objectives on an individualized basis.

Effectiveness of Individualization

The evidence supporting the value of the various individualized strategies is mixed. Under certain conditions, for example, research suggests that the mastery learning approach does lead to higher student achievement.

When used as the only method of instruction, however, such methods have not proven superior to traditional methods.

Individualized strategies tend to leave students on their own too much. Only the most motivated and self-directed students stay on task for extended periods of time. Therefore, with most students, a lot of time is wasted. Also, most students lack skill at analyzing and thinking reflectively about studied materials. They need the direct teaching and explanations provided by the teacher. Instead, the teacher's time is too often devoted to the preparation of materials and correction of individual assignments.

If carefully designed and monitored, individualization can be effective at providing needed remediation or enrichment. Students can work at their own pace on assignments geared toward their abilities, for example, but receive direct instruction from the teacher with the rest of the class. This more active involvement in their own learning generally results in a higher level of interest, better motivation, and a feeling of independence and self-discipline.

Efforts at improving individualization will continue. Students can only benefit from such techniques. Therefore, you will want to individualize your instruction at times. Study the varied techniques and determine how you can incorporate them into your class. But be sure to remember that students need a teacher: They need your expertise and guidance.

Drill and Practice

Drill and practice provide (or should provide) exactly what their name indicates—systematic and repeated "workouts" in the intended skill areas with the purpose of achieving automatic accuracy and speed of performance. *Drill* can be distinguished from *practice* in that **drill** is concerned with the fixation of specific associations for automatic recall, while **practice** is concerned with improvement. Thus, one drills on writing the different shorthand symbols, but practices working through geometric proofs.

Individualized problem-solving processes are the key to drill and practice. They are based on further development of initial whole-class learning. Seen in this light, drill and practice should be a basic part of the curriculum, not merely a time filler. As such, they should give students opportunities to apply their knowledge in solving problems or to refine their skills. Such practice and/or drill, when designed properly, will give you good feedback on how students are progressing. Therefore, you should plan your drills and practice carefully and communicate their importance to students.

Students should not have to interrupt drill or practice frequently to get help. Students who are supposed to work independently must understand what they are to do with little or no help. First, make sure assigned drills and practices are appropriate and not too difficult. Next, give clear expectations about what students should do when they finish their work. Last, make sure students are held accountable; when applicable, all seat work should be checked.

Computers, with their nearly limitless patience and endurance, can be quite effective at providing drill and practice (see chapter 6). Computers

TABLE *8.4*   Individualization

Method	Description
Individualized Instruction	Instruction tailored to interests, needs, and abilities of students
Independent Study	Activities carried out with little or no guidance
Mastery Learning	A diagnostic-corrective-enrichment model, where students work on objectives until mastery is achieved
Drill and Practice	Development of automatic and/or improved performance

Application Guidelines ▼

Individualization

Structure Your Instruction for Diverse Populations

Examples:
1. Provide a variety of opportunities throughout the year for students to participate in individualized instruction.
2. Create instruction sheets for activities so students can work at their own pace.
3. Give students options for achieving intended learning outcomes. Vary your assignments.
4. Create reading lists for suitable topics of interest to students.
5. Form learning groups when students will benefit from group study and/or tutoring.
6. Use multilevel textbooks, and base your assignments on the results of student preassessment.
7. Start where students *are:* Assess their readiness for unit objectives.
8. Have a multitude of materials and resources available, and be ready to suggest other sources of information.

Be an Active Observer and Assist Students over Roadblocks

Examples:
1. Vary your involvement in the learning process as the occasion requires: At times be the dominant figure, at other times a retiring one.
2. Plan and conduct student conferences so you can give one-on-one assistance and evaluate academic progress and personal attitude and feelings.

can drill students as long as the students can hold up. Math programs, for example, use a random-number generator to create new problems—as long as students make requests.

This completes our discussion of the various individualized techniques. Table 8.4 summarizes these techniques as well as the related drill and practice. Also, various teacher-tested suggestions are listed in the Individualization Application Guidelines. Review table 8.4 and the guidelines, and check your knowledge of this section by completing exercise 8.3.

Application of Knowledge

Exercise 8.3   Individualization

Test yourself on the following section concepts. Appropriate responses can be found in appendix A.

1. Which of the following should you do when individualizing instruction?
    a. Vary the objectives to be mastered.
    b. Vary the materials used in achieving mastery.
    c. Vary the methods for accomplishing the desired outcome.
    d. Let students work at their own pace.
    e. All of these represent ways to individualize.

2. Define *independent study:* _____

3. Independent study has proven to be inappropriate for most secondary students. (True/False)

4. Which of the following are components of both the traditional and mastery learning models?
    a. Unit objectives.
    b. Summative evaluation.
    c. Preassessment.
    d. Enrichment.
    e. Primary instruction.
    f. Formative evaluation.
    g. Alternative instruction.

5. Individualized methods have proven to be the superior technique of instruction for the secondary school. (True/False)

6. Drill and practice can be viewed as a form of individualized instruction. (True/False)

CHAPTER SUMMARY

Traditional classroom methods often stress structure too much and are less oriented to critical thinking and independent inquiry. These shortcomings can be overcome to some extent through the use of more indirect participatory methods.

You can design and use classroom discussions not only for stimulating students' thinking, but for helping students articulate their own ideas and teaching them how to listen to the ideas of others. Your role in discussion sessions is to be less directive and less obtrusive: Simply set discussions into motion and monitor their progress.

One of the major problems of whole-class discussions is that a few students tend to dominate. This problem can be overcome to some degree through the use of small-group discussions. Because small-group discussions foster more student-to-student interactions, they provide greater opportunities for the development of discussion and in-

terpersonal skills. However, small-group discussions require careful planning.

Panels, debates, and role-playing are special variants of the discussion method. Their main function is the involvement of students in limited self-directed learning. Role-playing is especially useful in getting students to consider the motives behind actions and behaviors.

Heuristic methods actively involve students in their own learning and result in higher degrees of intrinsic motivation. The heuristic modes of discovery, inquiry, and simulation essentially represent different types of problem solving. While discovery follows an established pattern of investigation, inquiry does not follow such an established pattern. Simulations, on the other hand, are problem situations that are intended to represent reality. Your function in using the various heuristic methods is that of facilitator. You must be prepared to provide assistance when needed and remove roadblocks to students' investigations.

Instruction can be geared to the needs and abilities of students. Individualized strategies such as individualized instruction, independent study, mastery learning, and drill and practice are tailored to fit students' needs and abilities. Having students work at their own pace on different objectives, work with different materials, and work on essays or projects represent a few ways a teacher can individualize.

Mastery learning is a model of instruction where students continue their work on unit objectives until mastery is achieved. Mastery learning represents a diagnostic-corrective-enrichment approach to instruction: Students are given a pretest that determines where they are relative to objectives, which is then followed with instructional and enrichment activities until all students have reached the criteria level.

Drill and practice help students fine-tune their accuracy and/or speed. Drill usually is concerned with the recall of associations, whereas practice more often is concerned with improvement.

Effective teachers use all available resources—one of which is the knowledge of how to implement a variety of methods. Alternative methods provide much-needed variety and flexibility, which will lead to higher achievement. Thus, you should be well versed in both direct and indirect methods of instruction.

Discussion Questions and Activities

1. **Indirect methods.** When is it appropriate to use indirect methods? Consider the objectives and purpose of the instruction as well as the students themselves. Would mastery learning be appropriate for secondary schools?

2. **Discussion topics.** Generate a list of topics that would be appropriate for discussions. Once you have compiled your topics, separate them as appropriate for whole-class or small-group discussions. Give your reasons and justify them.

3. **Classroom observation.** Visit several public school classrooms. Keep a record of the different methods used. What indirect methods did you observe? Was there a pattern? Was drill and practice used extensively?

4. **Individualized strategies.** If individualized strategies are so important and beneficial, why are they not implemented by all teachers? Give your reasons and justify them.

5. **Teaching.** Prepare and teach a minilesson using an indirect method. Use the microteaching guidelines and forms in appendix B in planning and analyzing your minilesson.

6. **Teaching analysis.** Make a videotape of your miniteaching lesson, then critically analyze it with your peers.

9   Teaching Learning Strategies

✎ **Wise teachers do not attempt to guide students in wisdom, but rather they open minds to wisdom.**

Overview

It is necessary, and even desirable, to provide students with a sound education in basic skills. A complete education, however, must emphasize thinking skills that will enable students to function responsibly and solve problems in ways that will be sensitive and caring of others, society, and the world. Undoubtedly, this goal will require that teachers of all disciplines explicitly teach those thinking skills deemed necessary for a lifetime of continuous learning.

In the 1923 work *The Prophet*, Kahlil Gibran tells us, "If the teacher is indeed wise, he does not bid you enter the house of his wisdom, but rather leads you to the threshold of your mind." These words suggest that thinking skills must be placed high on our agenda as one of the most basic of all skills needed today. In fact, thinking skills can be regarded as essential skills.

This chapter will focus on teaching students how to think and assume responsibilities. A wide variety of thinking skills will be examined; however, critical and creative thinking will be emphasized. We will attempt to examine some of the ideas, methods, and issues related to responsibility, critical thinking, and creative thinking.

Objectives

After completing your study of chapter 9, you should be able to do the following:

1. Provide a definition for *thinking*, and differentiate among the various categories of thinking skills.

2. Discuss the association between thinking skills and responsibility.

3. Explain creativity as a process and product, and describe the four stages of creative thought.

4. Describe various difficulties that can hinder the creative process.

5. Describe different approaches and activities that can be used in teaching thinking skills.

6. Explain the eight behaviors that exemplify "nonthinking."

7. Explain the role of the teacher and how modeling is used in the teaching of thinking skills.

Chapter Terms and Key Concepts

Creative Thinking
Creativity
Critical Thinking
Deductive Thinking
Inductive Thinking
Infusion Approach
Responsibility
Separate Approach
Thinking

R esearch (Sadler & Whimbey, 1985) has led educators to question the meaning of "basic skills" for learning, and many have suggested that "thinking skills" are the basis on which all other skills are developed. That is, individuals need thinking skills for remembering information, incorporating knowledge, learning and using motor skills, and developing values and attitudes. Some of these skills are generic and can be taught as general learning strategies, without reference to content.

The research findings tend to confirm that when thinking skills become an integral part of the curriculum and instructional practice, test scores in academic areas increase. It is now widely accepted that teachers of every discipline must teach thinking skills explicitly, in addition to their content area. However, it is also generally agreed that students must assume much of the responsibility for developing these skills. Students must take an active role in the learning process, but the teacher must provide opportunities for using thinking skills and not inhibit such activity. Indeed, responsibility can be thought of as a core thinking skill.

Implicit within the notion of responsibility is the concept of decision making, which involves making choices from among a number of competing appropriate responses. Not all problems have answers that are clearly "right" or "correct." In such situations, a person must choose from a variety of acceptable alternatives. This process of making choices involves skill at thinking (Beyer, 1988). Thus, responsibility is essential to the functioning of the broader dimensions of decision making and thinking. Because responsibility is central in developing learning for learning skills, a brief look at this core thinking skill seems in order.

Responsibility

What every teacher in every classroom wants and needs is responsible students. Indeed, one of the major goals of education is the direction of our society's youth toward social and self-**responsibility**—that is, toward a state of being not only accountable or answerable for one's actions, but able to meet obligations or act without direct guidance. But what creates human responsibility? Can it be taught? How important is responsibility teaching anyhow?

Teaching means helping students develop responsible ways of thinking, believing, and acting. The goal is not the indoctrination of students, but the provision of a climate of thoughtful examination—where wise convictions regarding responsibility can be formed. This climate of responsibility should have several important characteristics.

1. A climate of responsibility is concerned first with communication. You must inspire students to hold positive visions of their abilities: A student's belief that he or she can be a successful thinker, problem solver, and creator helps that student develop confidence to become so. Communicating and using different teaching and learning styles with students will often help individual students find the ones that work well for them. Simple awareness of their own learning styles can benefit students in dealing with the demands of critical and creative thinking. They begin to see how they can learn more effectively and efficiently;

Students must learn to be responsible for the way they behave in the classroom.

therefore, they are better able to take responsibility for their own learning. Moreover, helping students understand learning styles lets them see new perspectives and increases their tolerance for each other's differences.

2. The law of effect is used in a responsible climate. Nothing succeeds like success. Students tend to accept and repeat satisfying experiences. If students are trying new skills and quickly find they are learning them and can move ahead, the sky's the limit on what they can and will do.

3. Teachers are models of responsibility. They should model desired skills and guide students in the formation of thinking skills. Experiences should be such that students can duplicate observed responsible behaviors with a resultant feeling of assurance and competency.

4. Climates that foster responsibility should be active, not passive. Students should be involved in the processes of decision making. They should be given opportunities for testing their ideas and weighing the different options available to them. Open and sensitive classroom discussions about choices and their ramifications should be conducted.

5. A responsible climate helps students make connections between what they learn and how it is used in the thinking process. Students often see no connection between what they must learn and how it pertains

to their lives. They must be shown that learning is for living and decision making, that education means developing the capacity for making judgments and forming convictions.

Management of a classroom is often considered the responsibility of the teacher, and the task sometimes can be overwhelming. But why not share the responsibilities with students?

Let us now consider one scenario where a teacher successfully shared classroom responsibilities with students. This teacher felt so overwhelmed by the demands of recordkeeping needed in the classroom that she formulated a shared-responsibility system with her students. Each class was divided into three groups, and student elections were conducted. Each group elected an officer who handled recordkeeping for their group.

Students quickly learned to value honesty and accountability. As a result, each group requested additional officers so they could ensure more of a "check and balance" system. Now, each of the groups elected three officers—governor, assistant, and secretary—and assigned them each specific responsibilities. For example, the secretary of each group recorded and collected all makeup work for absentees in the group. When students returned after being absent, they were directed to their secretary for makeup work. Thus, the group held the secretary accountable for all makeup work. Subsequently, another interesting occurrence that happened with this system was that peer responsibility began to expand and be expected among students. Often, secretaries would talk with a group member when absenteeism was frequent or affecting the member's performance in class. Moreover, whenever an officer failed to provide a student member with accurate records, other issues evolved. For instance, should a student be "impeached" from office when found in error? To what extent should peers be tolerant of shortcomings?

The classroom teacher in this situation continued to insist on a shared-responsibility role and required that students use problem-solving and decision-making skills in resolving these problems. Thus, the system provided students with opportunities for practicing and refining responsibility learnings.

When you convey to your students that you view them as responsible persons, you give them an "I can!" sense that helps them view themselves as successful thinkers. So, nurture different ways in thinking, believing, and acting. Develop the vital sense of responsibility for their own accomplishments and of their capacity for finding solutions to complex problems.

Thinking Skills

What are thinking skills? How does one go about teaching them? These are difficult questions to answer. Indeed, there are as many definitions of *thinking* as there are thinkers. Do not all cognitive acts require thinking? While it is true that all cognitive acts require thinking, it is also important to distinguish between the ability to use one's mind in simply reproducing rote facts and the creative ability to use higher thinking skills in generating new information.

Many now believe that it is possible to teach students the skills that will enable them to produce the creative thoughts that lead to finding solutions to problems—a skill much needed in preparing the youth that will be tomorrow's leaders. In fact, authorities in the field of education have expressed strong feelings about what it means to "think" beyond the mere level of replication of information. For example, in a 1990 Association for Supervision and Curriculum (ASCD) video, David Perkins of Harvard University says that **thinking** is "problem solving, it's decision making, reading, reflecting, making predictions about what might happen." Matthew Lipman (ASCD, 1990) suggests that thinking is processing our experiences in the world, to edit, or rearrange, or examine experiences, and to think about the process of thinking about your experiences. On the other hand, Ernest Boyer, president of the Carnegie Foundation, stated that thinking could not be separated from good language. Finally, Webster's Twentieth Century Dictionary, Unabridged, Second Edition, defines thinking as follows: "a bringing of intellectual faculties into play; of making decisions, and the drawing of inferences; it is to perform any mental operation, or to reason, judge, conclude, to choose, hold an opinion, to believe, or to purpose, or to muse over, to meditate, to ponder, to reflect, or to weigh a matter mentally." While all of these reflective thoughts describe many important aspects of the operation of thinking, it seems important to establish that there are, indeed, many areas to approach in the teaching of thinking.

Indeed, there appear to be many views of thinking. For purposes of clarifying a definition of thinking for teachers searching for ways to create thinking students, we will encompass all of the definitions cited and summarize **thinking** here as the act of withholding judgment in order to use past knowledge and experience to find new information, concepts, or conclusions. Let us now look at the different types of thinking.

Categories of Thinking

Your first task in teaching thinking skills is determining which skills are appropriate for your class. In doing so, you should consider the maturity level of your students along with the special needs of your content subject. It is commonly believed that it is better to teach a few skills well and thoroughly rather than many skills superficially.

All teachers who teach thinking skills should refer to Bloom's Taxonomy of thinking levels for assistance in the formation and understanding of various thinking levels. Indeed, almost all content areas can provide instruction at six levels of thinking: knowledge, comprehension, application, analysis, synthesis, and evaluation.

At the knowledge level, most thinking tasks require that students recognize or remember key facts. The knowledge level calls on students to be attentive to information, or repeat information verbatim, to recite facts such as math rules and formulas. Activities that ask students to recall, define, recognize, practice drills, or identify concepts are a few knowledge-level thinking tasks.

Students translate, interpret, or explain given information at the comprehension level. Comprehension-thinking tasks might involve interpreting the meaning of a graph or diagram or decoding a word. Knowledge and comprehension levels are not representative of the higher-order thinking-skill levels, because students are not required to come up with new information, but are called on to translate the information that has been given.

Students at the application level can transfer known information to applicable situations. In effect, they must think and decide how information can be applied to situations other than those presented. Students are given generalizations and are required to make applications or explain relationships. For example, students could be asked to solve equations by applying a correct formula, or to transfer known skills to another area in solving a problem.

At the analysis level, students must think about how to divide a whole into component elements. Generally, this level includes finding comparisons and relationships between the parts to the whole concept. Students are required to break down complex information or ideas into simpler parts. Thinking tasks that call on students to identify the underlying structure of complex ideas or information and to compare similarities and differences would fall into the analysis level.

Thinking tasks at synthesis levels require that students take parts of previously learned information and create completely new products, or wholes. Both inductive and deductive thinking and reasoning fall in this category. With inductive thinking, students are provided evidence or details and then asked to use thinking skills to make generalizations. Conversely, students using deductive thinking are given a generalization and are asked to provide evidence that explains the generalization. Hypothesizing, predicting, and concluding are examples of deductive thinking.

Finally, evaluation-level thinking tasks are those in which students judge quality, credibility, worth, or practicality. Students thinking at this level generally must provide evidence, logic, or values in support of their conclusions. It is easy to make swift judgments that do not require the evaluation level of thinking. However, tasks at this level also demand that students use all the previous levels of thinking. The key in determining whether students are actually at this level lies within their ability to withhold judgments until they are able to explain the logic or provide the evidence in support of their judgments.

Critical Thinking

Critical thinking is not the same as intelligence; it is a skill that may be improved in everyone (Walsh & Paul, 1988, p. 13). Also, many educators differentiate between ordinary thinking and critical thinking. According to Lipman (1988), ordinary thinking is usually simple and lacks standards, while critical thinking is more complex and is based on standards of objectivity and consistency. He suggests that students must be taught to change their thinking (1) from guessing to estimating, (2) from preferring to evaluating, (3) from grouping to classifying, (4) from believing to assuming,

(5) from inferring to inferring logically, (6) from associating concepts to grasping principles, (7) from noting relationships to noting relationships among relationships, (8) from supposing to hypothesizing, (9) from offering opinions without reasons to offering opinions with reasons, and (10) from making judgments without criteria to making judgments with criteria.

Critical thinking tends to require higher levels of thinking—that is, more evaluation and synthesis than application or analysis. Indeed, it should be remembered that Bloom's Taxonomy is hierarchical; therefore, operation at the evaluative level requires use of the previous thinking levels as well.

Creative Thinking

All persons have the potential for experiencing those feelings of, "Aha!" or "Wow, guess what I just figured out?" Such thinking is creative thinking. It occurs as the result of questioning and learning beyond the gathering of rote information. Research indicates that the "creative" right brain generates ideas and images, whereas the "logical" left brain critiques and evaluates. It is during the creative processes that the two halves of our brain seem to communicate best. Before we can decide how we can develop creativity, however, we must discuss what, exactly, *is* creativity.

Some degree of **creativity** occurs whenever a person assembles information to discover something not previously taught or understood. To the individual, this may be the discovery of a new relationship between two unlike concepts. This concept of creative thinking is often associated with creative thinking as a process.

When creativity is defined as a product, the result embraces the idea of the production of a new invention or theory. This type of creative thinking is associated with the realization of an original concept. For the student, this could be the creation of a poem, a song, a game, or some unusual use for a common item. Ideally, all creative thinking takes the individual "beyond where they have ever gone before."

Curiosity, imagination, discovery, and invention are all equated with creative thinking. Although it may not be possible for one person to teach another person how to be creative, it is possible to provide activities that will enhance opportunities for thinking. Frequently, there is a high level of frustration associated with creative thinking as individuals travel through the four stages of creative thought.

Creative thinking is generally thought of as putting together information to come up with a whole new understanding, concept, or idea. The four stages generally identified with the development of creative thought are preparation, incubation, illumination, and verification. Numerous thinking skills are used during each of these stages of the creative process. In fact, the greater the flexibility in thinking, the greater the possibility for creative thinking.

During the first stage, preparation, the creative thinker collects information and examines it using many of the thinking processes previously mentioned. However, the creative thinker will question and investigate

Figure 9.1 *Stages of Creative Thinking*

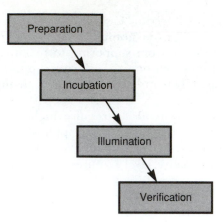

until a major relationship seems to appear among events, objects, or ideas. Usually a hypothesis of some sort will emerge in the thinker's mind, which causes the individual to ponder and meditate in a questioning manner. This begins what is known as the second stage of creative thought, incubation. The individual may spend quite some time allowing images from the subconscious to surface. At other times, this stage may be short-lived, moving the creative thinker into the "Aha!" or illumination stage. Suddenly, the "I've got it" or "Now, I know" may emerge. At this stage, the individual may feel confident and regain some degree of equilibrium, which can be followed by new questioning and a need for elaboration. Next, the individual will begin to seek out ways of verifying and testing the idea. This is called the stage of verification. Figure 9.1 summarizes the four stages of creative thinking.

Creative Difficulties

Eminent creative persons, and others less prominent but no less creative, have expressed frustration and disconcerting feelings while struggling with a puzzling concept that later led them to a discovery or "Eureka!" feeling. The following list of difficulties has been reported (Torrance, 1983) by many who have studied the process of creative thinking.

1. Difficulty in finding words that describe original images is one of the frequently reported frustrations given by creative thinkers. Sometimes ideas or images are too complex for them to put into words. Certainly, not all creative insights must be expressed in words, but can also be expressed visually or kinesthetically.

2. Inability to let the imagination "go" can be a problem. Many cannot permit themselves to "let go" in childlike play even momentarily. The ability to relax, laugh, and play with new ideas with an unrestricted attitude is an important characteristic of creative thought.

TABLE 9.1	Thinking Skills
Concept	**Description**
Thinking	The act of withholding judgment in order to use past knowledge and experience in finding new information, concepts, or conclusions
Responsibility	A core thinking skill: A state of being not only accountable or answerable for one's actions, but able to meet obligations or act without direct guidance
Critical Thinking	The ability to analyze complex situations critically using standards of objectivity and consistency
Creativity	The capacity for producing imaginative, original products or ways of solving problems

3. A tendency to analyze rather than synthesize is a common mistake that can hinder creative thinking. While analysis is helpful during the early stages of creativity, synthesis is necessary in pressing forward through the development of new, original ideas.

4. Creative thinkers sometimes ''jump the gun'' to synthesize before analysis of the facts is complete. This can create ''thinking blocks,'' which will hinder the consideration of other valuable possibilities.

5. Many have communicated fears of expressing new ideas they were generating in their own minds. Some are afraid to let others see their inventions and express doubt that their ideas will be appreciated by others. It takes courage to be an independent thinker! This does not mean, however, that independent thinkers will never experience doubt or misgivings. Even the most eminent creative thinkers of our time have experienced these feelings.

6. A frequent complaint of creative thinkers has been that they get too many ideas at one time. The flood of information becomes a form of stress and gives the individual an ''avalanche effect.'' Successful completion of one or more of these ideas will require the thinker to shelve some of these ideas and focus on what is needed for the moment.

If you are to confront and overcome the above cited difficulties, you must provide students opportunities for creative successes in the classroom. Moreover, avoid judging students' creative endeavors and provide support and encouragement for their attempts.

Few people would argue with the importance of improving critical thinking and creative skills of students in subjects such as mathematics, English, or history. Of course, some students will develop learning skills on their own, but most students need assistance in developing these skills.

The concepts regarding thinking skills are summarized in table 9.1, and the Thinking Skills Application Guidelines offer additional suggestions. Review the summary and guidelines, and complete exercise 9.1.

Application Guidelines ▼

Application of Knowledge

Exercise 9.1   Thinking Skills

Test yourself on the following section concepts. Appropriate responses can be found in appendix A.

1. Define *thinking:* _____

    _____

2. Responsibility can be viewed as a core thinking skill. (True/False)

3. Critical thinking is the same as intelligence. (True/False)

4. What does the law of effect state? _____

    _____

5. There are, in general, six hierarchical thinking levels, which get progressively more complex as one moves up the hierarchy. (True/False)

6. Creativity can be viewed as a _____ or a _____.

Thinking-Skills Instruction

The teaching of thinking skills requires open-mindedness on behalf of those that teach them. Every rock of information must be turned over, every avenue of learning must be explored. You must be willing to explore, question, take risks, and experiment; otherwise, how can you lead students through the same processes?

Many suggest that you begin the teaching of thinking skills by selecting only a few individual lessons, which focus on particular skills. Then, as experience and confidence grow, you should consider extending the emphasis on thinking skills and integrate these skills into your content area.

Should you teach thinking skills separately or infuse them into your content area? Indeed, there are pros and cons to both approaches. Those favoring the separate approach maintain that, like reading and writing, thinking skills are enabling disciplines and deserve separate instruction (Lipman, 1988, p. 143). Conversely, advocates of the infusing approach argue that certain cognitive skills are specific to particular disciplines and therefore should be taught in context (Ashton, 1988, p. 4). Therefore, perhaps the answer to this issue is to use both separate instructional programs along with infusion programs. Let's look at these two approaches.

The Separate Approach

Reuven Voyerstein (ASCD, 1990), an internationally known cognitive psychologist, points out that many students lack the basic skills and abilities for seeing relationships or comparisons between ideas. He suggests that these students need special programs of focused instruction on specific skills—that is, separate instruction on thinking skills. Many educators prefer this **separate approach** when introducing a new skill, because it may be difficult for students who are unfamiliar with a skill to focus on the learning of a new skill and on learning of content at the same time.

Modeling is an important component in the separate approach. In fact, when using this approach you should always begin the teaching of a skill by modeling it. For example, when teaching students about classification, you should demonstrate the skill by doing a whole-class classification activity. Although you may demonstrate how to classify, you would be wise to create a thinking exercise wherein the students' answers diverge. Guidance can be provided, for instance, by presenting the classification steps on the overhead projector or chalkboard. For example:

1. Skim over all the objects to find two that have something alike.

2. Choose two that are alike, and label them as a group.

3. See if any others fit into that group.

4. Find two more that have similarities, and label them a group.

5. Skim over the others to see if they fit into this group.

6. Continue the process until all items have been classified.

You should call for whole-class responses to each of the steps, which in turn will demonstrate that the skill allows for many correct responses. Class input is one of the most important aspects of teaching the classification skill as a thinking skill. As students make suggestions and form their own classified groups, you gradually need to release responsibility to students by allowing them to arrive at answers. Afterward, students should give explanations to the logic that led to their conclusions. Once the initial introductory activity has been completed with the group, you should provide students an opportunity for practicing the skill individually so their understanding of the skill modeled can be evaluated.

The Infusion Approach

The **infusion approach** calls for the use of the desired skill in conjunction with the regular curriculum. In effect, this approach requires that students transfer the newly acquired skill to the regular content being studied. If teaching students the skill of classification, for example, after the skill has been taught, it would be applied to the regular curriculum. That is, once students are taught to classify through introductory activities, they are asked to apply it to the content being studied. You might simply ask them to synthesize different ways the content being studied can be classified. If necessary, direct them toward items in your content area in which classifying may be of use. For example, the outlining of a chapter requires grouping information under headings and categories. Once another use has been established, go through the whole-class collaboration steps once again—using the skill in this new context. Afterward, the procedure of infusing the thinking skill into your content needs can be finalized by assigning students a situation in your content area in which they may apply the skill.

Critical Thinking Instruction

Stephen Brookfield (1987) purports that there are two activities central to critical thinking: (1) identifying and challenging assumptions and (2) exploring and imagining alternatives. Moreover, Brookfield defined *assumptions* as the unquestioned givens or rules that individuals have assimilated as self-evident truths into their value systems—"taken for granted" truths established by the culture that the individual has accepted as their own. These assumptions influence how we interpret situations and how we perceive solutions to problems. Consequently, one of the basic behaviors we develop through critical thinking is open-mindedness and a willingness to explore other possibilities. In effect, we must teach students to examine old ideas in new ways and to consider alternatives to old ways of thinking. This task is not an easy one, because it is often inherently disruptive to personal values and beliefs. This personal disruption may be one reason critical-thinking activities are at times so strongly resisted.

Direct and specific instruction is often useful in teaching critical thinking and should be used in assisting students in dealing with assumptions so that a more open-minded attitude toward new modes of thinking can be developed. Without such instruction, there is little hope for dismantling those truths our society has outgrown—for example, previously held conceptions about racism and sexism. Although many misconceptions about areas such as these still exist today, an important aspect of teaching thinking is the modeling of the open-minded attitude you hope to foster. This will not be possible if you become a dictator of your most comfortable ways of thinking and behaving. Indeed, you must provide opportunities for students to think about their views and the views of others, and yet the final decision should be left to students as respected thinkers. Without this atmosphere of respect, it is impossible to model the concepts you desire to teach.

One good way of providing opportunities for students to examine assumptions is by having them work in small groups with a list of "loaded" statements—statements about which the groups must gather responses from each member and then report their areas of agreement and disagreement during whole class discussions. The following statements are examples of loaded questions.

1. When we see a person who is wearing shabby clothes, what assumptions might we make about him or her?

2. When we see a picture of a rock star, what assumptions might we make about his or her lifestyle?

3. When we see a classmate get a D on his or her report card, what assumptions might we make about him or her?

4. When we see a woman running for the presidency of the United States, what assumptions might we have about her abilities?

5. If a substitute teacher is in the classroom on a particular day of school, what assumptions might you make about how to conduct your behavior for the day?

6. When we hear someone has AIDS, what do we think?

Developing societal consciousness is a starting point in developing a line of reasoning skills needed for producing thoughtful citizens for our future. Certainly, one of the critical aspects of critical thinking is the challenge of these basic assumptions. And yet a word of caution is in order, lest we isolate the very foundation on which we desire to develop. Indeed, Stephen Brookfield (1987) points out that challenges of the assumptions underlying our value systems can be both "liberating" and "threatening." He further suggests that questioning internalized truths, whether actually true or not, is a part of one's personality. However, it may seem demeaning to our capacity for valuing, believing, and developing moral codes when we discover that the absolutes we hold to be true are not necessarily absolutely true. The development of completely new thought patterns that differ from past thinking structures can even create momentary imbalance. Therefore, you might often find it necessary to implement ways for helping students broaden their thought structures beyond the confines of their own culture, without weakening their desire to believe in and form values. The goal is not to destroy, but to refine. Above all, remember that sometimes you too will pass through these same disruptive processes as a teacher-learner.

Regardless of the approach you choose for teaching critical thinking skills, there are eight nonthinking behaviors (Raths, 1986) frequently reported by classroom teachers. These eight behaviors will negatively impact the development of thinking skills. As such, you must learn to diagnose and prescribe appropriate thinking activities that will enable your students to overcome the following behaviors.

1. **Impulsiveness**

   These students respond before the question is completed. They do not take time to consider the problem or alternatives. In other words, they "leap before they look" or "jump the gun" without adequate thought. These students think, but fail to consider consequences of their inferences, hypotheses, or decisions on information presented. They blurt out the answer without having enough information, or they impulsively base decisions on the first thing that enters their minds.

2. **Overdependence on the Teacher**

   Students sometimes raise their hands as soon as the teacher finishes explaining the assignment and begins the independent work. These students won't try the concept first, but rather say, "I don't understand this"—before even attempting to read the instructions. These students often fail to pay attention during group instruction and will insist that the teacher provide individual instruction at their desks.

3. **Inattentive Behavior**

   These students start working but don't stay on task. They often need constant prompting; their attention span is short; and their attention constantly wanders, seemingly into "space." These students rarely finish assignments and demonstrate a lack of self-motivation.

4. **Restless, Rusher**

   Restless rushers get very little meaning out of assigned tasks; rather, they often rush through their work, concentrating only on turning in the assignment. These students frequently finish the work first, but lack accuracy. When asked questions pertaining to the assignment just finished, they may pause and reply, "I don't know." If the student is prompted further to redo the work, he or she usually rushes through the second time just as quickly as the first time. These students differ from your impulsive students in that they usually won't base their responses on past or similar experiences and jump the gun as impulsive students do, but instead concentrate only on turning in the work.

5. **Dogmatic, Assertive Behavior**

   These students fail to consider another's point of view. Conceived basic assumptions are never questioned, and they always think their perceptions are the only, correct ones. Because they think their views are already perfect, they see no reason for considering or listening for other possibilities.

6. **Rigidity, Inflexibility of Behavior**

   These students are reluctant to give up old strategies that have worked for them in the past, even when they prove inadequate in the new situation. For example, students might be requested to perform a certain task, and they may reply that it's not the way they learned to do that last year.

7. **Fearful, Lack of Confidence**

   These students rarely respond to questions that require anything other than one right answer! They are fearful of expressing their own views and opinions, as they lack confidence in their own thinking. When asked to answer a question that calls for higher-order thinking skills or to voice their thoughts during a brainstorming activity, these students are afraid to express themselves. These students may seem to be the opposite of the overdependent student in that they usually won't seek extra help.

8. **Responsibility Forfeiture**

   These students want the teacher to provide one right way of accomplishing all learning tasks. Again, fear of taking risks or assuming responsibility is evident. These students frequently are grade-conscious individuals who are not afraid to approach their teacher for specific guidelines; by obliging the teacher in this way, the students shift responsibility to the teacher and relieve themselves from thinking for themselves.

Often you will need to prescribe thinking activities that alter the behaviors cited above and promote self-confidence and mental growth. Let's now look at some of the activities that could be used in correcting faulty thinking habits.

Thinking-Skills Activities

Teaching thinking skills requires open-ended activities where no single, correct answers are sought. Although there are many areas, categories, and thinking operations that could be approached, let's examine some of the concepts that could be prescribed for the eight nonthinking behaviors.

Brainstorming

Brainstorming is an excellent way of promoting fluent thinking (see chapter 8). The goal of brainstorming is to produce as many responses as possible. It is crucial that all responses be accepted and appreciated during the activity. You should withhold praise or judgment and provide an accepting atmosphere throughout the activity. Encourage your students to "hitchhike" on each other's ideas. Emphasize that not all responses will be of high quality because the aim is for quantity, and hitchhiking on each other will generate additional ideas. Brainstorming activities of this type can also encourage flexible thinking.

Flexible Thinking

With flexible thinking, activities stretch the mind into considering possibilities beyond the usual responses. During these activities, you will need to define the area for examination. Ask students to put their five senses to work in thinking about how many different ways a concept could be used. For example, ask your students questions that will help them consider alternate possibilities—perhaps, for the use of a water hose, should they be stranded on a deserted island! Inspire them to ask themselves questions that take forms such as these:

What if . . .

Suppose that . . .

How is ____ like _____ .

If you were . . .

Such questions or statements will help define new possibilities and foster flexible thinking.

Another outstanding thinking skill that will improve students with impulsive behaviors is cause-and-effect consideration. Forecasting activities can help students generate causes and effects of a given situation.

Forecasting

Instruct students to brainstorm all possible causes and effects of getting good grades! This will require that students make inferences about cause and effect. The idea, once again, is to forecast what could or might be. Afterward, students should examine the quality of each prediction and choose the best cause and effect, and then they should provide reasons for their choice. Providing explanations for choices that students determine to be the best helps promote inductive thinking.

Inductive Thinking

Inductive thinking activities can be helpful for those students that frequently fail to check their responses to determine whether their generalizations can hold up against data. During **inductive thinking,** students collect, organize, and examine data, then they identify common elements, and finally they make generalizations based on the common or general elements. Once students have examined the data, they should be encouraged to state generalizations that are based on inferences found in the data. For example, encourage students to "read between the lines" when reading a selected newspaper article, and then to state a generalization based on information known about the article. If possible, provide students with newspaper articles from different areas and by different authors to further check the generalization against data. Making inferences is closely related to finding generalizations.

Making Inferences

When a person makes an inference, that individual must provide a possible consequence, conclusion, or implication from a set of facts or premises. Inference making requires that thinkers provide a rationale for their thoughts. These thoughts are personal beliefs about a situation that will be based on similar associations with past experiences. Basic assumptions held by the individual will play a key role in inferences given. Questions that call for inference making ask the student to provide their personal opinion. "Why do you suppose?" and "What do you think someone should do?" and "What do you suppose was meant by that?" are questions frequently used in promoting inference making. Yet, as with forming generalizations, it is important that you ask students to supply evidence or provide reasons for the inferences they make. Even when basic assumptions are examined, it may be necessary to determine whether or not inferences are based on clear, meditative thinking or whether they are the product of assertive, dogmatic rigidity. Therefore, students also will need practice in logical thinking.

Logical Thinking

Logical thinking is believed to be a left-brain function that organizes and associates ideas. Activities that require logical thinking begin with assumptions or concepts and generate step-by-step ideas to arrive at an end point or solution. Logical thinking is based on previous knowledge or acquired patterns of thinking. Logic will require that students interpret information in deriving the intended meaning from a source. Students must examine the main idea presented and follow the supporting details to arrive at a conclusion. For example, samples of logic skills can be taught, and then thinking activities—such as the one shown in figure 9.2—can be developed by students. Indeed, such activities can be developed by students and exchanged with other classmates for solving.

Figure 9.2 *Sample Logical Thinking Activity*

Crawling Caterpillars

1. The caterpillar crew is enjoying an out-of-school crawl.

2. Read the clues below carefully. Then write each crew member's name in logical sequence.

Assumptions
(clues)

1. Rick Reader loves to read.

2. Rick Reader is between Duff and Shades.

3. Shades is following Carrie the Carrier.

4. Carrie the Carrier is following Headphones Hector.

by Raul Acosta
Seventh-grade student
Anadarko Junior High

Deductive Thinking

Whereas inductive thinking calls on a student to make generalizations based on data, **deductive thinking** asks the student to consider the generalizations given and provide supporting data. Most thinking activities will be incomplete until students provide some kind of rationale for their responses.

Deductive thinking is crucial in a democratic society that demands a responsible citizenry in decision making. Deductive thinking often requires that students evaluate the merit or worth of an activity, object, or idea. Therefore, teaching students to identify possible outcomes, define standards of appraisal, and make judgments based on careful consideration become all-important elements of instruction. When students are called on to decide among objects or alternatives, decision-making and problem-solving steps will be helpful to them in reaching their conclusions.

Problem Solving

Complex thinking processes often involve problem solving and decision making. As pointed out in chapter 8, problem solving involves six steps: (1) defining the problem, (2) collecting data, (3) identifying obstacles to the goal, (4) identifying alternatives, (5) rating alternatives, and (6) choosing the best alternative. Problem-solving models can be developed that guide students through these important steps. For example, divergent questions might be developed that discourage students from supplying one "right" answer. Also, brainstorming should be an important aspect of each step. Students should consider the following questions as they carry out the problem-solving steps:

1. What is fact and what is opinion?

2. Is there only one right way?

3. Do the examples presented prove the rule?

4. Just because two things happened together, does this prove one is the cause of the other?

5. Is it possible that personal feelings might be causing you to rule out possibilities?

Sometimes a guide with questions similar to those cited above will help new problem solvers organize problem-solving activities. In using such a guide, students should be asked to record alternatives and then asked to critically consider their choices.

Decision Making

Decision making involves the thinking skills needed in choosing the best response from several options. It involves examining advantages and disadvantages, considering all of the steps of problem solving, and evaluating the final decision in relation to available alternatives and consequences. Basic to decision making is the ability to observe, interpret, compare, and analyze information.

Observation Observation demands that students watch for a purpose and note objective changes, details, or procedures. Students must use their five senses if they are to record data accurately. This activity can help students check the accuracy of a match between what is seen, heard, smelled, and so on. The proposition that you can't believe anything you hear and only half of what you "think you see" will become a reality, as students not only examine their own perception of things, but also attempt to understand the point of view of others. A good way of practicing careful observation techniques is by observing television commercials for underlying messages being developed and conveyed through various techniques. Close observations of this type will lead students to recognize the power of effective persuasion and help develop open perceptions when attempting to interpret information.

Interpretation Interpreting requires that students use their perceptions in examining their assumptions when making a judgment or reaching a conclusion. Perceptions are developed through associations with personal experiences and are, therefore, quite unique to each individual. Interpreting is an important skill to teach directly, as people tend to generalize on the basis of insufficient evidence in their repertoire of basic assumptions. Our interpretations sometimes can become hazy when we experience doubt in our attempts to attribute causation and validity to data. Causation and validity must be closely examined before deriving conclusions. Explain to students that the skill of interpreting depends on drawing inferences from *valid* data. Warn them about the tendency to generalize on the basis of insufficient evidence. Guide them in critically examining information and in differentiating between what is true and what they may believe to be true. Students' first activities of interpreting might begin with your presentation of a large poster with a visual graph or picture. Begin by asking students to list at least four or five statements that can be made through observing the picture. Afterward, ask them to share with the class their interpretations of what the picture was telling. After the first student gives personal responses of interpretation, search for other responses that might be interpreted differently. This particular activity prompts examination of the many different ways individuals perceive and interpret information. It can further develop students' ability to withhold judgments of absolutes and consider other alternatives. Thinking-skills instruction must include training that fosters open-mindedness, so that students reach an understanding that what seems to be unconditionally true in one situation may not be completely true in another.

Comparison Comparison requires that students examine two or more situations, objects, ideas, or events and seek out relationships or similarities or differences. The degree (or level of Bloom's thinking level) needed will vary with the assignment of tasks for comparison. Once differences and similarities have been determined, designate opportunities for the students to practice the skill independently. Above all, link the thinking skill taught to some practical use, and encourage students exhibiting nonthinking behaviors to keep an open mind and compare their answers and beliefs to opinions expressed by others.

Analysis During analysis, students take apart, identify elements, and find relationships when examining the problem to be solved. Instruct students to identify useful ways of breaking problems into parts, ask them to define each part clearly, and request that they organize the data related to each part and examine relationships in determining their conclusions. If you prefer the infusion method of instruction, you should ask students to consider each of these elements in relationship to the problem needing solving. If, however, you prefer to step your students through the skill of analysis before asking them to apply the skill to a real problem for solving, you might simply present an item for analysis and give them four steps to follow. For example: First, identify the whole; second, define each part of the whole; third, organize data related to each part; fourth, state a conclusion based on your analysis. Keep in mind the difference between asking an analysis question and asking a knowledge-level recall question.

While analysis is an important aspect of problem solving and decision making, it is not intended for confining the individual to categorizing only presented information. That is, students should be encouraged to analyze information for relationships that might otherwise go unnoticed.

Again, the teacher's role in developing students' skills in decision making is to create an atmosphere of acceptance and support in the

TABLE *9.2*	Thinking-Skills Instruction
Concept	**Description**
Separate Approach	Program that focuses instruction on thinking-skill development without regard to content
Infusion Approach	Development of thinking skills in conjunction with regular curriculum, where thinking-skill instruction is followed by applying the skill to the content being studied

forming of values and beliefs, lest students experience despair and turn off from a feeling of "overloaded" disequilibrium. You need to reassure students constantly that even though it is important to withhold judgments temporarily, it is important to never "bail out" until they feel comfortable with their own personal interpretations and perceptions. You, too, may feel some disequilibrium and may be tempted along with students to shut down or bail out because the challenges your students present have become intense.

This completes our examination of various activities for developing students' thinking skills. Table 9.2 summarizes the two thinking-skills instructional approaches, and the Thinking-Skills Instruction Application Guidelines give some further suggestions. Review the summary and guidelines, and complete exercise 9.2.

CHAPTER SUMMARY

Thinking can be viewed as the act of withholding judgment in order to use past knowledge and experience to find new information, concepts, and conclusions. This act requires responsibility. Teaching students to think and be responsible is a universally accepted idea; however, the misconception is often voiced that *all* activities teach thinking because their mere implementation calls on people to use their own thoughts. But the ability to think at a level other than that where factual information is recalled demands planned experiences and practice.

Thinking can take place at any one of Bloom's Taxonomy levels: knowledge, comprehension, application, analysis, synthesis, and evaluation. The level most appropriate for a specific class will depend on the maturity of the students and the needs of the content area. The most commonly taught thinking skills are critical and creative thinking.

The teaching of thinking skills requires open-minded teachers. Thinking skills can be taught separately (separate approach) or by infusing them into the content (infusion approach). Moreover, direct and specific instruction often proves useful in fostering critical and creative thinking skills.

Eight behaviors have been identified that often negatively impact the development of thinking skills: impulsiveness; overdependence on the teacher; inattentive behavior; restless rusher; dogmatic, assertive behavior; rigidity, inflexibility of behavior; fearful, lack of confidence; and responsibility forfeiture. Teachers must learn to diagnose and prescribe appropriate activities to overcome these behaviors.

Application Guidelines ▼

Application of Knowledge

Exercise 9.2   Thinking-Skills Instruction

Test yourself on the following section concepts. Appropriate responses can be found in appendix A.

1. The teaching of thinking skills can take place through the _____ or _____ approach.

2. Direct instruction can prove useful in teaching critical thinking. (True/False)

3. Challenges to our value system seldom represent threats to the development of critical thinking skills. (True/False)

4. Thinking skills are best taught through the use of open-ended activities. (True/False)

5. Describe the type of thinking operation each of the following promotes:
    a. Brainstorming _____
    b. Forecasting _____
    c. Logical thinking _____
    d. Analyzing _____

Discussion Questions and Activities

1. **Teaching methods.** What teaching methods and procedures can improve students' sense of responsibility? critical thinking abilities? creative thinking abilities?

2. **Thinking.** What type of thinking is emphasized in most secondary schools? Is critical thinking rewarded? creative thinking? Is school success based on students' ability for thinking critically? creatively?

3. **Environment.** What type of classroom environment would be conducive to developing responsibility? critical thinking? creative thinking? What problems can you foresee in establishing this environment?

10 Evaluation and Measurement

✎ **Evaluation, like teaching, is both an art and a science. It requires creativity and imagination. It calls for sound judgment. It demands knowledge.**

Overview

Today, evaluation occurs more frequently in schools than it did thirty years and more ago. The heavy emphasis on evaluation is a result of the accountability and reform movements that have impacted this nation's schools. Therefore, it is critical that beginning teachers build a repertoire of effective evaluation strategies for assessment of knowledge, behaviors, skills, and abilities in the cognitive, affective, and psychomotor domains.

Like every other aspect of the teaching-learning process, assessing the outcomes of teaching and learning is a complex and sometimes confusing endeavor. Nonetheless, teachers, administrators, and parents need information about the general impact of their programs and instruction.

Although the terms *evaluation* and *measurement* are closely related, they are not synonyms. In this chapter you will examine the difference between these terms as well as some of the kinds of evaluation and measurement techniques. The information presented should make teaching more productive, learning more engaging, and explaining the outcomes more tenable.

Although certain evaluation techniques are beyond the scope of this chapter, many of the basic concepts will be addressed. Thus, it will provide beginning teachers with a basic grasp of evaluative topics and procedures.

Objectives

After completing your study of chapter 10, you should be able to do the following:

1. Define *evaluation,* and explain the purposes of student evaluation.

2. Distinguish between the concepts of evaluation and measurement.

3. Explain the purposes of evaluation.

4. Compare and contrast diagnostic, formative, and summative evaluation.

5. Create a plan for the appropriate use of the three different kinds of evaluation.

6. Differentiate between the competitive, noncompetitive, and performance assessment systems.

7. Explain what is meant by the possibility of bias in the assessment process.

8. Differentiate between the concepts of reliability, validity, and usability.

9. Describe the various sources of evaluative information.

10. Identify advantages and limitations associated with the use of the different sources of evaluative information.

11. Explain the purpose and advantages associated with the use of rating scales, checklists, and questionnaires.

12. Define the following evaluative terms: *competitive evaluation, noncompetitive evaluation, performance assessment, norm-referenced evaluation, criterion-referenced evaluation, standard scores,* and *percentile.*

Evaluation is a vital part of the instructional process. Evaluation must be conducted in order to determine whether students are learning, gauge the appropriateness of the curriculum for a given group of students, identify what must be retaught, ensure proper placement of individual students within a program of instruction, and make sure that state guidelines for achievement have been met. Viewed in this context, evaluation performs a dual function in the educational process. Essentially, it provides not only information about student achievement, but information that can be used in future curriculum planning.

As you can see, evaluation serves many roles in the teaching-learning process. It is important to decide the purpose of every evaluation effort prior to implementing a plan of action. If you wish to determine the level of student learning, then the approach to evaluation will differ from the approach you would take if your purpose of evaluation is to determine the effectiveness of a particular teaching technique. Likewise, you would not use a pencil-and-paper test in ascertaining whether a particular performance skill, such as creating a poster using the computer, has been achieved. How you plan for and carry out evaluation and the methods of measurement you use can help determine how effective you are as a teacher.

Evaluation must also be more than a measurement of academic achievement. It will be necessary to determine the quality of student work beyond a minimum standard. You may want to gauge how well students work in small and large groups. You may want to evaluate students' abilities to work with very little supervision on projects of interest to the students. You may have the need to identify which students display leadership potential in group situations. Perhaps you will need to know the attitudes of your students toward a particular learning experience. Whatever the need that you identify, there are appropriate strategies for finding out what you need to know.

The identification of learner difficulties is a basic skill that successful teachers must possess. No matter how much planning goes into your lessons, some students will experience difficulty in mastering desired learning outcomes. Without proper identification and remediation, such difficulties may compound until the student becomes frustrated and turns off to your subject altogether. Thus, evaluation and measurement are essential components of effective teaching.

No process is more central to teaching than evaluation. But evaluation is not just testing. Evaluation is much broader. It demands that you make a qualitative judgment regarding some type of measure. **Evaluation** is the process of making a judgment about student performance; **measurement** provides the data for making that judgment. Valid evaluations will depend on accurate measurement. Evaluation often involves more than simply measuring academic achievement. It requires some type of decision. In other words, information is used in making some type of decision. Thus, in the classroom, evaluation can be related to how well students carry out specific actions (performance) or to what they can produce (product). Sometimes you will be interested only in how well a student performs, whereas at other times you may be interested only in an end

Evaluation is an integral part of the instructional process.

product. For example, you may want to evaluate how well your students participate in group work, how well they can perform algebraic equations, or how they go about adjusting a microscope in an experiment. Also, because attitudes and feelings can have an effect on learning, you may want to focus on such subjective factors in your teaching and in your evaluation.

Evaluation must be viewed as a two-step process. First, you must gather pertinent data regarding the desired outcomes. During this step, the tools and techniques of measurement are applied in gathering relevant information about students' acquisition of the intended instructional outcomes. Second, once the data has been gathered, the information is used in making reasonable judgments concerning students' performance.

Measurement comes in different types and with different precision. For example, you can compare the loudness of two sounds or the height of two objects, use a scale to determine your weight, use a ruler to find the length of an object, or watch a speedometer on a trip. What these measurements have in common is that the perceptual processes of hearing and sight are used in gathering some type of data. However, these measurements differ greatly in terms of their precision.

As a teacher, you will take hundreds of measurements daily. But, like all measurements, they will differ in type and have varying degrees of precision. For example, you will collect data as you observe your students' behaviors, when you ask questions and hear responses, and when you give and analyze an examination. There will be differences in the accuracy of the data, however, because of the differences in what is being measured and how it is being measured.

Evaluation requires that judgments and decisions be made. Ten-Brink (1986) suggests that the evaluation process consists of four steps:

1. **Preparation**
   Determine the kind of information needed as well as how and when to collect it.

2. **Information Collecting**
   Select techniques for gathering a variety of information as accurately as possible.

3. **Making Judgments**
   Compare information against selected criteria to make judgments.

4. **Decision Making**
   Reach conclusions based on formed judgments.

These four steps require that you develop an understanding of the different kinds of evaluation and the different data-collection techniques, and that you sharpen your decision-making skills. These understandings and skills will be addressed in this chapter and the next.

The ultimate question in the instructional process is whether or not you have taught what you intended to teach and whether students have learned what they were supposed to learn. Can they demonstrate the outcomes specified in your original objectives? That is, do they meet the acceptable level of performance as specified in the criteria of your objectives? These objectives will call for the demonstration of cognitive skills, performance skills, and in some cases attitudes or feelings. Thus, you may be required to perform evaluations in the cognitive, psychomotor, and affective domains. These different evaluations call for different evaluation techniques.

Evaluation in the three domains of learning will demand that you collect different types of information. Before we focus our attention on the gathering of evaluation information in the three domains, however, let us briefly look at the different evaluation types and the different sources of evaluation information available to classroom teachers.

Evaluation Types

Continuous feedback is needed throughout the planning, monitoring, and evaluation of instruction. This feedback may be obtained through any one of three different types of evaluation: diagnostic, formative, and summative (see table 10.1). These three primary types of evaluation differ in terms of their nature and chronological position in the instructional process.

TABLE *10.1* Relationship between Diagnostic, Formative, and Summative Evaluation

	Diagnostic	Formative	Summative
Purpose	To identify difficulties and place students	To promote learning through feedback	To assess overall achievement
Nature	Many questions related to general knowledge	Few questions related to specifics of instruction	Many questions related to specific and general knowledge
Frequency of Administration	Varied—usually before instruction	Frequently—usually during instruction	Once—usually final phase

Diagnostic Evaluation

Diagnostic evaluations normally are administered before instruction in order to assess students' prior knowledge of a particular topic for placement purposes. However, diagnostic evaluations may become necessary during the course of study when the teacher feels students are having difficulty with the material. The purpose of diagnostic evaluations generally is to anticipate potential learning problems and, in many cases, to place students in the proper course or unit of study. A common example of diagnostic evaluation is the assignment of high school students to basic mathematics or remedial English based on entrance assessment. Such pre-assessments are often designed for checking the ability levels of students in designated areas, so that remedial work can be planned or an instructional starting point can be established.

Diagnostic evaluation provides valuable information to teachers about the knowledge, attitudes, and skills of students. The results will assist the teacher in planning effective lessons in terms of appropriate activities and the level and pace of class instruction. Diagnostic evaluation can be based on teacher-made tests, standardized tests, or observational techniques.

Diagnostic information gives curriculum planners invaluable information regarding the appropriateness of instruction. Unfortunately, most school districts use diagnostic information for determining the achievement levels of students rather than for evaluating the curriculum. Achievement test scores, for example, are often devoted to making comparisons of school district group scores with national norms, whereas they could be interpreted for the purposes of making needed improvements in curricula and for redesigning curricula in areas found to be below the national norms.

Diagnostic information can also be used for the correct placement of students in curricular tracks and courses. One critical piece of diagnostic information often needed by secondary teachers is reading ability and comprehension. If your students have reading difficulties, modification in instruction must be planned to address these deficiencies.

*Evaluation is a
continuous process
fostered by daily
teacher-student
interaction.*

Formative Evaluation

Formative evaluation is carried out during instruction for providing feedback on students' progress and learning. It is used in monitoring instruction and promoting learning. Formative evaluation is a continuous process. However, comparatively little use has been made of formative evaluation.

Diagnostic information should be revised as formative information is gleaned from students' performance on oral and written work. This permits teachers to monitor and modify their instruction as needed. As individual student deficiencies or program problems are noted, remedial work or changes should be planned that will bring the slower-learning students up to the level of their peers or that will correct program weaknesses. Thus, although initial evaluation alone usually is considered diagnostic, formative evaluation is also diagnostic in that it provides information about the strengths and weaknesses of students.

Students sometimes will require more assistance than you can provide. On such occasions, you should seek outside assistance from available, qualified specialists. Finally, the information gained from formative evaluation might lead you to correct any general misconceptions that might be observed or to vary the pace of your instruction.

Formative evaluation generally focuses on small, independent pieces of instruction and a narrow range of instructional objectives. Essentially, formative evaluation answers your question "How are you doing?" and uses checkup tests, homework, and classroom questioning in doing so. You should use the results obtained from formative evaluation to adjust your instruction or revise the curriculum, rather than to assign grades.

Summative Evaluation

Summative evaluation is the final phase in an evaluation program. Because it is primarily aimed at determining student achievement for grading purposes, it is generally conducted at the conclusion of a chapter, unit, grading period, semester, or course. Thus, **summative evaluation** is used for determining student achievement and for judging teaching success. Grades provide the school with a rationale for passing or failing students and are usually based on a comprehensive range of accumulated behaviors, skills, and knowledge.

Summative evaluation, as the term implies, provides an account of students' performances. It is usually based on test scores and written work related to cognitive knowledge and rarely addresses such areas of learning as values, attitudes, and motor performance.

Student performance on end-of-chapter tests, homework, classroom projects, and standardized achievement tests are commonly used in summative evaluation. Summative evaluation can be used in judging not only student achievement, but the effectiveness of a teacher or a particular school curriculum as well. The data collected and instrumentation used in collecting the data will differ depending on the type of summative evaluation being considered.

Devices such as tests and homework are used most often in summative evaluation. However, these devices can also help diagnose learning problems and promote learning. In short, some evaluation devices can be employed in diagnosing learning problems, promoting learning, and deriving a grade. For example, tests can identify areas of difficulty (diagnose problems), feedback can be given when you return the examination and discuss the items (promote learning), and test grades should be recorded (derive a grade). Likewise, homework should be analyzed for problem areas; feedback comments written in the margins can promote learning; and finally, grades can be taken.

Evaluation should be a continual process as you go about the daily classroom routine. Many times you will gain valuable information regarding achievement, ability skills, or attitudes prior to or during class. Difficulties can be noted, and on-the-spot feedback can be provided to remedy the situation. Lack of response to questioning, for instance, often reveals that material is misunderstood. Trouble with a written assignment may suggest that students need further instruction. A spot check of student term papers during seat work might reveal problem areas.

Systems of Evaluation

Evaluation systems can be grouped into two categories: competitive and noncompetitive. **Competitive evaluation** systems force students to compete with other students (norm-referenced), while **noncompetitive evaluation** systems do not require interstudent comparisons, but rather are based on established sets of standards of mastery (criterion-referenced). We will take a closer look at norm-referenced and criterion-referenced tests later in this chapter. Traditionally, secondary schools have required competition among students because of the belief that it stimulated motivation.

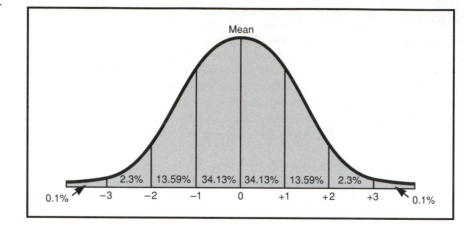

Figure 10.1 *Normal Probability Curve*

Mean

0.1%   2.3%   13.59%   34.13%   34.13%   13.59%   2.3%   0.1%

-3   -2   -1   0   +1   +2   +3

Competitive Evaluation

Most evaluators concerned with students' standing within a group make use of the *normal curve*. This curve is commonly called the *natural curve* or *chance curve* because it reflects the natural distribution of all sorts of things in nature. This distribution is shown in figure 10.1. Such a curve is appropriately used when the group being studied is large and diversified.

The **normal curve** is a mathematical construct divided into equal segments. The vertical line through the center of the curve (the mean) represents the average of a whole population on some attribute. For example, in a large population, the average (mean) IQ would be 100. Because this number represents the mean, it would occur most often and fall under the highest point on the curve. To the left of the highest point, each mark represents one standard deviation below the average. To the right of the highest point, each mark represents one standard deviation above the average. Neither side of the curve would touch the baseline, thus showing that some extreme IQ scores might exist. As shown in figure 10.1, about 34 percent of the named population on an attribute will be within one standard deviation below the mean, and about 34 percent of that population will be above the mean. About 13.5 percent of the identified population will be in the second deviation range below the mean, and 13.5 percent of the population will be in the second deviation range above the mean. About 2 percent of the population will fall in the third unit or deviation below the mean, and an equal portion will fall in the third deviation unit above the mean. Finally, about 0.1 percent of the population will fall in the extreme fourth deviation unit below the mean, and 0.1 percent will be in the fourth deviation range above the mean. Some of the many things that are subject to the normal distribution are weights and heights of animals, average temperatures over an extended period of time, and margins of error on measurements. Indeed, most schools use normal curves and standard scores when reporting the results of standardized tests.

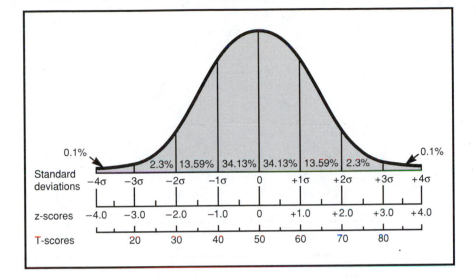

Figure 10.2
*Characteristics of the
Normal Curve*

An understanding of standard scores requires a basic knowledge of the concept of variability; that is, you must understand standard deviation. The **standard deviation** is a measure of the extent to which scores are spread out around the mean. The greater the variability of scores around the mean, the larger the standard deviation. When all the scores are identical, the standard deviation will be 0.

Standard Scores and Percentile

Most schools report student performances in terms of **standard scores,** such as z-scores, T-scores, and stanine scores, as well as in terms of percentile. These methods use the normal distribution curve to show how student performances compare with the distribution of scores above and below the mean. Standard scores provide a standard scale by which scores on different evaluative instruments by different groups may be compared reasonably (see figure 10.2). The various standard scores and percentile say the same thing in slightly different ways.

Note that z-scores and T-scores correspond to the standard deviation of the population scores: They indicate the number of standard deviations that a particular raw score is above or below the mean of the raw score distribution. Thus, a score falling one standard deviation below the mean would have a z-score of −1, a score falling two standard deviations above the mean would have a z-score of +2, and so on. The use of negative numbers is avoided by converting z-scores to T-scores. This is done by multiplying the z-score times 10 and adding a constant of 50:

$$T = 10z + 50$$

Many schools use stanine (standard nine) when reporting student performance. This technique uses the normal distribution in grouping

Figure 10.3 *Normal Distribution Curve and Stanine Scores*

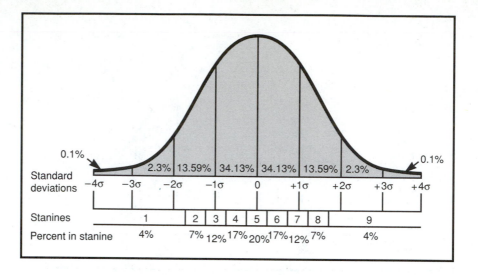

scores into nine categories, with a mean of 5 and a standard deviation of 2. Figure 10.3 gives the stanine score distribution and the percent of scores that will fall in each category.

Another type of score is the percentile. The **percentile score** indicates the percent of the population whose scores fall at or below that score. A score of 20, for example, would have 20 percent of the group falling at or below the score and 80 percent above the score. Of course, the fiftieth percentile would be the mean (see figure 10.2).

Noncompetitive Evaluation

Some researchers suggest that criterion-referenced evaluation (which do not force competition among students) contribute more to student progress than norm-referenced evaluation (Fantini, 1986). In effect, these researchers are suggesting that not all students are motivated through competition. In fact, they suggest that competition can discourage less able students who are forced to compete with more capable students. Competition can even be harmful to more capable students, because it often teaches that winning is all important.

Today, many educators feel grades should reflect a student's efforts. No one should receive an A without really trying, nor should students who are exerting themselves to their fullest potential receive an F. There is now a national call for change in how students are assessed. The feeling is that grades should reflect student progress. Performance assessment through the use of portfolios shows promise as a more viable assessment technique.

Performance Assessment Using Portfolios

Educators are trying to redesign schools to reflect changing world conditions. An essential element of that redesign is the way student learning is assessed. Much attention is being directed toward "performance" assessment.

In **performance assessment,** students demonstrate the behaviors that the assessor wants to measure (Meyer, 1992). For example, if the desired behavior is writing, students write; or if the desired behavior is identification of geometric figures, they draw or locate geometric figures. In effect, samples of students' work are compiled for evaluation. The students, the teacher, or both can select items for assessment of performance. These items are often accumulated in portfolios.

A **portfolio** can be thought of as a systematic, organized collection of evidence that documents growth and development and that represents progress made toward reaching specified goals and objectives. Portfolios enable students to display their skills and accomplishments for examination by others. Some teachers also ask that students provide a reflection on their skills and accomplishments as part of their portfolios.

Problems with Evaluation

We all like to view ourselves as fair, even-handed people. We believe it is possible and desirable to fairly evaluate our students' performance. But in order for fairness to prevail in student evaluation, we must recognize and plan for biases built into human nature and into the nature of schooling (Sax, 1980; Lyman, 1991).

A lot of research evidence suggests that certain groups of students fail to be assessed fairly because of predetermined notions on the part of primarily white, middle-class teachers about what constitutes successful school performance. Girls fare better than boys in the evaluation process partly because the structure of schools and classrooms favors the more passive socialization often demonstrated by girls. At the same time, some evidence suggests that boys begin to perform better than girls, particularly in mathematics and sciences, beginning in the middle school years (Murphy & Davidshofer, 1991). Many believe that this phenomenon is accounted for partly because boys tend to be given specific feedback regarding their academic performance, while girls are more likely to receive nonspecific feedback for both academic performance and classroom behavior. Whatever the reasons, girls and boys need to receive equal recognition and feedback for academic performance. Equally important is providing an environment that values individual and group differences within any given classroom.

Likewise, poor and minority students often do not fare well in the classroom setting. Teachers need to be aware of cultural and socioeconomic differences that may negatively influence how students are evaluated and then take every possible opportunity to reduce the influence of those factors.

Children who are creative, especially in ways not recognized within the ordinary structure of the classroom and the school, are often evaluated unfairly on the basis of pencil-and-paper tests. Children with behavior problems and other special needs are also often assessed unfairly. Poor behavior should never be a factor for determining grades. Special-needs students who have been mainstreamed should be evaluated against their own performance, not against the performance of the class as a whole.

Fairness issues and ethical issues must be considered before methods of assessment are determined. Criteria for evaluation should be related to the learning objectives. Performance standards should be established prior to assessment, not on the basis of the best example you receive. The purpose of the evaluation (diagnosis, formative, or summative) should be clear to you and clear to the students before the learning experience takes place. The results of assessment should be shared only with the students and their parents or guardians. Some circumstances will call for sharing results with the principal or counselor. The point to be made here is that assessment results are not to be shared indiscriminately. Everyone who sees the results of student assessment should have a legitimate need to know.

Clearly, if you are to make accurate judgments about student performance, you need to have confidence in the data you have collected. In other words, you must learn to employ measurement devices that provide reliable and valid information and that are usable.

Measurement Accuracy

Reliability, validity, and usability are three important qualities to every measurement device. If a teacher-made test revealed that 50 percent of an algebra class was unable to solve algebraic equations, should the teacher be concerned? The answer depends on the reliability, validity, and usability of the test—that is, the ability of the test to consistently measure what it is supposed to measure: problem-solving ability. Let's take a brief look at the three essential elements of measurement: reliability, validity, and usability.

Reliability

Reliability refers to the consistency with which a measurement device gives the same results when the measurement is repeated. In other words, it refers to the trustworthiness or dependability of the measurement device. A reliable bathroom scale, for example, would give identical weights for each of three separate weighings in a single morning. If, on the other hand, the three weighings differ by 5 pounds, the scale would not be very reliable. Likewise, a true/false test that is so ambiguously worded that students are forced to guess would probably yield different scores from one administration of the test to the next. In short, it would be extremely unreliable.

Measurement devices must provide reliable information if they are to be of value in decision making. However, no evaluation is perfect. There is always some measurement error; for example: (1) poor construction could affect the score (sampling error), (2) the attribute being measured may vary over time (trait instability), (3) scoring or recording inaccuracies will affect scores (scoring error), and (4) variables such as motivation, health, and luck can cause variance. The extent to which such errors can be minimized will determine the reliability of the measurement device.

How can teachers increase the reliability of their measurement devices? Basically, the reliability of measurement instruments can be improved by incorporating the following suggestions into their construction:

1. **Increase the Number of Evaluative Items**
   Reliability can be improved by increasing the amount of data collected. Because you will have a larger sample of the trait being evaluated, chance errors will tend to cancel each other out. Thus, a test of 30 items is more reliable than one of 20 items.

2. **Establish Optimum Item Difficulty**
   Reliability can be increased by making the items being evaluated (test or observational) of moderate difficulty. In effect, moderate item difficulty gives a moderate spread of scores, which allows you to better judge each student's performance in relation to other students. Conversely, difficult and easy items result in bunched scores, which makes it more difficult to differentiate between scores. Thus, tests made up of moderate items spread the data over a greater range than devices composed mainly of difficult or easy items. In the case of observational scales, an item with a 5-point scale would give more reliable information than a 7- or 3-point scale because it would give more consistent results than would larger or smaller scales.

3. **Write Clear Items and Directions**
   Reliability will be improved when students clearly understand what is being asked. Ambiguities and misunderstood directions lead to irrelevant errors.

4. **Administer the Evaluative Instrument Carefully**
   Reliability will be improved when students are not distracted by noises or when they are not rushed.

5. **Score Objectively**
   Reliability will be greater when objective data is collected. With subjective data, internal differences within the scorer can result in identical responses or behaviors being scored differently on different occasions.

Validity

Validity is the extent to which an evaluative device measures what it is supposed to measure. Otherwise, it measures what was taught and learned. For instance, if social studies content knowledge was taught and learned, but students scored low on the test over the content because they could not understand the questions, then the test would not be valid. We all have had teachers who taught one thing and tested over something else, or who have made the test so difficult that we performed poorly.

Although there are several types of validity, the most important one to secondary teachers is content or face validity. *Content* or *face validity* is established by determining whether the instrument's items correspond to the content that was taught in the course. Teachers sometimes construct tests that seem to address what was taught but in fact do not. For example, if instruction focused on developing issues and trends, the test should give students the opportunity for demonstrating their understanding of issues and trends. If the test focuses on names and dates, it would not have content validity. In the case of standardized tests, test inspection is carried out by subject experts. Similarly, the content validity of a teacher-made test should be evaluated by checking the correspondence of the test items with the teacher's stated outcomes. However, this simple process alone will not guarantee content validity. For example, the objectives may have been prepared by making a superficial examination of the textbook and writing objectives at random, rather than by carefully matching objectives to what was taught in class. In short, content validity requires that a teacher's test items match the actual class instruction.

Any measurement device, whether it is a test or observation instrument, must be valid to supply usable information. But an instrument is not simply valid or invalid; rather, its validity is a matter of degree, with each instrument having low, satisfactory, or high validity. Thus, the adequacy of an instrument involves a judgment regarding the usefulness of the information it provides for future decision making. Although most teachers lack the expertise or time to do extensive validity checks, they can at least make sure their test items match their stated learning objectives.

Usability

Usability is how well a measurement device is suited for gathering the desired information. For example, a 2-hour science test would not be suitable for a 50-minute class period. A test should be easy to administer and score, within budget limitations, suitable to the test conditions, and have the appropriate degree of difficulty.

Reliability, validity, and usability are all interrelated. In fact, a measurement device must be reliable and suitable for the proposed purpose before it can be valid. For example, if you cannot get consistent height measurements from a yardstick, you cannot expect it to be accurate. However, the measurements might be very consistent (reliable) but not accurate (valid). Moreover, a pencil-and-paper test would hardly be suitable for evaluating the ability to hit a tennis ball. Clearly, if a measurement device is to be used in making decisions, it is essential that the information be both reliable and valid, as well as suitable.

This concludes our discussion of the assessment process. Table 10.2 gives a review of the major assessment concepts. Before you continue, review table 10.2 and the Assessment Concepts Application Guidelines, and complete exercise 10.1.

Information Sources

Evaluation is the result of measurement. That is, evaluation requires that a judgment be made, and this judgment requires information. Therefore, you must become familiar with the different sources of evaluative information.

TABLE *10.2*   Assessment Concepts

Concept	Description
Diagnostic Evaluation	Evaluation administered prior to instruction for placement purposes
Formative Evaluation	The use of evaluation in supplying feedback during the course of a program
Summative Evaluation	A judgment made at the end of a project that determines whether it has been successful or not, and commonly used to give grades
Competitive Evaluation	Evaluation that forces students to compete with each other
Noncompetitive Evaluation	Evaluation that does not force students to compete with each other
Performance Assessment	Assessment where students demonstrate the behaviors to be measured
Portfolio	A systematic, organized collection of evidence that documents growth and development and that represents progress made toward reaching specified goals and objectives
Standard Scores	A score based on the number of standard deviations an individual is from the mean
Percentile	The point on a distribution of scores below which a given percentage of individuals fall
Reliability	The extent to which individual differences are measured consistently, or the coefficient of stability of scores
Validity	The extent to which measurements correspond with criteria—that is, the ability of a device to measure what it is supposed to measure
Usability	Suitability of a measurement device for collecting desired data

Application Guidelines ▼

Assessment Concepts

Relate Evaluation to What Is Taught

Examples:
1. Make sure assessment covers all instructional objectives.
2. Specify evaluation standards clearly.
3. Be certain that instruction and assessment are aligned.
4. Begin instrumentation preparation by determining the type and form of information desired.

Use Evaluation Appropriately and Creatively

Examples:
1. Use evaluation to enhance learning.
2. Use criterion-referenced evaluation to get students to compete with themselves.
3. Use evaluation for motivating students and providing feedback.
4. Design an assessment system that gathers information in all three domains (cognitive, affective, and psychomotor).
5. Use competition with care, because it can be damaging to less capable students.
6. Remember that all evaluation is subject to some error.

Application of Knowledge

Exercise 10.1   Assessment Concepts

Test yourself on the following assessment concepts. Appropriate responses can be found in appendix A.

1. The only purpose served by evaluation is to give grades. (True/False)

2. The two steps in the evaluation process are the following:
   a. _____   *b.* _____

3. Match each definition on the left with the appropriate term on the right.
   a. _____ Judgment made at end of project   1. Formative evaluation
   b. _____ Evaluation prior to instruction   2. Summative evaluation
   c. _____ Evaluation to supply feedback   3. Diagnostic evaluation

4. Whenever possible, competitive evaluation should be used in the classroom, because the normal curve can then be used in assigning grades. (True/False)

5. Performance assessment can only be used when measuring growth and development in the psychomotor domain. (True/False)

6. The accuracy of the information provided by any measurement device depends on the _____ , _____ , and _____.

7. All evaluation requires that some kind of judgment be made. (True/False)

Cumulative Record

Cumulative records hold the information collected on students over the school years. These records usually are stored in the guidance center office and contain such items as academic records, health records, family data, vital statistics, and other confidential information, as well as scores on tests of intelligence, aptitude, and achievement. Cumulative records also often contain behavioral comments from past teachers and administrators. These comments can prove useful in understanding the reasons for students' academic problems and disruptive behaviors. Treat these comments with great care, however, because teachers sometimes let them color their judgment or expectations. Indeed, it is recommended that you consult students' cumulative records only with good reason. An awareness of the information contained in students' files may affect your own observations and lead to the formation of inaccurate judgments. Moreover, exercise care in interpreting student test scores. Sadly, many teachers misinterpret test scores because of insufficient training.

The test scores found in cumulative files are usually those from standardized tests. As such, students' scores will be given in terms of how they compare with a large (usually national) group of students used in establishing norms for the test. That is, the scores will generally be reported in the form of standard scores, such as z-scores, T-scores, or stanine or in the form of percentiles.

Individual scores or a group of scores may vary from established norms for many reasons. For example, the content and skills addressed in a course may differ from that examined in the selected standardized test, or the test may be inappropriate for the individual students or a group in terms of difficulty, clarity of instruction, and so forth. Therefore, when you use a standardized test for collecting evaluative information, make sure it is appropriate for the group being evaluated; this isn't always an easy task.

You should also be aware that federal legislation permits the records of any student to be inspected by parents or guardians. Parents or guardians also have the right to challenge any information contained in the file. As a result, some teachers and administrators are reluctant to write comments or reports that may be considered controversial. This reluctance sometimes leads to the omission of important information that would be useful to other teachers and administrators.

Personal Contact

Information can be gathered as you interact with students on a daily basis. Your observations of students as they work and interact and your conversations with students provide valuable information that will be of assistance in planning your instruction. Indeed, observational information is available continuously in the classroom, as you watch and listen to students in numerous daily situations. For example, you can observe your students during guided practice, while they work in small groups, as they use resource materials, and as they participate in questioning sessions.

Accurate observation provides information about work habits, social adjustment, and personality that cannot be collected through pencil-and-paper tests. Observations can help you answer some of your own questions: Are students confused? Can they apply the concepts? Should I plan more activities to teach this concept? Are some students in need of special assistance?

Based on your observations related to your own instruction, you can draw certain conclusions about the academic progress of your students. Your observation during questioning, for example, might reveal that certain students have trouble with a concept, or appear to need special help, or need additional activities related to lesson concepts. Therefore, observe your students closely and be alert as they go about their daily activities. In fact, you may want to develop observational devices such as rating scales or checklists to ensure that your observational information is more accurate.

The information obtained through careful observation needs to be recorded and organized in a way that ensures accuracy and ready access, so insights can be gleaned about learning and development. Without a written record, you are often left with only general impressions of classroom actions. Over time, classroom impressions will fade, become distorted, or blend into one another—which will result in an inaccurate and biased picture of what has transpired. The development and use of an anecdotal record form, such as that shown in figure 10.4, can prove useful in recording some of your observations.

It is important that you include students in the evaluative process. Students can be asked whether or not they understand material or how they feel about a particular topic of discussion. They can also report best

Figure 10.4 *Anecdotal Record Form*

```
Student: _____          Date: _____

Description of environment/class: _____
_____
_____


Description of incident: _____
_____
_____
_____
_____


Reported by: _____
```

on their beliefs regarding the value of what they have learned, of what they are still unsure, and of their readiness for formal testing on a topic. In fact, information about student problem areas can often be obtained from casual conversations before and after class. Formal and informal conversations with students may be among the best techniques for gaining diagnostic and formative evaluative information. Therefore, pay close attention to students' comments when they want to talk about needed help or academic concerns. Such exchanges and questions will give you the opportunity for gaining valuable information not readily available from other sources. However, exercise caution when considering the reliability of the information gleaned from students: They may choose to tell you what they think you want to hear. So combine your observations with the students' self-reports before making instructional judgments.

The use of observation is not without its critics. Many believe that observation is too subjective to provide reasonable evaluation and, further, that keeping good observational records is too time-consuming to be practical. Simple observational instruments, however, can be devised prior to the lesson under observation, which in turn reduces recordkeeping concerns. The simple instrument of making several copies of the classroom layout, for example, could be used for a variety of purposes (see figure 10.5). You could record the physical movement of students during seatwork time. Who was out of their seats and why? Did they go to the pencil sharpener? the stack of dictionaries? the wastebasket? the teacher's desk for help or materials? In this way, you could analyze potential problem areas that might keep students from remaining on task.

The same instrument (figure 10.5) could be employed in following the flow of a questioning session. By devising a simple code, you could indicate who answered and who asked questions. You could break it down further by noting whether the questions answered were higher- or lower-order questions. Later analysis could reveal which students demonstrated understanding of the material and at what level of performance. It also

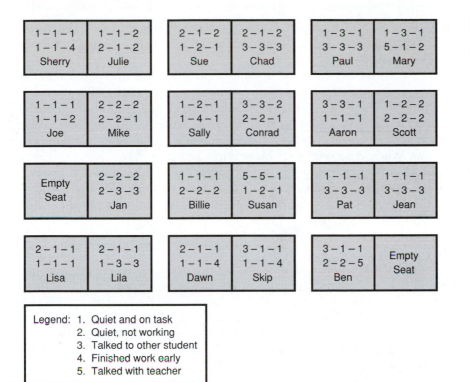

1 – 1 – 1 1 – 1 – 4 Sherry	1 – 1 – 2 2 – 1 – 2 Julie		2 – 1 – 2 1 – 2 – 1 Sue	2 – 1 – 2 3 – 3 – 3 Chad		1 – 3 – 1 3 – 3 – 3 Paul	1 – 3 – 1 5 – 1 – 2 Mary
1 – 1 – 1 1 – 1 – 2 Joe	2 – 2 – 2 2 – 2 – 1 Mike		1 – 2 – 1 1 – 4 – 1 Sally	3 – 3 – 2 2 – 2 – 1 Conrad		3 – 3 – 1 1 – 1 – 1 Aaron	1 – 2 – 2 2 – 2 – 2 Scott
Empty Seat	2 – 2 – 2 2 – 3 – 3 Jan		1 – 1 – 1 2 – 2 – 2 Billie	5 – 5 – 1 1 – 2 – 1 Susan		1 – 1 – 1 3 – 3 – 3 Pat	1 – 1 – 1 3 – 3 – 3 Jean
2 – 1 – 1 1 – 1 – 1 Lisa	2 – 1 – 1 1 – 3 – 3 Lila		2 – 1 – 1 1 – 1 – 4 Dawn	3 – 1 – 1 1 – 1 – 4 Skip		3 – 1 – 1 2 – 2 – 5 Ben	Empty Seat

Legend: 1. Quiet and on task
2. Quiet, not working
3. Talked to other student
4. Finished work early
5. Talked with teacher

Figure 10.5 *Seating Chart Record of Classroom Behaviors*

might indicate the level of interest in the topic if, for example, the questions were answered on an all-volunteer basis. Thus, once teachers have refined their observational skills, the objectivity of personal-contact information can be greatly enhanced through appropriate instrumentation. (We will address this issue later in the chapter.) Moreover, the time committed to personal-contact recordkeeping can be kept under control by opening a portfolio for each student and adding a few descriptive phrases periodically. Examples might include such phrases as ''Mary has difficulty remembering to bring her book to class,'' ''John must be continuously reinforced to study,'' and ''Ron has trouble with fine motor adjustments in chemistry lab.''

The point to keep in mind is that observation is only productive if it has a clear purpose (e.g., determining if students are on task); if all students have the opportunity to be observed equally; if the rating of performance is consistent with previously established criteria; and if the information gathered is later contemplated, analyzed, and used for improving instruction and learning.

Analysis

Teachers monitor students' work on a regular basis; that is, they analyze it for possible errors. Analysis of students' work can take place during or following instruction, and, as with other techniques we have discussed, analysis has the advantage of not being a formal test with its accompanying pressures. However, analysis is more formal than personal contact.

Analysis is important in that it provides the opportunity for correcting faulty beliefs or practice. A teacher can reteach skills during the learning process by analyzing the students' work as it is produced, probing for understanding, and suggesting new approaches to problem solving. This practice can enhance the students' abilities to self-analyze their performances. When combined with observation and inquiry, analysis can provide useful clues into the students' thinking processes and skills acquisition. For this reason, a good rule to follow is to not assign work unless it is going to be graded immediately by the teacher, another student, or the student himself or herself.

Students can and should be involved in the evaluation process. They can be called on to reflect about and critique their own work and the work of their peers. If this type of evaluation is to be successful, the criteria for performance should be clearly outlined prior to the exercise. The teacher must determine if the students understand the criteria for review before allowing such an exercise to take place. Peer critiques are especially effective in a cooperative-learning exercise. After a peer review session, students should be afforded the opportunity to revise their work before a grade is assigned.

Analysis is a useful tool for demonstrating progress or the lack of progress to parents. Samples of each student's work should be kept in a file. This file can be reviewed periodically, and progress can be noted. Students should have the opportunity to review and critique previous work. Many students will enjoy the chance to improve on something they did earlier in the year. Both samples should be kept to show improvement. Any written critique or analysis done by the teacher needs to be as objective as possible. Once again, planning and determining criteria prior to analysis improves the quality of the analysis.

Open-Ended Themes and Diaries

Secondary teachers have long been aware of the influences that peer groups and out-of-school activities have on classroom learning. Therefore, knowledge about the social climate and activities in which students live can be indispensable in the evaluation process. This information will make it possible for adjusting the curriculum so that it better addresses out-of-school differences in students' lives. For example, if most of the students in your class have after-school jobs, it may not be wise to assign a lot of homework.

One technique that can be used for gaining valuable information about students is simply to ask them to write about different in-school and out-of-school topics. You might ask students to react to questions such as these:

1. What profession would you most like to make your life work? What profession would you least like to make your life work?

TABLE *10.3*	Steps to a Successful Conference
Step 1	*Planning ahead.* Establish your purpose. Plan what you intend to say, what information you want to obtain, what are your concerns. Plan what your next step will be in the classroom as a result of the conference.
Step 2	*Starting the conference.* Be positive. Begin the conference with a positive statement.
Step 3	*Holding the conference.* Establish a positive sharing relationship. Be an active listener. Be accepting with regard to input and advice. Establish a partnership so all concerned can work toward a common goal.
Step 4	*Ending the conference.* End the conference on a positive note. Communicate the fact that in working together the common goals will be reached.
Step 5	*Conducting follow-up contact.* Keep all parties informed. Send notes and make phone calls to share successes and/or further concerns.

2. What do you want to do with your life?

3. What is your favorite leisure pastime? Why?

4. What persons do you most like to spend your free time with? Why?

5. How do you feel about the students in this school?

Of course, many of the comments and views expressed in students' writing will be distorted to some extent; nevertheless, students' views of reality will often be revealed when their writing is analyzed.

Diary writing on a periodic schedule (for example, once a week) is another method for obtaining evaluative information. A diary can consist of a record book in which students write about their concerns and feelings. Under conditions of good positive rapport, students will often communicate their true concerns and feelings openly and freely.

Conferences

Parental conferences may be needed for gathering evaluative information. Parents sometimes can shed light on students' social and academic problems. Parent conferences, however, are most beneficial when they are scheduled ahead of time and when they are well planned. Table 10.3 offers some helpful steps on holding parental conferences. Such conferences should not be a time for lecturing parents or for giving them advice on the proper rearing of the student. The overall atmosphere should be positive.

Information useful in making evaluative judgments can often be obtained from other teachers who have had your students in their classes. These colleagues can share the difficulties these students had in their classes, some techniques that were used to correct problems, and their evaluative judgments. Like conferences with parents, however, conferences with other teachers should be scheduled and well planned so that sufficient time will be available for productive meetings.

Finally, the school's support personnel—such as counselors, assistant principals, and even secretaries—can be an excellent source of information. For example, counselors can help interpret and shed light on test results, as well as on personality factors that might affect student performance.

Testing

All of you have taken tests. You have taken weekly exams in English or history, and you have taken state-mandated achievement tests during most of your school years. If you examine the purposes of tests, then you have some idea of how testing can be used most effectively. You will also develop an understanding of the limitations of testing for determining some aspects of learning.

According to Sax (1980, p. 13) a **test** may be defined as "a task or series of tasks used to obtain systematic observations presumed to be representative of educational or psychological traits or attributes." This definition implies that a test must be developed systematically (using specific guidelines) and must provide a specific description of the traits or attributes being measured as well as an established procedure for responding and scoring. Tests are classified according to (1) how they are administered (individually or in groups); (2) how they are scored (objectively or subjectively); (3) the emphasis of the response (speed or accuracy); (4) the type of response (performance or pencil-and-paper); and (5) the comparison groups (teacher-made or standardized).

Tests are generally constructed to provide one of two types of interpretations: norm-referenced and criterion-referenced. A **norm-referenced** test interpretation is made when you compare a student's score with that of a norm group (a large representative sample) in obtaining meaning. That is, a norm-referenced test compares individuals with one another. This comparison is made when you need to know how your students perform in relation to others at the same age or grade level. A **criterion-referenced test** interpretation is made when you compare an individual's score against a predetermined standard. In effect, students are compared with an absolute standard, such as 60 percent or 80 percent correct. Teacher-made tests generally belong in the criterion-referenced group, because students are compared with criteria specified by the teacher.

Tests are given for many reasons. The most common reason is for determining cognitive achievement. Tests are also often used in measuring attitudes, feelings, and motor skills.

There are many types of testings carried out in the classroom, including pretests, posttests, chapter exams, unit exams, midterms, final exams, standardized tests, and quizzes. The type of testing will depend on your needs and the purpose for collecting the data. Because of problems associated with reliability, validity, and usability, however, extra care must be taken in selecting tests that measure attitudes, feelings, and motor skills.

Good tests are carefully constructed and administered, but have certain limitations. For example, most tests do not measure environmental factors or student motivations. Moreover, you must guard against tests that are poorly administered and vulnerable to student guessing. Unless tests are carefully constructed and administered, the danger of testing superficial learning exists. Even under the best of conditions, pencil-and-paper tests—which are used more often than other kinds of assessment techniques—tend to place more value on knowing than on thinking, on verbalizing than on doing, and on teacher expectations than on student beliefs and values. With careful thought, however, you can construct tests that assess thinking ability. The problem is that most teachers lack either the skill or time to construct proper tests. Although important and probably the most common measurement technique used by teachers, testing should be thought of as only one of several techniques that you can implement for obtaining information about student progress. We will deal with test construct in greater detail in chapter 11.

Objective Observation

Observation can be an effective evaluative technique. But as we noted earlier, observation often lacks reliability and validity. For example, you may view students you like differently than those you dislike, let the time of day affect your observation, or allow your perceptions to change with time. Lack of objective observation can be overcome to some extent through the use of rating scales, checklists, or other written guides that help objectify observations. Let us look first at the design and use of rating scales.

Rating Scales

Some instructional objectives require students to engage in performance activities that preclude assessment through standard pencil-and-paper tests. In such cases, proficiency often can be assessed through rating scales. Rating scales can be extremely helpful in enhancing your observations' validity and reliability. They can be used in judging skills, products, procedures, social behaviors, and attitudes.

A **rating scale** is nothing more than a specific set of characteristics or qualities that are arranged in order of quality. Indications are made along the scale in such a way that a judgment can be made about the degree to which the attribute being assessed is present. For example, a scale for assessing student involvement in a group project might have 5 steps, with the lowest category labeled Uninvolved and the top labeled Involved. It might look like this:

The rater would develop the criteria for what to look for in group involvement and mark students against the criteria. The scale shown above could be modified and additional scales added to construct a more detailed instrument for assessing total group involvement. This instrument might be similar to the one shown in figure 10.6.

Scales similar to those presented in figure 10.6 can be developed for observations of students' social behaviors, attitudes, or products. You

Figure 10.6 *Rating Scale for Group Involvement*

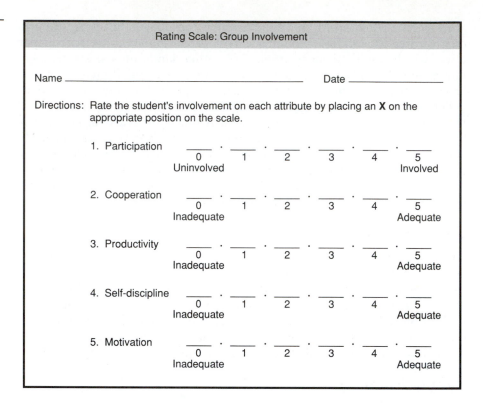

Rating Scale: Group Involvement

Name _____ Date _____

Directions: Rate the student's involvement on each attribute by placing an **X** on the appropriate position on the scale.

1. Participation

0	1	2	3	4	5
Uninvolved					Involved

2. Cooperation

0	1	2	3	4	5
Inadequate					Adequate

3. Productivity

0	1	2	3	4	5
Inadequate					Adequate

4. Self-discipline

0	1	2	3	4	5
Inadequate					Adequate

5. Motivation

0	1	2	3	4	5
Inadequate					Adequate

need only change the attributes assessed and perhaps change the scale classification. For example, you might want to change the 0-to-5 scale values shown in figure 10.6 to a more appropriate scale value, such as this:

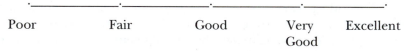

Poor   Fair   Good   Very   Excellent
                                          Good

Rating scales let the observer separate a total performance into various subskills, and, with appropriate scale judgments, a more objective determination of a student's performance can be obtained. However, even though more valid and reliable observations will result, some uncertainty will still exist.

Checklists

Checklists are similar to rating scales in that both are used for gathering information about physical kinds of student behaviors. However, a **checklist** differs from a rating scale in that it indicates the presence or absence of identified attributes. A checklist basically is a list of the criteria against which a student's performance or end product is judged. With a checklist, a teacher simply checks off the criteria items that have been met.

Figure 10.7
Performance Checklist for an Oral Report

```
┌─────────────────────────────────────────────────────────────┐
│                 Performance Checklist: Oral Report            │
│                                                               │
│  Name _____    Date _____         │
│                                                               │
│  Directions:  Check Yes or No as to whether criterion level is met.│
│                                                               │
│     Did the student:                           Yes      No    │
│     1. Use correct grammar .....................  ____    ____ │
│     2. Speak clearly ...........................  ____    ____ │
│     3. Use appropriate posture .................  ____    ____ │
│     4. Use correct vocabulary ..................  ____    ____ │
│     5. Make presentation interesting ...........  ____    ____ │
│     6. Use visual(s) ...........................  ____    ____ │
│     7. Use appropriate voice projection ........  ____    ____ │
│                                                               │
└─────────────────────────────────────────────────────────────┘
```

Figure 10.7
Performance Checklist for an Oral Report

The ways in which responses are recorded on a checklist can vary. The simplest way is to use a check mark when indicating that a listed action has occurred. For example, a checklist for assessing student readiness for a lesson might look like this:

___ *1.* Reading assignment completed.

___ *2.* Completed homework.

___ *3.* Has book, pencil, and paper.

___ *4.* Demonstrates understanding of related vocabulary.

You would simply check those items that had been demonstrated.

Some checklists use a simple *yes* or *no* response for recording the occurrence (or nonoccurrence) of an action. The *yes* is checked when an action has been observed at the required criterion level; the *no* is checked when the action has not been performed at the criterion level. An example of this type of checklist used to judge an oral report is shown in figure 10.7. You would check the appropriate column on each item to indicate whether the performance level has been met.

Checklists sensitize the observer to the various parts of desired student actions. By collecting reliable data on the component parts, you are able to evaluate the overall performance with greater accuracy.

Questionnaires

Attitudes, feelings, and opinions are often difficult for teachers to evaluate. Indeed, some attitudinal behaviors may not occur on a daily basis. One technique for overcoming this difficulty is to have students complete a questionnaire. **Questionnaires** call on students to examine themselves and react to a series of statements about their attitudes, feelings, and opinions. Because questionnaires require self-reporting of these attributes, it is important that you recognize the potential for persons to choose socially correct responses rather than indicate true beliefs. Nonetheless, questionnaires, especially those administered anonymously, can provide valuable information. The questionnaire designer decides what information is wanted and then writes statements or questions that will elicit this information. Questionnaires' response styles can vary from simple checklist-type responses to open-ended statements. Whenever possible, design your questionnaires so that they call for short answers only.

Questionnaires requiring checklist-type responses usually provide a list of descriptive or value-laden adjectives, or a list of features following a stem, or a guiding statement and instructions to mark those that apply. For example, a checklist-type questionnaire designed to evaluate a science lesson might include statements such as these:

1. The lesson was
   ___ important.
   ___ interesting.
   ___ boring.
   ___ unimportant.

2. I find science
   ___ fun.
   ___ exciting.
   ___ boring.
   ___ difficult.

The scoring of the checklist type of test is simple. The number of negative statements checked is subtracted from the number of positive statements checked. The result is the positiveness of the attribute being measured.

A second type of questionnaire usually involves a 7-point scale that links an adjective to its opposite. This scale is called a **semantic differential** and is effective for assessing degrees of attitudes, beliefs, and feelings—from very favorable to highly unfavorable. An example of a semantic differential used in assessing students' attitudes toward school might look like this:

School is:

Exciting ____:____:____:____:____:____:____ Boring

Good ____:____:____:____:____:____:____ Bad

Safe ____:____:____:____:____:____:____ Unsafe

Pleasant ____:____:____:____:____:____:____ Unpleasant

The composite score for each student on the total questionnaire can be determined by assigning numbers to the scale options and adding responses for each scale on the instrument.

A frequently used response style in attitude measurement is the **Likert scale.** Likert scales are 5-point scales that link the options "strongly agree" and "strongly disagree" as follows:

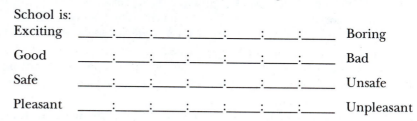

| Strongly disagree | Disagree | Undecided | Agree | Strongly agree |

```
┌─────────────────────────────────────────────────────────────┐
│                   Attitude Scale: Mathematics                 │
│                                                               │
│  Name _____  Date _____       │
│                                                               │
│  Each of the statements below expresses a feeling toward      │
│  mathematics. Rate each statement on the extent to which you  │
│  agree. For each you may strongly agree (A), agree (B), be    │
│  undecided (C), disagree (D), or strongly disagree (E).       │
│                                                               │
│    (A)        (B)        (C)         (D)           (E)         │
│  Strongly    Agree    Undecided   Disagree      Strongly      │
│   agree                                         disagree      │
│                                                               │
│    Mathematics is fun to do. ..........................  ____  │
│    I don't like mathematics. It is too difficult. .....  ____  │
│    Mathematics is easy to understand. .................  ____  │
│    In general I have good feelings toward mathematics. .  ____  │
│    I approach all mathematics with hesitation. ........  ____  │
│    I feel at ease when doing mathematics. .............  ____  │
│    Mathematics make me feel uncomfortable,                    │
│    irritable, and impatient. .........................  ____   │
│    I feel a definite positive reaction toward mathematics. ____│
│                                                               │
└─────────────────────────────────────────────────────────────┘
```

Students respond to statements by checking the options that most closely represent their feelings about the statements. An example of a Likert scale instrument is shown in figure 10.8. The Likert scale is generally scored by assigning a value between 1 and 5 to the available options. The value 1 is usually assigned to the option "strongly disagree" and 5 to the option "strongly agree." Assigned scale values usually are reversed when the statement is negative. A composite score for students can be calculated by adding all the scale values.

Another type of response style that can be used on questionnaires is the open-ended question. Open-ended sentences are presented, and students are asked to complete them with words that best express their feelings, for example:

I find social studies to be _____ .

This class is _____ .

The responses are then scored as to content for each respondent.

There are several advantages associated with using questionnaires: They can be administered in a relatively short period of time, they can help students clarify their feelings, they generally are easy to score, and they can often be used in helping students improve their vocabulary. A problem associated with the questionnaire, however, is that one cannot be absolutely sure that true feelings are being expressed.

TABLE 10.4   Information Sources and Evaluation Instruments

Concept	Description
Cumulative Record	File that holds information collected on students during the school years
Personal Contact	The collection of data through daily interactions and observations of students
Analysis	An examination of students' work
Open-Ended Themes and Diaries	The periodic writing of students on in-school and out-of-school topics
Conference	Meeting between individuals regarding issues of common concern to both parties
Testing	A task or series of tasks used in obtaining systematic observations
Rating Scale	Set of characteristics arranged in order of quality so that performance can be better judged
Checklist	Listing of characteristics used for indicating presence or absence of identified attributes
Questionnaire	Statements to which students react in order to examine their attitudes, feelings, and opinions

Application Guidelines ▼

Information Sources and Evaluation Instruments

Use a Variety of Data Sources Wisely

Examples:
1. Think through your comments before writing on the student's paper.
2. Use multiple sources when evaluating student performance.
3. Collect and carefully review samples of students' class work periodically to determine their strengths and weaknesses.
4. Regularly review students' diaries or journals.
5. Develop students' self-evaluation skills through the use of peer editing groups.
6. Listen carefully to parents' questions and concerns.

Use a Variety of Techniques to Improve Assessment Judgment

Examples:
1. Record and organize observational data in a way that ensures accuracy and ready access.
2. Record observations in a timely fashion so recollection remains vivid and thus accurate.
3. Avoid the halo effect—that is, always rating good students high.
4. Develop checklists to help students develop appropriate behaviors or acceptable products.

This concludes our formal discussion of information sources and evaluative instruments. Table 10.4 gives a summary of the information sources and evaluative instruments addressed in this chapter. Review table 10.4 and the Information Sources and Evaluation Instruments Application Guidelines, and complete exercise 10.2.

Application of Knowledge

Exercise 10.2 Information Sources and Evaluation Instruments

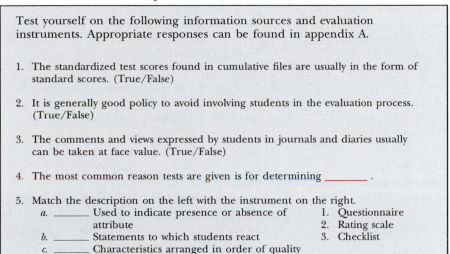

Test yourself on the following information sources and evaluation instruments. Appropriate responses can be found in appendix A.

1. The standardized test scores found in cumulative files are usually in the form of standard scores. (True/False)

2. It is generally good policy to avoid involving students in the evaluation process. (True/False)

3. The comments and views expressed by students in journals and diaries usually can be taken at face value. (True/False)

4. The most common reason tests are given is for determining _____ .

5. Match the description on the left with the instrument on the right.
   a. _____ Used to indicate presence or absence of attribute
   b. _____ Statements to which students react
   c. _____ Characteristics arranged in order of quality

   1. Questionnaire
   2. Rating scale
   3. Checklist

CHAPTER SUMMARY

Evaluating student learning is a complex endeavor that demands the same careful planning necessary for teaching content. Evaluation is an essential tool for teachers, because it gives them feedback concerning what their students have learned. Evaluation helps you become a better planner, and it enables you to better understand students, their abilities, interests, attitudes, and needs so that you can better teach and motivate them.

The three types of evaluation are diagnostic, formative, and summative. Diagnostic evaluation is carried out prior to instruction for placement purposes. Formative evaluation is used during instruction for promoting learning. Summative evaluation follows instruction and is used in judging the end product of learning.

Evaluation can be competitive, noncompetitive, or performance-based. With competitive evaluation, students must compete with each other, whereas with noncompetitive evaluation, students compete with themselves. Unlike most evaluation techniques, performance assessment demands that students demonstrate skills and accomplishments.

Evaluation requires information. Therefore, you must develop skills in using various information-gathering devices and the best data-recording instruments. You must develop an awareness of the information that is obtainable from cumulative records, personal contacts, analysis, open-ended themes and diaries, conferences, and testing.

The recording of reliable data calls for the selection of appropriate instrumentation. This selection will be related to the specific domain under study. For example, the desired data may require measurement in the cognitive domain (achievement), the psychomotor domain (process or performance), or the affective domain (attitudes, feelings, or opinions). Measurement in the cognitive domain generally requires a test (achievement or teacher-made) or some type of written work, whereas measurement of processes and performances usually is carried out best through rating scales, checklists, and questionnaires.

The measurement of achievement is usually achieved through teacher-made tests. In contrast, measurements of feelings, attitudes, and options are the most difficult to obtain and are usually measured through observations or questionnaires.

Discussion Questions and Activities

1. **Test-bank critique.** Examine and critique the test materials included in a published program of study for the subject area and grade level you would like to teach. What changes would you make before using the materials?

2. **Evaluation purposes.** List five purposes of evaluation. Why should there be a match between the method of evaluation and the purpose of evaluation?

3. **Evaluation systems.** Study the evaluation system of a teacher in the subject area and grade level you would like to teach. Determine the extent to which the teacher uses norm-referenced and criterion-referenced evaluation.

4. **Observation.** Develop a simple observation instrument to keep track of the questions answered by students in a classroom. Use the instrument in an actual classroom. Did your observational instrument make it easier to keep track of the question-and-answer sequence? How would you modify the original instrument?

5. **Conferences.** Plan a general conference with a parent for the first time. Discuss what topics might be important to include in a conference.

6. **Rating scales.** Develop a rating scale for assessing a common classroom behavior problem. Use the scale in an actual classroom. How helpful was your rating scale?

7. **Evaluating students.** List all the evaluation practices you think are beneficial to students and their learning. Now list all the practices you think are harmful to students and learning. Reflect on the two lists you have generated.

11 ▼ Test Construction and Grading

✎ **You groan when you realize that the "end of the nine" weeks is again approaching. You will be called on to justify a grade for each student's performance. Assigning grades is so complex that it is difficult to explain. Or is it really that complex?**

Overview

Teachers must test. These tests can be commercially produced or teacher-made. Therefore, teachers must be aware of how standardized tests are produced, as well as how to write test items and design tests.

The final step in the evaluation process is the interpretation of collected information in assigning grades. To do so, teachers must be able to arrange information in an objective and impersonal way.

This chapter has been designed to help prospective teachers better understand testing, to improve test-construction skills, and to better understand grading and the assignment of grades. To these ends, the focus will be on test types, test item construction, and the assignment of grades based on evaluative data.

Objectives

After completing your study of chapter 11, you should be able to do the following:

1. Given the purpose of the test, correctly determine the best type of test for that purpose.

2. Compare and contrast standardized tests and teacher-made tests.

3. Compare and contrast the different types of teacher-made test items and the advantages and disadvantages associated with each.

4. Construct the different types of items that can be included in teacher-made tests.

5. List the purposes for assigning grades.

6. Assign letter grades for participating students, and provide a valid rationale for this assignment.

Most secondary schools put their primary emphasis on learning in the cognitive domain. Although there are a number of ways of measuring knowledge in the cognitive domain, the most common is through the use of tests. These tests can be published by commercial testing bureaus, or they can be designed and constructed by individual teachers.

Tests are designed and administered for various purposes. Some are given for diagnostic purposes, while others are given for determining grades. As such, tests are sometimes given before instruction; others, after instruction. Indeed, at times a single test may be given before instruction for diagnosis (pretest) and again after instruction for determining student progress (posttest). Tests are also designed and administered for measuring student achievement. The measured achievement can be used in comparing students' scores with one another (norm-referenced tests) or in comparing students' scores with predetermined criteria (criterion-referenced tests).

As a teacher, you will be responsible for selecting the tests for your classroom. This will not always be easy.

Types of Tests

The compilation of evaluative information requires the use of some form of data-recording instrument. Of course, the most popular instrument in secondary schools today is the test. Consequently, we will discuss in this section the general characteristics of two commonly used testing devices: standardized tests and teacher-made tests. Detailed guidelines for constructing these tests are beyond the scope of this book. For more information on test construction, we recommend that you consult a basic textbook that details the construction, validation, and administration of tests.

Standardized Tests

Ebel and Frisbie (1991) define a **standardized test** as one that has been constructed by experts with explicit instructions for administration, standard scoring procedures, and tables of norms for interpretation. Standardized tests measure individual performance on a group-administered and group-normed test. Standardization means that the examinees attempt the same questions under the same conditions with the same directions, the time limit for taking the test is the same for everyone, and the results are scored with the same detailed procedure.

The preparation, editing, and analysis of standardized tests are undertaken commercially by experts in the respective field covered. First, these experts write a battery of content questions related to the subject field that should be answerable by the average, well-informed student at the targeted grade level. These questions are then tried out on a representative sample of students in the subject area at the specified grade level from all kinds of schools in all parts of the country. Based on the results obtained from the representative sample, the test is revised, and a final version of the exam is written. The exam is then administered to a sample of students that is larger and more carefully selected to represent the target subject area and grade level. This latter sample of students form the norming group against which all subsequent student scores will be compared. The final step in the development of the standardized test is the production of a test manual that provides clear directions for administration and scoring of the test, as well as certain information related to the test characteristics and interpretation of scores.

Standardized tests are particularly useful in comparing the performance of one individual with another, of an individual against a group, or of one group with another group. Such comparisons become possible because of the availability of the norming-group data and the uniformity of the procedures for administration and scoring of the test. Thus, you could compare a single school with other schools in a district, compare districts, compare states, or compare students in one state with all students in the nation. For example, suppose a student scored 80 percent on a physics test. For most purposes, this is sufficient information for evaluation purposes, but at times you might want to know how a physics score of 80 percent compares to the physics scores of other students in the district, state, or nation.

Standardized tests come in the form of test batteries and single-subject tests. Some standardized tests are used in assessing personality, but the most commonly used secondary school standardized test measures knowledge in specific areas, such as English, social studies, psychology, or chemistry. These tests are usually referred to as *achievement tests,* because they measure how much a student has learned in a particular subject area. Other secondary school standardized tests that are commonly used are those that measure students' aptitudes or abilities for performing certain activities. These tests are designed to measure an individual's potential in a given field—such as journalism, mathematics, law, drafting, teaching, or auto mechanics—and are given a variety of labels, including general ability tests, intelligence tests, or scholastic aptitude tests.

Standardized test results generally include a percentile norm, an age norm, and a grade-level norm, or some combination of these norms. Teachers are often called on to interpret these norms for parents. Therefore, you need a basic understanding of their meaning. At the most basic level, a percentile rank (see chapter 10) of 85 indicates that 85 percent of the norm group performed more poorly and 15 percent performed better than the individual in question. An age rank of 15.6 means that, regardless of chronological age, the student got the same number of right answers as did the average 15 1/2-year-old in the norm group: The number to the left of the decimal point represents years, and the number to the right of the decimal point represents months. Grade-level norms are the most widely reported and the least useful of the measures. Grade-level norms are reported as grade equivalent scores, with the tenths place representing the months in a 10-month school year. The only real value of grade equivalent scores is that they determine if the test was too easy or too difficult for students scoring at a particular level.

Sax (1980) and Ebel and Frisbie (1991) report that standardized achievement tests are most properly used when making these decisions:

1. Determining placement in differentiated instructional tracks.

2. Individualizing instruction for remediation or acceleration.

3. Diagnosing areas of strength and weakness.

4. Gauging the effectiveness of an instructional program or group of programs.

5. Evaluating the extent of student progress.

6. Determining teaching emphasis and effectiveness.

While the above reasons present a strong case for using standardized tests in educational decision making, it is important to recognize that a too narrow or too broad interpretation of results can lead to oversimplifying a complex situation. For example, one English class performs more poorly on grammar than another. Can you assume that the teacher is doing a poor job of teaching grammar concepts? Probably not. And certainly not without more information about the composition of the two classes. The poor performance could be explained by a large number of mainstreamed special-needs students in the first class, or by the fact that all school assemblies and announcements occur during second period, reducing instructional time during that period.

Standardized tests and teacher-made tests are given for different reasons. Standardized tests generally cover a much broader range of a content area than a teacher-made test, which is designed to measure achievement in a particular unit of work. Thus, achievement tests in the classroom should supplement teacher-made evaluation. The use of standardized tests will continue to play an important role for educational decision making and for public reporting on the state of school learning. But standardized tests are only one method for evaluating learning. The tests can give valuable information on how well your students are doing overall in comparison with other student groups.

Certain limitations are also associated with the use of standardized tests. For example, their validity is often questionable in situations in which they do not measure what was taught; that is, they may not be consistent with the goals and objectives established by the teacher. Moreover, standardized tests are likely to have some social and cultural bias, which means that the test may discriminate against certain social and cultural groups that lack prerequisite language, background experience, or testing experiences.

Teacher-Made Tests

Teacher-made tests are the most common of all secondary school evaluative instruments. There are three basic reasons for the popularity of teacher-made tests in the secondary school. First, they can be constructed so they are consistent with classroom goals and objectives. Second, teacher-made tests present the same questions to all students under nearly

identical conditions. This means that the test results provide the means and basis for making comparative judgments among students. Third, teacher-made tests generate a product that can be evaluated and easily stored for later use. This means that tests and results can be readily accessible for review by students and parents when explaining how grades were determined. In addition, teacher-made tests are much less expensive to construct and administer.

Although teacher-made tests have their advantages, the bulk of these tests will have unknown or low reliability, and most secondary teachers lack the skill for designing valid tests or writing appropriate test items. However, they remain an important part of the instructional process. Consequently, you should further develop and refine your skills in test construction.

Teachers have three basic alternatives in constructing tests: They can construct an objective test, an essay test, or possibly a combination. Objective tests comprise alternative-choice, multiple-choice, matching, and completion items, whereas essay tests include supply items. Furthermore, these supply items can be written either as brief- or extended-essay questions; that is, the students must supply short or elaborate responses. Brief essay items ask students to write a sentence or short paragraph, solve a problem, or give a proof, while the extended essay items require that students write at length. The item type or types used in the construction of a particular test will depend on your objectives and the nature of the behaviors being measured.

Test items should be written at the taxonomical level of your objectives. Contrary to common belief, this can be accomplished with almost any type of test item—objective or essay. Although it is more difficult to write objective items at the higher levels, it is also difficult to write high-level essay items.

Instructional objectives usually suggest the best type of test item. For example, an objective that involves solving physics problems would probably be best evaluated through the use of brief-essay items, while knowledge of the definitions of terms would probably be best evaluated through the use of multiple-choice items. In general, however, when objectives lend themselves to more than one type of test item, most teachers prefer objective items over essay types because of their scoring ease and reliability.

Tests in the secondary classroom generally should not contain more than two different types of test items. Students may have trouble when they must shift to different types of responses. Therefore, if your objectives can be evaluated by one or two different test types, then limit your test to these types.

The purpose of testing is to check student mastery of the stated objectives. Therefore, one overall principle applies to the writing of all test items: Every item should separate those students who have mastered the objectives from those who have not. Students who cannot respond should not be able to guess or bluff their way to success on a test. Moreover, "test wiseness" (the ability to answer questions through the use of clues from the question) should be guarded against when constructing a test. Let us now briefly consider the various types of test items commonly used by secondary teachers.

Alternate-Choice Items

The simplest form of objective test item is the alternate-choice type. The true/false format is the most common form of alternate-choice item. Variations on the basic true/false item include yes/no, right/wrong, and agree/disagree items.

Alternate-choice items tend to be popular because they appear to be easy to write. These items, generally, are simple declarative sentences. Unfortunately, writing good alternate-choice items requires skill, if you are to avoid triviality and discourage guessing. Writing good true/false items is difficult because there are few assertions that are unambiguously true or false. Therefore, because of this particular sensitivity to ambiguity, it is especially crucial that your alternate-choice items be stated as clearly as possible. For instance, consider the following:

Poor: The value of pi is 3.14.   T F

This question is ambiguous; 3.14 is not the exact value of pi, but it is a commonly used value. A totally clear question could be rewritten as follows:

Better: The value of pi is approximately 3.14.   T F

This question is better because it allows for the small difference between what is commonly used as the value of pi and the exact value. Here are some further suggestions for improving the writing of alternate-choice items.

1. Avoid the use of negative statements and double negatives. Such statements can be confusing and may cause knowledgeable students to get them wrong.

2. Make sure an item is not dependent on insignificant facts. Make sure that your items ask something important and worth remembering. For example, a statement should not be false because an individual's seldom-used first name is asked. Do not use trick items that appear to be true but are false because of an inconspicuous word or phrase.

3. Don't make your false items more lengthy than your true items (or vice versa). If you find it necessary to write a few lengthy true items, make sure that you supply approximately the same number of lengthy false items.

4. Watch for item response patterns. Generally, the proportion of true and false items in a test should not be too different. Similarly, guard against correct-response patterns—such as T T T F F F or T F T F T F—that could help students achieve a misleading number of correct answers.

5. Be clear and concise. Use simple grammar in item construction. Avoid dependent clauses and compound sentences.

6. Limit each statement to only one central idea. Don't mix true and false ideas in a single statement.

7. Be especially sensitive to the use of certain key words that can divulge the correct response. Words such as *always, never, all,* and *none* indicate sweeping generalizations, which are associated with false items, whereas words like *sometimes, often, probably, usually,* and *generally* are associated with true items.

8. Avoid quoting exact statements from the textbook or workbook. Exact quotations can have different meanings when they are taken out of context or may make students think that you prefer rote learning.

Alternate-choice items permit teachers to take a broad sampling of behaviors in a limited amount of time. Moreover, the scoring of alternate-choice items tends to be quick and simple. But it is often difficult to write good items. Also, some kinds of learning cannot be evaluated so easily through alternate-choice items. For example, problem-solving situations often are difficult to evaluate using alternate-choice techniques. Finally, students have a 50 percent chance of guessing the correct answer, thus giving the items poor reliability and validity.

Multiple-Choice Items

Probably the most useful and flexible form of test item is the multiple-choice item. It can be used successfully in measuring achievement of almost any objective of interest to the secondary teacher. Moreover, like alternative-choice questions, a multiple-choice test enables a teacher to ask many questions and thus cover many objectives on the same test. It can be used for measuring almost any type of cognitive behavior, from factual knowledge to the analysis of complex data. Undoubtedly, the multiple-choice format is the most versatile of all objective item formats. Moreover, it has the added advantage of being easy to score.

The basic form of the multiple-choice item is a *stem* or *lead,* which sets up the problem or asks a question to be completed with one of a number of alternative answers or responses (usually three to five). One of the responses is the correct answer; the other alternatives are called *distractors* or *foils* and should be plausible but incorrect. Writing good multiple-choice items is not as easy as many beginning teachers believe. It often takes a substantial amount of patience and creative ability to write good distractors. Unless you know your course content well, the number of items that can be constructed is limited.

Multiple-choice items should be constructed so they are straightforward, clear, and concise. Consider the following example:

> **Poor:** Who was president during the Civil War?
> *a.* Robert E. Lee
> *b.* Abraham Lincoln
> *c.* U.S. Grant
> *d.* George Washington

The correct response depends on whether you are asking for the president of the United States or of the Confederacy. In other words, there are two possible correct responses to the question. However, the question could be reworded as follows:

> **Better:** Who was president of the United States during the Civil War?
> *a.* Robert E. Lee
> *b.* Abraham Lincoln
> *c.* U.S. Grant
> *d.* George Washington

Additional guidelines that can be followed in writing better multiple-choice items are described here.

1. The central issue or problem should be stated clearly in the stem. It should be stated in the form of an incomplete statement or question, and there should be no ambiguity in terminology.

2. Avoid writing a stem at the end of one page and the alternatives on the next, or placing choices in a linear sequence.

3. Avoid providing grammatical or contextual clues to the correct answer. For example, the use of *an* before the choices suggests that the answer begins with a vowel. Instead, use the form *a(n),* which means "either *a* or *an.*"

4. Use language that even the most unskilled readers will understand. Keep the reading required in a question to a minimum. Write concise stems and precise choices.

5. Avoid absolute terms (such as *always, never,* and *none*) in the stem and alternatives. Test-wise individuals are usually sensitive to these terms.

6. Alternatives should be grammatically correct. The use of *is* or *are,* for example, can help students guess the correct response. All alternatives should fit the stem, in order to avoid giving clues to its incorrectness.

7. Avoid the use of negatives (such as *not, except,* and *least*) and double negatives in the stem and alternatives. If negatives are used in the stem, put them as close to the end of the stem as possible.

8. Avoid giving structural clues. For example, try not to use one letter more often than the others or create a pattern of correct responses.

9. Use "all of the above" and "none of the above" with care. "All of the above" is usually a poorer response than "none of the above" because all alternatives must be correct answers. It is often difficult to write four or five correct responses to a stem.

10. Avoid pulling statements directly from the textbook. Test students for understanding, not memorization.

11. Alternatives should be plausible to less knowledgeable students. Write distractors that include common errors, errors that are likely, and erroneous common-sense solutions.

Once you have written a pool of multiple-choice items for a unit of instruction, you generally will find it easy to modify the items based on feedback data. Moreover, multiple-choice items are relatively insensitive to guessing; however, they are more sensitive to guessing than are supply items.

Matching

Matching questions are designed to measure students' ability to recall a fairly large amount of factual information. Students are presented two lists of items (phrases, concepts, dates, principles, or names) and asked to select an item from one list that most closely relates to an item from the second list. Essentially, a matching item is an efficient arrangement of a series of multiple-choice items with all stems (sometimes called *premises*) having the same set of possible alternative responses. Thus, matching items can be used anywhere multiple-choice items can be used. They are best suited for measurement of verbal, associative knowledge.

Matching items are relatively easy to construct, especially if they are intended for measuring lower-level learning. Conversely, the chief disadvantage is that they are not effective for evaluating higher-level thinking.

Writing good matching questions is often difficult. Another problem associated with matching items is the tendency for one part of the item to give away the answer to another part. Consider, for example, the following:

Poor:

a. Alex Haley	1. *Wheels*
b. James A. Michener	2. *The Exorcist*
c. William Golding	3. *Lord of the Flies*
d. William Peter Blatty	4. *Cujo*
e. Arthur Hailey	5. *Centennial*
f. Stephen King	6. *Roots*

There are exactly six premises and six responses; if each statement is to be used once and only once, the students need only answer five of the premises correctly to correctly identify the sixth response for the last premise. It is better to allow each response to be used more than once or, even better, to add extra responses. For example:

Better:

a. Alex Haley	1. *The Exorcist*
b. James A. Michener	2. *Wheels*
c. William Golding	3. *The Grapes of Wrath*
d. William Peter Blatty	4. *Lord of the Flies*
e. Arthur Hailey	5. *Cujo*
f. Stephen King	6. *Centennial*
	7. *Roots*
	8. *1984*

Many multiple-choice questions can be easily converted to matching items. In fact, you should think of matching items as a set of multiple-choice items with the same set of alternatives. Each response is then appropriate for each premise. Also, the guidelines listed below will aid in the construction of better matching items.

1. Indicate in clear, concise words the basis for matching the premises with the responses.

2. Design the entire matching item so it is contained on one page. That is, don't put the premises on one page and the responses on the back or on the next page.

3. Keep the number of items to be matched short. Limit the number of items to ten or so. The more premises, the more difficult it is to avoid giving inadvertent clues.

4. Put premises and responses in some logical order. That is, be sure that premises and responses are easy for students to find.

5. Be sure items include statements, words, or phrases that have a high degree of homogeneity. Both the premises and the responses should fall in the same general topic or category.

6. The length of statements should be consistent. In fact, longer statements and phrases should be listed in the left column and shorter ones in the right column.

7. If names are to be matched, use complete names. Using only last names sometimes causes confusion.

Completion

Completion items require that students write responses in their own handwriting. They generally ask students to supply a word or phrase recalled from memory. A completion test item usually contains a blank, which the student must fill in correctly with one word or a short phrase.

Completion items are not easy to write. Skill is needed in writing such items so that there is one and only one correct response. Some teachers eliminate this problem by providing students with a selection of answers, some correct and some incorrect, from which students select a response.

Completion items are most useful for the testing of specific facts. However, they are less powerful than essay items in terms of the kinds of thinking they can evaluate.

Placement of the blank is of prime importance in writing completion items. Consider the following glaring example:

Poor: _____ , _____ , and _____ are three large cities in _____ .

In general, it is best to use only one blank in a completion item, and it should be placed near the end of the statement. Thus, the example would be better rewritten as follows:

Better: Dallas, Houston, and Austin are three large cities in the state of _____ .

Other guidelines associated with writing better completion items are detailed here.

1. Give clear instructions. Indicate how detailed answers should be, whether synonyms will be correct, and whether spelling will be a factor in grading.

2. Be definite enough in the incomplete statement so that only one correct answer is possible.

3. Do not adapt direct statements from the textbook with a word or two missing. Such usage encourages students to memorize the text.

4. Make sure all blanks are of equal length and correspond to the lengths of the desired responses. All blanks for all items should be of equal length and long enough to accommodate the longest response.

5. Write items that can be completed by a single word or brief phrase.

Some subjects lend themselves better than others to testing through completion items. For example, subjects that focus on the recall of specific, unambiguous facts or that require students to perform certain calculations to fill in the blank in the statement are more suited for evaluation through the use of completion items.

Essay

Essay items give students the opportunity for formulating answers to questions in their own words. Essay questions are said to measure what students know, because they permit students to select from their own storehouse of knowledge in answering a question. In effect, essay questions can successfully determine students' ability to analyze, synthesize, evaluate, and solve problems. Some specialists advocate placing words such as *why, how,* and *what consequences* in essay questions because, they claim, such terms call for a command of essential knowledge of concepts in order to integrate the subject into an appropriate response. Other test specialists urge teachers to use words such as *discuss, explain,* and *examine* because they prompt responses that provide a glimpse of how students think. Still other specialists advocate more precision and structure through the use of words such as *identify, compare,* and *contrast.*

Essay test items come in two basic forms: brief and extended. The brief-essay item generally requires a short answer or that a problem of some sort be solved, whereas the extended-essay item calls for several paragraphs of writing. Because of time constraints, extended essays are seldom used in the secondary classroom. In fact, most teacher-made tests are a combination of objective items and brief-essay items.

Essay items continue to be misused by teachers. Teachers often take less time in writing essay items than objective items. In fact, essay questions appear to be so easy to write that teachers often prepare them too hastily. Consider the following example:

Poor: Discuss Shakespeare's work.

This question is unclear. You should tell students what to discuss, and tell them in descriptive terms. "Describe the use of metaphor in Shakespeare's works" or "Analyze the political ramifications of Shakespeare's works" are more specific questions. Notice that the following phrasing makes the requested task much clearer.

Better: Analyze the use of humor in Shakespeare's *Twelfth Night.*

You should give careful consideration to the construction of essay questions so that students will know what is required of them. The following guidelines should be of further assistance in writing better essay questions.

1. Make directions clear and explicit. If spelling and grammar are to be considered in grading, tell the students. Also, if organization, creativity, and content are to be considered in grading, share this information as well.

2. Allow ample time for students to answer the questions. If more than one essay question is to be answered during a period, suggest a time allotment for each question.

3. Students should be given a choice of questions. Such a choice avoids penalizing students who may know the subject as a whole, but happen to have limited knowledge in the particular area of a single question.

4. The worth or weight of each question should be determined as the test is being written. Convey this information in the test instructions, and grade accordingly.

5. Explain your scoring technique to students before you give the test. It should be clear to them what you will be looking for when you grade the test.

A common problem associated with essay tests is content coverage. Because of the time students need for responding to essays, fewer topics can be covered. Realistically, only a few essay items can be included on a given exam.

Essay items are difficult to score. There is often no single right answer to a question. Because of this tendency, essay items tend to be less reliable and less valid than other types of tests. With care, however, biases associated with essay grading can be controlled to some extent. Several guidelines are offered below.

1. Write a sample answer to each essay question ahead of time, and assign points to various components of your answer.

2. Skim through all responses to a question before beginning the grading of the question. Establish a model answer for each question, and grade each question for all students before proceeding to the next question.

3. Grade essays blindly. Have students write their names on the back of the exam so it can be graded without knowledge of the identity of the respondent.

4. Establish a reasonable page limit and time limit for each essay item. This will indicate the level of detail desired and help students finish the entire test.

5. If time permits, read student responses several times. This will reduce the chances of making serious errors in judgment.

Despite grading drawbacks, unrestricted essay items are usually required to evaluate higher-order knowledge and thinking. Therefore, they should be used, but used with care.

This section has focused on several different types of test items. Keep in mind, however, that the different kinds of items can be written to sample almost any behavior. Even so, there are certain advantages and disadvantages associated with the various types of teacher-made test items. Table 11.1 illustrates these advantages and disadvantages.

TABLE *11.1*   Advantages and Disadvantages of Various Test Items

Type	Advantages	Disadvantages
Alternate Choice	Large sampling of content Easy to score	Guessing Writing clear items difficult Tends to test memorization
Multiple Choice	Large sampling of content Scoring simple and fast Measures wide range of cognitive levels Reduces guessing	Question construction time-consuming Often used to test trivial content
Matching	Large sampling of content Can test associations Easy to construct and score	Tests for recognition Guessing
Completion	Large sampling of content Easy to construct Limited guessing	Tests for memorization Writing good items difficult Difficult to score
Essay	Measures higher cognitive levels Less time needed to construct	Scoring difficult Questions sometimes ambiguous

Although not technically a teacher-made test item type, quizzes represent an important source of evaluative information for teachers. Moreover, quizzes often can be used in motivating students.

Quizzes

Classroom quizzes can be used for evaluating student progress. In fact, quizzes are an excellent technique for checking homework and for finding out whether concepts from the preceding lesson were understood.

Teacher quizzes differ from regular teacher-made tests in that they usually consist of three to five questions and are limited to the material taught in the immediate or preceding lesson. They are easy to develop, administer, and grade, and thus they provide prompt evaluative information to both students and teacher.

Quizzes encourage students to keep up with their homework and show them their strengths and weaknesses in learning. In addition, quizzes help teachers improve instruction by providing feedback related to their effectiveness. Problems identified through quizzes serve as early warning signals of teaching or learning problems. Early identification allows the teacher to focus on problems before they worsen.

Published Test Banks

Many textbooks and programs of study include publisher-produced test banks. These test banks vary in quality. Some test banks are provided in the form of masters for copying and typically include chapter and unit tests. Many of these tests are geared toward factual information and, consequently, ease of grading. If you have planned a set of instructional objectives independent of those suggested in the textbook, it is likely that the published test will fall short of serving your needs.

TABLE *11.2*   Evaluative Instruments

Concept	Description
Standardized Test	A commercially developed test that samples behavior under uniform procedures
Teacher-Made Test	An evaluative instrument developed and scored by a teacher for classroom assessment
Alternate-Choice Item	A statement to which respondents react either positively or negatively
Multiple-Choice Item	A test question with a stem that poses a problem or asks a question to be answered by one of several alternative responses
Matching Item	An arranged series of premises, each of which is matched with a specific item from a second list of responses
Completion Item	A statement with a missing word or phrase that must be supplied by the respondent
Brief-Essay Item	Questions to which respondents formulate a short-answer response in their own words or solve a problem
Extended-Essay Item	Questions to which respondents formulate responses of several paragraphs in their own words

A more promising development is the advent of test bank databases. Schools that purchase this service for teachers are provided with a phone number that allows teachers to order customized tests from the test bank. Use of this tool certainly requires advance planning.

A summary of the different testing concepts covered to this point is given in table 11.2. Study table 11.2 and the Evaluative Instruments Application Guidelines, and complete exercise 11.1 to check your understanding of the concepts presented in this chapter.

The gathering of data is not the end of the evaluative process. You now must interpret this data and assign grades. The importance of grades cannot be overemphazied because of their influence on the lives of students. For example, grades are often used for college entrance, courses of study, and job recommendations.

Grading Systems

Assigning grades is a responsibility most teachers dislike and feel uncomfortable in doing. There is no way of assigning grades that will be fair to all students. Most school districts assign grades of A, B, C, D, or F. Regardless of the system used, however, assigning grades to students' work is inherently subjective.

You will be required to make judgments when grades are assigned. How many tests should be given? How many As or Cs or Fs should be given? Will grading be absolute or on a curve? Will students be allowed to retake exams? Can students use extra-credit assignments to modify grades and to what extent?

Homework is a special consideration. Should it be counted in the grading system? Who should grade homework—students or teachers? The grading of homework by students provides immediate feedback and allows the teacher to decide what materials need to be retaught. On the other hand, when the teacher grades the homework, work loads are increased and feedback to students is delayed. Moreover, there is some question as

Application Guidelines ▼

Evaluative Instruments

Constructing Tests

Examples:
1. Phrase essay test items carefully; define your answer expectations specifically.
2. Some test items should be so easy that almost all students can answer them, while others should challenge even the most capable students.
3. Use both objective and essay questions on tests. Students differ on their success with each type of testing item.
4. Make sure your tests are reliable and valid.
5. Plan the number and type of items on the test with care. The number of items will depend on the type of items used.
6. Test all teaching objectives in proportion to their importance.
7. Use only a few types of test items; too many different kinds of items confuse students.
8. Group all test items of the same type together, and arrange the items from easiest to more difficult within each group.

Giving and Scoring Tests

Examples:
1. Test appropriately every two weeks over most important material taught.
2. Organize the learning environment for conducive test taking; make sure all students are comfortable and have ample room.
3. Avoid undue test competition and time pressures. Make sure your slowest student has time to finish an exam.
4. Use humor and simple relaxation methods to reduce test anxiety.
5. Write sample answers to all essay questions ahead of time, and make sure students are made aware of point distribution.
6. Conduct a formal review session a day or two before an exam is to be given.
7. Tell students what to do once they finish the test, so they do not disturb other students still taking the exam.
8. Discourage cheating by administering two or three versions of the test in which the order of the items varies.

to whether homework should be counted in the grading system. Some will say no. Indeed, it is generally not a good idea for a teacher to assign a grade to work that has been graded by students; instead, only the fact that the work was completed should be recorded.

A distinction must be made between the grades you give to students on tests, quizzes, and classroom activities and the grades issued for grade cards. As a teacher, you must grade students' examinations and quizzes. Basically, these grades can be assigned in one of two ways: an absolute grading system or a relative grading system.

Application of Knowledge

Test yourself on the following evaluative instruments concepts. Appropriate responses can be found in appendix A.

1. A test constructed by a classroom teacher is called a _____ , while a test constructed by experts is labeled a _____

2. Standardized tests are useful for making comparisons between groups. (True/False)

3. Teacher-made tests generally have high reliability. (True/False)

4. Match the teacher-made item characteristic on the left with its type name on the right.

   a. _____ A stem presented along with several alternative responses
   b. _____ A question with only two response choices
   c. _____ Questions that permit students to answer from their own knowledge and in their own words
   d. _____ Questions that test students' knowledge of associations

   1. Essay items
   2. Matching items
   3. Multiple-choice items
   4. Alternate choice

5. The best objective type of test item to use to limit guessing is _____ .

6. The two forms of essay tests are the _____ and the _____ .

7. Quizzes generally are limited to the material taught in a one-week instructional period. (True/False)

8. Every test item should separate students who have mastered the objectives from those who have not. (True/False)

9. When determining how often to administer tests, remember that you generally should test over the important material taught approximately every _____ .

Absolute Grading Standards

Grades may be given relative to performance against an established set of grading criteria. An illustration of an **absolute grading standard** is shown in table 11.3. In this system, grades are assigned based on the number of items answered correctly. This system, in theory, makes it possible for all students to make high grades. In fact, each student is potentially capable of achieving any grade; that is, no one needs to fail, and all students can make good grades if they put forth the effort. Grading is simple: A student either does get an established percent of the responses correct or does not. Student scores will depend on the difficulty of the test.

There are major limitations associated with an absolute grading standard: (1) the establishment of a standard for each grade is often difficult; (2) the standard established for each grade may vary from time to time, according to the content being taught, and with respect to curriculum changes; (3) teaching effectiveness may vary; and (4) the level of examination difficulty may vary. Despite these limitations, however, most

TABLE *11.3*   Examples of Absolute Standards of Grading

Grade	Percentage Correct		Percentage Correct
A	90–100		85–100
B	80–89		75–84
C	70–79	*or*	65–74
D	60–69		55–64
F	Less than 60		Less than 55

teachers use the absolute standard of grading. The major advantage of such a system is that it puts the control of test scores in the hands of students.

Relative Grading Standards

Teachers frequently use a **relative grading standard,** in which they assess student performance with respect to the performance of other students. Accordingly, they often employ a curve when assigning grades. In this type of system, students are compared with each other. Of course, the best-known curve is the normal curve (see chapter 10). When this curve is used, you would expect to give 3.5 percent of the students As, 23.8 percent Bs, 45 percent Cs, 23.8 percent Ds, and 3.5 percent Fs. However, the normal curve is applicable only when the group is large and diversified. Moreover, when the normal curve is used, some students must get As, some students must fail, and most of the students must be given Cs.

Because of its lack of flexibility, few teachers use the normal curve. Instead, they implement a relative grading system based on a simple ranking system. In a ranking system, the teacher establishes a fixed percent for each assigned grade. For example, you might set up the following curve:

A = Top 10 percent

B = Next 20 percent

C = Next 40 percent

D = Next 20 percent

F = Next 10 percent

Another common method of grading with curves is the inspection method. When using this method, a frequency distribution of raw scores is set up on a vertical or horizontal line, as shown in figure 11.1. Grades are then assigned according to natural breaks in the distribution. It is possible that this type of system will not yield A or F grades. For example, if the lowest grade in figure 11.1 had been 14, few teachers would assign an F grade for this work. As you see, the inspection method will yield different grades for different individuals. There is no correct or incorrect division. Figure 11.2 shows three possible inspection grading patterns for grade distribution.

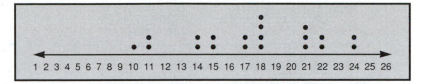

Figure 11.1 *The Inspection Method*

Figure 11.2 *Examples of Inspection Grade Distributions*

100	100	100 A
95	95	95
94 (1) A	94 (1) A	94 (1) B
91 (1)	91 (1)	91 (1)
90 (1)	90 (1)	90 (1)
85 B	85	85
81 (2)	81 (2) B	81 (2)
75	75	75
74 (4) C	74 (4)	74 (4) C
70 (3)	70 (3)	70 (4)
65	65 C	65
64 (2) D	64 (2)	64 (2)
60 (1)	60 (1)	60 (1)
55	55	55
50	50 D	50 D
45 F	45	45
44 (1)	44 (1)	44 (1)
43	43	43
42	42 F	42 F

The relative grading standard has a major limitation in that it does not take into account differences in overall ability of students. Thus, some students will always receive As, and some always Fs.

Assuming one of the above methods is used in arriving at grades, the next task you will face as a teacher is to assign nine-week or term grades. As you might imagine, this can present a real challenge.

Assigning Final Grades

Final term grades are generally determined by combining all the results of students' work for a grading period. There are three major ways of accomplishing this end: a point assignment system, a weighted assignment system, and a percentage system.

Point Grading System

A **point grading system** is fairly simple and easy to use. The importance of each assignment, quiz, or test is reflected in the points allocated. For example, you may decide that assignments will be worth 10 points, quizzes 25 points, and tests 100 points. At the end of the grading period, the points are added up and grades are assigned according to the established grade range. This system is illustrated in Figure 11.3.

Figure 11.3 *Example of Point Grading System*

Student work	Points
Assignments (25 x 10 pts.)	250
Quizzes (6 x 25 pts.)	150
Tests (3 x 100 pts.)	300

Total points possible = 700

Grade range

A 650–700
B 600–649
C 550–599
D 500–549
F Less than 499

Figure 11.4 *Example of Weighted Grading System*

Student work	Points
	25%
Quizzes (6)	25%
Tests (3)	50%

Total 100%

Weighted Grading System

A **weighted grading system** is more complex than the point grading system. Every assignment is given a letter grade, and all grades are then weighted to arrive at a final grade. An example of this system is illustrated in figure 11.4.

The determination of a final grade can be made simpler and more objective by changing grades to numerical values: A = 4; B = 3; C = 2; D = 1; F = 0. Once numerical values are assigned, an average score is calculated for homework, quizzes, and tests. For example, you would calculate a homework average for seven homework assignments with the grades of A, B, B, C, C, D, and A by carrying out the following computation:

$$(4 + 3 + 3 + 2 + 2 + 1 + 4) \div 7 = 19 \div 7 = 2.71$$

A quiz average for four quizzes graded B, B, C, and D would be computed as follows:

$$(3 + 3 + 2 + 1) \div 4 = 9 \div 4 = 2.25$$

Calculation of a test average for three tests with grades of C, C, and D would carry out the following computation,

$$(2 + 2 + 1) \div 3 = 5 \div 3 = 1.67$$

Now, applying the weights outlined in figure 11.4, you would calculate a final grade as follows:

Homework: $2.71 \times 25\% = 2.71 \times 0.25 = 0.68$

Quizzes: $2.25 \times 25\% = 2.25 \times 0.25 = 0.56$

Tests: $1.67 \times 50\% = 1.67 \times 0.50 = 0.84$

_____

Total numerical grade = 2.08

Thus, the final grade for the student would be 2.08 or a C. Of course, if other student exercises—such as class projects, term papers, group projects, and so on—were included in a grading period, they would be part of the grading system and be accounted for in the weights.

Percentage System

The **percentage system** is probably the simplest of all grading systems and the most widely used. The system typically relies on the calculation of percentage correct of those responses attempted. For example, a student who gets 20 of 25 correct on a homework assignment would have a score of 80 written in the grade book; 6 of 8 correct on a quiz would have a 75 recorded in the grade book; and 40 of 60 correct on an examination would have a 67 written in the grade book. You typically would calculate an average of these and other term scores in arriving at a final score on which to base the term grade. The problem with this system is that all student exercises carry the same weight, even though the type of exercises are markedly different—homework, quiz, and examination.

Even with the noted flaw, teachers tend to use the percentage system extensively for two reasons: First, it is simple to use and understand, and second, parents and students prefer the system because of its simplicity and their ability to understand it.

Contracting for Grades

Most schools give teachers considerable freedom in establishing grading standards. Some teachers have used this flexibility in implementing a contract approach to grading. With a contract, the teacher promises to award a specific grade for specified performance. Students know exactly what they must do to receive a certain grade; depending on the amount of work they wish to do, they receive a particular grade. For example, a simple contract could be this:

> To receive a grade of D, you must satisfactorily complete activities 1 through 6, satisfactorily complete half of the homework, and pass the posttest.

> To receive a grade of C, you must complete activities 1 through 6, satisfactorily complete 60 percent of the homework, do one of the optional activities satisfactorily, and receive at least a C on the posttest.

> To receive a grade of B, you must complete activities 1 through 6, satisfactorily complete 80 percent of the homework, do two of the optional activities very well, and receive at least a B on the posttest.

> To receive a grade of A, you must complete activities 1 through 6, satisfactorily complete 90 percent of the homework, do four of the optional activities excellently, complete at least one of the major project activities satisfactorily, and receive at least a B+ on the posttest.

Even though the above contract outlines the requirements for a D, it is unlikely that students will want to contract for the low grade. However, it sets the baseline for those activities required for a higher grade.

When you establish a contract system, you must develop sets of objectives that correspond to specific letter grades. You then decide the activities and assignments that will be required at each level. These objectives, corresponding letter grades, and requirements are shared with students in writing, so students can study them and make decisions on a contract grade.

Some teachers like to write a more detailed contract, which is signed by both student and teacher. A sample detailed contract is illustrated in chapter 13, figure 13.2.

This section has described grading systems and the assigning of grades. But as noted earlier, grading is a very subjective undertaking. It should be carried out with care and planning. Review table 11.4 and the Assigning Grades Application Guidelines, and complete exercise 11.2.

TABLE *11.4*   Assigning Grades

Concept	Description
Absolute Grading Standard	Performance compared with established set of criteria
Relative Grading Standard	Students' performance compared with each other, including grading on the curve
Point Grading System	Student work is allocated points, and grades are assigned according to established grade range
Weighted Grading System	Assignments are given a letter grade, and all grades are weighted to determine final grade
Percentage System	Percentage correct is recorded for each assignment and an average is calculated in determining final grade
Grade Contract	Written agreement between student and teacher as to what students will do to earn a specific grade

Application Guidelines ▼

Assigning Grades

Establish Guidelines for Testing and Scoring

Examples:
1. Because teacher-made tests are seldom designed to give a normal distribution, it usually is unwise to give grades on the normal curve.
2. Make grading procedures explicit. They should be written down and communicated clearly to students early in the year.
3. Make your grading procedures as objective as possible.
4. Makeup exams should be taken within a week of the regular examination.

Make Sure Term Grades Reflect Student Performance

Examples:
1. Use the amount of time spent on work as an indicator of its point value.
2. Grade cards should reflect a variety of types of students' performance.
3. Use grades for communicating achievement to students and parents.
4. The final decision about what grade to assign to a student should be based on what is best for the student.
5. Do not burden yourself with having to devise extra-credit work for students who did not do the regular assignments.

Application of Knowledge

Exercise 11.2 Assigning Grades

Test yourself on the following grading concepts. Appropriate responses can be found in appendix A.

1. Assigning test grades and term grades usually is quite objective. (True/False)

2. The use of a relative grading standard is referred to as grading on a _____ .

3. If a teacher decides to use a curve for grading purposes, the normal curve is the best option available. (True/False)

4. Match the description on the left with the appropriate grading procedure on the right.
   a. _____ Grades assigned according to established grade range
   b. _____ Number correct on all assignments used to determine grades
   c. _____ Importance of assignment used to determine grades

   1. Percentage system
   2. Weighted grading system
   3. Point grading system

5. Extra credit should be made available to all students so they can improve their grade. (True/False)

6. Grade contracts usually are too complex for implementation in most secondary school classrooms. (True/False)

CHAPTER SUMMARY

This chapter has focused on two important concepts to teachers: testing and grading. Testing and grading represent two critical, but unpopular, challenges for teachers.

Teachers generally use either standardized tests or teacher-made tests in the classroom. Standardized tests are tests prepared and published by assessment specialists, while teacher-made tests are developed by teachers to address specific classroom situations. Standardized tests are used for providing some indication of how individual students and classrooms compare with local, regional, or national averages. Teacher-made tests are employed for gathering information and making judgments regarding the achievement of students.

Formats for teacher-made tests are varied and widespread. Examples commonly found in the secondary classroom are alternative-choice tests, multiple-choice tests, matching tests, completion tests, essay (brief and extended) tests, and a combination of the different types. Each type of teacher-made test has inherent strengths and weaknesses.

The absolute grading system and relative grading system are two principal grading systems commonly used in the secondary classroom. An absolute standard compares student performance against an established set of criteria. Conversely, the relative standard compares students with one another.

Teachers must assign nine-week or term grades. Three different systems are available to teachers for accomplishing this task. First, the point grading system assigns points based on the importance of the students' work. These points are then added at the end of the grading term, and a grade assigned according to established grade ranges. Second, a weighted grading system assigns a letter grade to every student assignment. These letter grades then are weighted in arriving at a final grade. Third, a percentage system is the simplest of all grading systems. The teacher typically calculates the percentage correct for each assignment completed. An average of these percentages is then calculated in establishing a term grade.

Contracts can be used effectively in the grading process. With contract grading, the teacher outlines exactly what students will do to earn specific grades. Contracts can be used for improving a teacher's communication with students.

In the long run, successful evaluation will hinge on a teacher's ability to ensure that measurement is as objective as possible. It is objective data that will best lead you to sound judgments regarding achievement and grades.

Discussion Questions and Activities

1. **Standardized tests.** Describe three important characteristics of commonly used standardized tests. Briefly describe at least three standardized tests for a subject area.

2. **Test items.** Make up several examples of alternate-choice, multiple-choice, matching, completion, and essay test items. Ask your class to critique them. Discuss which types of items were the most difficult and the least difficult to construct.

3. **Test construction.** Examine a standardized test and teacher-made test in terms of construction, clarity, and readability. Are there major weaknesses in either test?

4. **Grading systems.** Compare the major advantages and disadvantages associated with absolute and relative grading standards. Do you prefer one system over the other? Defend your choice.

5. **Teacher interview.** Interview several classroom teachers about their tests and homework. How do the teachers deal with the following issues?

   a. Test construction.

   b. Test and homework scoring and grade assignment.

   c. Test and homework makeup for absences.

   d. Homework for extra credit.

   e. Late or missing homework.

6. **Grading objectivity.** Can a teacher be objective in assigning grades? Explain.

7. **Grading procedures.** Outline a grading procedure that you expect you will follow and implement as a teacher.

PART 3

▽   ▽   ▼   ▽

Implementation of Instruction

nce lessons have been planned, they must be implemented. Even the best-laid plans, however, can fail in the classroom. A successful teacher is one who can ably communicate, motivate, diagnose, and manage a classroom. Therefore, teachers must be aware of the influences that the communication process, motivation, reading ability, and management skills will have on the success of a lesson. Part 3 will focus on these implementation issues.

Without communication and motivation, there would be no teaching or learning. Chapter 12 will focus on the important process of communication. Various verbal and nonverbal techniques will be addressed, as well as the often-overlooked skill of listening. Chapter 13 will focus on motivation. Learning will only take place when there is a desire to know, to understand, to learn. Thus, teachers must develop students' desire for learning. They must motivate!

The textbook is still central to instruction in most secondary classrooms. Therefore, students must be able to read their textbooks. Chapter 14 will focus on this important skill. Diagnostic techniques, comprehension strategies, and textbook evaluation will be the focus of the chapter.

Skillful classroom management is indispensable to a career in the classroom. The establishment of an environment conducive to learning will not be an easy task. If you are to do well, you must have a repertoire of management techniques from which to choose. Chapter 15 will outline several approaches to classroom management.

Communication

✎ **We talk. But do we teach? We hear. But do we listen? Because we talk and hear, do we communicate?**

Overview

Communication is essential in helping students learn. As a teacher, you must be sensitive to cultivating excellent communication skills and to monitoring the effectiveness of your interactions with students.

Unfortunately, teachers often do most of the talking in classrooms, and students do most of the listening. Perhaps because of this, teachers tend to not really listen to what students are saying or not saying.

This chapter is about communication. As such, it will address both the sending and receiving of information and messages.

Objectives

After completing your study of chapter 12, you should be able to do the following:

1. Explain the importance of the communication process.

2. Diagram the model of the communication process.

3. Differentiate between the verbal, vocal, and metaverbal components of a message.

4. Identify variables associated with the verbal and vocal components of a message.

5. Explain the role nonverbal communication plays in the communication process.

6. Provide examples of various nonverbal behaviors commonly used in the classroom.

7. Identify and explain the four spatial distances.

8. Explain how color communicates.

9. Explain the importance of listening.

10. Identify and define the different types of listening.

11. Identify and describe variables that interfere with listening.

12. Explain the importance of feedback in the communication process.

Chapter Terms and Key Concepts

Communication

Hearing

Listening

Metaverbal Component

Nonverbal Communication

Verbal Communication

Verbal Component

Vocal Component

Of all the knowledge and skills you possess as a teacher, those concerning communication will be among the most significant and the most useful. Through communication, you interact with students, you teach, and students learn. Without communication, teaching could not occur.

As a practical skill, communication consists of the ability to speak, write, and read. Of equal importance to the communication process, however, is the ability to listen. Most teacher preparatory programs place a great deal of emphasis on the ability to read and write, with little attention put on speaking, and almost no attention given to nonverbal communication and listening. The most persuasive communicators do not rely exclusively on reading and writing; they talk, they observe, and they listen. Thus, the skills we will examine here are verbal and nonverbal communication as well as the art of listening, which serves an important function in the communication process.

The Communication Process

Communication refers to the act, by one or more persons, of sending and receiving messages that are distorted by noise, have some effect, and provide some opportunity for feedback. The communication act, then, would comprise the following components:

1. Source(s)—receiver(s).

2. Messages.

3. Noise.

4. Sending or encoding processes.

5. Receiving or decoding processes.

6. Feedback.

7. Effects.

These elements are the universals of the communication process. They are present in every communication act, regardless of whether the communication is with oneself, parents, colleagues, or students. As a teacher, therefore, you will be intimately involved in this communication process as you interact with students and colleagues on a daily basis. This process is illustrated in figure 12.1.

As shown in figure 12.1, the communication process can be viewed as a five-phase process, with each individual performing two functions: sending and receiving. First, you as a source encode (compose) a desired message into a form that, hopefully, will be understood by the receiver. Second, you transmit this message, which can be sent by speaking, writing, gesturing, smiling, and so on. Third, your transmitted message is accepted and decoded by a receiver. The message can be received by listening, reading, seeing, smelling, and so on. Fourth, the receiver then becomes a source and encodes some form of reaction to your message. The receiver's reaction generally will be in some nonverbal form. Fifth and finally, the

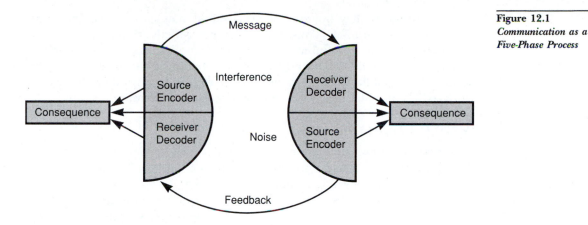

Figure 12.1
*Communication as a
Five-Phase Process*

nonverbal message (feedback) tells you, the sender, whether the received message was understood or not. Thus, as you send messages, you are also receiving messages in the form of feedback and must constantly decode and react to this feedback. Your reaction may be to continue with more information, to clarify the original message, or to repeat the message.

A typical classroom situation will illustrate the communication model. Suppose you want to emphasize specific information for your students. Therefore, you encode and send this message: "This information should be included in your notes." The transmitted message is received and decoded by students as meaning you will ask about the information on the next exam. They, therefore, add it to their notes for future reference. Because you observe (feedback) the information being written in the students' notes, you feel your communication has been successful and continue with your lesson. If on the other hand, you were to observe that students did not add the information to their notes, you might want to reemphasize its importance with a message such as this: "That information is so important that I had better write it on the board!" This example illustrates the importance of accurate messages, and it points to how critical your attention to feedback is to the communication process.

Communication always has some effect or consequence. In fact, there are three classes of communication consequence: The receiver can acquire new information or awareness (cognitive effect), change attitudinal or emotional states (affective effect), or learn a new skill (psychomotor effect). Often, however, the consequences will involve all three types of effects.

Noise and interference sometimes will distort or interfere with our ability to communicate. The hum of an air conditioner, hall noise, the sunglasses a person wears, cars passing in the street, student movements, clothes students wear—these all may be regarded as classroom noise, because they can interfere with the effective transmission of your messages to the class. Noise can also be psychological. Biases and prejudices, for example, can distort or interfere with getting an accurate message across. These sources of noise and interference must be overcome if your messages are to be received and decoded accurately by students.

Messages may be sent or received in many forms: verbal, vocal, physical, or situational. Thus, you must be skilled at sending messages through any one or combinations of these modes. But of equal importance is your ability to decode messages (feedback) transmitted by students. This ability is directly related to your listening skill. Before we address listening, let's look at verbal and nonverbal communication.

Verbal Communication

Teachers communicate information to students by talking. However, learning does not take place only through teacher talk and words. Nonverbal variables sometimes will determine whether or not something is learned.

Goodall (1983, pp. 14–15) breaks spoken messages into three components: verbal, vocal, and metaverbal. The **verbal component** refers to the actual words spoken and their meanings, the **vocal component** includes such variables as voice firmness, modulation, tone, tempo, pitch, and loudness, while the **metaverbal component** refers to what may be implied or intended by the spoken words.

The Verbal Component

Words can be interpreted in many ways, and these interpretations can be the basis for misunderstandings. Indeed, the message communicated in any interaction will depend on both the words and the meanings attached to the words spoken. These meanings are learned as a result of experiences, and thus are often arbitrary. For example, a class discussion of terms such as *feminism, religion,* or *democracy* will have varying outcomes, depending on students' past experiences. Despite the formal dictionary definitions, you must make sure that your verbal instruction is related as much as possible to the experiences of the learners. This determination calls for an assessment on your part of what students bring to the learning situation—for example, intelligence, prior learning history, and learning ability. This information may show that the verbal aspects of your messages are outside the experience base of your students. (A word of caution: Don't let your assessment of students influence your expectation of their ability. Students tend to behave in a way congruent with how they are viewed.)

Another problem associated with words is their misuse, which may stem from a lack of knowledge of their meanings. Indeed, it is often possible to talk endlessly about a subject and sound quite knowledgeable when, in fact, you haven't the slightest idea of the word meanings. These bluffing behaviors with words should be avoided in the classroom. Students usually will see through the lack of knowledge, and you will lose their respect.

Hurt, Scott, and McCroskey (1978, p. 76) suggest several other variables that may have some affect on whether a message is received and decoded accurately:

1. **Organization**
   Good or well-organized verbal information tends to be learned more thoroughly, as does the information presented first or last in a lesson.

2. **Message Sidedness**

   Two-sided messages that present opposing views tend to be learned best.

3. **Language Intensity**

   Verbal information that deviates from a neutral position appears to be learned best.

4. **Concreteness and Ambiguity**

   The more concrete a message, the better. You must take care, however, that your message isn't made so concrete that the basic concept is lost.

Generally, variables such as those discussed earlier and those suggested by Hurt, Scott, and McCroskey tend to increase the attention of the listener, which is your primary aim in the classroom. The increased attention should result in increased learning.

The Vocal Component

How you say words is extremely important. The voice brings words to life. Changes in tones, voice loudness or strength, rate, inflection, or pitch can change a message emphasis as well as its very meaning. For example, messages such as "I agree!" or "Yes!" can communicate different meanings, depending on the tone and modulation.

As a teacher, you will interact with groups and will often want to emphasize points with your voice. Therefore, it is essential that you develop and project a strong voice, so that you are heard by all students. This will take practice, but is well worth the effort. Often the practice of talking over a little distance or the practice of inhaling and exhaling air will improve both the strength and projection of your voice.

The rate at which you speak will impact students as well. When you speak rapidly, you might convey the message that the subject isn't really important and should be finished with as soon as possible. In contrast, words spoken at a slower rate can indicate their importance and, therefore, that they should be considered carefully by your students. This fact is important to remember, because you might be required to teach subjects that interest you little or to teach in areas in which you lack preparation. With such subjects, you must watch carefully your rate of presentation.

The tone, inflections, and pitch of the voice often impact words. Tone or inflection can communicate word seriousness or validity. For example, the seriousness of such messages as "I mean it!" or "Be quiet!" or even "I am losing my patience!" will be affected by your tone and inflection. Moreover, as Hennings (1975, p. 17) points out, "the high-pitched voice can grate on a decoder's nerves so that the listener turns off to words spoken; the very deep voice can distract from the message." You therefore must guard against using an incorrect tone, inflection, or pitch that might distract from your messages.

Voice volume, rate, tone, inflection, and pitch will often send emotional information. Loudness, rate, and pitch can communicate excitement or enthusiasm, whereas a slow rate and even pitch can communicate disinterest. Joy, eagerness, anger, wonder, awe, displeasure, determination, and indecisiveness can be communicated through variations in the voice. Skill at varying your voice can assist you greatly in keeping students on task and with the general management of the classroom environment. Therefore, practice with your voice; it will continue to serve you in your instruction if you know how to use it effectively.

You must be aware of the effect that a monotone voice can have on students. It can put them to sleep, cause their minds to wander, and, in general, result in a loss of student attention. Diversity in the voice can overcome these negative effects to some extent. Indeed, you can be a more effective teacher and keep students' attention by varying your voice volume, rate, tone, inflection, and pitch.

The Metaverbal Component

When you speak, there often is an implied or intended message that cannot be directly attributed to the meaning of the words or how they are spoken. This is referred to as the metaverbal component of a message. You may, for example, ask a student to drop by after school for a visit about an issue brought up in class, when actually you want to discuss the student's falling grades.

Metaverbal messages often are tricky, because you are trying to communicate an implied message. That is, students are being asked to hear beyond the words. Sometimes what you mean to imply when you speak is not how your words and actions are interpreted.

As you teach or listen, all basic components of verbal communication contribute to the messages received by students. Thus, students are hearing what you say at three levels: what is said, how it is said, and why (implied) it is said. Therefore, exercise care in the act of communicating, and match your intent with your message.

Nonverbal Communication

Communication can be nonlinguistic. That is, we can send messages without using words. This form of communication is referred to as **nonverbal communication.** Because some researchers in the area of communication claim that more than 80 percent of our communication is nonverbal in nature, it is important that teachers be proficient with its use (Sathrè, Olson, & Whitney, 1977; Miller, 1986).

Nonverbal communication is a vital component of the expression of attitudes and feelings.

You constantly send messages through the way you dress, your posture, the way you look, move, work your voice, and use space, as well as the way you use words. These nonverbal messages can reinforce, modify, or even contradict your verbal messages as, for example, when you say with a sigh of relief, "I wish you could stay longer." In fact, the nonverbal part of communication often is more important than the verbal part, in that it expresses real feelings. Sometimes nonverbal information plays a role in determining what our reaction will be in certain situations or in deciding what our future behavior will be. For example, when a friend says, "I'd like to get together again soon," that person may state it in such a way that you suspect otherwise. Thus, actions often do speak much louder than words.

Sometimes nonverbal communication is designed very carefully for evoking a particular response, while at other times it occurs naturally or accidentally. In either case, it can influence perceptions, attitudes, or feelings. These nonverbal cues are often not taken at face value; rather, inferences are made from them in determining what to believe. Thus, teachers and students often unwittingly reveal attitudes and feelings toward each other and toward school in general through nonverbal cues. In other words, you must be alert to your nonverbal expressions and the effect they can have on students. An awareness of nonverbal communications and their consequences is a step toward controlling them. We now will look at some elements of the different languages.

Facial Language

The face and eyes are probably the most conspicuous parts of our body, and, as such, we communicate a great deal of information through our facial expressions. In fact, according to Miller (1986), the face is second only to words in communicating our internal feelings. Miller further suggests that these facial expressions can be readily visible or fleeting, involuntary or voluntary. Whatever the type, facial expressions can reinforce, modify, or contradict what is said verbally.

Facial expressions that are readily visible are usually intentional. They send a message (e.g., a smile of pleasure) or mask our true feelings (e.g., a stern look of displeasure). These expressions are formed by movement of facial muscles around the forehead, mouth, eyebrows, chin, cheeks, or nose. Wrinkling the forehead, for example, communicates deep thought, lifting the eyebrows reveals wonder or surprise, a sneer shows anger or displeasure, and a jutting chin demonstrates firmness. Conversely, fleeting facial expressions are often unintentional and usually are quickly covered up with other expressions. For example, you may feel sudden disgust, anger, or dislike for someone you meet, but do not want to communicate this impression to the individual. Therefore, you quickly mask your true feelings or emotions with other intended expressions.

Involuntary facial expressions usually take place under some type of traumatic or delightful circumstances. Such microexpressions can flash across your face in situations where you are fearful, angry, happy, or surprised. In the classroom, these expressions are often fleeting in that you attempt to cover them up with other expressions as soon as possible. However, under certain circumstances you may want to retain such expressions to convey a message to students. For example, teachers often use expressions of displeasure or anger for controlling misbehavior in the classroom and expressions of humor for relieving tension or improving student attention.

Teachers commonly use voluntary facial expressions when communicating with students. In fact, effective teachers have perfected their facial expressions to a high degree. They convey a message with a look—for example, the smile of approval and the frown of displeasure.

The eyes can send several kinds of messages. As Miller (1986, p. 13) notes, your eyes "can be shifty and evasive, conveying hate, fear, and guilt, or they can express confidence, love, and support." Also, with eye contact you can open communication, prolong communication, or cut off communication entirely.

Eye contact, as most teachers know, can be used in controlling interaction in the classroom. When they want an individual student to speak, they make direct eye contact with that individual. Conversely, when they want to continue talking, they refrain from making direct eye contact with anyone who may want to speak. Moreover, most of us can remember trying to avoid a question we couldn't answer by glancing away from the teacher. At such times, we would become very interested in our textbook or our assignment. Thus, teachers sometimes gauge eye contact in determining when students are lying, or when students can't answer a question, or when students have failed to complete their homework. Indeed, you probably have heard it said often that when people are lying or when they haven't done as they should, direct eye contact is avoided. However, this hypothesis generally hasn't been supported by research. In fact, watch your use of such often unproven generalizations, for they may influence you inappropriately. For example, we may tend to distrust persons who do not make direct eye contact when speaking to us. But a shy person who does not like or finds it difficult to make direct eye contact may be completely trustworthy.

Very direct eye contact—a stare—often can change student behavior. A stare used in conjunction with silence can be quite effective in gaining the attention of misbehaving or inattentive students. Indeed, the stare alone often will result in appropriate student behavior.

Body Language

Kinesics, or the study of body movements and gestures in communication, represents an important source of information to listeners. Indeed, gestures with the head, arms, hands, and other body parts are most pervasive as nonverbal communicators. Gestures may provide information, as when you point when giving directions; they may communicate feelings, as when you nod your head in agreement as someone speaks; they may emphasize a point, as when you tap something you have written on the chalkboard; they may call for attention, as when you stomp your foot. Indeed, we often interpret an individual's body movements as an indication of his or her character (as in an authoritative or nonchalant walk). Our physical actions, then, are sending information constantly to those who are observant and attentive.

The overuse of body movement and gestures can be a deterrent to effective communications. When you gesture too often, the listener finds it difficult to discern the peaks and cannot really tell what is important in a message. Also, too many gestures can prompt a listener to attend to the gestures themselves rather than the message.

Stance and general posture is another type of kinesic communication. A tense, rigid body tends to convey closedness and insecurity, whereas a relaxed body denotes strength, openness, and friendliness. The

way you stand can also communicate information. A body orientation toward the listener tends to suggest security and comfort in the communication interaction.

The use of touch is a very powerful nonverbal communicator. Touch in communication is influenced by who does the touching. Teachers of young children, for example, often use hugs as reinforcement, whereas touch is often inappropriate with middle and secondary school students.

Although it is usually unwise for you to touch a student of the opposite sex, remember that an appropriate pat on the back is a good reinforcer for students. You should use your best judgment as to whether or when to touch in communicating with your students.

The way you dress sends a variety of messages. It is often difficult to take a speaker seriously, for example, if he or she is dressed in ill-fitting, wrinkled clothing. Conversely, we tend to pay attention to an attractively dressed speaker. Teachers, then, would be well advised to dress as befitting their roles as classroom leaders.

The Language of Space and Motion

The arrangement of your classroom and your use of the space can shape communication. How you place objects within your classroom, as well as where and how you choose to move within the confines of the space, are significant.

The Environment The physical makeup of the learning environment can create moods and, in doing so, affect the interaction within the environment. Indeed, the attractiveness of a room appears to influence the happiness and energy of people working in it. Such findings are supported by Miller (1986, p. 23) in his summary of research related to student reactions in ugly and beautiful classrooms. He states that "subjects in the ugly room had reactions of monotony, fatigue, headache, irritability, and hostility, while subjects in the beautiful room responded favorably with feelings of comfort, pleasure, importance, and enjoyment for completing the assigned tasks." Thus, Miller's findings suggest that a well-decorated, pleasing classroom is more conducive to open communications and is more effective at keeping students on task.

Colors can affect the behavior of students. For example, it has been shown that blue is more soothing and red more active than other colors (Snider & Osgood, 1969). Perhaps color can be used in influencing actions within the classroom. It may be that a combination of such colors as blue and red will result in more productive communication patterns.

Territoriality Territoriality is commonly observed in the classroom. Indeed, learning environments are too often arranged into territories, with the teacher's desk forming the teacher's territory and each student's seat or desk forming the individual student's territory. Such arrangements can lead to the understanding that each is to remain in his or her own territory. This too often leads to a restricted environment with little interaction. Also, such restricted environments can convey messages of closedness and separation between teachers and students.

Territoriality can also be observed in classrooms or other areas where seats are not assigned. For example, when a student takes the seat normally occupied by another student, the regular occupant often becomes disturbed and resentful. Likewise, in a library, you may mark your territory with a jacket or books when you leave the room.

Teacher Motion Teacher movement within the classroom can aid or hinder the communication process. Movement toward a student who is speaking can, for example, convey a message of interest, while movement away from the student can communicate lack of interest. A teacher's movements, then, can often prolong interaction. Indeed, teacher movement throughout different areas in the classroom often helps keep student attention directed toward the teacher. (See chapter 13 for a more detailed discussion of this topic.)

Proxemics Proxemics is the study of the use and meaning of space. Studies (Hall, 1959; Montagu, 1977) indicate that people engaged in interactions tend to choose a particular separation distance, depending on their feeling toward the other person or persons at the given time, the context of the conversation, and their personal goals. For example, conversations between intimate people usually take place within 18 inches (intimate distance). Friends in conversation usually stand 3 to 4 1/2 feet apart (personal distance). Business and social interactions usually take place with a separation of 4 to 7 feet (social distance). For most presentations, a distance of 15 feet or more is most common (public distance).

Even though the generalizations about "appropriate" interaction distances are tentative, you should recognize the value of the use of space in your interactions with students. In general, teachers want to work within the personal and social distance ranges in their interactions with students. Interactions with individual students should take place at a personal distance, while whole-class interactions usually will occur at the social distance.

The Language of Time

Time and its subtleties can be wisely used for successful communication. How you decide to spend class time conveys important attitudinal information. When you spend little time on a topic, or pass it by completely, you communicate that the topic is unimportant or that you have little interest in it. Such actions can unintentionally translate into similar attitudes by students.

Pauses or silence represent another way that time can be used in communicating. For example, pausing just before or after you make a specific point often signifies that the point is important. In addition, pauses can cue students that an important point is going to be made or that the last point made was important enough for them to reflect on it.

Time can also communicate a variety of emotional responses. Silence, for example, can reflect fear, a determination to be uncooperative, or an attempt at defiance. And, of course, silence is often used for showing lack of interest. In fact, your discussions will often result in silence when your topic lacks interest or when you fail to motivate.

Teachers ask many questions; however, they may find it difficult to allow for sufficient time between the asking of their questions and the reception of a student response. Teachers too often expect almost instant responses to their questions, and, when not forthcoming, they tend to answer the questions themselves. These teachers must learn to increase their wait-time so they may improve classroom interaction. (See chapter 7 for a detailed discussion of wait-time.)

Finally, reverence for silence and the sense of time varies with different cultures, subcultures, and regions (Gilliland, 1988; Berger, 1991). The Apache, for example, encourage silence. For some African cultures, time is only approximate. The Midwest has a reputation for punctuality. In New York City, people are on the go, and time is money. However, punctuality is perhaps not as revered as it may be in the Midwest; indeed, lateness can be "fashionable" for social gatherings. On the notoriously laid-back West Coast, on the other hand, being late is not a serious problem. Teachers, then, should take a close look at their students' concept of time before they react to situations that involve time. Perhaps their students are running on different clocks.

The Language of Voice

As mentioned earlier in this chapter, the vocal cues that accompany our spoken language exert a great deal of influence on a listener's perception. Indeed, vocal intonation can reveal prejudices, emotions, or background information about a speaker; it can communicate excitement, fear, or some other strong emotions. These perceptions are generally based on experiences and stereotypes associated with various vocal qualities, intonations, characteristics, and so on.

TABLE *12.1*   Communication Process

Type	Description
Verbal Communication	Communication with the spoken word through verbal, vocal, or metaverbal components
Nonverbal Communication	Nonlinguistic communication; or the sending of messages without words

Application Guidelines ▼

Communication Process

Communicate with Care

Examples:
1. Communication is irreversible: Think before you speak.
2. More communication is not always best; some things are best left unsaid.
3. Use language that students can understand. Be aware of students' background experiences.
4. Make sure your verbal and nonverbal messages are congruent when you interact with students.
5. Send positive messages through your dress, classroom arrangements, classroom decoration, and body language.

Attend to Feedback

Examples:
1. Be cognizant of nonverbal messages that reveal reactions to what you are communicating.
2. Interpretation of feedback isn't always accurate. Check the validity of the feedback you receive.

The adage is often true: "It's not what you say. It's how you say it." A vibrant "That's an excellent idea!" will convey a different message than a simple monotone "That's an excellent idea." As noted earlier, when a contradiction occurs between a verbal and vocal message, the latter message is usually believed.

As a teacher, you must watch your vocal messages. Your various vocal intonations sometimes will communicate meanings different than those you intended. Your messages can be modified by varying the loudness or softness, by using high pitch or low pitch, or by varying the tone or the quality of speech. You must be aware of and pay attention to the effect of these voice intonations. That is, you must learn to speak so your verbal and vocal messages are congruent.

This concludes our discussion of verbal and nonverbal communication. Table 12.1 summarizes the material presented in this section, and the Communication Process Application Guidelines offer some helpful suggestions. In the next section, we will consider another very important topic related to the communication process: the art of listening. Before moving on, however, review the summary and guidelines, and complete exercise 12.1.

Application of Knowledge

Exercise 12.1   Communication Process

Check yourself on the following section concepts. Appropriate responses can be found in appendix A.

1. Your major communication concern as a teacher should be the sending of information. (True/False)

2. It is possible to *not* communicate. (True/False)

3. The three components of the spoken word are _____ , _____ , and _____ .

4. Define *nonverbal communication*.
   _____
   _____

5. We can communicate unintended messages through our expressions, appearance, and mannerisms. (True/False)

6. Briefly describe five nonverbal languages that we often use in communicating during our daily interactions with others.
   a. _____
   b. _____
   c. _____
   d. _____
   e. _____

7. In general, teachers should interact with students at the personal or social distance. (True/False)

Listening

Hearing and listening are not the same thing. Hearing is automatic, while listening is an art. *Hearing* occurs when eardrum vibration caused by sound impulses is transmitted to the brain. **Listening** occurs when the brain assigns meaning to the transmitted impulses. Thus, listening is an active process.

Many times you hear but do not listen. You hear boring lectures, for example, but seldom listen to them. It is hard work to *really* listen—and it is much harder than talking. Although listening takes effort and discipline, the dividends that result will continue to reward you as a teacher, both inside and outside the classroom.

Virtually everyone listens; however, few do it well. Basic to the improvement of your listening ability is your awareness of the need for improving the skill. When you compare all the training you receive in reading, writing, and speaking with that provided in listening, you will find your listening training to be lacking. This is ironic when you realize that 60 percent of your communication involves listening (DeVito, 1985; Friedman, 1986).

Listening requires that you first learn to cut down on your talking. Although when we were younger we tended to ramble on and on, oblivious as to what others around us were saying, we soon learned from adults that others did not look favorably toward those who talked continuously. But cutting down on our talking is only the beginning to becoming a good listener.

Listening is more than just being silent. Like thinking, listening is an intense, active process. It takes concentration, self-discipline. In fact, Barker (1971, p. 4) describes the listening process as having four components: hearing, attending, understanding, and remembering.

Hearing

Hearing is physiological. It is the nonselective process of sound waves striking the eardrums with the resultant electrochemical impulses being transmitted to the brain. Therefore, any aural information you wish to process and understand will be accompanied by noise. This noise will mask the desired message. In fact, hearing can be affected by exposure to continuous loud tones or noise. Loud music and city noises can indeed lead to auditory fatigue, a temporary loss of hearing, or even to a permanent loss of hearing.

Attending

Although listening starts with the physiological process of hearing, it quickly becomes a psychological one as you decide whether to focus on or *attend* to what is heard. This decision is directly related to your needs, wants, desires, and interests, as well as the relevance of the message, the setting, the intensity of the message, the concreteness of the message, and the duration of the message.

Listening involves focusing on the speaker and the message being transmitted. In some cases, you may not like what the speaker is saying or you may not see the importance of the message to you, but you will never truly know unless you sit it out and listen. Although you will not be able to control all the variables that affect listening, your awareness of such variables will enable you to take a step toward controlling them. You must focus your attention, stop talking, stop fidgeting, and stop letting your mind wander. You must "lock in" on what the speaker is saying while blocking out everything around you.

Blocking out external stimuli is not an easy task and, in fact, is not always desirable behavior for teachers who must be aware of everything that is happening in the classroom. Indeed, teachers must learn to both be aware of what is going on in the classroom and pay attention to students when the situation calls for it.

The way we view a speaker will also affect our willingness to listen. If a speaker is described as very intelligent or as someone of importance, we tend to listen with greater intensity. This tendency also applies to speakers who are attractive and who hold ideas, attitudes, and values similar to our own. Other factors such as size, dress, and name may also have an effect on our capacity for listening. We must control these affecting variables as much as possible if we are to enhance our ability to truly listen.

Listening, like talking, consists of both a verbal and nonverbal component. The words we hear are only one aspect of listening. We also gain information through nonverbal means—that is, through the constant interplay of gestures, feelings, body movements, and so on inherent in human interaction. Thus, people sometimes believe they are sending one message (verbal), but their voice, choice of words, and gestures (nonverbal) send a completely different message.

Sokolove, Sadker, and Sadker (1986, p. 232) identify four nonverbal cues that will affect communications. These writers suggest that attentiveness can be improved by giving special attention to the following:

1. **Eye Contact**
   Focus your eyes directly on the speaker, while taking care that the direct eye-to-eye contact does not make the speaker uncomfortable.

2. **Facial Expressions**
   Let your facial expressions show that you are really listening. These expressions should give feedback (positive and negative) to the speaker as to whether the message is being communicated.

3. **Body Posture**
   Relax as a listener. A relaxed listener tends to relax the speaker and stimulate the person to say more. In fact, a listener who is relaxed and leans toward the speaker communicates interest and involvement.

4. **Physical Space**
   Locate yourself so that you and the speaker have comfortable separation.

Although much of the nonverbal information we receive is on a conscious level, we also glean information from others at the subconscious level—for example, when we know someone isn't really interested in what we are saying. This subconscious information plays an important part in producing our impressions and helps in developing an understanding of the messages being sent, even though we may not be aware of them. Indeed, inferences—sometimes inaccurate—regarding people are often formed based on the subconscious information we receive.

Understanding

Understanding involves the mental processing of the received information. During this phase, the listener must actively judge the worthiness of the message and the relevance of the information as well as select and organize the information received (Friedman, 1986, p. 7). You must consider the information and decide "Am I really interested?" This judgment is based on several elements. First, it involves recognition of the rules of grammar that were used to create the message. Second, judgment often is based on our knowledge about the source of the information—whether the source is reliable, a friend, a professional, and so on. Third, understanding can hinge on the social context. For example, the same message delivered in the teacher's lounge and at a principal's meeting would most likely elicit different judgments. Finally, we often judge the merit of a message by our ability to organize it into a recognizable form.

Remembering

Remembering is the last phase of the listening process. However, your recall of information is directly related to how you evaluate it. In other words, before you send the information to long-term memory, you must decide that it is worthy of remembering. In this evaluation process, you are "weighing the message against personal beliefs, questioning the speaker's motives, challenging the ideas presented, suspecting the validity of the message, holding the speaker's ideas up to standards of excellence, wondering what has been omitted, thinking how the message could have been improved, and in other ways evaluating what is being said" (Friedman, 1986, p. 7). This evaluation generally takes place with respect to the internal beliefs and values one holds. You must learn, however, to evaluate information on its own merit. This ability is difficult, and it takes self-discipline. But it is well worth the effort, especially to teachers.

Past experiences and internal feelings will often have an effect on our evaluation. We all have emotional filters, which affect how we evaluate what we hear. These filters may block words or phrases or, conversely, allow certain words or phrases to rush in and overly impress us. They may at times even change what we hear, as with such terms as *AIDS, test,* or *radical.* Like observing, listening can be selective to some degree.

Nichols and Stevens (1957, pp. 102–103) offer three guidelines for reducing the effects of one's filters on evaluation:

1. Be self-disciplined. Withhold evaluation until you receive the total message.

2. Hunt for negative evidence related to the received message. Don't take what you hear at face value.

3. Make a realistic self-analysis of the information you hear. Test the information against your own biases, values, and feelings.

The ability to recall information is also related to how often you hear the information and to whether the information has been rehearsed. Of course, the more you hear any piece of information, the better it will be retained; similarly, rehearsed information is more often remembered.

Some people are poor listeners because they have developed bad listening habits. These bad habits include the following:

1. **Pseudolistening**
Pseudolistening is an imitation of listening. Good pseudolisteners often will look you in the eye, nod and smile in agreement, and even may answer questions occasionally. In other words, they give the appearance of attentiveness, but, in reality, they are usually thinking about other things.

2. **Insulated Listening**
Some of us avoid listening when we do not want to deal with an issue or when it takes mental exertion to understand what is being said. If you have such a habit, you must make special efforts to practice listening to difficult-to-understand information.

3. Selective Listening

Selective listeners attend only to a speaker's remarks that interest them. Such people automatically cease listening when the message is of little interest. They equate "interest" with "value." The fallacy associated with this habit is that the message is often worth hearing. Of course, all of us are somewhat selective at times—for instance, when we screen out media commercials and background noise as we work.

4. Attribute Listening

Attribute listeners are more interested in the delivery and/or the physical appearance of the speaker. Such individuals are often more concerned with criticizing the speaker's style of delivery or physical appearance. They associate the importance of the message with the way it is delivered or with the appearance of the speaker. It should be remembered that the content of most messages is more important than the method of delivery or the appearance of the deliverer.

5. Stage Hogging

Stage hoggers want to talk. They are only interested in expressing their own ideas. If they allow others to speak, it seems to be only while they catch their breath. Many teachers, for example, want to do all the talking in the classroom. These teachers seldom give students the opportunity for voicing their opinions, and when they do, they often cut off student remarks. In a word, teachers must be especially sensitive to the habit of stage hogging. Remember: Stage hogging isn't really conversing; essentially, it's speech making.

6. Defensive Listening

Defensive listeners take innocent remarks as personal attacks. Teenagers are notorious for being defensive listeners. They often take parental or teacher remarks about their behaviors as being distrustful snooping, and teachers must be aware of this. Similarly, teachers must also realize that teenagers tend to be overly sensitive and defensive regarding the remarks made by other teenagers about their appearance, physical attributes, and/or teaching abilities. Teenagers can be extremely cruel at times.

In most cases, an awareness of the bad habits associated with the listening process is enough in itself to assist one in overcoming their effects. Still, you should practice working on such bad habits if you want to become a better listener.

Thinking often affects listening. It is a well-established fact that we can process information at a faster pace than it can be delivered to us. Therefore, when we listen we have time for taking in our environment and for thinking—for meandering off on mental tangents. This extra thinking time would be better used in reflecting on and analyzing what is being said.

Although we want to be better listeners, we often lack the skills. These needed skills might be better understood through an examination of the different styles of listening.

Styles of Listening

We often listen for different reasons and with different ends in mind. Indeed, listening does and should vary from situation to situation. Listening to a student recitation, for example, would call for a different style of listening than would helping a student with his or her problems. Here we will address three styles of listening: one-way, two-way, and empathic.

One-Way Listening

One-way listening occurs when you are not actively taking part in the exchange of a message. In a word, it is passive listening. You listen without talking and without giving nonverbal directions to the speaker. One-way listening gives speakers the opportunity for developing their thoughts and ideas without being unduly influenced by the listeners. Common examples of one-way listening are watching television or taking in a lecture.

One-way listening gives a speaker free reign. The listener becomes a sounding board for the speaker's ideas or problems. Teenagers often need such a person, who will just hear them out without giving a reaction. The occasional need for a sounding board explains why some people enjoy talking to inanimate objects or pets.

You are also taking part in one-way listening when you just sit back, relax, and let the auditory input stimulate your senses. Listening to music for pure enjoyment is an excellent example of this type of listening.

One-way listening has limited value to teachers. Indeed, except for the few cases we have addressed, it isn't very effective for the simple reason that listeners often misunderstand at least some of a speaker's ideas. Messages, for example, that are overly vague will often be interpreted incorrectly by listeners. In other cases, speakers can send incorrect information, or a listener can simply get the information wrong. Thus, a speaker can say "eight grams" instead of "five," or a listener can transform eight grams into five. On the whole, although one-way listening has its uses, complete understanding of the speaker's message isn't always a sure thing. Fortunately, there are other, better listening styles.

Two-Way Listening

Two-way listening actively involves the listener in the exchange of information. In practice, listeners provide feedback to the speaker by asking for more information or by paraphrasing the speaker's message.

Asking for additional information when a message is unclear is a valuable tool in seeking understanding. Often, you simply ask the speaker to elaborate on the information presented. For example, you might want a student to provide more details on the method used in solving a math word problem, or a student might ask you to repeat your directions for writing a theme, or students in class might ask you for clarification on how to use a piece of laboratory equipment.

Restating the speaker's message in your own words is another technique for providing feedback. One example of rephrasing might be "So you're telling me that you have problems with your parents because they are too restrictive." The thing to remember in restating the speaker's message is to paraphrase the words, not parrot them.

Although active listening usually involves verbal feedback, the feedback can be nonverbal in form—for example, a smile or nod of comprehension, or a frown that shows a lack of understanding. If the speaker is observant, active nonverbal listening techniques can be as effective as the more common verbal techniques.

Two-way listening offers some real advantages for teachers. First, it boosts the odds that they will accurately and fully understand what students are telling them. In effect, active listening serves as a double check on the accuracy of your interpretation of student statements. A second advantage of active listening is that it often stimulates students to explore issues in greater depth. Lastly, your use of listening encourages students to solve their own problems by giving them the opportunity to talk through them.

Empathic Listening

Empathic listening is listening with feeling. It is an earnest attempt at experiencing what the speaker is experiencing or feeling and responding to those feelings. Only through such listening can you fully understand another's meaning. Empathic listening calls for careful attention to the verbal and nonverbal cues given by the speaker. The listener gleans the full meaning of the speaker's message by putting these cues together into a statement that reflects the content as well as the associated feelings.

During the response portion of reflective listening, the listener is attempting to avoid misinterpretation of the speaker or to clarify the message. Sokolove, Sadker, and Sadker (1986, p. 230) suggest that the teacher's function in reflective listening is like holding up a mirror for the student's words, feelings, and behaviors. Through the process of empathic listening, you try to provide direct feedback regarding the success of student communication. This response can take the form of simple paraphrasing of the speaker's words, or it can be an actual interpretation of the speaker's message as reflected in the verbal and nonverbal behaviors. For example, if a student conveys that he or she dislikes your science class, your reflective response to the content of this message might be, "I believe you are saying that you dislike science because you find the experiments too difficult."

Your response to a student statement can be related to the content component of the message or the affective component of the message. For example, your responses to the content of a message might begin with phrases such as "I believe you are saying" or "You appear to think," whereas with responses that reflect the affective component of a message, you might begin with "I think you are feeling" or "You appear to feel."

There are no quick methods for achieving empathy with your students. But it is important to work toward this end. You must learn to see the student's point of view. For example, if students turn in their work late, you should attempt to put yourself in the place of the students in understanding reasons for the lateness. You will often see behaviors that you will consider foolish and ridiculous. What you need to do, however, is consider such situations from the viewpoint of the students.

TABLE *12.2*	Listening	

Type	Description
One-way	Passive listening with no interaction between speaker and listeners
Two-way	Active listening with exchange between speaker and listeners
Empathic	Listening with an attempt at experiencing speaker's feelings

In summary, skill in the various types of listening is an essential tool for effective teaching. Indeed, the importance of good listening on the part of teachers has become more acceptable and recognizable today than ever before. Listening skill is now acknowledged as directly related to teacher effectiveness. All teachers must be proficient listeners.

Listening Feedback

Classroom communication requires that the specific messages you encode and transmit are received and accurately decoded by students. This is generally a continuous and two-way process. Students continuously decode the information you send and send you messages in return. These student-feedback messages, in general, are usually nonverbal in nature.

Students are constantly sending nonverbal messages of understanding or uncertainty, agreement or disagreement, liking or distaste, concern or lack of concern, attention or inattention. When you receive this feedback, you should interpret it and incorporate it in modifying or clarifying your original message; namely, you should respond by reexplaining, offering further examples, or changing your mode of instruction. Identifying and responding to such student feedback is a skill you must master.

The successful utilization of feedback in the learning environment is an effective way of improving instruction. Sadly, many teachers indicate that they rarely, if ever, use feedback as part of their teaching strategy. But feedback is so important to the total learning process, it must not be avoided or ignored.

Table 12.2 summarizes the different types of listening, and the Listening Application Guidelines offer some helpful hints. Review the summary and hints, and complete exercise 12.2.

Application Guidelines ▼

Application of Knowledge

Exercise 12.2   Listening

Check yourself on the following section concepts. Appropriate responses can be found in appendix A.

1. Hearing and listening can be regarded as the same process. (True/False)

2. Name and briefly describe the four components of the listening process.
   a. _____
   _____
   b. _____
   _____
   c. _____
   _____
   d. _____
   _____

3. How we view a speaker will affect our willingness to listen. (True/False)

4. Some people are poor listeners because of bad listening habits. (True/False)

5. Match the listening styles on the right with the appropriate descriptive statement on the left.
a. _____ Active listening	1. One-way listening
b. _____ Listening with feelings	2. Two-way listening
c. _____ Passive listening	3. Empathic listening

6. Empathic listening requires that you pay close attention to _____ and _____ speaker cues.

7. Effective speakers use feedback in determining whether they have been successful at communicating their information. (True/False)

CHAPTER SUMMARY

Communication is central to the learning process, for without it, learning could not take place. Classroom exchanges consist of both spoken and nonverbal messages, with the spoken message comprising the verbal, vocal, and metaverbal components. The verbal component is the actual words spoken; the vocal component is the meaning attached to the words, depending on such things as pitch, loudness, tone, rate, and so on; and the metaverbal component is the implied or intended message. Most teachers are aware of the importance of verbal communication. However, students also learn through nonverbal communication; that is, they learn from a teacher's facial language, body language, use of space and motion, use of time, and use of the voice.

Teachers and students alike need to develop better listening skills. Listening is a four-step process: hearing, attending, understanding, and remembering. Learning is impossible unless you are skilled at all four of these listening steps. Many people have developed bad habits that must be overcome if they are to be effective listeners. Indeed, teachers must overcome bad habits and become proficient at one-way, two-way, and empathic listening.

Teachers generally do most of the talking in the classroom. They have not learned to use nonverbal communication effectively, and rarely—if at all—have they learned to use feedback and to *really* listen to students. Because teachers fulfill their function through the exchange of ideas, it is essential that they develop an understanding of and skill in all facets of the communication process.

Discussion Questions and Activities

1. **The communication process.** Communication, even when effectively carried out, can have good or bad results. Recall several incidents in which communication improved a situation and several in which communication made a situation worse.

2. **Listening habits.** Use the bad habits described in this chapter to describe faulty listening behaviors you use daily. In what circumstances are you guilty of these habits? Around whom? In what settings? At what times?

3. **Vocal communication.** Play a tape of an instructional episode with audio and without video. List the information being exchanged through vocal communication.

4. **Nonverbal communication.** Play the tape in question 3 with only video (no audio). List information being exchanged by the teacher or the students through nonverbal communication.

5. **Metaverbal communication.** Play the tape in questions 3 and 4 with audio and video. Did you notice any implied messages? If so, what were they? Give your reasons for making these conclusions.

6. **Classroom observation.** Complete several observations in secondary school classrooms. Collect data related to communication acts such as these:

   a. The effective use of verbal communication.

   b. The different nonverbal languages used by the teachers.

   c. The teachers' skills at listening.

13 Motivation

✎ Oh, to convert the apathy, the cynicism into a search for meaning in life! Indeed, to connect the classroom to a world of wonder!

Overview

One of your greatest teaching challenges will be to develop students' desire for learning—that is, to motivate students. The traditional approach to motivation was one of preaching to students about learning and the benefits they would derive as well-informed citizens. Needless to say, this approach was ineffective.

Lack of motivation and problems with classroom management are often cited as the major causes for the apathy in the secondary classroom. Thus, motivation and classroom management are two keys to effective instruction. Classroom management will be addressed in chapter 15.

This chapter will focus on the meaning of motivation and will consider three basic orientations: cognitive, stimulation, and reinforcement. Through these three orientations, we will address internal and external factors that affect motivation. Emphasis will be put on techniques that will help keep students interested, involved, and on task.

Objectives

After completing your study of chapter 13, you should be able to do the following:

1. Describe the concept of motivation from the cognitive, stimulation, and reinforcement points of view, as well as explain the interrelationship between the three viewpoints.

2. Identify examples of intrinsic and extrinsic motivation.

3. Discuss student attitudes and needs and their motivational effect on learning.

4. Explain the possible effects of stimulus variation on learning as well as techniques for varying the stimuli in the teaching-learning environment.

5. Define *reinforcement,* and describe the different types of classroom reinforcement.

6. Differentiate between the concepts of positive and negative reinforcement.

7. Identify and discuss three techniques that can be used in providing feedback to students.

8. Describe the characteristics of reward-mechanism systems, and explain the advantages associated with their use.

9. Describe common ways of identifying viable reinforcers for use with secondary school students.

10. Describe contingency contracts and their appropriate classroom use.

Chapter Terms and Key Concepts

Attitude

Being Needs

Contingency Contract

Deficiency Needs

Extrinsic Motivation

Intrinsic Motivation

Modeling

Motivation

Natural Motives

Need

Negative Reinforcement

Nonverbal Reinforcement

Positive Reinforcement

Qualified Reinforcement

Reinforcement

Reward Mechanism

Stimulus Variation

Verbal Reinforcement

Vicarious Motivation

Adolescents today have been raised with television, high-production movies, and highly stimulating musical productions. Having grown accustomed to such highly stimulating experiences, adolescents often expect such experiences when they enter the classroom. Needless to say, they are usually disappointed and often find the classroom less than exciting. Consequently, there is limited motivation to learn in many secondary school classrooms.

All teachers will undoubtedly agree that motivation is a critical factor in classroom learning. But what is motivation, and, more importantly, how do you go about developing students' basic physiological drive to learn? Sadly, attempts at explaining motivation have led to disagreement because of the complexity of the concept of motivation. Let's begin our study of motivation by looking at its source.

Intrinsic versus Extrinsic Motivation

Motivation can be defined as something that energizes and directs our behaviors. Obviously, such influences can come from within (internal) or outside (external) the individual. Internal or **intrinsic motivation** is what learners themselves bring into the learning environment—that is, their internal attributes (attitudes, needs, personality factors, and values). We shall refer to the emphasis on these internal factors as the *cognitive* approach to motivation. Essentially, this view will be concerned with the unique internal attributes that direct individual behaviors. In contrast, external or **extrinsic motivation** originates in the learning environment, where persons are offered the right incentives for doing certain things. This use of rewards represents a *reinforcement* approach to motivation.

Internal motives often are difficult to change, and when change does occur, it occurs slowly. Indeed, what with the short time you will have with students, the likelihood of your changing students' internal motivational patterns will be slim at best. Thus, you must learn to stimulate the motivational attributes that already exist.

External motivation makes use of incentives in getting students to modify behaviors. These incentives represent artificially devised techniques for prompting students to work harder. Ideally, incentives should never become the primary reason for doing classroom work; that is, you should use incentives only sparingly and phase them out as soon as possible.

Many theorists assume that intrinsic and extrinsic motives are interrelated and will interact. This viewpoint, which will be referred to as the *stimulation* approach to motivation, suggests that external environmental factors can be used in influencing internal factors. Figure 13.1 shows how the different motivational viewpoints interact to influence student motivation. Let's look at these approaches more closely.

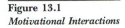

Figure 13.1
Motivational Interactions

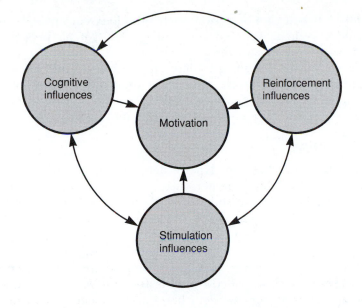

The Cognitive Approach to Motivation

Like most people, students have a tendency to react according to their perceptions of events. These perceptions will result in differing desires, based on variations in attitude, need structure, curiosity level, task interest, satisfaction with learning, sense of well-being, and so on.

Student Attitude

Some students will love school and your subject at the outset, while others will hate it all. These predetermined **attitudes**—or mind-sets toward certain persons, places, or things—are the results of prior experiences with school and similar subjects: Some will love school and your subject because they find it interesting or easy, while others will hate school and your subject because they find it boring or difficult. Your job is to deal with negative attitudes and to bring about change. Because you cannot force students to like school or your subject, this task will not be an easy one. Indeed, you cannot compel students to change their attitudes against their will. Your best strategy is to entice change through the use of innovative motivational techniques.

First, it is important that negative mind-sets regarding school and learning be reversed. Thus, you must show students that school is worthwhile. In other words, you must show students that the learning acquired in school is important to the development of life skills and of the skills necessary for accomplishing career goals. One way of accomplishing this task is by inviting respected community leaders and business people into the school for a discussion about the importance of school and learning.

Second, students often are concerned with subject relevance. Therefore, you should be prepared to respond to those age-old questions: "Why do we have to learn this stuff?" or "What good is this stuff going to be for me?'' If you cannot answer such questions convincingly, perhaps you should reevaluate your course content. You, of all people, should know why your subject is worthwhile.

Finally, if you are going to develop positive attitudes toward school and learning, you must involve students in their own learning and stimulate their interest. We will consider involvement and interest techniques in the next section, when we discuss stimulation motivation.

Student Needs

A **need** can be defined as ''any type of deficiency in the human organism or the absence of anything the person requires, or thinks he requires, for his overall well-being'' (Kolesnik, 1978, p. 149). Obviously, students will enter your class with a wide variety of needs. Indeed, Maslow (1970) has suggested that human needs function on seven hierarchical levels. The first four lower-level needs, labeled **deficiency needs,** represent the needs for survival, safety, belonging, and self-esteem, whereas the three higher-level **being needs** comprise the needs for intellectual achievement, aesthetic appreciation, and self-actualization. The being needs, unlike the deficiency needs, are never truly satisfied; that is, the quest for their fulfillment only motivates individuals to seek further fulfillment.

Maslow's needs hierarchy can provide valuable insight as to the reasons for some students' behaviors. In a word, students' desire to fulfill lower-level needs may interfere with your desire that they achieve higher-level goals. A student's longing, for example, to belong to the peer group and maintain self-esteem within the group may interfere with achievement. Indeed, students sometimes may break rules, or even openly defy a teacher, simply for recognition from peers. Furthermore, the intensity of various needs will vary from individual to individual and even change with time and circumstances.

The need for safety has important ramifications for teachers. Essentially, because it is usually more difficult to learn when there is a feeling of insecurity, you would probably avoid using fear and excessive anxiety as a motivating device. That is, you should avoid shaming students when they make mistakes or judgment errors, and you should avoid overemphasizing tests and grades. Indeed, students are often motivated when they feel secure enough to share their ideas and opinions. An atmosphere tempered with a little anxiety can motivate students, but exercise care when you use fear and anxiety with your students.

All students have the need to achieve and the need to avoid failure. Consequently, the overall tendency (resultant motivation) of students will be to take risks in order to achieve or to avoid threatening situations that might lead to failure. Therefore, when you plan, consider which students have high achievement needs, low achievement needs, and fears of failure. You may want to provide challenging optional assignments for high achievers and provide encouragement and reinforcement for those students with an acute fear of failure.

TABLE *13.1*	Cognitive Approach to Motivation
Factor	**Description**
Attitude	Mind-set toward person, place, or thing
Need	Deficiency, real or imaginary, that a person requires for well-being
Natural Motives	Internal desires of individual, many of which are believed to be innate

Application Guidelines ▼

Cognitive Approach to Motivation

Recognize Importance of Internal Factors to Learning

Examples:
1. Urge students to think about and select realistic long-term goals.
2. Emphasize that learning can be enjoyable, that doing well in school opens opportunities.
3. Make classroom experiences as positive as possible.
4. Try to be a sympathetic, responsive person; build up positive associations.
5. Try to allow for and alleviate discomfort.
6. Make your classroom physically and psychologically safe.
7. Show students they are worthy of esteem.
8. Avoid public comparisons; stress self-competition and self-improvement.
9. Try to strengthen need for achievement.
10. Try to strengthen self-concept; help students succeed after initial failure.
11. Make sure students have sufficient opportunities for fulfilling their need for affiliation and belonging.
12. Help students who are overly concerned with achievement and grades to relax.

Natural Motives

By nature, people are curious, are stimulated by suspense, and have a natural desire for action, adventure, and to do things of interest. Therefore, you should harness these **natural motives** in planning your learning activities. For example, educational games, puzzles, computers, and simulations represent viable strategies for capturing the natural motives of most students. Finally, as much as is feasible, select activities that will give individual students the opportunity for pursuing individual interests and desires.

To this point we have focused on the internal motives of students. Table 13.1 offers a review of the major concepts, and the Cognitive Approach to Motivation Application Guidelines give further cognitive motivational suggestions.

What can you do to influence students' perceptions of events? How can you stimulate the internal motives of your students? To answer

Application of Knowledge

Exercise 13.1   Cognitive Approach to Motivation

Test yourself on the following section concepts. Appropriate responses can be found in appendix A.

1. Internal changes usually occur rapidly. (True/False)

2. Intrinsic and extrinsic motives are interrelated and often interact. (True/False)

3. Match the definition on the left with the term on the right.
   a. _____ An innate internal desire   1. Attitude
   b. _____ A deficiency required for well-being   2. Natural motive
   c. _____ A predisposition regarding an idea,   3. Need
            place, or thing

4. Maslow's two categories of needs are _____ and _____ .

5. Maslow's higher-level needs are never completely satisfied. (True/False)

6. Teachers should never try to weaken students' need for achievement. (True/False)

7. Anxiety should be avoided at all cost in the classroom. (True/False)

these questions we must turn to the stimulation approach to motivation. Before you continue, however, complete exercise 13.1, which will check your understanding of the concepts presented to this point.

The Stimulation Approach to Motivation

It is rather easy to teach when students are internally motivated to learn. Sadly, this usually is not the case; most secondary school students are not overly excited about learning. Thus, you must learn to stimulate the desire to learn. Let's look at some techniques that can be used in accomplishing this end.

Classroom Atmosphere

The school and classroom atmosphere often set the tone for learning. Such factors as leadership style, physical environment, room arrangement, and classroom communication often can make the difference between a motivated learner and a bored, reluctant learner.

Leadership Style

What type of leader do you want to be? Do you want to be stimulating, warm, caring, fair, funny, and interesting? Or would you prefer to be commanding, dominating, sharp, critical, and harsh? Or perhaps you might choose to be lackadaisical and completely permissive? These characteristics often determine your leadership style: authoritarian, democratic, or laissez-faire. The type of leader you become will also depend on the policies of the school, your students, and your personality. Some teachers feel students lack the maturity and ability to be involved in decision making, and therefore they rely heavily on the authoritarian style of leadership.

The *authoritarian* style of leadership is characterized by power, domination, pressure, and criticism. The authoritarian teacher assumes the sole responsibility of making all decisions for the class and uses pressure, a sharp voice, and fear in forcing compliance. Accordingly, the authoritarian teacher uses criticism and "put downs" for motivating students, which often results in an atmosphere of hostility, a feeling of powerlessness, competitiveness, high dependency, and a feeling of alienation from the subject matter (Schmuck & Schmuck, 1988). Students in this type of atmosphere often develop a fear of failure, a low self-esteem, and a defeatist attitude. Consequently, students tend to give up when new or difficult tasks are encountered.

The *democratic* teacher is kind, caring, and warm, but also firm. The democratic leader tries to provide stimulation from within through a sharing of responsibility and through encouragement, rather than demands. Self-esteem is developed by a sharing of responsibility, and students are encouraged when mistakes are made. The democratic classroom atmosphere is one of openness, friendly communication, and independence, with a resultant high level of productivity and performance.

The *laissez-faire* leader is completely permissive. Anything goes, which generally leads to chaos. The classroom is often disorganized, which causes student frustration, a high level of stress, and a feeling of being totally overwhelmed and lost.

Change from the obsolete authoritarian approach of demanding submission to a more democratic approach based on freedom, choice, and responsibility would do much for helping students develop a positive feeling toward school and your subject. Students hopefully would learn to be truly responsible individuals.

Physical Environment

Will your classroom be attractive and colorful, or will it be bleak and drab? Sadly, many secondary school classrooms tend to be on the bleak side. An attractive room, however, is often more conducive to learning. Compelling bulletin boards and displays can add much to the atmosphere of your classroom. Indeed, such bulletin boards and displays can be designed to be both informative and colorful; and when students are allowed to design and construct them, classroom bulletin boards and displays can be quite motivating.

The arrangement of the classroom coupled with the seating of students can also be an effective motivating device. That is, your room arrangement can foster group cohesiveness, which can lead to a high level of group belonging. Because a sense of belonging represents a basic need, it will have a positive influence on motivation. Even better, give students an occasional opportunity for rearranging their own seating.

Communication

Communication is a topic covering a broad range of complicated human relationships. Lack of classroom communication definitely can be the cause of poor motivation. Indeed, when motivational problems arise, communication becomes essential. However, communication means more than

the "teacher talks and students listen." Real communication is an open, two-way street; you talk, but you also listen. You must learn to listen, and you must allow students to talk and have input in finding solutions to classroom motivational problems. You must constantly strive to improve your communication skills and to listen with an open mind to the feelings, ideas, and opinions of your students.

Modeling

Modeling is a motivational technique in which persons admired by students demonstrate, through their actions, the values and behaviors you want students to acquire. These actions usually take the form of subtle suggestions that are communicated through noted nonverbal body language. Students, for example, who role-play or observe others role-play political leaders, musicians, poets, and scientists sometimes develop related interests. Furthermore, students at times will serve as role models for each other. That is, when students see certain desirable behaviors in respected or admired peers, they may learn these behaviors themselves. Consequently, group work sometimes will result in the transfer of desirable behaviors.

The most notable model in most classrooms will be you, the teacher. Indeed, the enthusiasm and sense of wonder you show for your subject will often be passed on to your students. Consequently, if you appear interested and excited about a lesson, students often will become transfixed, eager to find out what is so interesting. Indeed, research

suggests that enthusiastic teachers produce higher academic achievement by students. (Silvernail, 1979, pp. 27–28). Thus, teacher enthusiasm appears to be directly related to the students' need for achievement.

Stimulating Interest

Students naturally seek stimulation as they constantly search for interesting things to do, for variety, for challenge. They constantly seek stimulating thrills and prefer settings that will provide these stimuli. Thus, students will prefer environments rich in stimuli over those that are monotonous and dull; doing *something*—no matter how trivial—generally is more interesting than doing nothing.

The human need for stimulation has important motivational implications. The learning environment typically is under continuous bombardment from such external stimuli as street traffic, hall traffic, and school-yard conversation. All these stimuli take students' attention and interest away from the classroom to some degree. You therefore must compete continuously for students' attention with irrelevant external stimuli. If the irrelevant external stimulus is viewed by the students as more interesting or novel than the learning activity, attention and interest more than likely will be directed toward the external source.

Students are notorious for their inattentiveness and short attention spans. If periodic changes in stimuli do not occur in the learning environment, students often lose interest. In other words, unless students are extremely engaged in the class proceedings, their attention will soon turn to external stimuli or to inner thoughts. Thus, you must vary or change your behaviors or your learning activities so students receive new stimuli that will keep their attention directed toward the lesson. In effect, you must consciously incorporate **stimulus variation** into your lessons for the purpose of gaining, maintaining, and increasing student attention and interest. Allen, Ryan, Bush, and Cooper (1969) suggest several behaviors or behavior patterns that can help accomplish this end: gestures, focusing techniques, varying interaction styles, shifting sensory channels, and movement.

Gestures often capture and focus our attention. A tap on the desk, a hand movement, or shift of the body position, for instance, is often all that is needed to refocus attention back on a lesson. Such gestural movements represent a change in stimuli to the students, which usually prompts them to direct their attention back to the lesson. Indeed, an added emphasis can be communicated through various general movements of the body, head, and hands. A snap of the fingers or a nod of the head will often focus student attention on you as you teach.

Focusing is the technique of directing students' attention to what you have said or will say through verbal statements or through gestures. Verbal focusing can be used effectively in directing students to pay closer attention to specifics in a lesson presentation, or it can be used when you notice that student attention is beginning to wander. Examples of verbal statements that are commonly used in focusing students' attention are "This point is well worth remembering!" and "These are today's major issues!" or even "Make sure you include this point in your notes." Even greater impact can be obtained when a verbal focusing statement is used in conjunction with some form of gesture—for example, a tap on the chalkboard in conjunction with a verbal statement such as "Remember these definitions!"

You can use any one of four basic interaction styles with your students: teacher-group, teacher-student, student-student, and student-group. The *teacher-group interaction* style should be used when you want to address the class as a whole—for example, when you are giving a lecture over some content or when giving some form of demonstration. If, on the other hand, you want to address or question a specific student, the *teacher-student interaction* style would be appropriate. When used wisely, this style will often enhance student interest in a lesson through involvement.

Sometimes you may want to redirect a student comment or question to another student for a response or for clarification. Such *student-student interaction* can be used when it is desirable to acknowledge a student's knowledge in the area being discussed or when it is desirable to direct an inattentive student's attention back to the lesson. At other times, you may want to withdraw from a discussion and direct a question or a request for clarification to a student, which would require that the student address the entire group. This style of *student-group interaction* should be used only with students who can assume a central role in a group discussion; avoid putting your students in uncomfortable situations.

Although most classroom communication is oral, you have four other vital communication channels: seeing, touching, tasting, smelling. You can often stimulate interest by shifting between these sensory channels. When you make such shifts, you prompt students to make a shift in reception modes, which in turn causes them to refocus their attention.

The use of an overhead projector, for instance, is a typical example of effective refocusing, with students being required to shift their "primary" reception between aural and visual modes.

In most cases, you will be the most significant person in the classroom environment. Thus, any action on your part will draw students' attention. Consequently, you can refocus student attention during your lessons by incorporating simple movement into your teaching actions. For example:

1. Move to the left or to the right within the classroom.

2. Move to the back or to the front within the classroom.

3. Move out among the students.

In general, you should avoid remaining stationary (or hiding) behind a podium or desk when you teach. Most of you have been exposed to teachers who stood rigidly behind a podium and spoke in a low monotone voice; you probably had trouble maintaining attention and interest. Clearly, such experiences reveal the importance of developing skills in focusing student attention and interest on a lesson.

Finally, teacher enthusiasm should not be overlooked as a focusing technique. When you are enthusiastic, you keep students' attention as a result of your energy and excitement. As such, students will often become interested and attentive.

Although focusing techniques are used for drawing students' attention and interest toward your lessons, they can serve to refocus attention and interest *away* from the lesson if they are overused. That is, if you implement refocusing techniques too often, students may become more interested in the novelty of your presentation rather than in the lesson content. A continual "uh" or "okay," pacing, or the tapping of your foot, for example, can detract from your lesson. Indeed, even overly enthusiastic teachers can detract from their lessons when they exhibit excessive emotional behaviors.

Set Induction

Typically, you must get students' attention and interest at the outset of your lessons (see chapter 5). That is, you must get the undivided attention of every student in your class and prepare them to listen (establish a cognitive set).

Many factors will influence student attention and interest at the onset of a lesson—namely, the weather, holidays, school sports, and so on. Therefore, you must develop a repertoire of techniques that will gain student attention and interest. For example, as pointed out in chapter 5, the act of facing the class in silence is often all that is needed for gaining the attention and interest of your class. This technique is especially effective when you have a small group within the class that is inattentive. Silence and an intense stare in the group's direction will soon get their undivided attention. The use of silence and pauses are effective tools for gaining student attention.

Another often-used method that can be employed in fostering student attention and interest is by beginning your lesson with a topic that is of vital interest to the class. Indeed, the topic itself need not even be closely related to the lesson of the day. For example, an interest in cars can lead into a study of motion or friction. A discussion of the beach can lead into a discussion of the solar system. This technique needs to be developed; it is an art.

Such techniques as the use of gestures, teacher movement, suspense, models, and pictures can be quite excellent attention getters. An interesting demonstration, a discrepant event, or a picture usually will attract students' attention. Even better, let your students conduct the introductory demonstration, lead in the discrepant event, or show the pictures. You should experiment with various attention-getting techniques when determining which ones will be the most effective with your students. Classes will often differ, based on such factors as course content, socioeconomic level, background, motivation, grade level, and class size.

Motivational Methods

Many of the teaching strategies described in chapter 8 will heighten student motivation through their direct involvement of students in their own learning. In addition, many of the strategies are motivational in that they can influence students' cognitive needs. The need for belonging, for example, can be met through cooperative learning—that is, through a classroom structure where groups of students work together toward a common goal, with individual group members contributing for the benefit of the individual and the group. The interaction and sharing of responsibility in cooperative learning represents a form of social motivation in that it greatly enhances the sense of belonging. This sense of belonging can be accomplished in many of the instructional strategies that involve experiences that satisfy the need for affiliation and acceptance from others.

When students use their own initiative in exploring concepts and they meet with success, a sense of competence (an intrinsic need to cope with the environment) often results and the level of aspiration often rises. Therefore, the use of strategies that maximize student involvement in learning may well stimulate a sense of competence along with a sense of accomplishment. Moreover, if students can help select and plan their own activities, they will find them even more interesting. Consequently, some forms of individualized instruction represent effective motivational strategies.

Students desire variety, action, excitement, and novelty. Indeed, they would much rather read a story with many subplots or a lot of action over a slow-moving, single-plot story. Furthermore, they will prefer stimuli that are new or represent new experiences to stimuli that are routine or familiar. In other words, you should try to add life to your lessons by keeping your lessons lively, by introducing interesting, stimulating materials and teaching techniques, and by using approaches ranging from pauses to humor. Humor, for example, will give your students a change of pace. The pauses will give students time to think, ponder, and reflect.

Teacher Expectations

Students tend to perform better and feel more personally adequate when you set high expectations and hold them to these expectations (Good & Brophy, 1987). This self-fulfilling prophecy holds important ramifications for teachers; namely, students will behave and achieve in accordance with your expectations.

Classroom interaction studies suggest that teachers tend to favor students they perceive as high achievers. Indeed, high achievers are often given more time to answer questions, receive more positive feedback, and have more and higher-quality interaction with their teachers. In fact, Cooper and Good (1983, p. 10) offer several common ways that teachers respond differently to high-achieving students ("highs") and low-achieving students ("lows"):

1. Seating lows far from the teacher.

2. Paying less attention to lows in academic situations (using less eye contact, nods, winks, and smiles).

3. Calling on lows less often to answer classroom questions.

4. Waiting less time for lows to answer questions.

5. Criticizing lows more frequently than highs for incorrect classroom responses.

6. Praising lows less frequently than highs after successful classroom responses.

7. Praising lows more frequently than highs for marginal or inadequate classroom responses.

8. Providing lows with less accurate and less detailed feedback than highs.

9. Demanding less work and effort from lows than from highs.

10. Interrupting performance of lows more frequently than highs.

These findings suggest that teachers tend to give more support to those students they view as more capable. As a result, the interactions between more capable students and their teachers tend to be more positive.

Students' motivation, aspiration, and self-concept can be affected to a considerable extent by your viewpoints and actions. When you expect students to do poorly, you may unconsciously give them less encouragement, less time to answer questions, and less attention. As this pattern continues over the year, students move closer and closer to your expectations. Be aware, then, that students are using your actions as a mirror of themselves. So challenge your students and communicate a belief in their abilities—and mean it.

This concludes our discussion of the stimulation approach to motivation. Table 13.2 reviews the major concepts covered, and the Stimulation Approach to Motivation Application Guidelines offer some further suggestions. Review the table and guidelines, and complete exercise 13.2, which will check your understanding of the concepts presented in this section.

TABLE *13.2*	Stimulation Approach to Motivation

Factor	Description
Classroom Atmosphere	The climate of the classroom, which generally is related to leadership style, environmental arrangement, and communication
Stimulation	Engaging and interesting factors that attract and involve students
Modeling	The demonstration of desired values and behaviors by a person admired by students
Set Induction	Gaining students' attention and interest at the outset of lesson
Teacher Expectation	Perception of how well students will do, which often leads to self-fulfilling prophecy

Application Guidelines ▼

Stimulation Approach to Motivation

Provide a Supportive Atmosphere

Examples:
1. Support students' attempts. Let them know that you see and want them to do their best.
2. Encourage students to cooperate with you in planning their own learning activities.
3. Be enthusiastic.
4. Personalize your classroom. Treat students as individuals; talk with them about their problems and interests.
5. Build students' trust in you: Be fair, but firm.
6. Encourage students to identify and solve their own problems.
7. Play down comparison between students; urge self-improvement.

Offer Stimulating Instruction

Examples:
1. Provide an assortment of appealing activities, materials, and content. Make sure that this selected content is relevant and worthwhile.
2. Never start off an activity without gaining the attention of the total class. Carefully plan orientation set inductions.
3. Implement active rather than passive activities. Novelty is important, so introduce a variety of activities and keep your activities lively.
4. Keep students' ideas and interests in mind: Appeal to their desire for fun, social interests, curiosity, and need for achievement.
5. Make learning fun, and try to have a happy classroom: Make your content attractive, and use humor once in a while.
6. Employ a variety of interesting strategies and activities. Try an occasional surprise in your lessons.
7. Use audiovisual materials that will be relevant and interesting to students.
8. Create failure-proof situations for slow learners as well as challenging activities for high-ability students.
9. Put the textbook aside occasionally, and instead teach from the newspaper, which can be used for any content area.

Application of Knowledge

Exercise 13.2   Stimulation Approach to Motivation

Test yourself on the following section concepts. Appropriate responses can be found in appendix A.

1. Match the leadership style on the left with its characteristic on the right.
   a. _____ Teacher assumes sole responsibility for   1. Authoritarian
                      decisions   2. Democratic
   b. _____ Students do almost anything they wish   3. Laissez-faire
   c. _____ Encouragement of stimulation from within
                      the student

2. Secondary teachers generally do not place major emphasis on room attractiveness. (True/False)

3. Define *modeling*: _____
   _____

4. The most influential model in most secondary classrooms is the teacher. (True/False)

5. Describe some techniques that you can use for gaining and keeping students' attention and interest in your lessons.
   _____
   _____
   _____
   _____

6. The set induction is used for attracting and establishing students' attention and interest at the outset of a lesson. (True/False)

7. Name and describe some teaching strategies that would heighten students' desire to learn.
   _____
   _____
   _____
   _____

8. The self-fulfilling prophecy applies only to low-achievement students. (True/False)

The Reinforcement Approach to Motivation

Reinforcement, or the rewarding of desired actions, is a long-recognized motivational technique. This technique is based on the principle that actions that induce pleasure tend to be repeated. Essentially, we tend to behave in ways that result in some type of valued payoff or reward. Thus, if a student will work at obtaining something, the something (event, object, action, etc.) acts as a reinforcer for that student and will be a motivator. However, a particular reinforcer may serve as a motivator for one student, but not for a second. In other words, the reinforcement is proven to be a motivator only if the desired behaviors are increased or enhanced. Grades, for example, are not motivators to all students. Any repeated student actions, appropriate or inappropriate, are being reinforced in some way with a payoff; that is, the student is being motivated by a reward to behave as he or she does. Reinforcement, then, can be an effective motivator when used appropriately. Let's now take a close look at teacher reinforcement and its function as a motivator.

Positive versus Negative Reinforcement

Reinforcement can be positive or negative. **Positive reinforcement** occurs when something valued by the student is presented as a result of some student action. Possible positive reinforcers are grades, praise, stickers, and social recognition.

Negative reinforcement, on the other hand, involves the removal of an aversive stimulus, such as a test or the threat of detention. In effect, students are placed in an undesirable situation from which they are motivated to escape by means of appropriate actions. Note that the student is in control with negative reinforcement; that is, the negative situation can be escaped with appropriate actions.

Reinforcement Techniques

What types of reinforcement typically are best for motivating secondary students? Unfortunately, this is not an easy question to answer. The most effective technique in any given situation will depend on such variables as the grade level, individual student, learning activity, and you as the teacher. Four reinforcement sources, however, have proven to be effective at motivating secondary school students: teacher approval, observing other students, knowledge of results, and reward mechanisms.

Teacher approval can come in one of two forms: verbal and nonverbal. **Verbal reinforcement** occurs when you follow a student action or response with some type of positive comment. Typical examples are the one-word ''Good!'' or brief-phrase comments, such as ''That's right!'' and ''Great idea!'' and the like. You should take care not to overuse such brief-phrase reinforcers, for they can lose their effectiveness if you use a single one exclusively. Therefore, be a wise verbal reinforcer: choose a variety of comments, and make sure you use them only for appropriate actions or responses. Also, don't overlook how student ideas may be used as reinforcers: You should apply, compare, and build on contributions made by students. Consequently, when you show that what students say is important, they are motivated to participate even more.

When a physical action is used for sending a message of approval for some student action or response, it is referred to as **nonverbal reinforcement.** A nod of approval, a smile, eye contact, movement toward a student, or any positive gesture, for example, show students they are correct or on the right track. Nonverbal reinforcement is a powerful motivator—perhaps even more powerful than verbal reinforcement.

When student actions are only partially acceptable, you want to motivate the student so that he or she will continue to attempt the desired action. For example, you might want to reinforce an attempt at solving a geometry proof or the fact that the procedure used in investigating a problem was correct. In effect, you want to differentially reinforce the acceptable parts of a student action or the attempt itself. In such situations, you are using the technique of **qualified reinforcement.** Qualified reinforcement can be an effective technique for getting your shy and less able students more involved in class activities.

Vicarious Motivation

Students can be motivated by seeing other students being reinforced for their action. That is, if a student sees another student reinforced for certain actions or behaviors, he or she tends to act in the same way if the reinforcement is desirable. For example, if a student is given exemption from the unit test for doing well on the chapter tests, that reinforcement may serve to motivate other students to do well on chapter tests. The term applied to this type of motivation is **vicarious motivation.** In effect, the first student serves as a model for the desired behaviors.

Vicarious motivation usually is quite efficient in that desired actions are learned immediately; no teaching is required. Therefore, with properly chosen reinforcers and appropriate application, vicarious motivation can initiate desired new actions and behaviors.

Feedback as Motivator

Three techniques can be employed in providing feedback to students: praise, disclosure of results, and grades. If they are to be effective, these feedback techniques must be carefully and systematically applied. Simply "handing out" positive feedback will, in time, destroy any techniques's effectiveness as a motivator. Appropriately used feedback, therefore, is contingent on the desired action, specifies clearly the action being reinforced, and is believable (O'Leary & O'Leary, 1977). In other words, positive feedback should be a sincere recognition of student work that has been well done.

Teachers have long acknowledged and recognized the power of praise as a compelling motivator. Brophy (1981), in a comprehensive analysis of praise, attests to the importance of teacher praise as a reinforcement technique. Indeed, Brophy suggests that praise is more powerful than general reinforcement, because it generally calls for teacher attention and energy beyond the use of the standard one-word or short-phrase response ("Good," "Fine answer," or "Okay"). Finally, praise can lay the foundation for lasting internal change because it works to improve students' self-esteem.

Providing students with the results of assigned tasks motivates some students, because it communicates the correctness of responses. Results that indicate success lead to renewed vigor, while indications of needed corrective measures communicate what actions or efforts are needed for improving performance. If you are to ensure that students benefit from the motivational effects of work results, you must return papers and tests to students immediately—with more than a simple grade marked on them. Indeed, it is suggested that teachers can achieve maximum incentive from marking papers if each returned paper is

Providing feedback on how well a student did on assigned work is often an effective motivator.

personalized with comments about strengths and weaknesses. Simple comments written in the margins should be sufficient for offering students needed guidance.

Teachers have always considered tests and grades as highly motivational sources. Unfortunately, the research does not support the conjecture that tests and grades motivate students to learn, but rather, that tests typically motivate students to cram—that is, learn for the test. Actually, tests and good grades seem to be motivational only to top students, while offering only limited incentive to low-ability students. Therefore, you would be wise not to make grades your primary source of motivation. Instead, you should appeal to students' intrinsic motives, and rely more on cooperative and individualized strategies. Such structures are more likely to be motivational for students.

Reward Mechanisms

As used here, a **reward mechanism** is a more formal system of reinforcement. It is an agreement where students earn certain specified rewards for displaying certain types of behaviors. In one such successful system, students earn tokens, points, stars, or checks—or anything else that seems appropriate—for performing desired academic and classroom behaviors. These tokens are then periodically exchanged for some desirable reward, such as free time, less homework, tangible objects, educational games, or anything else desired by the students that is deemed appropriate.

You can also offer a menu of rewards in a reward-mechanism system. Students then purchase the rewards for different numbers of tokens, for instance; few tokens yield less desirable rewards, and many tokens yield more desirable rewards. For example, students might be excused from a homework assignment for a few tokens and be allowed to listen to music in class for several tokens.

An advantage to the more formal reward mechanism is that students are not inadvertently overlooked from receiving reinforcement. However, it is sometimes difficult to find adequate reinforcers for secondary school students. Two common ways of identifying such reinforcers is to simply ask students directly or have them fill out a questionnaire about desired reinforcers. Moreover, simply observing students during their free time or after they finish their work will often give you valuable clues as to what can be used for reinforcement. The best reinforcers frequently will depend on the students, the subject, and the situation.

Contingency Contracts

Contingency contracts are formal written agreements between a teacher and student that describe exactly what the student must do to earn a desired privilege or reward. These contracts can be written up by the teacher and presented to the student for agreement, or the student can work out the contract and present it to the teacher. However, contracts are usually best when they are written by the teacher and student together as a negotiating process. Regardless of the contract-development process followed, the contract should specify exactly what the student will do to earn the privilege or reward. A sample contingency contract is shown in figure 13.2.

Contracts should encourage students to make realistic expectations of their abilities. Accordingly, you can have a stipulation that the contract can be changed, but there should be a built-in penalty for any alterations.

No matter what your specific explanations for the sources of motivation, you should be aware that no one is completely unmotivated. Even doing nothing takes motivation. Table 13.3 gives a review of the major concepts in this section, and the Reinforcement Approach to Motivation Application Guidelines give some further suggestions. Review the table and guidelines, and then focus your attention on exercise 13.3, which will check your understanding of this section.

Figure 13.2 *A Sample Contract*

Read through the listed items and check those you would like to do. Then decide for what grade you would like to contract. Grades will be given as follows:

   D The starred items plus one more from each group
   C The starred items plus two more from each group
   B The starred items plus three more from each group
   A The starred items plus four more from each group

Discuss your choice with your teacher, and sign your name in the proper place.

I, _____ , agree to complete the following
        (Name)

work on the unit at a level of _____ or better:
                    (Grade)

   * Read assigned text chapters
   * Complete in-class and out-of-class assignments
   * Complete unit test at or above contracted grade level

Group I

   * Do one library assignment

   1. Prepare an outline of unit content
   2. Write a one-page paper on a unit topic
   3. Complete an optional writing assignment
   4. Develop an annotated bibliography related to the unit
   5. Review a textbook that addresses the unit topic and
      write a short report on its contents

Group II

   * Give one class demonstration

   1. Conduct a short project related to the unit content
   2. Lead a class discussion of a topic related to this unit
   3. Locate and present to class unit-related newspaper articles
   4. Draw some conclusions relative to the importance of the
      unit topic to your everyday life

_____
Date

_____
Student's signature

_____
Teacher's signature

TABLE *13.3*   Reinforcement Approach to Motivation

Factor	Description
Positive Reinforcement	Presentation of a desired stimulus to strengthen likelihood of a behavior or event
Negative Reinforcement	Removal of an unpleasant stimulus to strengthen likelihood of a behavior or event
Verbal Reinforcement	Presentation of positive comments as consequence to strengthen student behavior or event
Nonverbal Reinforcement	Using a physical action as a positive consequence to strengthen behavior or event
Vicarious Motivation	Strengthening of behavior because of desire to receive consequences received by others who exhibit that behavior
Feedback	Disclosure of correctness of response
Reward Mechanism	Formal system of reinforcement
Contingency Contract	Formal written agreement between student and teacher as to what students will do for receiving reward

Application Guidelines   ▼

Reinforcement Approach to Motivation

Use a Variety of Reinforcement Techniques

Examples:
1. Encourage students through use of peer recognition: Display students' good work, or have them share with each other.
2. Have students keep charts of their daily and weekly grades and encourage them to show improvement.
3. Give students the opportunity to work together for rewards.
4. Use educational games as reinforcement.
5. Write brief messages to students when you return papers.
6. Use a mix of reinforcers, tangible rewards, social rewards, feedback, and teacher actions.
7. Employ contingency contracts whenever appropriate.
8. Try to use peers as models for desirable behaviors or actions.

Correctly Apply the Principles of Reinforcement

Examples:
1. Use continuous reinforcement when reinforcing new behaviors.
2. Once a behavior has been established, switch to intermittent reinforcement.
3. Use rewards that are suitable for each student.
4. Make sure you are offering meaningful reinforcement.

Application of Knowledge

Exercise 13.3   Reinforcement Approach to Motivation

Test yourself on the following motivational concepts. Appropriate responses can be found in appendix A.

1. Repeated behaviors or actions usually are the result of some type of reward or payoff. (True/False)

2. When students receive a desirable stimulus for an appropriate behavior, positive and negative reinforcement has occurred. (True/False)

3. List four actions or behavior patterns through which students can attain reinforcement and, in turn, become motivated.
    a. _____
    b. _____
    c. _____
    d. _____

4. Teachers generally should remain stationary when teaching so students' concentration isn't broken. (True/False)

5. It is best to use only continuous reinforcement in the secondary school classroom. (True/False)

6. It is usually unwise to use peers as reinforcers in the secondary school classroom. (True/False)

7. Define *vicarious reinforcement:* _____
    _____

8. Grades are always an effective motivator for secondary school students. (True/False)

9. A reward mechanism is a formal system for the reinforcement of student behaviors and actions. (True/False)

10. Define *contingency contract:* _____
    _____

CHAPTER SUMMARY

Motivation is not easy. It does not exist or occur in isolation. Indeed, motivation is influenced to a large extent by internal factors, the actions of the teacher, and the physical environment. Motivation often will come from a person's active search for meaning and satisfaction in life. And you must help students with this search. However, there is no surefire method of motivating students. Techniques that may work in one situation may be totally ineffective in another.

Motivation can come from within (intrinsic motivation) or outside (extrinsic motivation) an individual. Intrinsic motivation is related to an individual's attitudes, needs, personality factors, and values. Conversely, extrinsic motivation comes from stimulation within the environment and from the application of desired incentives. Although diverse in their view of motivation, the intrinsic and extrinsic explanations are essentially interrelated and commonly interact.

We are motivated by our perceptions of events. These perceptions will be related to such internal attributes as attitudes, needs, curiosity, interests and sense of well-being. Thus, a student's desire to learn will be related to the student's internal attribute structure.

Students must be motivated to pay attention. Thus, you must learn to gain and keep student attention directed toward a lesson. Often central to the desire to attend to the learning process is classroom atmosphere. You should establish a democratic classroom that is attractive and characterized by open communication.

Students seek stimulation. Therefore, you must employ various stimulus variation techniques for gaining and maintaining student attention. Commonly used techniques for providing the needed changes in stimuli include the use of gestures, the refocusing of student attention, varying classroom interaction styles, shifting students' sensory channels, and using teacher movement. These techniques should vary the stimuli for students, which should focus their attention back on you and your lesson. Teacher enthusiasm can also be an effective motivator. When you show excitement and interest in your lesson, that excitement often is communicated to students. Enthusiasm can be contagious.

A strong beginning for your lesson is crucial for motivating students' desire to learn. Therefore, begin with some attention-getting device that will stimulate interest in the coming lesson. This beginning then should be followed up with other stimulating devices that will keep students interested. Finally, students are motivated by your expectations. When you expect the best, you often get it.

Reinforcement is a long-recognized technique for motivating students. The nature of reinforcement, however, is critical if you are using reinforcement for motivational purposes. Select your reinforcers based on your knowledge of the students and subject. For instance, letting students know how well they are doing can be an effective motivator. But don't rely on grades exclusively for providing such feedback; offering praise and disclosing the results of assigned work can also motivate students.

Reward mechanisms and contingency contracts offer more formal motivational systems. They give students the opportunity for becoming directly involved in determining incentives for classroom behaviors and actions.

Discussion Questions and Activities

1. **Classroom observation.** Complete several secondary school observations. Plan your visits to collect viable observational data related to motivation:

   a. The use of stimulus variation.

   b. The different types of stimulus variation utilized by the teachers.

   c. Examples of teacher enthusiasm displayed.

   d. The use of positive and negative reinforcement.

   e. The different types of reinforcement utilized by the teachers.

   f. The use of praise and encouragement.

2. **Teaching.** Teach a 20-minute minilesson to a group of secondary students or to peers. Try to use as much stimulus variation and as many reinforcement techniques as possible in your lesson. If possible, videotape the lesson.

3. **Teaching analysis.** Study the videotape you made in question 2. Record your uses of stimulus variation and reinforcement. Draw some conclusions regarding your proficiency in the use of stimulus variation and reinforcement.

4. **Reinforcement menus.** Develop a list of incentives that could be used in your subject area. Arrange them in ascending order of value.

5. **Contingency contracts.** Set up a sample contingency contract for a unit in your subject area.

Reading

✎ **To read is to open the gateway to the world—to the joys, the wonders, the satisfactions that can be found.**

Overview

All teachers, including secondary school teachers, are reading teachers in the sense that they must help students read and understand classroom reading materials. Indeed, most school learning depends on the ability to understand written material. But many students have difficulty reading textual materials and, consequently, are frustrated in trying to complete assigned work. Printed materials assigned by teachers are too often written at reading levels not suitable for students in their classroom. As such, teachers must learn to guide students toward the ability to be independent readers.

This chapter will be concerned with the often-overlooked issue of reading in content courses. The chapter will address the concerns of identifying reading strengths and weaknesses of students, the use of effective teaching strategies for making textbook reading a viable option for students, the implementation of techniques for students using textbooks, and the use and evaluation of textbooks.

Objectives

After completing your study of chapter 14, you should be able to do the following:

1. Explain the importance of a knowledge of reading to secondary school teachers.

2. Identify and describe several different reading levels that might be found in a given secondary school classroom.

3. Describe several different techniques that can be used for identifying students' reading levels.

4. Identify and describe different strategies that can be used in promoting students' comprehension of classroom reading material.

5. Describe the structure of the typical secondary school textbook, and compare the student's edition and teacher's edition.

6. Outline the typical textbook-adoption procedure.

7. Evaluate a secondary school textbook according to a given rating system.

Chapter Terms and Key Concepts

Anticipation Guide

Cloze Procedure

Content-Area Reading Inventory

Frustration Level

Independent Level

Instructional Level

Listening Capacity

Option Guide

Oral Reading Assessment

Prereading Plan

Silent Reading Assessment

Student's Edition

Teacher's Edition

Textbook Adoption

Three-Level Reading Guide

Secondary school teachers too often take the reading ability of students for granted. However, reading is a complex skill that takes years to truly master. If teachers expect students to reach the desired level of competence in their subject area, they must address how well their students read and how people learn through reading. Most of your students probably will be efficient, effective readers; but some will have reading problems. Someone must teach those students who have reading problems how to read better. More than likely, that someone must be you.

The process of becoming a proficient reader often continues well into adult life. Even then, many individuals continue to have problems with reading. It is no wonder secondary school teachers report that many of their students have reading problems.

Reading Problems

Most secondary school teachers view themselves as content experts and therefore are content-oriented. "I have to teach my subject matter. If I don't teach the math concepts, where will they learn them?" "I must reach the end of World War II in 16 weeks. If I don't cover this much material, I won't be teaching the textbook and students won't get all they should out of this course." These and other similar statements are expressed frequently by secondary teachers whose primary assignment is to teach a specific content area. How can they possibly be concerned with teaching "reading"? There simply isn't time.

Most secondary school teachers presume that all students can read the text material provided in their classes. Unfortunately, such an assumption is not well founded. Indeed, classrooms are filled with students who are still struggling to decipher print into meaningful concepts. Still other students are confused by the demands of reading expository text, which requires skills in reading *to learn,* as opposed to narrative text, which is reading for the purpose of learning *to read.*

There is a cognitive shift from learning to read into reading to learn around the fourth grade. At this time, students are confronted with concepts and facts that are presented in an expository format. The demands on vocabulary, prior experience, text structure, and complexity of ideas increase dramatically. As such, it is the content teacher's responsibility at the secondary school level to ensure that students progress in their transition from learning to read to reading to learn.

Thus far, only the act of reading itself has been addressed as a potential problem for adolescents. Problems with motivation also impact reading. Indeed, motivation not only impacts whether students read, but also how they read. One survey (Rieck, 1977) of students who did not read textbook assignments revealed that students did not choose reading as a viable means of obtaining information (see table 14.1). This study also indicated, however, that these students could not say with certainty that reading was a priority of their teachers. Is it possible that the content-area teachers are part of the problem in communicating the importance of reading by the way assignments are given, by their lack of modeling, and

TABLE *14.1*   Survey of Nonreaders

Question	Response	
1. Do you like to read?	52%	Yes
	38%	No
	10%	No response
2. Do you read your assignments in this class?	15%	Yes
	81%	No
	4%	No response
3. Do your tests mainly cover lecture and discussion, or reading assignments?	98%	Lecture and discussion
4. Are you required to discuss your reading assignments?	23%	Yes
	73%	No
	4%	No response
5. Does your teacher give you a purpose for reading or are you only given the number of pages to read?	95%	Pages
	5%	Purpose
6. Does your teacher bring in outside material for you to read and recommend books of interest for you to read?	5%	Yes
	95%	No
7. Does your teacher like to read?	20%	Yes
	33%	No
	47%	Don't know

Source: Rieck, B. J. (1977). How content teachers telegraph messages against reading. *Journal of Reading, 20,* 646–648.

by their method of classroom instruction? What you do in the classroom to motivate students in reading to learn often makes a major difference in how and whether they read textbook assignments.

Should all teachers be teachers of reading? Perhaps not, but they must face up to the necessity of making sure that students can read and understand the content of their courses. Indeed, the major concern of content teachers should be with teaching their subject matter. But in so doing they must teach students to view reading as a realistic option for acquiring, maintaining, and extending concepts within their specific content field. That is, content-area teachers should be concerned with teaching their students how to learn from text. Before you can do this, however, you first must ascertain what students can and can't do. You must make a diagnosis of students' reading abilities.

Diagnostic Strategies

The selection of appropriate instructional materials and activities will depend on what students are capable of understanding. Thus, as pointed out in chapter 3, the first step in effective instruction is the diagnosis of students' entry level. This diagnosis should include the reading-proficiency level of students as compared to the reading difficulty of class materials.

Student Reading Levels

Reading ability often varies greatly among secondary school students. In fact, students in a single classroom may vary by as much as eight years in their graded reading levels. A formula you could use for estimating the possible range of reading levels in your classroom is this: Grade level + 1 = Range of years. Thus, the range of reading levels for a class of ninth graders could be calculated as such: 9 + 1 = 10. If you divide the range in half (5) and then consider the grade placement (9) as the middle, the range of reading levels could be from grades 4 to 14. For a class of tenth graders, the range could be from 4.5 to 15.5 grade levels. While this formula will give you a general estimate of the amount of diversity within one class, it is important that you realize that the variation in reading ability occurs within individual students as well.

Betts (1946) established a way of considering the variation in reading ability within the student according to four reading levels: *independent, instructional, frustration,* and *listening capacity.* At the **independent level,** the highest level, the student reads fluently and with excellent comprehension. Independent-level students need no assistance, make few word-recognition errors, and have good recall. The **instructional level** is the highest level at which students can make progress in reading with instructional guidance. At this level, students require preparation and supervision, make infrequent word-recognition errors, and have satisfactory comprehension and recall. The **frustration level** is the level at which students are unable to pronounce many of the words and are often unable to comprehend the material satisfactorily. This is the lowest level at which readers are able to understand. At this level, the basic reading skills break down—fluency disappears, word recognition errors are numerous, comprehension is faulty,

TABLE *14.2*   Reading Level Criteria

Reading Level	Word Recognition	Comprehension
Independent	99% to 100%	90% to 100%
Instructional	95% to 98%	75% to 89%
Frustration	90% or less	Less than 50%
Listening Capacity		75% to 100%

recall is sketchy, and signs of emotional tension and discomfort become evident. Finally, **listening capacity** is the level at which students can understand material that is read aloud. This level is also known as the *potential level*, because it represents the level at which students would have no problem with comprehension if they could read fluently.

Students who are reading at their independent level typically exhibit a high level of confidence and interest in the task. At the instructional level, students can read somewhat smoothly, they understand with help, and usually are challenged but not overwhelmed. In contrast, students attempting to function at the frustration level often refuse to read or fail to continue to read. They lack expression during oral reading, which indicates a lack of understanding of the material. Finally, students functioning at the listening-capacity level are able to understand and discuss the material. Identification of students' listening-capacity level is especially useful for content teachers, because then other means of communicating information related to course content become possible.

Criteria for determining reading levels vary among reading specialists. However, perhaps the most widely accepted is the one Betts proposed more than forty years ago. These criteria are presented in table 14.2. Your goal should be to avoid instructional materials and strategies that force students to function at their frustration level. The only time a frustration level should be sought is in the diagnostic process of discovering that level.

Identifying Reading Levels

The reading-proficiency level of students in your classes will often vary depending on the course content. Perhaps the most efficient way of identifying reading levels among your students is through informal techniques, such as the oral and silent reading assessments, a cloze procedure, or a content-area reading inventory (CARI).

Oral and Silent Reading Assessments

Typically, you will not have time to hear all of your students read aloud in order to take an informal oral reading inventory. But in cases where a student has been identified through observation and standardized testing procedures as one who needs the more intense diagnostic analysis, an informal oral reading inventory can be extremely useful. When you prepare an **oral reading assessment,** you should select a 250- to 300-word passage from your classroom textbook. Devise a short introduction that provides the background necessary for understanding the passage and a statement that will help set a purpose for reading. You can estimate comprehension by using a free-response recall method or by asking specific questions. If you use a free-response recall method, say to the student, "Tell me the story in your own words," or perhaps say, "Tell me the major ideas presented in this passage." It is important that you set the criteria for determining the key ideas of the passage prior to giving the passage to the student to be read. Categories of Good, Fair, and Unsatisfactory are usually sufficient.

If you use questions for estimating the level of comprehension, five to ten relevant questions should be constructed that reflect a literal level of understanding and an inferential level of understanding. *Literal comprehension* means understanding explicit textual information, or information that is stated directly in the text. An *inferential comprehension* level requires applying reasoning abilities.

In addition to literal and inferential questions, questions that require critical and creative reading could also be included as part of the assessment when determining the level of comprehension. *Critical reading* requires evaluative decisions about text based on analysis and synthesis of ideas. *Creative reading* requires going beyond the text to arrive at innovative ways of relating what is learned from the text to new ideas or conclusions.

When conducting an oral reading assessment, you should set aside a private place for a one-on-one interaction with the student. Students need privacy if an accurate estimate of their reading levels is to be discovered. You should also be aware of other factors that might influence reading performance: interest and background experiences. Research (Estes & Vaughan, 1973) indicates that a student's reading level fluctuates depending on the level of interest in the reading material. Moreover, recent research in cognitive psychology continues to emphasize the importance of background experiences on reading ability and learning in general. A student's reading level may appear much higher when the material is of interest or when there is sufficient background knowledge for interpreting the information. The converse is also true. When a student lacks interest in a subject or a reading task or when there is a lack of appropriate background information, a lower reading level than what is actually correct may be indicated. Establishing a purpose statement prior to reading the passage can help address the potential interest and experience discrepancy. Furthermore, by listening carefully to students' recall statements or answers to comprehension questions, you will often be alerted to the need for probing for clarification or elaboration, which can increase the accuracy of your assessment. Remember, precise analysis of oral reading performance is not your goal. Your goal is to discover the approximate reading level of the student so that appropriate materials can be provided.

You may choose to gauge the reading levels of your students by using a **silent reading assessment.** The advantage of this method is that a group or entire class can be assessed at one time. Again, select appropriate passages from textbooks in your subject area. Devise comprehension questions as previously described. If you are assessing a group or class, you

must depend on written responses to the questions. There are advantages and disadvantages related to using this method of assessment. Of course, the ability to test many students at one time is a great advantage. In addition, the greater sense of anonymity associated with a group setting may prove to be extremely important, especially for self-conscious students. However, this procedure does not permit further probing and elaboration of responses. Furthermore, because responses must be written, some students will be at a disadvantage because of poor writing skills, which may affect their actual reading ability. Personal conferences with selected students after the testing and analysis of the results, however, could clarify any questions you may have concerning individual performances.

The Cloze Procedure

Perhaps an even more effective way of assessing individual reading level is to use the **cloze procedure.** *Cloze* is a term that refers to the psychological principle of *closure,* the human tendency to complete a familiar but not-quite-finished pattern. The purpose of a cloze procedure when used as a diagnostic tool is to estimate the match between the reading level of the student and the reading level of the textbook. The procedure involves the systematic deletion of words from a text passage and then the assessment of students' ability to supply the missing words accurately. A student's capacity for correctly supplying the deleted words is considered an indicator of how well he or she can read and construct meaning from the text, reflecting the extent of background knowledge and language fluency. Therefore, the cloze procedure functions as a measure of the *process* of reading, rather than merely the *product* of reading.

TABLE *14.3*   A Cloze Passage with Answers

Because no major publishing company has a "cloze closet" of its own, the catch is you have to make your own. There

is a bundle to be made in new _____ , and there is no reason to wait for handy _____ or attractive boxes.

　　　　　　　　　　　　　　　　1　　　　　　　　　　　　　　　　　　　　　　　　　　　　2

　　Now for the first step in _____ your new wardrobe, start with the next book you _____ to use in class. Select

　　　　　　　　　　　　　3　　　　　　　　　　　　　　　　　　　　　　　　　　　　4

the *three* most meaningful _____ of 100 to 200 words each. Almost any source can be _____ : Try classic

　　　　　　　　　　　　　5　　　　　　　　　　　　　　　　　　　　　　　　　　6

literature, fantasy fiction (the clozed *Hobbit* is _____ treat!), Greek myths, or science fiction, and choose which

　　　　　　　　　　　　　　　　　　　　　　　7

passages _____ reflect the import and content of the story.

　　　　　　8

　　Some _____ in making new cloze is common. Basically, you uniformly _____ one word in every ten (some

　　　　　9　　　　　　　　　　　　　　　　　　　　　　　　　　　　　　10

folks say every f_____ or every seventh word) throughout the passages and make _____ gaps 10 spaces long. On

　　　　　　　11　　　　　　　　　　　　　　　　　　　　　　　　　　　　　12

some materials, you may _____ to provide clues or cues to the cloze units, _____ blanks can have the same

　　　　　　　　　　　13　　　　　　　　　　　　　　　　　　　　14

number of spaces as _____ missing words. Initial or ending consonants can also be _____—as long as these aids

　　　　　　　　　15　　　　　　　　　　　　　　　　　　　　　　　　　16

help meet your need.

　　F_____ research or diagnostic purposes, keep the blanks and the _____ of the deletions internally

　　17　　　　　　　　　　　　　　　　　　　　　　　　　　　　18

consistent; for grammar, vocabulary, _____ syntax, vary them as suits your purpose. Researchers often _____ the

　　　　　　　　　　　　　　19　　　　　　　　　　　　　　　　　　　　　　　　　　　20

first and last sentences intact, but if the _____ chosen are interesting and meaningful enough, they will

　　　　　　　　　　　　　　　　　21

provide _____ the clues necessary for completion. **Good luck on furnishing your cloze closet!**

　　　　22

Cloze Key

1. cloze	7. a	13. want	19. or
2. kits	8. most	14. and	20. leave
3. designing	9. variety	15. the	21. passages
4. intend	10. delete	16. supplied	22. all
5. passages	11. fifth	17. for	
6. used	12. the	18. structure	

Source: Adapted from Beil, D. (1977, April). The emperor's new cloze. *Journal of Reading*, pp. 601–604. Reprinted with permission of Drake Beil and the International Reading Association.

The following steps can be followed to develop a cloze passage for assessment:

1. Select a reading passage of approximately 275 words from material that students have not yet read but that you plan to assign.

2. Choose complete paragraphs. Leave the first sentence intact as a lead-in to the passage. Starting with the second sentence, select at random one of the first five words. Delete every fifth word thereafter, until you have the desired total number of words deleted. (50 words simplify calculation.) Retain the remaining sentence of the last deleted word.

3. Leave an underlined blank, approximately 10 spaces long, for each deleted word as you reproduce the passage for duplication.

Table 14.3 depicts a typical cloze passage. When administering the cloze procedure as a diagnostic tool, you should be careful to inform your students that they are not to use their textbooks or work together on the passage. Explain the process for completing the task by placing an example passage on the chalkboard or the overhead projector. Be sure to allow as much time as necessary for completing the passage; this is not a timed assessment. It is also important that you warn students that it may be difficult to complete every blank. Explain that this is *not* an assignment that will be graded, but a way for you to determine the best materials and instructional procedures to use in teaching the class.

Here are the steps typically followed in scoring and interpreting the cloze procedure:

1. Count the correct words. Count as correct *only* the *exact* word for each blank. Do not count synonyms, even though they may appear to be acceptable. Misspellings are the only exception to this rule. Inappropriate word endings are incorrect.

2. Divide the total number of exact word replacements by the number of possibilities, and multiply the results by 100 to determine the student's cloze-procedure percentage.

3. Record the cloze-procedure percentage for each student on a class sheet divided by level. The results can be organized into one to three instructional groups, which can form the basis for differentiated assignments.

It is generally accepted that students with scores as low as 40 to 60 percent could be considered as functioning at the instructional level. That is, students who score within the 40 to 60 percent range could benefit from the text in question with appropriate instruction from the teacher. Guidelines for determining the level of student performance as matched to the level of the text follow.

Independent Level. A score of above 60 percent indicates that the passage can be read with a great deal of competence by students. They should be able to read the material on their own without reading guidance.

Instructional Level. A score of 40 to 60 percent indicates that the passage can be read with some competence by students. The material will challenge students if they are given some form of reading guidance.

Frustration Level. A score below 40 percent indicates that the passage probably will be too difficult for students. They need either a great deal of reading guidance to benefit from the material or more appropriate material.

If a student's score falls on the borderline between two levels, you should analyze his or her errors carefully. For example, a student who scores just below 40 percent but did so because he or she used synonyms may be better placed at the instructional level than at the frustration level. However, if the student's errors were the result of inappropriate endings or incorrect words, placement at the frustration level may be most appropriate, even if he or she "almost" scored at the instructional level. Because scoring as low as 61 percent places a student at the independent level, it is especially important to remember not to reveal the scores to your students. A low score can be extremely upsetting to a high school student. Remind your students that you are collecting information about them that will help you make instructional decisions that will lead to more effective teaching.

Content-Area Reading Inventory

A teacher-made **content-area reading inventory** (CARI) can be an effective means of assessing student reading performance through the materials actually used in class. The CARI can give you insights into how your students can handle reading assignments in several areas: locating information within the text, responding to questions from various levels of comprehension, using vocabulary skills, and adjusting the rate of reading to the demands of the text. These four areas of assessment can be addressed through the development of a teacher-made test. As with the cloze procedure, be sure to tell your students that this "test" is not for a grade, but for you—for making appropriate instructional decisions. Introduce the selected portion of the text to be read, and offer a purpose statement that will guide silent reading. Because the CARI is for assessing the student's ability to use the textbook, let it be an "open book" evaluation. Any discussion of the assessment results should occur during private conferences. An example of a content-area reading inventory for a science assignment is shown in table 14.4.

Content Reading Strategies

Comprehension is the key to reading to learn. Strategies used in promoting this comprehension of text can be organized around the concept that you should implement appropriate strategies *before, during,* and *after* reading assignments.

Before-Reading Strategies

Because comprehension of text is dependent on the interaction of the reader with the text, it is essential that the reader become aware of what he or she already knows about the subject before he or she begins reading. Encourage your students to ask themselves these two questions prior to reading an assignment:

1. What do I already know about this subject?

2. What do I need to know to complete this assignment?

TABLE *14.4*   Example of a Content-Area Reading Inventory in Science

General directions
Read pages 228–233. Then look up at the board and note the time that it took you to complete the selection. Record this time in the space provided on the response sheet. Close your book and answer the first question. You may then open your textbook to answer the remaining questions.

Student Response Form

Reading time: __ min __ sec

I. **Directions:** Close your book and answer the following question. In your own words, what was this selection about? Use as much space as you need on this page. Continue on the opposite side if you should need more room to complete your answer.

II. A. **Directions:** Open your book and answer the following questions.
   1. An insect has six legs and a three-part body.
      a. True
      b. False
      c. Can't tell
   2. Insects go through changes called metamorphosis.
      a. True
      b. False
      c. Can't tell
   3. Most insects are harmful.
      a. True
      b. False
      c. Can't tell
   4. Bees help flowers by moving pollen from flower to flower.
      a. True
      b. False
      c. Can't tell

B. **Directions:** Answers to these questions are not directly stated by the author. You must "read between the lines" to answer them.
   1. How is a baby cecropia moth different from a full-grown moth? _____
   2. Why does a caterpillar molt? _____
   3. What are the four stages of a complete metamorphosis? _____

C. **Directions:** Answers to these questions are not directly stated by the author. You must read "beyond the lines" to answer them.
   1. Why do you suppose the caterpillar spins a long thread of silk around itself? _____
   2. During which season would the full-grown cecropia moth leave the cocoon? Why? _____
   3. Why do you think they leave in that season rather than another? _____

Source: Developed by Maureen W. Moorehead Frederiksted, St. Croix, Virgin Islands. Used with permission.

The steps you take in preparing your students for reading or completing an assignment will have a significant impact on how well or even whether they will complete the task. Establishing this "cognitive readiness" for interaction with the text can be accomplished by using strategies **before** students complete the assignment. For example, you can **preview information** needed for understanding the text, or you can lead your students through a survey of the text features (e.g., title, subtitles, graphics, etc.) or through the introduction and summary information included in the text. In other words, attention should be given to the structure of the

Reading comprehension can be greatly enhanced when students are taught how to use their textbooks.

text and how it can aid in comprehension. Research by Armbruster and others (1987) has demonstrated the importance of text structure, which tends to be highly correlated to the level at which text is understood. This text structure comprises both internal and external structure. *Internal structure* signals the author's organization through the use of reading or word signals. Examples of these reading signals include terms such as *first, second, finally, nevertheless, however, as a result of, because,* and *since.* These signals should be pointed out to students before the reading assignment begins. In addition, the text's *external structure* provides organizational cues to text material. Features such as boldface print, subtitles, titles, graphics, and chapter divisions are examples of the different types of external structure. You cannot assume that your students will recognize the value of this structure on their own. Through a preview survey of text features, however, students can be taught to recognize the organization or structure that is in the text.

Furthermore, you can implement strategies that will help your students **activate and access their prior knowledge.** By calling attention to what students already know through brainstorming, discussion, and strategies such as PreP (Prereading Plan), students become aware of their existing schema. In addition, you can determine what information your students may be missing in their background experience and, accordingly, supply that information for them. The **Prereading Plan** (PreP), as suggested by Judith Langer (1981), is an excellent technique for use as an assessment/instructional activity by encouraging group discussion and awareness of the topics to be covered. Begin by analyzing the text to be read, and select key words or concepts that represent the major focus of the assignment. Langer proposes the following three steps for implementation of PreP:

1. **Initial Associations with the Concept**

   In this first phase, the teacher says, "Tell anything that comes to mind when. . . ." As each student tells what ideas initially come to mind, the teacher jots each response on the board. During this phase the students have their first opportunity for finding associations between the key concept and their prior knowledge.

2. **Reflections on Initial Associations**

   During the second phase of the PreP, the students are asked what made them think of their particular responses. This phase helps the students develop awareness of their network of associations. They also have an opportunity to listen to each other's explanations, interact, and become aware of their changing ideas. Through this procedure, they may weigh, reject, accept, revise, and integrate some of the ideas that come to mind.

3. **Reformulation of Knowledge**

   In this phase the teacher says, "Based on our discussion and before we read the text, have you any new ideas about [the concept named]?" This phase allows students to verbalize associations that have been elaborated or changed through the discussion. Because they have had a chance to probe their memories in elaborating their prior knowledge, the responses elicited during the third phase often are more refined than those during phase one.

PreP can facilitate the identification of those students who have much, some, or little prior knowledge about the concept. Those students who have significant background knowledge are able to define and suggest analogous situations that help expand the concept for the class, which leads to conceptual linking and categorical thinking. Those students who have some background knowledge can give examples and cite characteristics of the concept, but may not recognize relationships among ideas or make connections between what they know and the new materials. Finally, those students with a little background knowledge frequently have little to contribute to the brainstorming process and even offer misassociations with the topic. Recent research on learning, however, suggests that "mistakes" should be viewed as "errors" that serve as windows into the thinking processes. Lauren Resnick points out that "errors are frequently the result of a person's trying hard to make sense of something" (Brandt, 1989, p. 15). The PreP strategy actually can promote the risk-taking environment necessary for encouraging an openness where students are willing to make errors; and, in turn, it can provide you with clues for following your students' thinking processes.

Finally, you can prepare your students for the learning task by **focusing on interest and setting a purpose for the task.** Perhaps the focusing technique most widely used by teachers is that of asking questions.

However, you should use preparatory questions wisely and sparingly. A few higher-level "why" type questions, which stimulate interest, can be more effective than many lower-level questions, which move the questioning process into a recitation event rather than a thought-provoking one. Finally, you can lead students to anticipate what they will read by devising an anticipation guide.

Anticipation guides are also called *reaction guides* or *prediction guides*. They are designed for preparing students to react to a series of statements related to the content of the materials to be read. The process of anticipating what will be read helps students read with greater interest and attention. Erickson and associates (1987) suggest three benefits derived from the use of anticipation guides: (1) students will see that they already know something about the new information, which will help them comprehend better; (2) students tend to become interested and participate in lively discussion, which motivates reading; and (3) reading and writing instruction are easily integrated when anticipation guides are used. In addition, an anticipation guide can be used following a reading activity as a way of reflecting on what has been read. In effect, it becomes a tool for comparing students' prereading and postreading responses. Consider the following guidelines when constructing and using your own anticipation guides.

1. Read the content passage and identify the major concepts. Decide which of these ideas, both implicit and explicit, are most important for stimulating student background and beliefs.

2. Write those ideas in three to five short, clear declarative statements. These statements should reflect the students' world. Abstractions should be avoided.

3. Put these statements on the chalkboard, reproduced sheets, or the overhead projector. Give clear directions, and make sure students understand the process of predicting.

4. Discuss readers' anticipations prior to reading the text selection. During the discussion, encourage students to support their predictions and present arguments based on their past experiences.

5. Read the text, and evaluate the statements in light of what the author actually says.

6. Return to the anticipation guide to compare and contrast readers' predictions with the author's intended meaning.

Examples of anticipation guides used in social studies and in a high school developmental English class are illustrated in tables 14.5 and 14.6, respectively. You should learn to develop your own similar guides based on actual reading material from your class. The process of developing the anticipation guides will prove to be an excellent method for analysis of your classroom reading material. Remember, there is no right way of constructing an anticipation guide.

TABLE 14.5   Sample Anticipation Guide for Social Studies Class

Anticipation/Prediction Guide: Social Studies

Directions

Read these statements to yourself as I read them aloud. If you agree with a statement, be ready to explain why. We will check all statements we agree with in the prereading column. Then we will read to see if we should change our minds.

Prereading		*Postreading*
_____	1. Pioneers traveled west in search of adventure and a new and better life.	_____
_____	2. You can be a pioneer.	_____
_____	3. A community is a place where people live and work closely together.	_____
_____	4. More Americans live in the East.	_____
_____	5. There are only four necessities of life.	_____
_____	6. Much of the desert earth is rich.	_____

Source: Developed by Helen M. Lipscomb, Richmond, Virginia. Used with permission.

TABLE 14.6   Sample Anticipation Guide for Developmental English

Anticipation Guide: Developmental English Class

Directions

Read the following statements, and check whether you agree or disagree based on your own opinion. After you make your own decisions, share your responses with a neighbor. Before we read the short story by O. Henry, "The Green Door," we will discuss our responses.

Agree	*Disagree*	
_____	_____	1. It's easy to miss the obvious if you are not looking for it.
_____	_____	2. It's dangerous to go into rooms if you are uninvited.
_____	_____	3. Being adventurous is a safe way to live.
_____	_____	4. Asking questions helps to clear up uncertainty.

After you have read the short story by O. Henry, review the statements above. Did the author's point of view influence you to change your mind? Be ready to discuss your insights.

During-Reading Strategies

Helping your students complete their reading assignments successfully during reading begins with recognizing the purpose for reading. That purpose can be set by you or by the students themselves when they ask the question, "What do I need to know?" Students should be led to (1) confirm or redefine predictions, (2) clarify ideas, and (3) construct meaning for each segment of information. Study guides of various types, self-questioning, and structured note taking are three strategies that can help students assimilate new ideas, maintain interest, and withhold judgment of the text during reading. Students can become alert to key vocabulary in the text, generate new questions, and evaluate the ideas presented by the author and those constructed in the process of reading itself. Finally, attention to during-reading strategies can help students select important ideas, connect existing ideas to new ones, and organize those ideas.

Study guides can be constructed around three levels of comprehension: literal, interpretative, and applied. These "levels" should be

TABLE *14.7*   A Three-Level Reading Guide for *Lord of the Flies*

Part I: What the Author Actually Said

Directions
After you read chapter 7 in the novel, look at the statements below and put a check beside those statements that are true based on what the author has written.

_____ 1. When Ralph was scrutinizing himself, he noticed that his nails were long and dirty.

_____ 2. It really bothered Ralph to see the boys so dirty.

_____ 3. The ocean made Ralph feel helpless, and he thought the boys were never going to be rescued.

_____ 4. Simon told Ralph that they definitely would be rescued.

_____ 5. Ralph had at one time lived in a cottage on the edge of the moors.

_____ 6. When he was younger, Ralph loved to read about Topsy and Mopsy.

_____ 7. Jack hit the pig in the snoot with his spear.

_____ 8. Jack was concerned that Piggy might worry if the group went to look for the beast without telling him, and that is why Jack kept mentioning Piggy to Ralph.

_____ 9. When the boys started up the mountain, Ralph didn't really expect to find a beast.

_____ 10. At the top of the mountain, the boys saw an ape with its head between its knees.

Part II: What the Author Really Meant

Directions
Put a check next to each statement below that represents what the author meant by his words. You may have to read more than one page to arrive at your answer.

_____ 1. Jack wasn't kidding when he said he wanted to kill a "littlun" in the pig hunt game.

_____ 2. When the boys started out, they knew that hunting for the beast was going to take all night long.

_____ 3. Jack was jealous because Ralph had speared the pig.

_____ 4. The reason the boys wanted to go back to the shelters was that they were tired.

_____ 5. Jack was braver than Ralph because he went up the mountain first.

Part III: What Do You Think?

Directions
Put a check next to the statements below if you think they are a good representation of the chapter.

_____ 1. A fool and his gold are soon parted.

_____ 2. The soldier who runs away lives to fight another day.

_____ 3. The truly brave man feels no need to prove his courage.

Source: Developed by Vel Moss, Lawton, Oklahoma. Used with permission.

considered as general guidelines that represent general categories of cognitive functioning, rather than discrete, mutually exclusive classifications. Study guides that include statements within each category, however, are more likely to prompt students to process information beyond a literal understanding of text. One type of study guide, the **three-level reading guide,** can be constructed in a variety of formats by incorporating statements that focus on the main points of the reading selection and statements that support your content objectives. The three-level reading guide gauges students' perceptions of what the author said, what the author meant, as well as students' perceptions of reading content. Suggestions for creating such a guide follow.

1. Begin constructing the first set of statements for the guide at the second level, the interpretive level. Analyze the text selection by asking, "What does the author mean?" Write down in your own words those inferences that make sense to you. Make sure your statements are written simply and clearly.

2. Search the text for literally stated propositions and explicit pieces of information that support the inferences you have chosen for the second level. Put these into statements, which form the first level, the literal level.

3. Decide whether you want to add a distractor at the first or second levels. Some debate has been generated over the utility of distractors (Herber, 1978). However, Vacca and Vacca (1989, p. 168) point out that occasional distractors help maintain a higher level of interest and involvement in using a reading guide. However, you want to avoid using distractors so frequently that they reinforce a "right or wrong" mentality in responding to the statements.

4. Develop statements for the third level, applied level. These statements should represent additional insights, which demonstrate the connections between the author's ideas and the ideas of the reader.

5. Be flexible. Be creative. Offer different kinds of formats for different assignments. Keep it brief. Asking your students to read too much in the reading guide itself can detract from the original purpose—to get students to actively read the text with heightened interest and attention.

A typical three-level reading guide is illustrated in table 14.7.

Another type of study guide especially useful in social studies is the **option guide,** which differs from a three-level reading guide in that it requires that students function in an active, decision-making role. An option guide is discussed before reading but completed during reading. Readence, Bean, and Baldwin (1989) propose the following guidelines for creating an option guide:

1. Carefully analyze a text reading assignment for major concepts and key subheadings that foreshadow upcoming events.

2. Building on background knowledge acquired from previous readings, construct a brief background statement that will remind students of the material they have read.

3. Develop one or two central questions that ask students to consider various options open to specific groups of people within the particular historical context.

4. When students have completed reading up to the point where the option guide is to be used, group them in groups of 3 or 4 for about 10 or 15 minutes to discuss and complete the **before-reading** section

TABLE *14.8*   A Typical Option Guide

The Kamakura Shogunate (1192–1333) Began

Background

In 1156, civil war broke out between two large landowning families. Each family had a band of loyal warriors, called *samurai*. In 1192, one samurai, named Minamoto Yoritomo, became the supreme general of all Japan. The emperor named him the *shogun*.

During this period of military rule, what *options* for political influence do you think were available to the following groups?

1. Nobles?
   1.1 Before reading:
   1.2 After reading:

2. Farmers?
   2.1 Before reading:
   2.2 After reading:

3. The Samurai?
   3.1 Before reading:
   3.2 After reading:

4. If the Chinese try to invade Japan, how will they do?
   4.1 Before reading:
   4.2 After reading:

Source: Adapted with permission from Readence, Bean, & Baldwin. *Content area reading: An integrated approach* (4th ed.). Copyright 1992 by Kendall/Hunt Publishing Co., Dubuque, IA.

of the options guide. Then, when they finish reading the assignment, they should check their listed options against actual events in the text. Finally, they should complete the **after-reading** section of the options guide. A follow-up group discussion can clarify any sections of the guide that need further explanation.

A typical option guide related to Japanese history is shown in table 14.8.

In addition to study guides, students can be taught to use the technique of self-questioning during reading. You can teach your students to examine the relationship between questions and answers. This technique can be used whether the question's source is the textbook, the teacher, or self-generated from the student. Pearson and Johnson (1978) have proposed focusing on *textually explicit, textually implicit,* and *experienced-based* question/answer relationships as a means of comprehending text at multiple cognitive levels.

Textually explicit comprehension means that you are getting the facts of a passage as stated by the author. This information is explicit. Raphael (1984) uses the phrase "right there" to help communicate the notion that the answer to the question is stated specifically within the text. The student need only "read the lines" to answer the question. This is a "literal" level of question in terms of traditional classification systems of questions. During the reading process, the student should ask what information is "right there," or explicitly stated in the text.

Textually implicit comprehension involves getting information inferred by the author. The answer is derived directly from the language of the text, but also requires that the student read "between the lines" to

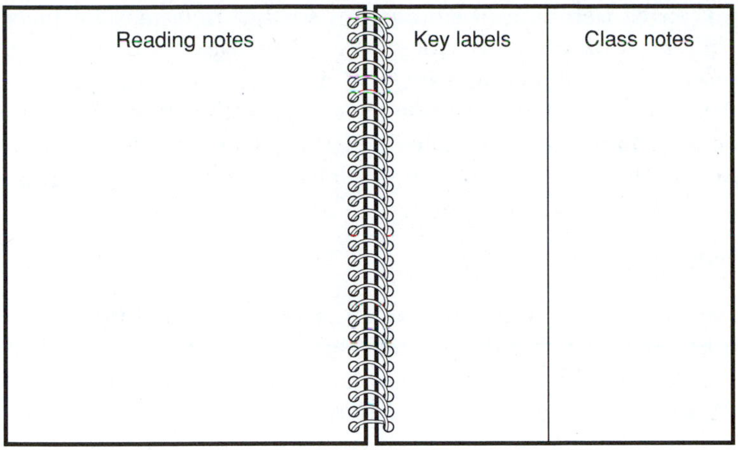

Figure 14.1 *Note-Taking Notebook*

make connections not explicitly stated. Raphael (1984) calls this the "think and search" component of comprehension. Answers to these questions require paraphrasing of facts presented by the author and the addition of information from prior knowledge in deriving a reasonable implicit relationship. Self-generated questions at this level encourage students to stay in touch with what they already know as well as search for what the author is implying.

Experienced-based comprehension, also referred to as *schema-based,* is a relationship between questions and answers that is based almost entirely on the student's previous knowledge. The question is one that requires an answer that, while initiated in the text, is "in memory"; therefore, the student is "on his or her own" (Raphael, 1984). By reading "beyond the lines," students are thinking beyond the constraints of the text—beyond the explicit and implicit notions of the author—and drawing on their own schemas in making connections.

Finally, note taking during reading can help students organize information for study and recall. A method developed by Palmatier (1973) is called the "note-taking system for learning." Not only does this system promote the processing of information during reading, but it also provides a way of combining notes taken during class with the related reading assignments. Thus, a unitary note-taking system makes preparing for tests easier and encourages integration of learning.

The procedure is simple. For both reading and lecture notes, tell students to use only *one* side of their notebook paper, as illustrated in figure 14.1. Pages used for class notes (right side of notebook) should be divided by drawing a line about 3 inches from the left side of the paper. All notes taken during class should be written on the right side of this paper. Encourage students to use subdivision and spacing for identifying important concepts and flow of ideas. Indentation, dashes, and so on may be used for subdividing ideas. As notes are reviewed, labels for key concepts should be written in the 3-inch left column of the page. Now, the notes taken during reading should be taken only on the "back" of the notebook pages (left side of notebook), so that they may be placed adjacent to the class notes. Thus, notes taken from class, coded later as *review,* can be seen in conjunction with the notes taken during reading. This method facilitates studying for tests, because all the pages may be laid out together for comparison. Furthermore, the pages may be laid out so that only the key labels are revealed, which forms question stems for test review.

After-Reading Strategies

What you do with students after reading is equally as important as what is done both before and during reading. Yet, the activity used most frequently after reading is simply an independent student activity or a group review. The independent activity typically consists of answering selected questions at the end of the chapter, and the reviews are often strictly teacher-centered, which tends to engender responses from students that are less than enthusiastic. In the drive to "cover the text," little thought may be given to after-reading activities.

You need to consider the essential learning processes that will be neglected if after-reading emphases are neglected. Focusing on what has been read helps students (1) **construct meaning for the whole passage,** (2) **assess achievement of purposes,** and (3) **consolidate and apply learning.** Underlying these goals are the critical processes necessary for learning to occur. If students learn from their reading, they should be able to categorize and integrate the information into their existing schema. Ideas should be summarized and connections clarified. When reexamining the purposes set for reading, students should be able to confirm predictions, identify gaps in learning, generate new questions, and extend their learning beyond the information presented in the text. Finally, students who have learned from text should be able to transfer the knowledge acquired to new situations. As students begin to take ownership of their own learning process, they begin to realize what "study" is all about: It is not just the memorization of facts and figures, nor is it the parroting of information to an authority in the classroom. But instead, through study, the actual cognitive structure of a student's schema has been molded, modified, confirmed, refined, extended, and changed. In other words, learning has occurred. Such lofty goals for reading can be more readily realized if you follow all the way through the teaching-learning process—from before reading, during reading, and to the after-reading stage. There are many strategies to focus on after reading currently being researched and implemented in middle and secondary schools across the nation. Although these strategies are being proposed as after-reading strategies, they may be used successfully throughout the reading process. Among the most widely used strategies are **cooperative-learning grouping, summarizing, creating graphic representations,** and **writing to learn.**

The advantages and characteristics of cooperative learning were discussed in chapter 8. Implementing this particular strategy after reading is especially effective. The process of discussing what has been read can be enhanced greatly by allowing students to share their ideas with one another, rather than just participating in a large-group discussion. However, two points are especially important. First, students need to be taught the various responsibilities of a being a group member. Second, methods for skillfully sharing their thoughts about what has been read need to be taught directly.

Clearly defined roles for the students will help the groups function efficiently. One student may be chair for the week, guiding discussion of study guides, for example. Other roles may include a recorder and a gatekeeper (timekeeper), who maintain the flow of discussion. The roles should rotate to ensure that all members have an opportunity to serve in the various capacities. Indeed, it has been found that students of different abilities tend to exhibit different strengths, which makes the group experience more beneficial than the individual-study experience. For example, locating specific facts may be a strength of a lower-ability student, while a higher-ability student may be better at making connections from specific information to generalizations. Most importantly, students are learning from each other.

Summarizing is a powerful strategy for students to use after reading, because the types of thinking needed for summarization are *selection* and *reduction*. The *selection* process means that judgments must be made about what text information would be included or rejected. The *reduction* process means that ideas must be condensed by substituting general ideas for lower-level and more detailed ones (Johnson, 1983). Students who can summarize a text passage demonstrate the ability to be selective about what is included and the ability to reconstruct the meaning of the text. Moreover, effectively written summaries can indicate that students understand superordinate and subordinate concepts and their relationships. Such an understanding goes well beyond simple memorization of facts.

Summaries may be of at least two types: writer-based and reader-based (Anderson & Hidi, 1989). A writer-based summary is written so that the writer may understand the text being summarized, while the reader-based summary is written for someone else to read. Because of the difference in purpose, the two summaries will appear quite different, and the processes involved in writing them will be different. A writer-based summary will probably include a great deal more detail, with little attention to the grammatical or sentence structure. In contrast, the reader-based summary is likely to be more polished as a product and reflect a greater understanding of the overall meaning of the text. Students need to be taught the difference and given opportunities for writing both types of summaries.

When you teach students to summarize, begin by choosing text of appropriate difficulty. In the beginning, excerpts should be short and clearly written so that the main idea is fairly explicit. Then, advance to longer and more complex text as students demonstrate their proficiencies. Let students refer to the text while writing their summaries. Focus attention on what is important to the author. Summaries should include important information; but, make sure your students understand that *important* means *author* importance, not importance to you. The author's text structure can signal what is important. Help your students look for introductory statements, topic sentences, summary statements, underlining, italics, repetition, boldface print, and so on. Begin with writer-based summaries, then gradually advance to summaries written for others to read—that is, reader-based summaries.

Furthermore, verbal summaries are part of a cooperative-learning strategy proposed by Palinscar and Brown (1984) and called "reciprocal teaching." In this strategy, students are taught to generate questions about the content being read, summarize the content, clarify points, and predict upcoming content from cues in the text or from prior knowledge on the topic. A dialogue is the mode of communicating this information in small (cooperative learning) groups. Verbal summarization will complement the task of creating written summaries.

Graphic representations can be used effectively as both before- and after-reading comprehension strategies. The purpose of a graphic representation is to visually portray the interrelatedness of ideas. These "visual illustrations of verbal statements" (Jones, Pierce, & Hunter, 1989) can take the shape of flowcharts, pie charts, family trees, spider maps, fishbone maps, network trees, compare/contrast matrices, and so on. Essential to your grasp of this strategy is the understanding that there is **no one correct way** of creating a graphic representation. Furthermore, you need to realize that teachers and researchers use many different terms when referring to graphic representations. Some of these terms are *webbing, semantic webbing, cognitive mapping, mapping, attribute web,* and *structure overview.* When using such graphic representations, remember that you need to be flexible and open to divergent ways of thinking. Representations are designed to reflect students' thinking. Students need a secure sense of acceptance if they ever are to develop the risk-taking position necessary for skillful thinking about text they have read. It is important to remember that "graphic organizers and outlines are fundamental to skilled thinking because they provide information and opportunities for analysis that reading alone and linear outlining cannot provide" (Jones, Pierce, & Hunter, 1989, p. 25).

Finally, writing-to-learn activities can be used as effective strategies for learning from reading, because of the interdependent nature of the reading/writing process. It's been said that reading and writing are like two sides of the same coin: Reading is not even possible without first the act of writing, and writing has no purpose if there is no reading. Readence and others (1989) have summarized the principles behind the reading/writing connection by emphasizing that the construction of meaning requires active interchange between readers and writers. When a student takes the position of a writer, he or she is better able to understand the demands of the reading task. Furthermore, the process of writing itself engages students in their own learning, because writing is a way of knowing what you are thinking. Edward Albee, the contemporary playwright, has been quoted as saying, "I write to find out what I'm thinking about." Thus, writing can uncover thinking. Indeed, clear, effective writing can foster clear, effective thinking. Thus, writing becomes not only a means of expression, but a valuable tool for "seeing" how your students are thinking. Yet, with all these apparent benefits of writing, little instructional time is spent on writing within the content areas.

A writing-to-learn strategy that has proven effective in diverse content areas is the journal. Journals, sometimes called *learning logs* or *reader's journals,* can be used by students for recording their reflections on their own learning experiences. The journal can also be the place for recording reactions to text that has been read, or responding to given topics for thoughts, or reviewing a previously discussed topic, or recording what is or is not understood about a math problem or a scientific problem, or recording predictions prior to reading. The various uses of a journal are endless. However, there are some general guidelines for journal writing suggested by Fulwiler (1986).

First, journal writing should become a regular part of your teaching. Students need to write in their journals on a daily basis. Students will probably find journal writing difficult at first, some will even resist. Therefore, it is important that you remain consistent in your emphasis. In general, practice will result in better-written journal entries, and interest in writing on the part of the students tends to increase as they become more comfortable with the process.

You should model journal writing by keeping your own journal and sharing entries aloud with students. Again, the value of cooperative learning is obvious. In smaller groups, there is more opportunity for more students to share what they have written in their journals. Fulwiler further suggests that you be part of that sharing process.

You should look at students' journals and respond to their thoughts. It is probably not possible, or even desirable, for you to read every single entry in every student's journal. However, random collection of journals several times a month will enable you to read some portion of all the journals over time. These journals should *not* be graded. The purpose is for the writer to explore ideas, not to be evaluated on those ideas or on writing style. A loose-leaf notebook will allow students to take out the pages they do not want you to read and will also allow you to ask for one particular journal entry without taking the student's whole notebook.

Finally, allot 5 to 10 minutes daily for journal writing. Be consistent so that students can learn to expect to write. But be creative with how the journal writing is used, so that the activity does not become so routine that it loses its effectiveness.

In summary, content-area reading strategies provided before, during, and after students read seem to be successful in promoting comprehension of text. Those strategies discussed should be viewed as suggestions, which can be adapted for your particular use to fit your unique situation. This concludes the diagnostic and strategies phase of our study of reading. Table 14.9 gives an overview of the major diagnostic and strategies concepts, and the Reading Diagnosis and Strategies Application Guidelines offer some further suggestions. We will now direct our attention toward the classroom textbook. Before you proceed, however, complete exercise 14.1, which will check your understanding of the major diagnostic and strategies concepts.

TABLE 14.9   Reading Diagnosis and Strategies

Concept	Description
Reading Level	Reading ability of students based on levels: independent, instructional, frustration, and listening capacity
Assessment of Reading Levels	Techniques for determining the reading level of students in relationship to course reading materials, including oral and silent reading assessments, the cloze procedure, and the content-area reading inventory (CARI)
Before-Reading Strategies	Activities designed to enhance comprehension that are carried out before assigned materials are read
During-Reading Strategies	Activities designed to enhance comprehension that are carried out during the reading process itself
After-Reading Strategies	Activities designed to enhance comprehension that are carried out after assigned reading has been completed

Application Guidelines ▼

Reading Diagnosis and Strategies

Recognize That Students Have Different Reading Abilities

Examples:
1. Plan individual writing projects geared to individual student's ability.
2. Assign more difficult materials to be read orally in class by better readers. Narratives that usually are at lower reading levels then can be read by all students.
3. Have tape recording of text for use by low-ability readers. Better readers can be asked to make these recordings. Low-ability readers will benefit from making and listening to their own recordings.

Assist Students with Reading Comprehension

Examples:
1. Train students in reading-comprehension strategies.
2. Introduce a chapter to students by surveying the major topics and sections.
3. Generate questions related to the reading purpose. Turn the headings and subheadings into questions.
4. Teach students to adjust their reading speed to the difficulty of the material and the purpose in reading.
5. Teach students to reflect on what they are reading. They should try to think of examples or create images of what is being read.
6. Teach students to skim and reread in trying to answer questions.
7. Teach your students effective note-taking techniques. Don't assume students know how to take notes.

Application of Knowledge

Exercise 14.1   Reading Diagnosis and Strategies

Test yourself on the following reading diagnosis and strategies concepts. Appropriate responses can be found in appendix A.

1. Most secondary school reading material is at the appropriate level for students. (True/False)

2. Match the reading level on the right with the description on the left.
   - a. _____ Little ability in reading with a breakdown in most reading skills
   - b. _____ Ability to understand material that is read aloud
   - c. _____ Ability to read fluently with excellent comprehension
   - d. _____ Ability to make progress in reading with guidance

   1. Frustration level
   2. Independent level
   3. Instructional level
   4. Listening-capacity level

3. Match the assessment tool on the right with the description on the left.
   - a. _____ Students read a textbook passage and respond to a teacher-made test
   - b. _____ Students supply words that have been deleted from a reading passage
   - c. _____ Students read a 150- to 300-word passage and recall what was read

   1. Cloze procedure
   2. Oral and silent reading assessments
   3. Content-area reading inventory

4. Strategies for improving the comprehension of text material can be carried out _____ , _____ , and _____ reading assignments.

5. It usually is a good idea to establish cognitive readiness before students complete a reading assignment. (True/False)

6. Label the following strategies as being appropriate before (B), during (D), or after (A) reading assignments.
   - a. _____ Option guides.
   - b. _____ Three-level reading guides.
   - c. _____ Graphic representations.
   - d. _____ PreP.
   - e. _____ Note taking.
   - f. _____ Anticipation guides.
   - g. _____ Writing-to-learn activities.

Secondary School Textbooks

As pointed out in chapter 6, the textbook historically has been the most commonly used printed material in the classroom, and in some classrooms it is the only source of information used by the teacher. However, this is presently undergoing some change. Today, although an adopted textbook still remains the primary source of information for most classes, other information sources are now common in secondary school classrooms.

Good textbooks serve an important function in the classroom. Indeed, a textbook is a viable tool for instruction, as long as it is selected with care and represents only one of many information sources. You must realize, however, that textbooks are written for broad, nationwide consumption and are geared toward "average" students. In addition, many textbooks tend to be general, noncontroversial, and bland and rarely address the abilities, needs, and interests of all students. Finally, in many cases, textbooks contain much more information than can be covered adequately in a one-year course.

Don't be afraid to be critical of textbooks. Despite the considerable effort that has been expended by authors and publishers in developing and refining their texts, some textbooks will contain inaccurate information, some will be poorly written, and some will be poorly designed. In short, some textbooks can bore or even misdirect students, and some may turn them off to learning. Therefore, when selecting your textbooks, make sure they are accurate, coherent, well organized, lively, and motivating to students.

Structure of the Textbook

Modern secondary school textbooks come in two forms: a student's edition and a teacher's edition. The teacher's edition contains everything included in the student's edition as well as additional aids that assist the teacher in the instructional process.

The typical **student's edition** includes a preface, an introduction, a table of contents, sections (or units) divided into chapters, a glossary, appendixes, and an index. The sections (or units) are written around a common theme, with the chapters within the specific sections (or units) relating to this theme.

Textbook chapters often begin with a list of objectives, which focus on desired learning outcomes. In addition, chapters are divided into subsections, which break the chapter's main topics down into subtopics. Many chapters also contain checkpoints, illustrations, graphs, and pictures to improve student comprehension and add to the overall attractiveness of the text.

The appendixes and index are found at the end of the text. A well-designed text will include appendixes that supplement the text in special areas. For example, a physics book may contain an appendix on the use of vectors, or a math text may contain an appendix with various statistical tables. Finally, a well-prepared index will prove invaluable in locating key words and concepts.

The **teacher's edition** commonly is a modified copy of the student's edition. In general, a teacher's manual is placed in the front of the student's edition. This manual usually gives a rationale for the program; a scope and sequence chart for below-average, average, and above-average classes; and background content information to update the teacher's knowledge. In addition, the manual may include (1) chapter pedagogical assistance, (2) answer keys to textbook questions and problems, (3) test questions, (4) reinforcement activities, (5) enrichment activities, (6) instructional objectives, (7) lesson plans, (8) bulletin board ideas, and (9) evaluation tips. Many teacher's editions also provide marginal annotations related to the major concepts being presented in the student's edition, as well as questions keyed to these concepts.

Using the Textbook

Textbooks should be regarded as "dispensers of information" (Readence, Bean, & Baldwin, 1989). That is, they should be viewed as tools for implementation by both you and the students in acquiring information about the concepts being learned. However, a textbook remains a closed book for many students, because they are unfamiliar with how to use one to the best advantage. You can help overcome this problem by beginning your course with an overview of the textbook. You should start this overview at the cover of the book, noting the title and any general statement of a theme presented in illustrations. Discuss the general format of the text—the table of contents, chapter divisions, end-of-chapter activities, glossary, index, extra helps, and so on. Be sure to point out other features of the text that help highlight important vocabulary and concepts, such as italicized words, boldface print, indentation, marginal notes, captions, and graphs. The idea is that you want your students to "walk" through the entire book, so that they have a sense of what the book is all about and what is in the book.

If you have a teacher's guide, use it for a resource, *not* a "recipe book" to be followed to the letter. The most valuable ideas for instruction are often included in the enrichment sections of the guide. Become familiar with the teacher's guide in much the same way that you helped your students become familiar with their text. Perhaps the most important step you can take in preparing for your lesson is this: **Always read the student's text prior** to assigning it to students. When you read the student's text, you have a clearer sense of what the students are reading. This will give you quite a different view of the text than if you merely read your "guide" with its number of aids for help in understanding. Try to start by seeing the text from the students' point of view. This will enable you to more effectively plan instruction that will help bridge the gap between the reader and the text.

Textbook Adoption

Textbook adoption for most secondary school classrooms is done by teachers serving on textbook-selection committees. These committees can be formed at the state, district, or school level for the purpose of identifying and selecting school textbooks worthy for use in the classroom.

In some states, textbook adoption begins at the state level. Each year a committee is formed that selects the textbooks in all subjects eligible for new textbooks that year. New textbooks generally are selected for all subjects every five years, on a staggered basis. For example, new math books and social studies books may be selected one year, and the new reading and English books may be selected the next year. Thus, all subjects would adopt new textbooks every five years. These state committees usually select several appropriate textbooks for each subject. Oklahoma, for example, selects five books for each subject. A local selection committee then selects one book from the state-approved list for district or school use for each subject. In most cases, the local district is free to select a textbook **not** on the state list, but state funds cannot be used for purchasing these books.

When adoption lies solely at the district level, committees of teachers and administrators are formed that select appropriate textbooks when subjects become eligible. These local committees select textbooks based on established district guidelines.

Evaluation of Textbooks

A course textbook must be selected with care. Merely flipping through a copy of the textbook does not offer an objective analysis of a book's appropriateness. In effect, the content, organization, and readability must be evaluated carefully.

First and foremost, a textbook must contain up-to-date and accurate content. Moreover, this content must be consistent with the school and community goals as well as the objectives of your course. Thus, when selecting your textbooks, keep in mind your broad class goals and the school community.

Ideally, a textbook should be organized in a way that is consistent with your philosophy. That is, the principles and concepts should be developed in a way that you feel will make it relevant and meaningful to students. This is especially important when the textbook is to structure the course of study.

When evaluating textbooks, you must seek to match as closely as possible the reading level of the text with the reading level of your students. Readability of text is addressed by using various readability formulas such as those proposed by Fry (1977) or Raygor (1977). You may refer to a reading text, such as Harris and Sipay's *How to Increase your Reading Ability* (1990), for a thorough description of various formulas and a discussion of their use. It is important to realize, however, that any readability formula measures only two variables: sentence length and word length. Critical features that make a text more or less readable—features such as conceptual density, syntax, semantics, interest, and so on—are not evaluated by formulas.

Your textbook evaluation will be more thorough if you conduct a formal evaluation system, such as that shown in figure 14.2. This system addresses the components of the good textbook; namely, it focuses on the content and organization of a textbook as well as the three key features related to text readability: utility, mechanics, and comprehensiveness.

Teachers can also use workbooks, duplicated materials, and newspapers to enhance classroom instruction. But remember to review these pedagogical aids carefully for their instructional value as well.

Workbooks, Duplicated Materials, and Newspapers

Pedagogical aids in the form of workbooks, duplicated materials, and newspapers can supplement a textbook. These aids can be used before students read the textbook to acquaint them with the information and concepts to be learned. While students read the textbook, the aids can focus attention on important concepts, provide examples, and supply

Textbook title: _____ Publisher: _____
_____ Year published: _____
Author: _____ Price: _____

Figure 14.2 *Textbook Evaluation Rating System*

Give each item listed in each category a rating of 1 to 5 based on the following scale: 1 point, unsatisfactory; 2 points, poor; 3 points, fair; 4 points, good; and 5 points, excellent.

The total number of possible points is 200. A partial score for each category should be determined first. These partial scores are then totaled to arrive at an overall score for each textbook under consideration. Refer to the following scale to interpret the overall rating of the textbook.

Scores between 161 and 200	Excellent
Scores between 141 and 160	Good
Scores between 121 and 140	Satisfactory
Scores between 101 and 120	Poor
Scores below 101	Unsatisfactory

1. Content	1	2	3	4	5
a. Content is up-to-date.					
b. Content is accurate.					
c. Content is appropriate for grade level.					
d. Content includes adequate development of concepts and principles and is appropriate for grade level.					
e. Content is relevant to students.					
f. Objectives are clearly stated.					
Partial score					

2. Organization	1	2	3	4	5
a. The organization and selection of topics or units fits the sequence of the course syllabus.					
b. Organization is flexible, permitting variation in sequence.					
c. Material within the chapters is well organized.					
d. Approach is suitable for a wide range of student abilities.					
e. Content is presented at a variety of cognitive levels.					
Partial score					

3. Utility	1	2	3	4	5
a. Chapter headings clearly define the content of the chapter.					
b. Chapter subheadings clearly break down the important concepts in the chapter.					
c. Topic headings provide assistance in breaking the chapter into relevant parts.					
d. Important terms are in italics or boldface type for easy identification by readers.					

Figure 14.2 *Continued.*

3. Utility cont.	1	2	3	4	5
e. Concepts are spaced appropriately throughout the text, rather than being clustered in too small a space or expressed in too few words.					
f. The author's style (word length, sentence length, sentence complexity, paragraph length, number of examples) is appropriate for the level of students who will be using the text.					
Partial score					

4. Mechanics	1	2	3	4	5
a. Chapter titles and subheadings are concrete, meaningful, and interesting.					
b. Writing style of the text is appealing to the students.					
c. Questions are well constructed and useful for review.					
d. Activites are interesting and suitable for a wide range of student abilities.					
e. Suggested activites are thought-provoking and challenging.					
f. Text provides positive and motivating models for both sexes as well as for other racial, ethnic, and socioeconomic groups.					
Partial score					

5. Appropriateness	1	2	3	4	5
a. Reading level of text is fitting for grade level of students.					
b. The text vocabulary level is suitable.					
c. New concepts explicitly linked to the students' prior knowledge or to their experience.					
d. Text introduces abstract concepts by accompanying them with numerous concrete examples.					
e. Text avoids irrelevant details.					
Partial score					

6. Illustrations	1	2	3	4	5
a. Illustrations are up-to-date.					
b. Photographs are clear and of good quality.					
c. Line drawings are well done and clearly executed.					
d. Illustrations are tied in with content of the text.					
e. Captions for illustrations are well written and appropriate.					
f. Illustrations are useful in classroom teaching.					
g. Illustrations are strategically placed within the text.					
Partial score					

Figure 14.2 *Continued.*

7. Teacher Edition	1	2	3	4	5
a. Teacher's manual is available with the text and is useful.					
b. Teacher's manual suggests ways the teacher can review and develop the student's grasp of concepts and experiences.					
c. Annotated edition of the text is available and is useful.					
d. Tests are provided.					
e. Teacher's manual lists accessible resources containing alternative readings for students who either need help with or are advanced in their reading.					
f. Teacher's manual provides introductory activities that will capture students' interest.					
g. Library resource materials are suggested.					
Partial score					
8. Indexes and Glossaries	1	2	3	4	5
a. Glossary is accurate and complete.					
b. Index is accurate and complete.					
c. Table of contents is accurate and complete.					
Partial score					
9. Physical Makeup of the Text	1	2	3	4	5
a. Textbook cover is attractive.					
b. Book is well constructed and durable.					
c. Textbook is not oversized or cumbersome.					
d. The print is attractive, and size is suitable for ease in reading.					
e. Page design is not cluttered.					
f. Paper is of good quality.					
Partial score					
Total Score _____					

TABLE *14.10*	Classroom Textbooks
Concept	**Description**
Student's Edition	The text used by students, which typically contains a preface, introduction, table of contents, chapters organized into units, a glossary, appendixes, and an index
Teacher's Edition	Text that contains everything in student's edition as well as instructional aids to assist teachers
Textbook Adoption	Procedure for selection of textbook, which can begin at state or local level

supplementary information. Pedagogical aids used after the textbook is read can reinforce learning through summaries, develop critical and reflective thinking, and provide remediation of problem areas.

Many textbook publishers provide a workbook to supplement the student textbook. These workbooks can be extremely helpful when used properly. You should be selective in assigning workbook exercises. There is no reason for all students to do the same exercises at the same time. As a matter of fact, there is no reason why all students have to do workbook exercises. However, if workbook exercises are assigned, they must be followed up; that is, they must be checked in some way. In some cases, you may want to develop an answer sheet and have students check their own work.

Some teachers provide students with a great deal of duplicated materials. These materials should be employed with the same care as workbooks. In other words, be selective! Make sure your supplementary activities are meaningful and have instructional value. Avoid giving worksheets as time fillers. Above all, when duplicated materials are supplied, make sure the instructions are clear and students understand what is to be done.

Interest and relevancy can often enhance instruction through newspapers and magazines. Students should be encouraged to bring in pertinent articles that will enrich and update subject areas being studied. Current materials from newspapers and magazines can also furnish materials for bulletin boards and other visual aids.

This concludes our study of secondary school textbooks and pedagogical aids. Table 14.10 gives a summary of the major concepts related to textbooks, and the Classroom Textbooks Application Guidelines offer further suggestions for the appropriate use of textbooks. Review the summary and guidelines, and complete exercise 14.2 to check your understanding of textbook-related issues.

Application Guidelines ▼

Classroom Textbooks

Adopt Textbooks with Care

Examples:
1. Complete a formal rating system on each textbook being considered for adoption.
2. A textbook should be selected on the basis of its usefulness to both students and teacher.
3. Make sure the selected textbook presents view of different sexes, cultures, and races.
4. Try to select more than one textbook for a course. Remember, a textbook presents only one point of view.

Use Your Textbook Wisely

Examples:
1. Teach students effective note-taking skills.
2. Become familiar with the organization of the materials before making assignments for students.
3. Establish a cognitive set (purpose) prior to giving students a reading assignment.
4. Avoid total dependence on a textbook for printed materials in the classroom.
5. Organize guide sheets and study guides with definitions, questions, review exercises, supplementary readings, and assignments for each chapter to be assigned to students.

Application of Knowledge

Exercise 14.2   Classroom Textbooks

Test yourself on the following textbook concepts. Appropriate responses can be found in appendix A.

1. Textbooks generally are written to meet the needs and abilities of students in a prescribed area of the country. (True/False)

2. The teacher's edition of a textbook usually is a modified copy of the student's edition. (True/False)

3. Textbook adoption can begin at the state or local level. (True/False)

4. A sufficient judgment of the worth of a textbook usually can be conducted by making an informal inspection of the book. (True/False)

5. An effective rating system of a textbook should focus on _____ , _____ , and _____ .

6. Three pedagogical aids that can be used for supplementing secondary school classroom instruction are _____ , _____ , and _____ .

CHAPTER SUMMARY

Secondary school teachers have an obligation to further students' ability to read and comprehend assigned class material. Part of this obligation requires that they determine the reading level of students and select teaching strategies that will help students with reading comprehension.

Students can be operating at four different reading levels: independent, instructional, frustration, and listening capacity. Typically, teachers use oral and silent reading assessments, the cloze procedure, or a content-area reading inventory (CARI) in determining the reading level of students. The cloze procedure and content-area reading inventory (CARI) have the added advantage of being applicable to a whole class at one setting.

Strategies can be planned and implemented for assisting students with their comprehension before, during, and after assigned material is read. Before-reading activities can be provided through preview information gleaned from a survey of the text, by calling attention to students' prior knowledge, and by focusing on students' interest and setting a purpose for the assignment. During-reading activities can be provided through various types of study guides and through note-taking techniques. After-reading activities can be provided through the use of cooperative-learning groups, summarizing, creating graphic representations, and writing to learn.

The selection of the classroom textbook can be critical to effective instruction. The textbook will come in two forms: a student's edition and a teacher's edition. Both forms should be analyzed carefully when selecting a classroom textbook.

Textbooks should be viewed as only one source of information available to students. Pedagogical aids such as workbooks, duplicated materials, and newspapers can be incorporated effectively in the classroom. Moreover, students should be taught to make optimal use of their textbook: They should be taught to use the organization, structure, and format of the textbook to assist them with comprehension.

Teachers are often asked to serve on textbook-adoption committees. The adoption procedure can begin at the state or local level. But despite the level at which textbook adoption begins, a formal rating system should be used for analyzing those textbooks being considered. In effect, textbooks should be examined with respect to content, organization, and readability.

Discussion Questions and Activities

1. **Teaching reading.** Examine and compare several textbooks from different grade levels in your content area. What differences do you see in teaching the reading component of your subject at the different levels? What strategies would you employ for motivating students to read the textbooks at the different levels?

2. **Study-guide construction.** Select a chapter from a textbook of your choice. Construct one or more of the following guides that will help students with their reading comprehension.

    a. An anticipation guide.

    b. A three-level reading guide.

    c. An option guide.

3. **The cloze procedure.** Select a textbook from your content area, and construct a cloze test for use with the selected text. If possible, administer the test in an applicable secondary school classroom.

4. **The textbook.** Examine the table of contents, chapter structure, and internal structure of several textbooks from your content area. How are they helpful to the reader? What other pedagogical aids to learning are included in the various texts? How would you use them in addressing reading problems in your classes?

5. **Textbook evaluation.** Apply the rating system in figure 14.2 to several textbooks from your subject area. Would the ratings derived support your decision to use all of the books in your course(s)?

Classrooom Management

✎ **The focus of teaching is on the total individual, but knowing when to say enough is a must.**

Overview

Conducting the business of the classroom for the achievement of learning intent is the function of a teacher, and one that requires skill at effective management. Management is often difficult in the classroom, which is a dynamic system of hundreds of interactions that must be monitored. In other words, classroom management is not an easy task. It takes planning.

All teachers will have management problems. Therefore, you must deal effectively with misbehavior if you are to accomplish your instructional goals. How you deal with misbehavior will depend on your management philosophy and the approach you tend to endorse. As such, this chapter will examine the principles of three current approaches to classroom management and some illustrative models.

Also, if classroom managers are to function effectively, they require an understanding of misbehavior. Therefore, we will address how to deal with misbehavior. We will examine such issues as how to start the year off right, the establishment of rules, the efficient monitoring of a classroom, the appropriate use of punishment, and so on. Finally, teacher-tested ideas for conducting the business of the classroom will be presented.

Objectives

After completing your study of chapter 15, you should be able to do the following:

1. Define *classroom management,* and identify its various aspects.

2. Identify and describe the self-discipline, instructional, and desist approaches to classroom management as well as characteristics of the different illustrative models of discipline associated with each approach.

3. Identify and discuss causes of secondary school misbehavior.

4. Discuss organizational techniques that lead to effective classroom management.

5. Identify and discuss teacher-tested techniques for effectively preventing classroom management problems.

6. Identify and discuss punishment and its appropriate use in secondary school classrooms.

Chapter Terms and Key Concepts

Assertive Discipline

Behavior Modification

Body Language

Classroom Management

Desist Approach

Discipline

I-message

Incentive System

Instructional Approach

Limits

Overlapping

Punishment

Reality Therapy

Ripple Effect

Self-Discipline Approach

Teacher Effectiveness Training

Withitness

Effective teaching requires effective management. Indeed, teachers, administrators, parents, and students report that misbehavior interfered a great deal with the ability of a teacher to teach and with the ability of students to learn (Baker, 1985; Gallup & Elam, 1988). Although such reports suggest that there are serious management and discipline problems in the public schools, it would be a mistake to assume that the secondary schools are out of control.

What is the role of classroom management? Before we can develop techniques for its improvement, we must know what its function should be.

The Role of Classroom Management

Classroom management is the process of organizing and conducting the business of the classroom relatively free of behavior problems. Classroom management is often perceived as related to the preservation of order and the maintenance of control. However, this view is too simplistic; classroom management means much more. Indeed, it involves the establishment and maintenance of the classroom environment so that educational goals can be accomplished.

Central to effective management is the ability to provide a positive social and physical environment conducive to the learning process. Although not its sole component, another highly important aspect of classroom management is discipline, which, as noted earlier, perennially appears as the major concern of teachers, administrators, parents, and students. Discipline should not be viewed as primarily concerned with punishment. **Punishment** involves the consequences of misbehavior, whereas **discipline** deals with the prevention of classroom misbehavior as well as the consequences of disruptive actions. This chapter will focus on discipline rather than punishment, because your success as a classroom teacher will depend on your adequacy in making sound decisions in both of these areas.

As a teacher you must be aware of the principles and consequences of any classroom management decisions and strategies you may wish to implement. For an overview of the various strategies, let's take a look at three such management approaches: the self-discipline approach, the instructional approach, and the desist approach.

Approaches to Classroom Management

The three approaches to classroom management form a continuum, from the self-discipline approach at one extreme to the instructional approach to the desist approach at the opposite end. The six representative models we will discuss are depicted in figure 15.1.

Self-Discipline Approach

The **self-discipline approach** is built on the premise that students can be trusted to evaluate and change their actions so these behaviors are beneficial and appropriate to the self and to the class as a whole. The approach

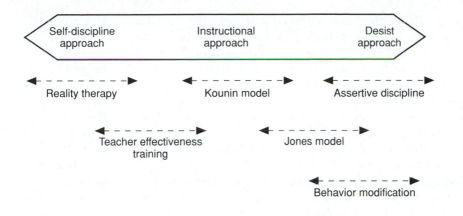

Figure 15.1 *The Continuum of Classroom Management Models*

Self-discipline approach — Instructional approach — Desist approach

Reality therapy

Kounin model

Assertive discipline

Teacher effectiveness training

Jones model

Behavior modification

views classroom management as a function of the teacher's ability to build and establish working teacher-student relationships. In a word, advocates argue that teachers need to recognize the dignity of students and that they must exhibit the attitudinal qualities of realness, trust, acceptance, and empathy. With these attitudinal qualities in mind, let's look at two class-room management models that focus on self-discipline.

Reality Therapy

Developed by William Glasser (1965, 1977, 1986), **Reality Therapy** is a strategy that helps students take the responsibility for examining and solving their own problems. Glasser believes that students are rational beings and can control their behavior if they wish. For example, witness the usual good student behaviors found on the first day of school.

Furthermore, Glasser suggests that students often must be assisted in making good choices rather than bad choices. Indeed, he feels that students must be guided so that they become responsible individuals able to satisfy their needs in the real world. That is to say, they must be guided toward reality. It is the teacher's job to provide the needed guidance so that students make good choices. The teacher must help students examine their behaviors in light of their benefit to self and to the class. If found inappropriate, the individual student must be assisted in devising a realis-tic, written plan for changing the inappropriate behavior. No excuses are acceptable for not carrying out the devised plan. The student has made a commitment and is held to it. If the original plan proves inadequate, it is essential that both the teacher and student be willing to reexamine the plan and to renew or change the commitment. If the student is unwilling to make the commitment, he or she should not be allowed to remain in the classroom.

Note that Reality Therapy places the responsibility on the student, not the teacher. The teacher does not punish. In fact, Glasser does not believe in punishment. He feels punishment hinders personal develop-ment and is ineffective. If a student disrupts the class, he or she simply is removed until a commitment for change has been worked out. Thus, the teacher's function is to assist students in becoming responsible, productive members of the classroom.

Rules that are enforced are essential to Glasser. Indeed, background and poor upbringing do not make poor behavior acceptable. Student responsibility must be stressed continually. Students are forced to acknowledge their behavior, and they should make value judgments regarding that behavior. For example, when a disruption occurs, the teacher should never ask why a student is doing what he or she is doing, but rather, the teacher should ask, "What are you doing?" The emphasis should be put on the *you* so that there is no misinterpretation as to who is responsible. This question should be followed up with queries such as "Is this behavior against the rules?" or "Is this behavior helping you or this class?" If the misbehavior persists, a conference (private) is needed for working out a commitment for change. If the disruptions continue or the commitment is not followed, the consequences should become progressively more severe: principal conference, followed by parent conference, followed by in-school suspension, followed by out-of-school suspension, and finally with permanent exclusion from school.

Classroom meetings are an essential element in addressing problems in the Glasser model. Students sit in a close circle and discuss classroom situations and problems. The teacher's role is to provide background information as needed by the group and to give opinions sparingly. Classroom rules, consequences, and classroom procedure are developed at such meetings, and all students are expected to participate in their formation. All students are expected to observe the agreed-upon rules and consequences. However, the rules are flexible and could be changed with another meeting as the situation changes.

Teacher Effectiveness Training (TET)

Teacher Effectiveness Training (TET), conceived by Dr. Thomas Gordon (1974), stresses the establishment of positive working relationships between teachers and students. Gordon believes that teachers can reduce disruptive student behaviors by using clearer, less provocative communication. Furthermore, he recommends that nonverbal language and listening should be stressed as the teacher interacts with students in an atmosphere of openness and trust.

According to Gordon, the key to Teacher Effectiveness Training is based on who owns the problem when one develops in the learning environment: teacher or student. If the teacher is blocked from reaching the instructional goals by the student's actions, then the teacher owns the problem. For example, if students continuously talk as the teacher tries to teach, the teacher owns the problem because he or she is kept from reaching the goal of teaching. On the other hand, if the teacher feels annoyed by a student's behavior or if the teacher wishes a student would change his or her behavior, the problem likely belongs to the student. The student who says he or she hates the teacher or hates the subject has a problem.

When the teacher owns the problem, an "I" message should be sent. An **I-message** tells the student how you feel about a problem situation and invites the student to change, to correct that situation—for example, "I am angry with this continuous talking in class," "I am disappointed in your behavior at the assembly," or "I can't hear myself think with the noise in this classroom." If the process works, the student (or class) should see the harm being done and change his or her (their) behavior. However, if an I-message does not correct the problem, the teacher and student (class) are in a conflict situation, which calls for finding a solution through problem solving. When this happens, Gordon recommends that a "no lose" problem-resolution tactic be employed. The no-lose strategy is a six-step form of negotiation where teacher and student (class) contribute relatively equally. First, the problem or conflict is clearly determined. Second, possible solutions are generated, with the teacher and student (class) presenting an equal number of ideas. These ideas are evaluated in the third step, and those unacceptable are rejected. During the fourth step, the remaining ideas are ranked and the best solution is selected. This is followed by the fifth step, determination of how to implement the selected solution so that all parties are satisfied. The sixth and final step entails an assessment of how well the solution works. In general, punishment is not recognized as a viable option in the no-lose tactic, because the student (class) would be placed in a losing situation.

A student-owned problem calls for active listening (or empathetic listening) on the part of the teacher. That is, the teacher should listen carefully and become a counselor and supporter for the student, who should be encouraged to express his or her views. As such, the teacher should reflect the student's point of view only and help the student find his or her own problem solution. The teacher's function is not to give or impose solutions to students' problems.

Instructional Approach

The premise that forms the basis for the **instructional approach** to classroom management is that well-planned and well-implemented instruction will prevent most classroom problems. Basically, the assumption is that students will not engage in disruptive behavior when lessons are geared to meet their interests, needs, and abilities. In other words, the instructional approach is predicated on the assumption that well-planned and well-implemented lessons that engage students in their own learning and afford them the opportunity to be successful learners will prevent and solve most management problems. Let's now look at two models of classroom management that focus on the principles of the instructional approach.

The Kounin Model

In a comprehensive comparison of effective and ineffective classroom managers, Jacob Kounin (1970) found that the teachers differed very little in the way they handled classroom problems once they arose. The primary difference was in the things the successful managers did that tended to prevent classroom problems. First, these teachers were environmentally aware. In other words, they knew everything that went on in their classrooms at all times. Second, the effective managers were skilled as group leaders and at keeping activities moving on task. That is, these teachers had students involved and doing something productive at all times. No one ever just sat and waited for work or watched others. The teachers had lessons that were well planned and conducted at a smooth, even, appropriate pace. Kounin concluded that some teachers are better classroom managers because of skill in four areas: "withitness," overlapping activities, group focusing, and movement management (Charles, 1986).

Withitness is the skill of knowing what is going on in all parts of the classroom at all times; nothing is missed. "Withit" teachers note and act quickly and accurately in curbing class disturbances. They prevent minor disruptions from becoming major and know who the instigator is in a problem situation.

Effective classroom managers are also skilled at overlapping. **Overlapping** means having the ability to handle two or more activities or groups at the same time. Essentially, it is the ability to monitor the whole class at all times. It involves keeping a small group on task, for example, while also helping other students with their seat work.

Finally, Kounin notes that successful classroom management also depends on movement management and group focus—that is, the ability to make smooth lesson transitions, keep an appropriate pace, and involve all students in a lesson. Moreover, efficient managers did not leave a lesson hanging while tending to something else or change back and forth from one subject or activity to another. They kept students alert by holding their attention, holding them accountable, and involving all students in the lesson.

The Jones Model

Frederick Jones (1979), in his more than ten years of researching the problems teachers encounter in the classroom, found that most management problems resulted from massive time wasting by students. In other words, most classroom problems were a result of students being off task. In fact, Jones estimated that teachers lose 50 percent or more of their instructional time through student time wasting (e.g., talking and walking around the room). Jones contends that this wasted instructional time can be reclaimed when teachers correctly implement four strategies: limit setting, good body language, incentive system, and giving help efficiently.

Limit setting is the establishment of classroom boundaries for appropriate behavior. According to Jones, these **limits** should include the formation of rules of behavior as well as descriptions of appropriate work behavior, procedures for getting supplies and materials, what to do when stuck on seat work, and what to do when finished with assigned seat work.

Ninety percent of discipline and keeping students on task, Jones contends, involves the skillful use of *body language*. **Body language** is a set of physical mannerisms that tend to get students back to work, the most effective of which are physical proximity to students, direct eye contact, body position (body orientation toward student), facial expressions, and tone of voice.

Jones contends that **incentive systems** also can be employed for keeping students on task and for getting them to complete their work. Indeed, he suggests that preferred activities such as time on the computer, free time, use of educational games, and free reading can serve as motivational rewards for desired behaviors. Furthermore, Jones adds that the use of peer pressure represents a quite effective motivator. For example, time

can be deducted from the class preferred-activity time when an individual student misbehaves. The deduction of time can be recorded, as Jones suggests, with a large stopwatch placed at the front of the room, so the whole class can see. If a large stopwatch is not available, a standard amount of time (e.g., 1 minute) can be deducted for each misbehavior.

Finally, Jones suggests that *giving help efficiently* is related to time on task. His research revealed that teachers on the average spend 4 minutes helping individual students who were having difficulty with seat work. Jones recommends that this time be cut to no more than 20 seconds per student. Doing so allows more students to be helped and reduces the tendency for students to work only when the teacher is standing over them.

Limit setting, the use of body language, implementing an incentive system, and giving help efficiently will not eliminate all behavior problems. When such problems do develop, Jones suggests, a back-up system such as in-class isolation or removal from the room is needed.

Desist Approach

The **desist approach** to classroom management gives the teacher full responsibility for regulating the classroom. The teacher makes use of and enforces a set of specific rules to control student behavior in the classroom. Because the desist approach models of classroom management give teachers power to deal forcefully and quickly with misbehavior, they can be viewed as power systems. The desist approach probably is the most widely used strategy in today's public schools. Two common desist models of classroom management are *assertive discipline* and *behavior modification*.

Assertive Discipline

Lee and Marlene Canter (1976) contend that teachers have a basic right to require decent behavior in the classroom. To this end, the Canters advocate **assertive discipline,** which calls for assertive teachers. Assertive teachers are those who clearly and firmly communicate needs and requirements to students, follow up their words with appropriate actions, and respond to students in ways that will maximize compliance, but in no way violate the best interest of the students (Canter & Canter, 1976, p. 9). Assertive teachers take charge in the classroom in a calm yet forceful way.

Assertive teachers do not tolerate improper behavior that interrupts learning. Commonly used excuses—citing peer pressure, home environment, and heredity, for example—are not accepted for misbehavior. The assertive teacher establishes rules and limits for behavior, along with consequences for proper behavior and improper behavior. Students who follow the established rules receive positive consequences, such as some kind of material reward, free time, or special privileges, while students who break the rules receive negative consequences, such as detention, giving up part of their lunch period, staying after school, or going to the principal's office. The rules, limits, and consequences are communicated to students and parents in clear terms at the beginning of the year.

Assertive teachers insist on decent, responsible behavior from their students. After establishing expectations early in the year, assertive teachers consistently reinforce the established procedures and guidelines. In other words, the teachers make promises, not threats. They do not *threaten* to enforce the rules and guidelines and apply the consequences to misbehavior, they *promise* to do so. It is assumed that all students, if they want, are capable of behaving; it is a matter of choice.

Behavior Modification

Behavior modification, based on the ideas and work of B. F. Skinner (1968, 1971), is an approach that evolves from the assumption that students will change their behavior in order to receive definite rewards.

The basic premise of behavior modification is that student behavior can be changed by altering the consequences that follow their actions and behaviors. Technically, reinforcement principles are used systematically for changing some aspect of educational practice or student behavior. Students who follow established procedures, who follow the rules, or who perform well on required work are given reinforcers or rewards. The reinforcers may be teacher praise, good grades, or even such tangible items as stickers or appropriate free movies. Students who do not follow the procedures, who misbehave, or who perform poorly are denied desired rewards or are punished in some way.

Basically, there are four general categories of consequences that can follow students' actions: positive reinforcement, negative reinforcement, punishment I, and punishment II. As noted in chapter 13, positive and negative reinforcement are used for maintaining or increasing the occurrence of a desired student behavior. In the case of positive reinforcement, a reward (e.g., praise, grades, or free time) is presented for desired

TABLE *15.1* Management Approaches

Approach	Description
Self-Discipline Approach	View that students can evaluate and change to appropriate behavior
Instructional Approach	View that well-planned and well-implemented instruction will prevent classroom problems
Desist Approach	View that the teacher should have full regulatory power in the classroom

behavior, while negative reinforcement involves the removal of an undesired stimulus (e.g., weekend homework, no visiting, or a change in the seating arrangement).

Inappropriate student actions can be discouraged through the use of punishment. Like reinforcement, punishment can be categorized into two categories, simply labeled I and II. Punishment I, the most commonly used form, involves the application of some undesirable stimulus. For example, undesirable student action can be followed by a private reprimand, or being placed in isolation, or being sent to the principal's office. Contrastly, punishment II involves the removal of a desired stimulus or the withholding of an anticipated positive stimulus. For example, inappropriate student behavior could be followed by a loss of free time, or exclusion from a school film, or loss of computer time for a week. If used appropriately, both punishment I and II should result in the elimination of, or at least a decrease in, undesired student behaviors.

Reinforcement also can be a complex system. For example, one such program is the token reinforcement system in which students earn tokens for both positive classroom behaviors and academic work. The tokens earned are then periodically exchanged for some desired activity or reward (see chapter 13).

Management approaches can be studied and analyzed. However, you must decide on your own modus operandi with regard to managerial style. These management approaches are summarized in table 15.1, and the Management Approaches Application Guidelines offer some additional management suggestions. How you respond to management problems will depend on which approach or approaches along the continuum of management strategies best fits your specific educational philosophy. Moreover, how you respond to student misbehavior should also be related to the cause of the misbehavior. Let's now look at some of the reasons students misbehave. But first, review the approach summary and the guidelines, and complete exercise 15.1.

Causes of Misbehavior

Classroom misbehavior can often be attributed to conditions that are not readily obvious. Therefore, if you are to deal successfully with misbehavior, you must try to identify the deeper problems that are causing the actions. That is, you must get to the root of the problems that are causing students

Application Guidelines ▼

to misbehave. A careful examination of students' classroom behaviors, desirable as well as undesirable, can reveal that they are influenced by forces and pressures inside and outside the classroom environment.

Home Environment

Relationships with parents and siblings often affect classroom behavior. Parents usually serve as models and communicate important attitudinal ideals and feelings to their children. If these parental influences are negative, students might develop these same negative ideals and feelings.

Parents, through daily interactions, establish the general acceptable conduct of behavior of their children and therefore will directly influence students' classroom behavior. Consequently, when parents are extremely tolerant and do not teach respect for others, or when they allow their children to talk back, or when swearing and fighting is tolerated in the home, these behaviors often will carry over into the classroom. Conversely, students who come from homes with overly strict parents may be

Application of Knowledge

Test yourself on the following management approaches. Appropriate responses can be found in appendix A.

1. Punishment deals mainly with the prevention of behavior problems. (True/False)

2. Match the approach on the right to the premise on the left.
   - *a.* _____ Teacher deals quickly and forcefully with classroom problems
   - *b.* _____ Students can be trusted to change to appropriate behavior
   - *c.* _____ Well-planned and well-implemented lessons prevent classroom problems

   1. Self-discipline
   2. Instructional
   3. Desist

3. Reality Therapy places responsibility for proper behavior on the student. (True/False)

4. Which of the following components is/are integral to Teacher Effectiveness Training (TET)?
   - *a.* Withitness.
   - *b.* I-messages.
   - *c.* Body language.
   - *d.* Punishment.
   - *e.* No-lose strategy.
   - *f.* Active listening.

5. Which of the following discipline models place(s) emphasis on the establishment of classroom rules?
   - *a.* Reality Therapy.
   - *b.* The Kounin Model.
   - *c.* The Jones Model.
   - *d.* Assertive discipline.
   - *e.* Behavior modification.

inclined to be followers who do not question authority, or they may resent anyone in authority—including the teacher. Therefore, you must try to determine the rules of conduct established in the home before you can deal effectively with misbehavior in the classroom.

Students from homes where there is constant family friction and a related lack of parental support sometimes will develop discipline problems. Constant involvement in the home's emotional turmoil and a too-often associated feeling of rejection can also lead to problems in the classroom. You should be sensitive to abrupt behavioral changes that might be a result of a student's problems at home.

Lack of supervision in the home is a common problem in our society. Many students come from single-parent homes or from homes where both parents are too busy with their own lives to be concerned with the children. Therefore, you may have students who work, or who stay out late at night, or who watch television late into the night. These students often fall asleep in class or are inattentive. Other students may live on junk food or come to school without breakfast. These students sometimes lack the energy to carry out assignments or to even pay attention. You need to counsel these students, and perhaps the parents, on the importance of rest and proper diet.

Parental attitudes toward schooling will influence students' behavior in the classroom. Parents who put little value on education, for example, will often instill these same attitudes in their children. Furthermore, parents who communicate negative feelings toward educators (classroom teachers as well as administrators) will often pass such feelings on to their children, who, in turn, will have little respect for educators.

Conversely, some parents value education so highly that they establish unreasonable expectations for their children—the parents, for example, who want and will accept nothing but straight-A work. Similarly, problems may develop when parents have unrealistic goals for their children—for instance, the parents who want their sons or daughters to be physicians and so insist that they enroll in advanced science courses. Problems often develop because of lack of interest or lack of academic ability. Both high expectations and unrealistic goals can result in poor motivation, low self-esteem, and behavior problems.

The Teacher

Teachers who do not plan well will have trouble with class control. Teachers who do not start class when the bell rings, or who are sidetracked from their lessons into unrelated talk, or who are not sure where they are going next in their lessons will communicate disorder to their students. Too often, such a message of disorder will lead to disrespect toward the teacher and a dislike of the subject.

Teachers must teach at the level of their students' ability. Lessons geared too low end up boring and irritating bright students, whereas lessons geared too high will frustrate low-ability students. However, the teacher who focuses on the average students, as many teachers do, are still not challenging the bright students and are not giving low-ability students a reasonable opportunity to be successful. As a result, both groups become mischievous, inattentive, and interruptive in class. In short, you must design lessons that offer challenge to your bright students, but at the same time give low-ability students reasonable opportunities for success.

Teachers must show respect for students as individuals with rights, values, and feelings. They must exercise control and refrain from ridiculing them, both in front of their peers and in private. Ridicule and sarcasm will back students into a defensive position to save face with peers, which can cause problems. Also, teachers should refrain from demanding an unreasonable degree of inactivity from students. Some talking, scuffling of feet, and paper shuffling is unavoidable. Remember that adolescents need some outlets for their energy. In fact, adolescents often find it difficult to be perfectly quiet, inactive, and attentive in the classroom for extended periods of time as some teachers insist. In short, don't be oversensitive to noise in the classroom, but let common sense be your guide. Establish your limits, however, and don't tolerate all the desires of students in your classroom.

Personality and Health Problems

Some student classroom problems can be attributed to immaturity and/or problems related to health. Immaturity is especially a problem with junior high school students.

Adolescents often feel insecure about their appearance, lack of peer recognition, and lack of parental respect. Such feelings may stem from a lack of self-respect and self-control, which results in constant talking, no consideration for others, immature actions, and a lack of responsibility. These behaviors, although usually viewed as minor, when exhibited daily should be addressed at once, so their escalation into more serious problems may be averted.

More serious problems, such as cheating on tests and talking back to teachers, often can be traced back to the home environment or even to some deep underlying causes, which may require expert assistance. Keep in mind, however, that some students will go to such extreme measures to obtain attention from their parents, teachers, or classmates.

Some students present problems to the teacher because of health concerns. Allergies, poor eyesight, respiratory ailments, and poor hearing can affect classroom behavior. It is difficult to concentrate when you have trouble breathing, or seeing, or hearing. Indeed, an illness may be so severe that students are not able to exert the energy needed for classroom activities or homework exercises. It is important that you be sensitive to the health problems of students and refer such students to the school nurse, principal, and/or parents so they become aware of the problem.

Once a philosophy of classroom management has been formulated and the cause of misbehavior understood, your managerial style must be implemented in such a way that it prevents problems from developing and deals with the misbehavior that does take place. This requires that you organize for the prevention of problems as well as deal with the ongoing management of the class.

Organizing for Effective Management

Effective classroom management takes organization. Indeed, much of what we have covered should prove useful in organizing your classroom for effective management. Such techniques as motivation and variety in instructional planning represent major factors in the prevention of management problems. However, let's look at some other key classroom problem–prevention areas.

Planning

Obviously, classroom order takes planning. Plans must be devised such that classroom problems will be minimized and learning time will be maximized. In other words, if you are to be effective, you should be well prepared: You should know exactly what and how you will teach and have all required materials ready for students. In fact, you should overestimate what can be accomplished in the allowed time. It can be extremely frustrating and embarrassing to find yourself with 15 to 20 minutes of class time and nothing to do. Needless to say, problems often develop. Therefore, overplan—with activities that are interesting, stimulating, and relevant—and keep your lesson moving at a brisk but appropriate pace. Finally, it is good practice to have alternative activities planned and available in case they are needed.

The school calendar should be consulted when planning, because certain days or weeks will require special steps to avoid potential behavior problems. For instance, the day before a major holiday, the day of an afternoon assembly or pep rally, the day of a big football or basketball game, or the week before Christmas or spring break are apt to require special attention and preparation. At such times, it is essential that students be involved in highly motivating and interesting activities that will compete successfully with other, external events.

Establishing Routines

Many school and classroom activities will be basically routine. For example, the taking and reporting of attendance, the issuing of passes for students to leave the room or building, and the distribution and collection of papers. Some of these routines are established by the school for all teachers, while others are established by individual teachers.

What are the standard school-operating procedures and routines? To find out, you should consult the school handbook and talk with your department head, other teachers, and the principal. In most schools, routines and procedures are established for (1) the taking and keeping of attendance, (2) dealing with tardy students, (3) the issuance of passes to leave the classroom or building, (4) having students in after school, (5) the recording and reporting of grades, (6) the use of the school library, (7) dealing with ill students, (8) the issuance of failing notices, and

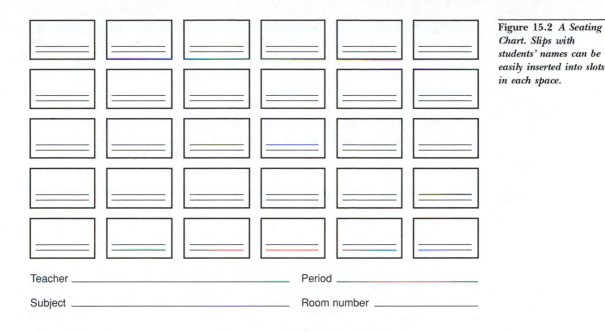

Figure 15.2 *A Seating Chart. Slips with students' names can be easily inserted into slots in each space.*

Teacher _____   Period _____

Subject _____   Room number _____

(9) conducting parental conferences. Such school routines and procedures must be adhered to by all teachers, because if each teacher were to establish individual school routines and procedures, the results would more than likely be student uncertainty and discipline problems. Therefore, if the established school routines and procedures are not known, you should find out *prior* to the reporting of students to class.

Routines and procedures must also be established for the classroom. Routines and procedures should be established for activities such as entering the classroom and starting class, checking attendance, passing out materials, and collecting and checking homework. You should, for instance, have a short activity ready when students enter the classroom (e.g., a problem or question on the overhead or a few pages to read) that they will complete as you take care of routine activities.

Attendance represents a problem area for many teachers in that they will spend as much as 10 minutes calling roll. This wasted time at the beginning of the period is usually used by students for talking and other mischievous activities. Instead of calling roll, you should prepare a seating chart for each class (see figure 15.2). A pocket-type seating chart works best, because you or your students themselves will request some changes in seating during the year. During the first class meeting, students should be given the opportunity for selecting a seat (do not assign seating at the secondary school level). Once the selection has been made, have students write their names—or you write their names—on slips, which are placed in the appropriate slots. You may have to change some seat assignments later, but in the beginning give them their choice.

The collection and distribution of papers should be streamlined as much as possible. Unnecessary amounts of time on such tasks often lead to student misbehavior. Collecting and passing out class materials can be accomplished by passing to, or from, the front of the seating rows. In other seating arrangements, some similar technique—for instance, assigning one student per group to collect or pass out materials—can be used.

Taking care of excused absences is another time-consuming administrative chore. In handling these, you must, of course, sign the admission slip, but you must also bring the student up-to-date as to missed classroom activities and assignments. When several students have been absent on a given day, the handling of missed work can often delay the start of class considerably. This delay usually will result in talking and general student misbehavior. A monthly calendar, such as that shown in figure 15.3, can be helpful in dealing with absences. Students know what classroom activities were completed on a given day; they know what assignment was given. The calendar also gives your better students the opportunity to work ahead so they can work on other individual projects. Indeed, announcements, messages of recognition, and motivational messages (e.g., awards, birthdays, and accomplishments) can be shared with the class through the class calendar. Computer programs are now available, and most are user-friendly, that will make the construction of class calendars a relatively easy task.

You should never become a slave to routine; however, when routines will be of assistance in carrying out classroom business efficiently, they should be followed. You should determine and use those routines and procedures that are appropriate for your particular classroom.

Managing Space

Your classroom should be arranged to be an environment where it is easy for you and students to work, and so that it does not encourage misbehavior. The pencil sharpener, for example, should not be positioned in a place where students must pass close to other students when going to sharpen a pencil. Secondary school students often can't leave each other alone as they pass nearby. In addition, it is usually unwise to place the wastebasket at the front of the room; it is an inviting target for basketball practice.

Most classrooms today have movable chairs. Therefore, don't get in the habit of only seating students in straight rows. You should try different seating arrangements (e.g., circles, semicircles, U-shapes, and squares). In fact, arrange your seating according to the activity to be completed by students. Experiment with various arrangements and see what works best with your students.

Constructive use of wall space makes a classroom more conducive to learning and evokes a more positive climate. For example, walls can display motivational statements, or materials to spark interest in a topic, or classroom procedures. Moreover, before school begins, put up a bulletin board and be prepared to change it periodically. Make your bulletin boards attractive, interesting, and colorful so they help promote a positive attitude toward your room and subject. However, you might want to

April 19??

S	M	T	W	T	F	S
1 Welcome back to class, Jesse.	**2** Text pages 450–451. Do practice 1–10. Do pages 452–453: Apply section.	**3** Text pages 454–455. Do practice work 1–10. Persevere, you can do it!	**4** Text 456–457. Do all practice work.	**5** Text pages 458–459. Do all practice work. This one is a "piece of cake."	**6** Spelling test. All assignments must be in baskets today!	**7** Birthdays this month are: Kevin, Kendra, Thomas, Alison, Jennifer, and Hope!
8 Failing notices go out Friday. Don't be caught off balance! Turn in all work NOW.	**9** Spelling. Text pages 462–463. Do all practice work.	**10** Text pages 464–465. Do all practice work. Stretch your neck out and try Part C.**	**11** Text pages 568–469 do A&B.	**12** Text pages 470–471. Do all practice work.	**13** DUCKING OUT FOR EASTER BREAK. NO SCHOOL TODAY!	**14** ALCOHOL IS A DRUG. COLORED EGGS ARE OKAY. Happy Easter Weekend.
15 HAVE A "HOPPY" EASTER.	**16** Tune into Spelling! 50 words this week for the spelling spin-off on Friday.	**17** Text pages 472–475. Do all practice work. Challenge** Try the Apply*	**18** Film today on preparing speeches!	**19** TIME FOR TALK. DISCUSS TOPIC FOR SPEECHES TODAY.	**20** SPELLING SPIN-OFF** Today!	**21** Character Comes from the Heart! Students Persevere** *************
22 "Write On" with Learning. Essay winners this month are Jay and Natalie****	**23** Library to begin research.	**24** Library work. Bibliography due end of class today. See page 339.	**25** Library work. Topic outlines due today!! See page 340 for help.	**26** Library work. Rough drafts due today. See page 343 for help.	**27** Library work. Final drafts due today. See pages 347–349 for help.	**28** Remember to say "NO" to drugs.
29 Don't forget to vote this month for the most improved student in your class.	**30** Text pages 502–504. Do all practice work.					

Figure 15.3 *Monthly Calendar*

devote one bulletin board to announcements, such as the bell schedule, the weekly lunch menu, news items of interest to the class, and classroom rules and consequences.

Establishing Usable Limits

Limits specify the expected and forbidden actions in the classroom. Students need and want limits (rules); that is, they want to know what is expected of them and why. Teachers who try to avoid setting limits and imposing necessary structure will often find that chaos results. But don't establish rules for the sake of having rules. Indeed, you should take care not to have too many rules, unenforceable rules, and unnecessary rules; only essential rules and limits should be set.

Clarity and consistency are vital in the establishment of rules. Your rules should always reinforce the basic idea that students are in school to study and learn. When no longer needed, a rule should be discarded or changed. But as long as they are retained, rules must be enforced. You should always explain and discuss with students why certain rules are necessary. You may even want to spend time negotiating the establishment of certain rules with students at the beginning of the year.

It is often better to have a few general rules (five or six) that cover many specifics, rather than to list all the specifics. However, if specific actions represent a problem area (e.g., chewing gum or using reference books), then a rule should cover the specific problem. Examples of appropriate general rules for secondary school classrooms that might be established and discussed are these:

1. *Be prepared with books, paper, pencil, and the like when you come to class.* You should discuss exactly what is to be brought to class.

2. *Be in your seat and ready to work when the bell rings.* You may want students to begin working on a warm-up activity that is written on the overhead, or you may require that they have homework ready to be checked, or you may ask that they have notebooks open and ready for taking notes when the bell rings.

3. *Take care of your classroom, and respect other people's property.* This means school, teacher, and fellow student property is to be left alone.

4. *Be polite and respectful.* This conduct covers verbal abuse, fighting, talking back, and general conduct.

5. *Obtain permission before speaking or leaving your seat.* Address exceptions—such as when to sharpen pencils, throw trash away, and going to the teacher's desk for assistance—to this rule.

Again, your rules should always be discussed and taught to students. In fact, some teachers require that students pass a test about classroom regulations at the beginning of the year. Specific behaviors that are included and excluded in each general rule should be explained and discussed at the beginning of the year. Indeed, you might be wise to have students record the rules for future reference. You should also consider sending parents a copy of your classroom rules.

As soon as you have established your rules, you must decide on the consequences for breaking a rule. It is often rather difficult to make this decision at the time the rule is broken. The appropriate response is often to have the student "do it right." For example, messes can be cleaned up, incomplete papers can be finished or redone, or broken property can be replaced. For other infractions, you may want to form a hierarchy of consequences, such as:

1st infraction: Name on board.

2nd infraction: Talk with teacher.

3rd infraction: Lunch detention.

4th infraction: Conference with principal.

5th infraction: Call to parents.

Once you have established the rules for your classroom and the consequences for breaking the rules, you have taken the first step in making students aware of what will and will not be tolerated in the classroom. You must now think about managing the classroom on a daily basis.

Managing the Class

Effective classroom management is a daily and essential challenge to teachers. Managing a class basically involves getting off to a good start, and then keeping the class moving smoothly toward established goals.

Getting Started

The first few weeks of school set the tone for the year. During these initial weeks, it is essential that you establish your credibility as a manager. In fact, student respect for you as a teacher will often be established during the first few weeks.

What do effective secondary school classroom managers do during those first critical weeks? Experienced teachers suggest the secret to successful management is organization. The focus during the first few weeks of school should be on the teaching of rules, the organizational system, classroom procedures, and expectations. Feedback on appropriateness of actions is essential in these early stages. In other words, you should create a positive classroom environment and establish rules and consequences. Planning is the key to management: Make sure your content is interesting and meaningful to students. Moreover, it is important that you clearly communicate standards for academic work and establish an atmosphere of free exchange. Indeed, involve students as much as possible in the learning process. Finally, monitor student behavior closely, and deal with misbehavior quickly and firmly.

Making full and meaningful use of time on the first day is especially critical. Therefore, it might be helpful to plan a schedule such as the following:

1. **Make Out Seating Slips**

   Pass out seating slips, and have students sign them. Collect them in order, separating each row with a paper clip. It is often wise to count and inspect the slips as they are collected. If you don't, you may find slips signed by Snow White or not signed at all.

2. **Distribute Books**

   Assign books to students, and keep an accurate record of assigned book numbers. Books sometime get lost or stolen. Remember, you or the student will replace any unreturned book. Have a short activity for students to complete as you distribute books.

3. **Assignment Sheet**

   Distribute an assignment sheet with at least one week's work on it. Explain it to students. Make your first assignment short, interesting, involving, and not dependent on the textbook.

4. **Class Discussion**

   Discuss the unique contributions of your subject that make it important and relevant to them.

5. **Homework**

   Discuss assigned homework topic. Pose some provocative questions.

6. **Marking System**

   Give a brief explanation of your grading system, of when you collect homework, of when tests are administered, and so on.

Admittedly, completing all these tasks will be difficult on the first day, but accomplishing a great deal the first day may serve you well. Students will be impressed with your organization and businesslike manner, and first impressions are important to adolescents.

Finally, leave about 2 or 3 minutes at the end of the period for closure. That is, save some time at the end of the period for needed cleanup and for giving any assignment. When—and only when—you are ready, you should dismiss the class. Don't let the bell dismiss the class. This should be understood from the first day.

Know the Students

It is good practice to know as much as possible about your students. Of course, with 25 to 30 students per class, you might have up to 150 students total in all your classes. Just learning names can be a chore. However, learning names as soon as possible shows definite interest. A seating chart will be helpful in remembering names.

Figure 15.4 *Information Card*

Family name: _____	First name: _____
Address: _____	Telephone: _____

Homeroom teacher: _____

Father's first name: _____

Occupation: _____

Mother's first name: _____

Occupation: _____

Number of siblings: _____

Interests (hobbies, clubs, sports, other activities): _____

_____

_____

_____

Understandably it is advisable to know more about students than just their names. An information card (figure 15.4), completed during the first class period, can provide some of this information. If more information is needed, student files are usually available to teachers. Information on students often proves helpful in understanding why students act the way they do.

Enforcement of Rules

Lax enforcement of established rules renders them worthless. In fact, students like to know where they stand and periodically will test your enforcement of the rules. When this happens, quick and firm application of the consequences should follow. If a student tries you—and one always will—you cannot ignore the breaking of the rules, because the behavior will ripple to other students, and they will also want to test you. Conversely, if you are firm when a student tests you, this action too will ripple out to other students, and they will be less likely to test you in the future.

The use of the **ripple effect** is especially effective with high-status students. Consequently, you should be firm with these students, and other students will give you fewer problems.

Be consistent and fair in your enforcement of the rules. Treat all students the same, but be humane. You sometimes must consider the reasons for misbehavior and make exceptions with regard to punishment. However, make sure the class as a whole understands the reason for an exception.

Monitoring

You should be aware of what is going on in the classroom at all times. Therefore, room arrangement is an important part of your ability to monitor the classroom: You must be able to monitor all areas of the classroom from your desk and from any other classroom area. When a potential problem is spotted, a simple pause in conjunction with eye contact (a stare) usually will curb the inappropriate activity.

Two aspects of room arrangement are critical to effective monitoring: your ability to see students at all times and the traffic patterns within the room. Your capacity for seeing students and moving quickly to be in the proximity of a potential problem will often control the misbehavior. Therefore, apply careful thought to your room arrangement. Eliminate barriers that may keep you from seeing certain areas of the room.

Monitoring the classroom as you teach is not an easy task. You must be well prepared, know your content thoroughly, and maintain contact with all areas of the classroom at all times. If you are uncertain about what you are to teach or if there are dead spots in your lesson, students may recognize the insecurity and become inattentive.

Punishment

Sooner or later, no matter how well you plan for preventing problems, student misbehavior is going to demand that you administer punishment. Some student behavior will be so severe that some kind of adverse stimulus must be employed to decrease the occurrence of a behavior. However, you must be aware that what is considered punishment by one individual might not be considered punishment by another—in fact, it may even be considered rewarding by the second individual. Also, when applying adverse consequences for misbehavior, be sure that you communicate to students that they have chosen the consequence. They should understand that by choosing to misbehave, they have also chosen the consequences.

The most common consequence used for curbing disruptive behavior is probably the verbal reprimand. But all too often these reprimands become mere nagging. As a rule, secondary school students are at an age when they react negatively to what they perceive as being treated as less than adults. Efforts to apply adverse stimulus such as criticism may provoke hostility. Indeed, the student may blow up and say something unintentional. Thus, criticizing, ridiculing, or embarrassing a student often results in a power struggle between the student and teacher, which does little for resolving the long-term behavior problem.

One way of avoiding a confrontation with offending students is to administer the reprimand privately rather than publicly. In this way, the student "saves face," and there is no need to engage in a power struggle. Moreover, a private talk gives you the opportunity for developing a closer, personal relationship with the misbehaving student. If the private talk fails to solve the problem, more severe consequences must be administered. Other consequences often applied when severe misbehavior occurs are, in order of severity, loss of privileges, detention, in-school suspension, and out-of-school suspension.

Loss of privileges is a common and effective form of punishment. Examples might be the loss of free time, or the loss of time on the computer, or the loss of a weekend free of homework, or the loss of any other preferred activities. Other options include requiring students to stay in the classroom when others attend an assembly or pep rally. Unfortunately, the problem with this form of punishment is the lack of privileges commonly available in most classrooms and, consequently, the shortage of privileges to be denied.

Detention is one of the most frequently used means of punishment, which generally comes in two forms. One type requires that all students serving detention report to a detention hall at a specified time (e.g., Monday after school or Saturday morning). The other kind requires that the students report back to the teacher's classroom after or before school. However, because many students ride buses or work, many teachers have students return to the classroom during some break during the day (e.g., part of their lunch break). When using detention as a punishment option, the student should be required to complete a serious academic task. Moreover, you should avoid engaging in conversation with students serving detention. Conversation with the teacher may be perceived as enjoyable, and, hence, the misbehavior might be repeated for more of the "enjoyable" detention.

On occasion, misbehavior becomes so serious or persistent that you must solicit outside assistance. As a general rule, assistance comes from two sources: the school administration (e.g., the vice principal or principal) and parents. When a student is sent to the principal's office, you should phone or send a message to the office informing them that a student is being sent and exactly why he or she is being sent to the office. A call to parents about a behavior problem usually has positive results. Most parents are concerned about the behavior and progress of their children and will be willing to work cooperatively in correcting any misbehavior. There are exceptions; some parents feel that taking care of school misbehavior is your job.

In-school suspension currently is becoming very common. This technique involves removing misbehaving students from a class and placing them in a special area where they do their school work. They generally are placed in a bare room, furnished only with a table and chair. They report to this room at the beginning of the school day and remain until the end of the day. Meals are sent in, and teachers send in the class work for the day. If the in-school suspension does not correct the misbehavior, out-of-school suspension usually follows. But out-of-school suspension should only be used with extreme cases and as a last resort.

Assigning extra work or deducting from academic grades for misbehavior should be avoided. Associating grades and subject work with punishment only creates a disliking for the subject. However, it is often good policy to request that students redo sloppy or incorrect work. Indeed, accepting sloppy work or incorrect work only encourages more of the same.

Punishment of the whole class for the misbehavior of one or two students sometimes will create negative effects. Indeed, such an approach may curb the inappropriate behavior, but other students often feel the teacher is unfair and, as a result, will develop a negative attitude toward that teacher. On the other hand, if the teacher is well respected and viewed as fair, the use of peer pressure can be an effective approach to discipline.

To this point, we have not mentioned the use of corporal punishment as an option. First of all, it is illegal in most states for teachers to administer corporal punishment. Second, secondary school students are too old for corporal punishment. Moreover, corporal punishment often fails to address the long-term problem. In short, corporal punishment has proven to be ineffective, and other techniques usually are more effective with older students. And if practiced, corporal punishment can lay you open to accusations of brutality and legal difficulties.

When used, punishment should be administered immediately after the misbehavior, and it should be fair—that is, the punishment should fit the crime. Certainly, the same punishment should not be administered for constant talking as for constant harm to other students. Of course, all misbehavior must be dealt with in some way. Therefore, keep your emotions under control, and deal with problems consistently, fairly, and professionally. In other words, when you do use punishment, make it swift, sure, and impressive.

When administered appropriately, punishment can be an effective deterrent to misbehavior. Punishment should only be used, however, when no other alternatives are available. If the misbehavior is not severe, a warning should first be issued. If a warning does not work, you should consider punishment.

This completes our study of classroom management. Table 15.2 summarizes the control aspect of classroom management, and the Control Techniques Application Guidelines give some teacher-tested suggestions. Review the summary and guidelines, and complete exercise 15.2.

TABLE 15.2	Control Techniques
Element	**Description**
Routines	Classroom activities that are repetitive and follow a common procedure
Limits	The accepted and nonaccepted actions in the classroom
Monitoring	Awareness of all that is happening throughout the classroom
Punishment	The application of a negative stimulus or removal of a positive stimulus for inappropriate behavior

Application Guidelines ▼

Control Techniques

Understand Reasons for Misbehavior

Examples:
1. Ask students to provide information on their background.
2. Try to determine the cause of student's behavior, and whether it's from internal or external sources.
3. Keep folders with notes and work samples of disruptive students. Such files are useful at parent conferences.

Plan for Prevention

Examples:
1. Determine how papers will be collected and returned.
2. Plan each class carefully, and have all materials ready before class begins.
3. Plan rules and consequences carefully. Involve students as much as possible in the establishment of rules and consequences.
4. Arrange your room to avoid problems; watch classroom traffic patterns.
5. Plan the use of audiovisual aids for stimulating interest in the lesson.

Keep the Class Moving Smoothly

Examples:
1. Start classes on time. Require that students be in their seats when the bell rings.
2. Set up a class routine or activity for the first 4 or 5 minutes of class. Students should begin the activity when the bell rings.
3. Establish a procedure for dismissing class. Require that students be in their seats and quiet before they are dismissed.
4. Stop misbehavior immediately, before it can escalate.

(*continued*)

Application Guidelines ▼

Control Techniques—*continued*

5. Make transitions between activities in a quick and orderly manner. Give all directions before activity begins or before materials are passed out.
6. Talk to the class, not the chalkboard; make eye contact with students.
7. Be firm, polite, and consistent with students. If a rule is broken, warn students only once, then follow through with consequences.
8. Do not take a position or make a threat you cannot carry out.
9. Be "withit." Move around the room, and know what is going on in all areas of the room.
10. Corporal punishment does not work well; its use is not advised.
11. Use reprimands with care, and try not to nag. Avoid public sarcasm, ridicule, and reprimands.

Application of Knowledge

Exercise 15.2   Control Techniques

Test yourself on the following control concepts. Appropriate responses can be found in appendix A.

1. Most causes of misbehavior are quite obvious. (True/False)

2. Teachers who have well-established routines usually will have fewer behavior problems. (True/False)

3. In responding to discipline problems, it is important for the teacher to respect the dignity of students. (True/False)

4. Which of the following will help to minimize management problems?
   a. Well-planned, well-implemented lessons.
   b. Getting a good start by establishing credibility as an effective manager.
   c. Calling roll to get students' attention.
   d. Administering harsh punishment for all misbehavior.
   e. Knowing your students.

5. It is usually poor policy to start the year off by acting too firm and strict. (True/False)

6. Avoid giving students rewards for desirable behavior, because it amounts to bribery. (True/False)

7. The ripple effect can be used effectively for preventing misbehavior. (True/False)

8. Nonverbal teacher behavior can be an important component of classroom management. (True/False)

CHAPTER SUMMARY

A classroom must be organized, orderly, and run smoothly for learning to take place. Handling management problems is an integral part of teaching. Positive management strategies are therefore essential to effective teaching and learning.

There are many schools of thought on effective classroom management. Three common schools are the self-discipline approach, the instructional approach, and the desist approach. Principles of the self-discipline approach are supported by Glasser's Reality Therapy model and Gordon's Teacher Effectiveness Training (TET) model. Principles of the instructional approach are emphasized by the Kounin Model and the Jones Model. Finally, principles of the desist approach commonly are applied through assertive discipline and behavioral modification.

Misbehavior has many causes. Misbehavior sometimes can be attributed to influences outside the classroom, such as home environment or the community. On the other hand, misbehavior can stem from characteristics associated with the teacher or with students themselves. Whatever the cause, an effective manager is one who understands the causes of misbehavior.

Effective classroom management requires organization as well as the ability to deal with an ongoing learning environment. You must plan well, establish routines, arrange your room to avoid problems, and formulate limits. Above all, you must try to foresee classroom problems and try to prevent their occurrence.

A class must be kept on task. This requires that you establish your credibility at the beginning of the year—and then keep it. In short, be fair, firm, and consistent with students. Monitor your classroom, and apply the necessary consequences to misbehavior. When severe misbehavior takes place, administer the appropriate punishment. However, use punishment only as a last resort. As a final thought, be strict in the beginning; you can always lighten up. Finally, establish a positive classroom atmosphere, where students have an opportunity for working on and developing a sense of self-discipline.

Discussion Questions and Activities

1. **Discipline approaches.** Analyze the three approaches to classroom management. Which approach, if any, do you prefer? Can you put together parts of the different approaches and come up with an eclectic approach that you think would work for you? Can you identify some basic concepts that appear to be true of all three approaches?

2. **Causes of misbehavior.** Think back over the classes you have attended in which there have been disciplinary incidents. List the possible causes for any misbehaviors. How might knowledge of the causes of these misbehaviors influence a teacher's action? Some behavior problems are teacher-created, and some are student-centered. Can you think of examples?

3. **Planning.** Plan a first day for a class you may teach. What activities would you try on the first day? The first few weeks? What rules and consequences would you plan to implement and discuss?

4. **Rules and consequences.** Prepare a list of rules for a secondary school classroom. After you have established a set of rules, prepare a list of consequences for breaking the rules.

5. **Behavior observation.** Complete several observations in various classrooms at different levels. How do the observed teachers control behavior? Observe the students as well as you consider these questions:

   a. Do the students seat themselves when the bell rings? Is there a warm-up activity?

   b. Do the students raise their hand before speaking?

   c. Do the students refrain from speaking during class?

   d. Do the students hand in papers in an orderly manner?

6. **Maintaining control.** What types of procedures would you use to maintain control throughout the year? What measures would you take for severe misbehavior problems?

PART 4 ▼ ▼ ▼ ▼

The Profession

H istorically, education has undergone constant change. Changes in society are often reflected in more demands being placed on our educational system. The final chapter in this textbook will address recent trends in education. The accountability movement, assistance to beginning teachers, the professional growth of practicing teachers, and recent reforms in education will be the main focus of the chapter.

Finally, chapter 16 will address the concerns, criticisms, and expectations being voiced regarding the role and performance of modern schools. Several national reports, the reforms being proposed for schools, and the preparation of teachers will be examined.

16

Recent Directions in Secondary Education

✎ **We are bombarded by criticism of the schools, and advice about how to make schools better abounds. Toward what end are we striving, and which direction should we take? And will we know when we have arrived?**

Overview

This chapter will explore some of the recent trends and reforms in secondary education. Among the trends we will consider are accountability and reflective teaching and how they contribute to the attainment of more effective teaching. Also, although the idea of either being mentored or providing mentoring is certainly not new, the many ways that states and local school districts are addressing the issue of mentoring for beginning teachers is discussed.

We will also focus on how beginning teachers become involved in the profession and the importance of graduate school. Which organizations are geared to the total process of teaching, and which are geared to special interests within the field of teaching? How important is it to become involved in professional organizations? What is the value of seeking a graduate degree? These questions will be explored in this chapter.

Finally, this chapter will focus on recent reforms in education. A wealth of reform reports since 1983 have described in detail the condition of schools and have put forth recommendations for the improvement of schools. Faced with such a large and diverse amount of reform-minded thinking, school people have found themselves juggling competing expectations about what schools should do and deliberating how they can *show* that students have mastered the curriculum and that teachers are teaching well. Compounding these pressures is the rapid advancement in the development of new technologies that have the potential for changing the organization of schools and of learning itself.

Objectives

After completing your study of chapter 16, you should be able to do the following:

1. Describe the characteristics of reflective teaching.

2. Describe the role of a mentor teacher, and give examples of how this concept is translated into specific programs across the country.

3. Identify two or three professional organizations that serve your needs as a professional educator.

4. Develop a strategy for continuing professional growth.

5. Enumerate the competing demands placed on schools.

6. Explain the rationale for increased standards for student performance and teacher performance.

7. Describe the impact of new technologies on education.

Chapter Terms and Key Concepts

Accountability

Alternative Certification

Core Curriculum

Mentoring

Minimum Competency Testing

National Teacher Exam

Reflective Teaching

School Choice

Staff Development

Teacher Testing

Vouchers

One of the primary purposes of American education is to respond to the needs of society. But what will school be like in the twenty-first century? Of course, no one can predict the future with certainty. But you can prepare for the future to some extent by keeping abreast of recommended reforms in education and by improving your teaching.

The teachers of today and tomorrow are and will be working with students who are dramatically different from the students of a generation ago. You must learn to cope with these changing students effectively. Also, if you make a point to be well informed on the new technologies and teaching techniques, as well as on the breakthroughs from research on teaching and learning, you will stay "on top" of the profession.

Recent Trends

This first section will focus on some of the recent trends that have impacted the secondary classroom. These trends fall into four categories (Green, 1987): those resulting from social influences, political influences, and educational influences, and those resulting from improvements in technology.

Social Influences

People expect teachers of today and those of the future to be prepared for meeting the challenges of society. They hold teachers responsible for preparing our youth for what will exist. In effect, people feel teachers are the key to effecting needed changes in our society.

Accountability

The public wants to hold teachers accountable for preparing the youth of today for the world of tomorrow. To date, the public appears to feel that teachers are failing in this capacity.

Public dissatisfaction with schools centers around low achievement scores, lax standards, and doubt as to whether schools are preparing students to meet the challenges of a changing society. The basic premise of the **accountability** movement is that professional educators should be held responsible for how well students learn. Thus, teachers should be held responsible for the learning outcomes of students in their classroom. However, the accountability movement is also extended to students: Students too are responsible for their own learning.

An outgrowth of the teacher accountability movement has been **teacher testing.** Most state legislatures have passed laws requiring that teachers pass a test before becoming certified. These tests come in two forms, national and local. The **National Teacher Exam** (NTE), a nationally standardized test designed by Educational Testing Service, currently is used by most states requiring testing. Other states have elected to develop their own tests. Those administered in Oklahoma and Texas are typical of these state-specific tests. Some of these states developed a single test, while others created a separate test for each certification area. The impact of these tests on teacher preparation is obvious: better-prepared teachers.

Another outgrowth of the accountability movement has been **minimum competency testing** for students. Many states have mandated or are mandating minimum competency testing. In many states, those students who fail the graduation competency test receive a certificate of attendance rather than a high school diploma.

Advocates of competency testing claim these tests will send a clear message to students about what they should learn before they will be granted a diploma. Implications for classroom teachers and test constructors is clear: They must coordinate and ensure a match between the content of the competency tests and the content of the high school curriculum.

Public pressure for improvement in education has also resulted in a movement for **school choice.** Parental choice of schools in its broadest interpretation implies parents may choose any school, public or private, either within or outside the school district. Parents have begun seeking alternative education programs within the public schools. This pressure along with pressure from influential educators has prompted the establishment of alternative programs within some schools, and has even opened doors for students to attend other schools within some school districts. In some school districts, there has been a movement for increasing the use of *magnet schools*—schools, usually junior high schools, that frequently focus on a specific content area, such as science and mathematics, the humanities, and fine arts.

Educational **vouchers** are another form of choice being urged by some parents. Under a voucher system, parents of all school-age children in a district would be given credit for funds (vouchers) that roughly represent their children's share of the educational budget. Students then use the vouchers to attend any school they choose, public or private, secular or parochial. However, voucher proposals that limit the use of the vouchers to public schools within a single school district have aroused less criticism. To date, because of the controversy over the appropriate use of public funds, proposals for the educational use of vouchers have met limited success.

Political Influences

Education is strongly influenced by political forces at the local, state, and federal levels. For example, during the Bush administration, a new education agenda for the United States was implemented. The agenda was spelled out in the six National Goals for Education (National Governors' Association, 1990) to be achieved by the year 2000.

1. All children in America will start school ready to learn.

2. The high school graduation rate will increase to at least 90 percent.

3. American students will leave grades 4, 8, and 12 having demonstrated competency in challenging subject matter, including English, mathematics, science, history, and geography; and every school in America will ensure that all students learn to use their minds well, so that they may be prepared for responsible citizenship, further learning, and productive employment in our modern economy.

4. U.S. students will be first in the world in mathematics and science achievement.

5. Every adult American will be literate and will possess the skills necessary to compete in a global economy and to exercise the rights and responsibilities of citizenship.

6. Every school in America will be free of drugs and violence and will offer a disciplined environment conducive to learning.

The Bush influence on education was extended in April of 1991 with *America 2000: An Education Strategy*. This plan included the following components:

1. Strategies for achieving the six 1990 national goals.

2. Establishment of funding to create a "New Generation of American Schools" (at least 535) around the country by 1996.

3. A 15-point accountability plan for parents, teachers, schools, and communities designed to measure and compare results among schools.

4. Creation of "New World Standards" in five core subjects for what students need to know and be able to do.

5. Creation of a voluntary system of national testing, the American Achievement Tests, based on the New World Standards.

6. Creation of incentives to states and local districts to adopt policies for school choice.

7. Governor's Academies for Teachers designed to assist teachers in helping students pass the American Achievement Tests.

8. The creation of a nonprofit organization called the New American Schools Development Corporation, which would oversee innovative school-reform efforts.

9. The creation of electronic networks to serve the New American Schools.

10. The creation of skill clinics to provide knowledge and skills needed for employment.

As a result of the federal influences on education, there has been renewed interest on the part of business and industry in upgrading education in the United States. Indeed, businesses and industries are making unprecedented grants to encourage reform and improvement in education.

Educational Influences

Educational influences on education come from three sources: higher education, school districts, and professional organizations. Significant changes on how to better prepare teachers, better assist them in making the transition from the university classroom to public school classrooms, and help them refine their skills after they begin teaching are being provided by all three of these sources (Galluzzo, 1988; Sears, 1988; Sikula, 1987; Stewart, 1987).

Reflective Teaching

The Reflective Teaching (RT) Model is being implemented in many institutions to better prepare teachers for the classroom. The Reflective Teaching Model of teacher preparation was developed at Ohio State University (Cruickshank, 1987) and is used in a good many schools of education to promote thinking about the nature of teaching and learning. **Reflective teaching** is the process of making informed, thoughtful judgments about the success or failure of our teaching efforts in real classrooms.

Constant reflection and assessment of what it is we do as teachers are imperative if we are to achieve the status of master teacher. The old cliché ''I pound my head on the wall because it feels so good when I stop'' fits the profile of the teacher who pulls out, dusts off, and uses the same old lessons over and over without giving any thought to whether or not teaching and learning have taken place. Round-robin reading of the chapter and answering the questions at the end of each section are not likely to produce lively inquiry into the material at hand. Yet we can witness this method of ''teaching'' in almost any school we choose to visit.

If you are to be a reflective teacher, you need to possess certain characteristics and certain kinds of knowledge. The reflective teacher is self-confident enough to embrace and value self-critique, colleague critique, and student critique. The reflective teacher seeks out information about personal teaching successes and failures, and he or she uses this information continually to improve the process and the product. The reflective teacher is innovative, tries new techniques, and takes risks, accepts successes and expects occasional failures. The reflective teacher takes responsibility for student learning. The reflective teacher is well prepared in his or her subject area, as well as in pedagogy. The reflective teacher remains a learner. The reflective teacher values diversity in the classroom and successfully conveys this value to students.

When you become a reflective teacher, you will have become a master teacher. Your teacher-preparation program will provide the best it can offer in the way of knowledge about the nature of teaching and learning. You will have opportunities for practicing what you have learned. You will have opportunities for observing veteran teachers at work. If you are to become a reflective teacher, you will have to synthesize and refine your practice in the classroom.

Research within the last two decades has strongly influenced education. Research into multiple intelligences and multicultural learning styles has broadened our understanding of learning and teaching. Also, research in the fields of neurophysiology, neuropsychology, and cognitive science has opened more doors by explaining further how people think and learn. Those persons who desire additional information on these research breakthroughs should seek material on such topics as brain research, cognitive science, and information processing, which is available in most current educational psychology textbooks.

Mentoring

Beginning teachers need help in their initial year of teaching. In other words, every beginning teacher needs a mentor, who can offer clues about how to get things accomplished in a particular school. Many states have implemented **mentoring,** teacher-induction programs that pair a beginning teacher with a veteran mentor or with a team of mentors. In Oklahoma, the Entry Year Assistance Program requires that each beginning teacher be assigned a committee, comprised of a consulting teacher (a veteran teacher in the school, preferably from the same grade level or content area), a school administrator, and an education instructor from a college or university. At the end of the first supervised year, the committee recommends whether or not the licensed teacher becomes certified.

The first year of teaching historically has been one of pure survival. Teacher-induction programs have grown out of the recognition that this trying situation could impede or even waste budding talent. But what if your first teaching job is in a state without an induction program? Seek a mentor on your own! Your preparation in the content area and your education courses have provided you with the foundations for becoming an effective teacher, but your practice (other than student teaching) has involved hypothetical situations and short teaching sessions. A veteran teacher can provide you with valuable advice and knowledge about the students, the school, and the community. A mentor can guide you when you need to know how to arrange a field trip, or raise funds for a special project, or get material for your classroom. Having a mentor during that first year of teaching can make the initial year more like a pleasant stroll through a meadow than a careful trip through a mine field.

Professional Organizations

There are a number of professional organizations geared for enhancing the professional life of teachers. Teaching is a somewhat isolated endeavor. You will discover that it is important to have opportunities for engaging in dialogue with colleagues about classroom issues, personal issues, and professional issues. Involvement with professional organizations provides such an opportunity and promotes professional growth.

Organizations for teachers basically are of three types: fraternal, political, and professional. *Fraternal* organizations typically identify themselves with Greek letters, and their missions encompass everything from research of teaching and learning to dissemination of information through publications and conferences. These organizations usually provide scholarship opportunities to those seeking to teach or to teachers interested in pursuing additional training. Delta Kappa Gamma and Phi Delta Kappa, for example, have numerous local chapters that contribute to the national organization's mission and pursue a local agenda. Both groups produce a variety of publications that address issues of interest to teachers and administrators. Organizations with a *political* mission are also involved in research and dissemination of information, but these groups typically engage in efforts at improving the standing of the profession through legislation, negotiation, and influencing public opinion. Teacher's unions, like the American Federation of Teachers and the National Education Association provide many services for their members. Both of these organizations have been influential in improving the professional lives of teachers. *Professional* organizations either are geared to the profession as a whole or are specific to a particular discipline. National Council of the Social Studies, National Council of Teachers of English, National Science Teachers Association, and the International Reading Association are representative of the group of organizations geared to a particular discipline. The Association for Supervision and Curriculum Development and the Association of Teacher Educators are examples of professional organizations concerned with the overall health of the profession. Regardless of their particular focus, all organizations seek, at some level, to improve teaching practice and enhance the professional life of teachers.

Growth as a Professional

With teaching certificate in hand, you are ready to go out and make a mark. You have spent a great deal of time and money preparing yourself for teaching. You have finished your education. Or have you? As you teach, you will discover that there are many things you still need to know. You must constantly revitalize your commitment to teaching. This is best accomplished if you have a plan. You will want to join and participate in some of the professional organizations mentioned earlier. You might find it difficult to suppress your enthusiasm after attending a stimulating conference where the latest innovations in teaching and the results of research have been reported. But your continuing education must not stop at group membership. You need to seek out opportunities for staff development and continuing education if you wish to remain current.

Staff Development

For our purposes, **staff development** is defined as any endeavor that increases professional knowledge and improves practice. It is critical that your learning continue. You may decide that for your own professional growth you will read every issue of a particular journal, or read a set number of books in your field in a given time frame. These certainly are staff-development efforts. You also may decide to engage in conversation with a group of colleagues about educational issues on a regular basis. You may choose to attend workshops or presentations sponsored by your school district or a professional organization to which you belong. These too are valid staff-development endeavors. But whatever form your efforts take, your continual involvement in self-improvement and school improvement efforts is critical.

A majority of teachers
return to school in the
summer to update their
knowledge and skills.

There is an ongoing trend for school districts or states to require certain staff-development efforts on the part of teachers. Many school districts require completion of prescribed staff-development components as a condition for promotion within the district. These endeavors often augment requirements that students complete college courses in the specialty area. Intern experiences for the aspiring administrator, counselor, curriculum specialist, or department chair are becoming commonplace. But even if your school district does not require staff development, you will need to plan for continued professional growth.

Graduate education also provides the opportunity for professional growth. Indeed, graduate education can enhance your knowledge of content or your knowledge of the educational process, or both. Graduate education can prepare you for assuming a new role within the school district. Administrators, counselors, reading specialists, curriculum supervisors and mentors, and master teachers are all required (in most states) to have a master's degree. Some districts also provide additional pay on the salary schedule or through a merit system for those teachers who pursue graduate coursework.

Technological Influences

One of the greatest influences on education has been the revolution in microelectronics. Computers, video equipment, and communication devices (satellite transmission) are having a profound effect on the classroom (see chapter 6). The impact of new technologies on the methodology of teaching is just beginning to be felt. Schools have expanded staffing choices because of

the availability of satellite transmission of courses from some central location. The possibilities for providing courses are only limited by the availability of equipment, space, and money. This technology could herald the end to the critical teacher shortages being experienced in some fields.

As noted in chapter 6, probably the greatest technological impact on the classroom in recent years has been the microcomputer. Most of the microcomputers are concentrated at the secondary level, with an emphasis placed on computer-literacy training. To this end, teachers must develop the skills needed for developing students' understanding of microcomputers and their use in both the classroom and society. Specifically, the computer competencies deemed necessary for teachers include the following:

1. The ability to read and write simple computer programs in some type of computer language, such as BASIC or Logo.

2. The ability to use educational computer programs and documentation.

3. A basic understanding of computer terminology, particularly as it relates to hardware.

4. The ability to locate information on computing as it relates to education.

5. The ability to manage instruction with computers and maintain sophisticated records about students.

6. Skill in software evaluation.

More than ever, teachers need to be computer-literate. It has been estimated that by the year 2000, 98 percent of all households in the United States will have computers. Computers are no longer just an instructional tool for teachers; they have become a part of everyday life.

TABLE *16.1* Educational Trends

Concept	Description
Accountability	Holding schools responsible for what teachers teach and students learn
Minimum Competency Testing	Exit tests designed for ascertaining whether or not students have achieved basic levels of performance in such areas as reading, writing, and computation
Teacher Testing	The requirement, usually legislatively mandated, that teachers pass a test prior to certification
School Choice	Policies in some districts that permit parents to choose the school that meets their individual needs
Vouchers	Credit system of funds allocated to students' parents, who then purchase education for their children in any public or private school
Reflective Teaching	Teaching style wherein a teacher critically reflects on the outcomes of his or her teaching efforts
Mentoring	The assignment of consultant teachers to assist beginning teachers during their initial year of teaching
Professional Organizations	Organizations geared for enhancing the professional life of teachers
Staff Development	Activities designed for increasing the professional knowledge and practices of teachers
Computer Literacy	A basic understanding of the general principles that underlie computer hardware, software, and the application of computer technology

In addition to satellite transmissions, integrated videodiscs hold promise for instructional use. Computers coupled with video displays potentially could infuse the latest advances in the sciences into the classroom, without the lag time associated with producing a new textbook.

Computer systems coupled with electronic mailing could provide needed services for homebound students. These students could "hook up" to their classrooms and continue to learn within the social environment of their peer group.

Many of the newer technological breakthroughs have been slow in gaining regular implementation in the classroom. This slowness has been mainly attributable to cost, lack of training on the part of teachers, and the dearth of educational materials available for use with the technology.

As you reflect on your role as a teacher, consider the challenges that technology has created for you and students. Are you prepared for the twenty-first century? Are you ready to turn some of the teaching over to technology?

Continuing to develop your skills as a teacher is an important step toward becoming a master teacher. Table 16.1 gives an overview of the major trends that you should be aware of that relate to education. Review table 16.1 and the Educational Trends Application Guidelines, and complete exercise 16.1.

Application Guidelines ▼

Application of Knowledge

Exercise 16.1   Educational Trends

Test yourself on the following educational trends. Appropriate responses can be found in appendix A.

1. The four sources of influence that have greatly impacted secondary education are _____ , _____ , _____ , and _____ .

2. There has been general public dissatisfaction with schools. (True/False)

3. Two outgrowths of the accountability movement have been _____ testing and _____ minimum competency testing.

4. As a result of the political influences on education, there has been renewed interest by business and industry in education. (True/False)

5. The Reflective Teaching Model (RT) is which one of the following?
   a. A mentoring program for beginning teachers.
   b. The process used in making judgments about classroom successes and failures.

6. Professional organizations and staff development are important only to high school teachers. (True/False)

7. It is becoming important that all teachers be computer-literate. (True/False)

No overview of recent directions in secondary education would be complete without a peek at the reform movement. During the last decade, there have been widespread efforts aimed at ensuring that all teachers and students are successful.

Reform and the Future

Schools and teachers are faced with competing demands for curricular emphasis, with one group lined up on the side of a core curriculum, and the other group calling for an increased emphasis on the liberal arts and critical thinking. Matters are complicated further by growing support for a national curriculum for students and national certification for teachers. Global issues as well as multicultural considerations place additional demands on the schools. Accountability is demanded of students and teachers alike, and, consequently, the schooling of youth and the preparation of teachers are often viewed in terms of a *product* that can be easily quantified. In other words, some believe that accountability prompts some educators to focus on the teaching of basic knowledge, with less emphasis on the teaching of inquiry and thinking skills. The demand for reform abounds, with various groups claiming they have the answers that will bring excellence back to education.

Since 1983, a number of reform reports have documented the condition of schools and have proposed measures to improve them. *A Nation At Risk: The Imperative for Educational Reform,* the initial report issued by the National Commission on Excellence in Education (1983), received the most press—partly as a result of its dramatic and highly quotable introduction that declared that our nation was at risk as a result of the poor performance of our schools. If a foreign power were to pose against our nation a threat of similar gravity, the report reasoned, it would be considered an act of war. The reports that followed *Nation At Risk* were equally critical of the job schools are doing. All of the reports issued made suggestions for improving the performance of schools. With such diversity in reform-minded thinking, it is not surprising that school people are faced with the difficult task of juggling competing expectations about what schools "should be doing." The competing expectations that schools must deal with have been manifested in an ever-changing view of the elements that constitute *evidence* that students have mastered the curriculum and that teachers are teaching well.

Competing Expectations

One area that has received considerable attention centers around the expectations of what ought to be taught in schools. *A Nation At Risk* called for a thorough grounding in the "five new basics"—English, mathematics, science, social studies, and computer science. With the exception of computer science, there is nothing new here. The same report called for increased standards for admission to college, better-prepared and better-paid teachers, more rigorous academic standards, and more standardized testing of students.

A Nation At Risk has gained widespread support from the public. The deterioration of the traditional family unit, concern about drug abuse, increased juvenile crime, and the belief that schools themselves have become chaotic have contributed to public acceptance of a more traditional view of schooling. Coupled with reports that American youth fare poorly when compared academically with Asian and European youth, these reports have sparked heated debate about what should be taught in schools, who should teach it, and what evidence is required to assure the public it has been taught.

Against the backdrop of a call by some for a **core curriculum** (Adler, 1982) that would require all students to complete the same program of studies, with electives eliminated and rigid tracking systems put in place, is the call by others to integrate the curricular offerings around a solid liberal arts model that produces youth educated in the common American heritage (Hirsch, 1987). While Mortimer Adler argues that a common set of requirements reduces the possibility of inequality, many believe such a system would herald a new wave of dropouts from the groups least likely to be successful in such a program. Still other educators express concern that the return to ''basics'' or a core curriculum could have a chilling effect on teaching students to think critically.

Most people are likely to report that they value the teaching of critical thinking in the schools. Critical thinking skills, however, are not easily tested through standardized achievement tests. But because student testing is relied on for determining progress, making decisions about promotion, and awarding diplomas, test results often are used like report cards of school effectiveness. Moreover, the widespread practice of reporting aggregate test results in the local newspaper has led to calls for a national set of standards for schools.

The call for national standards encompasses the curriculum and performance of public schools and the preparation of teachers. Reacting to public criticism of teacher-preparation programs, the Holmes Group (1986) and others have recommended that teachers receive a liberal arts degree and complete certification requirements in a fifth-year program, often in conjunction with a master's degree. The idea behind these proposals is to better prepare teachers for the challenges of the classroom. However, calls for alternative routes to teacher certification are competing with the call for increased standards, with many states implementing **alternative certification** plans. The details vary by state, but the pattern is similar in that anyone qualified in a specialized field with a college degree, usually in areas of critical shortage, can get a teaching certificate and receive on-the-job training. Teacher educators generally oppose these plans. These approaches are defective, they say, because they are market-driven, simplistic solutions to a long-term problem of underfunding schools, which makes it difficult to attract fully qualified people in fields that can demand more money in the business arena. The National Board for Professional Teaching Standards, while it holds promise for enhancing the status of teachers, is one more attempt to grant certification to qualified degree holders who may or may not have completed a teacher-preparation program. The rationale for the development of a national teaching certificate is the belief that national standards can be established in this way.

In finishing off this potpourri of competing expectations and demands, we must cite the growing concern for emphasis on the impact of a global economy and the need for multicultural education in light of the changing student population of the schools. Many American people still tend to view the United States as the central player in the global marketplace. Evidence suggests, however, that companies in Pacific Rim countries are competing more successfully than are U.S. companies (Naisbitt & Aburdene, 1990; The Race Is on to Ready Students for Globalization, 1990). Feeling the need to remedy this situation, our society has begun to examine the effectiveness of American schooling and to define it according to measurable results produced. A product, rather than a process, dictates the success of schools. The argument for increased multicultural education is predicated on two beliefs. First, there is a need within this country to draw the diverse population of young people into the mainstream of American life. This is particularly true when viewed against a backdrop of low birth rates among whites and high birth rates among minority groups. The second consideration revolves around the issue of a global economy. If Americans and American companies intend to compete in a global marketplace, then an understanding of culturally diverse groups is essential.

Changing Standards

In many ways, there has been a return to the reform efforts that followed the launch of Sputnik in 1957. It is becoming increasingly apparent that the call for higher standards is yet another attempt to produce a "teacher-proof" curriculum. The public demands accountability for what is done in schools, with accountability taking the form of acceptable scores on standardized tests. If the scores meet expectations, then it follows, in the public view, that students are learning and teachers are teaching. The potential exists for creating a fact-based, lockstep curriculum that assures "success" on achievement tests.

Teacher Preparation and Performance

As noted earlier, the majority of states now require some kind of minimum competency test for beginning teachers. The focus of these tests varies from state to state, with many states requiring the National Teacher Exam (NTE). Still other states now require that prospective teachers pass specialty-area (content) tests. Some states have developed their own tests for measuring general, professional, and specialty knowledge; in others, only subject-area knowledge is tested. The major criticism of this philosophy of testing teacher performance is that there is no evidence that an ability to pass the tests will ensure success in the classroom.

Beginning teachers need to be aware of the potential impact of competency testing on their professional lives. Prior to the advent of these tests, many states had reciprocal certification agreements, which meant that if you met the requirements for certification in state A, and state A had a reciprocal agreement with state B, you could get a certificate in state B. That is no longer the case. While reciprocal arrangements certainly still exist between states, the process is no longer a simple one. If you anticipate moving from one state to another, you need to contact the state's department of education to find out the requirements for certification. This situation helped spark the push for national certification.

Pursuing Reform

Teaching in the 1990s and the early twenty-first century will be influenced strongly by the reform movement. Indeed, these future teachers will be charged with implementation of the reform agendas. The following are possible agendas (Finn, 1987; Pipho, 1986) that could be the focus of future education:

1. Back-to-basics instruction with accompanying accountability.

2. Teacher empowerment, with greater professionalization of teaching.

3. More effective schools and teaching with the goal of attaining higher levels of student achievement.

4. A change in the content or subject matter taught.

Responsibility for reform now moves from legislatures and policymakers to school administrators and teachers. Schools will now decide what students need to learn and how best to teach that curriculum.

Schools also must change to address the reform agendas. Change will take place not just with respect to the teaching and learning sought within the schools, but in school governance and organization as well. In short, as the Carnegie Task Force (1986) suggested, schools must become places where highly skilled teachers decide and do what is called for to achieve appropriate student learning, rather than places where they follow a rigid, established curriculum.

The future depends directly on the abilities of the teachers available to teach students. These teachers must be not only knowledgeable in their content areas, but they also must be reflective thinkers and able organizers. They need to be informed on the latest technologies. And they must be able to handle complexity. Of course, none of these skill areas are new. Teachers have always needed these competencies to be effective. But now the need for teachers to be skilled in these areas is more pressing, and because of the new and higher levels of specification needed, the level of competence required seems to be more difficult to achieve.

This completes our brief discussion of reform in education. Table 16.2 offers a review of the major reform recommendations. Before continuing, review table 16.2 and the Education Reform Application Guidelines, and check your understanding of the ideas presented in this section by completing exercise 16.2.

TABLE *16.2*   Education Reform

Reform Recommendation	Description
A Nation At Risk	The major 1983 national report calling for educational reform in the school curriculum, expectations, time, and teaching
Five New Basics	The five areas of English, mathematics, science, social studies, and computer science recommended in *A Nation At Risk* for emphasis in the schools
Core Curriculum	The common set of requirements completed by all students
National Standards	Common national requirements relative to curriculum, student performance, and teacher preparation
National Teacher Exam (NTE)	An examination that covers communication skills, general knowledge, and professional knowledge, which is currently required for teacher certification in many states

Application Guidelines   ▼

Education Reform

Become Involved in the Reform Movement

Examples:
1. Keep up-to-date on various teaching and learning reform suggestions. Try those that show promise in your own classroom.
2. Keep up-to-date on curricular issues. Your teaching may have to be revised to meet the changing expectations of society or the profession.
3. Become involved in the establishment of new graduation requirements, new programs, and revisions in school-district policies.

Application of Knowledge

Exercise 16.2   Education Reform

Test yourself on the following education reform concepts. Appropriate responses can be found in appendix A.

1. The initial report that signaled the start of the reform movement was _____ .

2. Which of the following statements represent expectations from groups calling for reform in education?
    a. Children should be taught by parents in the home.
    b. Students should have a thorough grounding in "five new basics."
    c. There should be more standardized testing of students.
    d. There should be less emphasis on global and multicultural education.
    e. Alternative routes to teacher certification should be provided.
    f. National certification of teachers should be required.
    g. A lowering of standards for teacher preparation is needed.

3. The test most states require that teachers pass for certification is the _____ .

4. Because of the reform movement, there now exists no reciprocal agreement among states. (True/False)

CHAPTER SUMMARY

Schools and teachers are faced with competing demands for excellence. Accountability, demanded at every level, has prompted some to regard the schooling of youth and of teachers as a product that can be easily quantified. As a result of the accountability movement, there has been a call for teacher testing and minimum competency testing. Along with the accountability movement has come pressure for school choice and the issuance of school vouchers.

Local, state, and federal political groups have strongly influenced educational goals in recent years. The result has been the establishment of six national goals for American education to be achieved by the year 2000. The goals were later extended with *America 2000: An Education Strategy.* The political impact on education has resulted in renewed interest on the part of business and industry.

Reflective teaching represents a promising technique for bringing excellence to teaching. It calls for teachers to make reflective judgments about the successes and failures in the classroom. This information is then used for improving the process and product of teaching.

Teachers need assistance during the critical initial year of teaching. Many states are providing this assistance through induction programs that pair the beginning teacher with a mentor or a team of mentors.

Professional organizations often offer teachers the opportunities for working with colleagues and for upgrading their skills. Membership and participation in professional organizations can provide some of the stimulation teachers need for growth. Some professional organizations are geared to the profession as a whole, while others are geared to specific disciplines. Staff development and graduate courses are also important sources of professional development.

New breakthroughs in technology have brought a revolution to education. For example, microcomputers are now common in most schools. Indeed, microcomputers have become an important part of everyday life.

Educational change is inevitable. Within the last decade, change and reform have been the scenario. The first of a number of reform reports, *A Nation At Risk* (1983), decried the failure of American schools to effectively educate future generations. The wave of reform reports has called for higher standards, more rigorous curriculum, and more testing to prepare for worldwide economic and technological competition.

The call for excellence in teaching has impacted teacher preparation. It has been recommended that all teachers receive liberal arts degrees and complete the requirements for certification in a fifth year. At the same time, there has been a call for alternative routes to teacher certification. In effect, many organizations and states have urged that any person holding a college degree in a specialized field or area of content need be allowed to receive a teaching certificate.

Many states are now requiring some kind of minimum competency testing for initial teaching certification. Most states require a passing score on the National Teacher Exam (NTE). Still others have developed their own tests for measuring general, professional, and/or specialty knowledge.

As a future teacher, you will find it worthwhile to know about the reform movement. Education must continue to improve; continue to look to the future.

Discussion Questions and Activities

1. **Minimum competency testing.** Investigate the requirements for high school graduation in your state and two neighboring states. Are minimum competency tests required for graduation? How will you help students meet the standards?

2. **Reflective teaching.** Self-analyze the most recent lesson you have taught. What went particularly well? Why? What needs improvement? Why? What evidence do you have that demonstrates student learning and interest have been achieved?

3. **Teacher induction.** Investigate to see if your state has a teacher-induction model that provides a first-year mentor. If not, develop a strategy for seeking out a mentor.

4. **Professional organizations.** Choose a fraternal, a political and a professional organization in which you have an interest. Research these groups to discover if you would like to join.

5. **Professional development.** Make a list of professional areas about which you would like to know more. Develop a plan for improving your knowledge in these areas.

6. **Reform movement.** Research several reform reports. Note the similarities and the differences. Speculate on what effect these reports will have on your teaching life.

7. **Educational technology.** Visit the computer lab in a nearby school. List the ways the computers are being incorporated in the classroom. What percentage of students use the lab? Interview teachers about their use of the computers. Are teachers using the computers to reduce routine paperwork?

8. **Satellite courses.** Visit a nearby school that uses satellite transmission to offer one or more courses. Sit in on a session. Is the presentation interesting and understandable? Do the students like this method for taking a course?

Appendix A

Answer Keys

Chapter 1
Exercise 1.1 Purposes of Secondary Education
1. False. There is a variety of school organizational structures across the United States.
2. ministry, political leadership
3. True. Academies, junior high schools, and middle schools were first established in the United States.
4. *A Nation At Risk*
5. Progressive, Functionalist
6. maintain status quo, ensure economic prosperity, culturalize immigrants, teach basics

Exercise 1.2 Curricular Imperatives and Successful Teaching
1. True. This common learning is generally the development of basic skills.
2. *a.* 3 *b.* 1 *c.* 2
3. state, regional
4. False. American society is changing and, along with it, family structure.
5. diagnose the situation; evaluate and follow up.

Chapter 2
Exercise 2.1 Adolescence
1. The period beginning with the changes preceding the growth spurt and ending with achievement of adult status.
2. *a.* 3 *b.* 1 *c.* 2
3. True. Appearance is often of great concern to adolescents.
4. self or ego identity
5. concrete, formal
6. True. Many adolescents find school irrelevant and meaningless.
7. False. Sex education has made little impact on teenage pregnancy.
8. True. Teenagers often seek belonging and, to this end, become involved in undesirable behaviors.

Exercise 2.2 Teaching

1. The actions of someone who is trying to assist others in reaching their fullest potential in all aspects of development.
2. art
3. *a.* 4   *b.* 2   *c.* 1   *d.* 4
4. False. Plans should change when student feedback indicates a lesson is not going well.
5. True. Most teachers use seating charts to speed up the taking of class roll.

Exercise 2.3 Learning

1. A change in an individual's capacity for performance as a result of experience.
2. *a.* 2   *b.* 3   *c.* 1
3. True. An individual's teaching style will generally be consistent with the beliefs he or she holds about learning.
4. False. There is no one best learning style for secondary students.
5. True. The difference in observational patterns is a basic difference in cognitive styles of field-dependent and field-independent individuals.
6. False. There should be a balance between impulsivity and reflectivity.
7. *a.* Teach students to elaborate.
   b. Teach students to take notes related to main ideas.
   c. Teach students to write summary statements.
   d. Teach students to generate questions about what is read.

Chapter 3

Exercise 3.1 The Curriculum

1. *a.* 3   *b.* 1   *c.* 2
2. True. Teachers generally have little control over students' learning prior to their arrival in class.
3. True. Diagnosis should be a never-ending process.
4. False. Achievement tests are often used for making comparisons among groups of students.
5. *a.* What students know about the subject.
   b. Mastery of prerequisite skills.
   c. Students' reading level.

Exercise 3.2 Content Selection

1. *a.* 3   *b.* 2   *c.* 1
2. True. Most content selection is districtwide or schoolwide.
3. *a.* Major topics to be covered.
   b. Whether and how textbook should be supplemented.
   c. Grouping of topics to form units.
   d. Sequence of planned units.
   e. Emphasis for each unit.
4. True. A teacher cannot always predict the exact amount of time needed to complete a unit.
5. False. There is no rule that all chapters in a textbook must be covered.

Chapter 4

Exercise 4.1 Instructional Intent
1. True. Teachers must be able to verify that learning has taken place.
2. False. An objective represents a statement as to what students will be able to do after instruction.
3. *a, c, d*
4. educational goals, informational objectives, instructional objectives
5. performance, product, conditions, criteria
6. True. This element specifies what students are expected to do after they receive instruction.
7. False. There should be only one action or product specified in an informational objective.
8. performance, product

Exercise 4.2 Objective Domains
1. cognitive, affective, psychomotor
2. False. Because of the difficulty of writing affective domain objectives, most teachers avoid them.
3. True. The creation of a unique communication would represent a synthesis-level skill.
4. *a.* A   *b.* P   *c.* A   *d.* C   *e.* C
5. False. Most objectives will contain elements of all three domains.

Chapter 5

Exercise 5.1 Planning
1. *a.* Allows you to anticipate instructional needs in advance so materials can be gathered and organized.
   b. Provides a plan that directs classroom interactions.
2. *a.* 2   *b.* 4   *c.* 1   *d.* 3
3. *a.* Topic: The broad unifying theme to be studied.
   b. Goals and objectives: The broad and specific learning intent.
   c. Content outline: An outline of the content to be covered.
   d. Learning activities: The teacher and student activities that will lead to desired learning.
   e. Resources and materials: Materials to be selected or prepared for the unit.
   f. Evaluation: An outline of the unit's evaluation procedure.
4. False. A textbook is only one of many reliable sources available to assist in planning.
5. True. Daily plans should reflect the methods and procedures that will be used in bringing about the desired learning.

Exercise 5.2 Lesson Plan Structure
1. *a.* Set induction: What the teacher does at the beginning of a lesson to get students attention, arouse their interest, and establish a conceptual framework for the lesson content.
   b. Strategies: The methodology and procedure used in reaching the desired lesson outcomes. The methodology acts as a motivator and sets the tone for the lesson. The procedure is the sequence of steps designed to bring about the desired outcomes.

c. Closure: The lesson activity used for bringing the lesson to a logical conclusion. It should pull together and organize the lesson concepts.

2. False. Advance organizers are the introductory remarks that give students a "what to look for" frame of reference for a coming lesson.

3. *a.* S   *b.* T   *c.* T   *d.* S

4. *c*

5. Closure is needed to make sure students understand and integrate a lesson's main concepts into their existing cognitive structure.

6. Teacher as a reflective decision maker who analyzes past experiences in planning.

Chapter 6

Exercise 6.1 Classroom Printed Materials

1. abstract

2. True. The textbook is the only instructional aid used in many secondary classrooms.

3. True. The textbook can often dictate *all* that is taught in a classroom.

4. False. Textbooks can enhance independent study.

5. Material is presented in a series of carefully planned sequential steps.

Exercise 6.2 Nonprojection-Media Tools

1. True. Teachers and students alike can use the chalkboard to convey information.

2. False. Teachers should plan how they want to use the chalkboard before they begin to write.

3. motivate, inform, stimulate, decorate

4. True. Flat pictures have a multitude of uses in the classroom.

5. Pictures that have good composition, present clear messages, use color effectively, and offer good contrast and sharpness.

Exercise 6.3 Projection-Media Tools

1. False. With care, teachers can produce good transparencies.

2. True. Poor products and inappropriate use of equipment are the main problems associated with transparencies.

3. True. Filmstrip production requires special equipment.

4. True. Filmstrips can be employed successfully with any size group.

5. True. Because motion pictures are a multisensory media, they sometimes can make one feel like they are a part of the action.

6. False. Videodiscs can store vast amounts of information and material.

7. A video system linked to a computer system that empowers an individual to control images and sounds.

8. *a.* Drill and practice exercises, related to information, facts, and so forth.

   b. Tutorial programs, which present new information.

   c. Simulation programs, which present "real life" situations.

   d. Gaming programs, which are used to develop skills.

Chapter 7

Exercise 7.1 Exposition Teaching

1. False. Many secondary teachers use the lecture method incorrectly.
2. *c, d*
3. the lecture
4. *b, c, e, g*

Exercise 7.2 Exposition with Interaction Teaching

1. *a.* L *b.* L *c.* H *d.* H *e.* H *f.* L
2. *a.* 3 *b.* 1 *c.* 2
3. wait-time 1
4. False. Reinforcement can sometimes curtail student responses.
5. True. Students need to know the content before they can answer related questions.
6. False. You should designate who is to answer the question when a particular student is not paying attention or when you are directing the question to a slow or shy student.
7. *c*
8. True. The Socratic method is a technique that relies on a questioning sequence.

Exercise 7.3 The Demonstration

1. an inquiry demonstration
2. False. Most demonstrations are best done by students.
3. *a.* Dangerous for students to use equipment and materials.
   b. To save time.
   c. For showing how equipment is used.
   d. For outlining steps in a procedure.
   e. For getting a complex point across.
4. True. A follow-up should be used in checking for understanding.
5. True. Questions can direct attention, motivate, and check for understanding.
6. False. Student attention must be gained and directed for any type of demonstration.

Chapter 8

Exercise 8.1 Discussion Method

1. *d*
2. *a, b, c, d*
3. *a.* Goals and student preparation.
   b. Decision as to whether discussion should be large- or small-group discussion.
   c. Seating arrangement.
   d. Time allotment for discussion.
4. False. Student attention and interest must be gained and directed.
5. *c*
6. *b*
7. *d*

Exercise 8.2 Heuristic Methods

1. False. Discovery and inquiry are unique but related techniques.
2. Intentional elimination of uncertainty or doubt through direct experiences and under supervision.
3. *d*
4. False. Discovery and inquiry involves active student involvement, which generally results in intrinsic motivation.
5. *a.* Select problem. A problem is identified and stated in precise terms.
    b. Propose solutions. Hypotheses and solutions are generated based on data collected and analyzed.
    c. Collect data. Data is amassed to test hypotheses.
    d. Analyze and interpret data. Validity of hypotheses is tested through data interpretation.
    e. Test conclusions. Support for conclusions is generated and revisions are made.
6. *a.* Identify problem. Problem is identified and clearly stated.
    b. Work toward solution. Orchestrate process for solution of problem.
    c. Establish solution. Students apply themselves to finding a solution to a problem.
7. *d, f*
8. *c*
9. False. The heuristic method implies freedom for students to explore, with the teacher acting as a facilitator.

Exercise 8.3 Individualization

1. *e*
2. An educational activity that an individual carries out with little or no guidance.
3. False. Most normal-functioning students can benefit from independent study.
4. *a, b, e*
5. False. No method is superior to another in all situations.
6. True. Drill and practice work can generally be completed independently.

Chapter 9

Exercise 9.1 Thinking Skills

1. Withholding judgment in order to use past knowledge and experience in finding new information, concepts, or conclusions.
2. True. Responsibility is central to decision making and thinking.
3. False. Critical thinking is more complex; it is a skill.
4. Individuals tend to accept and repeat satisfying experiences.
5. True. Generally, thinking skills adhere to Bloom's Taxonomy of the cognitive domain.
6. process, product

Exercise 9.2 Thinking-Skills Instruction

1. separate, infusion
2. True. Direct instruction can be used in focusing on new modes of thinking.
3. False. Challenges to one's value system can cause imbalance, which can have a negative effect on forming new thought structures.

4. True. The best activities for developing thinking skills are those that have more than one answer.
5. a. Fluent thinking.
   b. Cause-and-effect thinking.
   c. Organization and association thinking.
   d. Thinking about relationship and elements of a whole.

Chapter 10

Exercise 10.1 Assessment Concepts
1. False. Evaluation has many uses in the teaching-learning process.
2. a. Gather pertinent data.
   b. Make reasonable judgments.
3. a. 2   b. 3   c. 1
4. False. Sometimes the normal curve is not appropriate in assigning grades—for example, when mastery of a subject is the desired goal.
5. False. Performance assessment can be used in evaluating any type of learning.
6. reliability, validity, usability
7. True. No assessment is completely objective.

Exercise 10.2 Information Sources and Evaluation Instruments
1. True. Because the purpose of giving standardized tests is to make comparisons, standard scores are needed.
2. False. Students should occasionally be involved in their own evaluation.
3. False. People tend to create situations that are congruent with their own values, beliefs, and attitudes.
4. grades
5. a. 3   b. 1   c. 2

Chapter 11

Exercise 11.1 Evaluative Instruments
1. teacher-made test, standardized test
2. True. The tests' construction, conditions of administration, and interpretation are standardized.
3. False. Most teachers lack the skill to design highly valid and reliable tests.
4. a. 3   b. 4   c. 1   d. 2
5. multiple-choice
6. brief, extended
7. False. Quizzes are generally limited to material taught in the preceding lesson.
8. True. This is one of the functions of a test.
9. two weeks

Exercise 11.2 Assigning Grades
1. False. Assigning grades always requires that a judgment be made.
2. curve
3. False. There are several good curving methods available to teachers.
4. a. 3   b. 1   c. 2
5. False. Grades should be indicative of achievement relative to objectives, not the amount of extra credit completed.

6. False. Contracts can be appropriately developed for any secondary classroom.

Chapter 12

Exercise 12.1 Communication Process

1. False. Teachers must also attend to receiving information.
2. False. We are always communicating in some form.
3. verbal, vocal, metaverbal
4. The sending of messages without the use of words.
5. True. We are always communicating nonverbally.
6. *a.* Facial language: Use of face and eyes in conveying information.
   b. Body language: Also referred to as *kinesics,* the use of body movements and gestures in sending messages.
   c. Language of space and motion: Communication through the arrangement of the environment and the movement throughout that environment.
   d. Language of time: How time is used in sending and sharing messages.
   e. Language of the voice: Using the voice for achieving meaning.
7. True. This is a comfortable distance for both students and teachers.

Exercise 12.2 Listening

1. False. Hearing is a purely physiological process, whereas listening is an active process in which the brain assigns meaning to what is heard.
2. *a.* Hearing: The physiological aspects of listening.
   b. Attending: The psychological aspects of listening.
   c. Understanding: The judgment of received information.
   d. Remembering: The decision on the worth of information and the judgment of whether it is worth remembering.
3. True. We all have filters through which we listen.
4. True. Many people have developed bad listening habits, which can effect what they hear.
5. *a.* 2   *b.* 3   *c.* 1
6. verbal, nonverbal
7. True. The most effective speakers actively use feedback in improving their communication.

Chapter 13

Exercise 13.1 Cognitive Approach to Motivation

1. False. Internal changes usually occur quite slowly.
2. True. Motives are generally influenced by both internal and external factors.
3. *a.* 2   *b.* 3   *c.* 1
4. deficiency, being
5. True. Fulfillment of a being need generally motivates an individual to seek further fulfillment.
6. False. Some students may have the need to achieve at all cost, which may prompt them to take undue risks or avoid situations that might threaten their success.
7. False. A limited amount of anxiety can be beneficial as a motivator.

Exercise 13.2 Stimulation Approach to Motivation

1. *a.* 1   *b.* 3   *c.* 2
2. True. Unfortunately, secondary teachers often see little need for an attractive room.
3. Persons admired by students who, through their actions, are used for demonstrating the values and behaviors you want students to acquire.
4. True. The teacher is the classroom leader.
5. Some possible ways you might attract and maintain student interest are these: involve students in their own learning; use focusing techniques, gestures, and different interaction patterns; be enthusiastic; and begin lessons with topics of interest to students.
6. True. It prepares students for the coming lesson.
7. You might heighten students' desire to learn if you involve them in their own learning; are a democratic leader; model excitement and interest; and add variety, action, excitement, and novelty to lessons.
8. False. The self-fulfilling prophecy applies to all people.

Exercise 13.3 Reinforcement Approach to Motivation

1. True. Generally, some type of reward is associated with repeated behavior.
2. False. Negative reinforcement is the removal of a negative stimulus.
3. Students may be motivated by a number of factors, such as these:
   a. Teacher approval.
   b. Observing other students.
   c. Disclosure of work results.
   d. Reward mechanisms (earning rewards for displaying desired behaviors).
4. False. Movement can be used for keeping students interested or reinforcing student actions.
5. False. Once an action has been established, you should switch to intermittent reinforcement.
6. False. Vicarious reinforcement can be an effective technique for establishing student actions.
7. Students exhibit desired behaviors because they see others being rewarded for those desired behaviors.
8. False. Some students care little about grades.
9. True. Certain rewards are given to students who display specific actions.
10. Formal written agreement between student and teacher that describes exactly what the student will do to earn desired privilege or reward.

Chapter 14

Exercise 14.1 Reading Diagnosis and Strategies

1. False. Many secondary students have trouble with classroom reading materials.
2. *a.* 1   *b.* 4   *c.* 2   *d.* 3
3. *a.* 3   *b.* 1   *c.* 2
4. before, during, after
5. True. You want to avoid asking students who are reading at the frustration level to complete reading assignments that are beyond their cognitive ability.
6. *a.* D   *b.* D   *c.* A   *d.* B   *e.* D   *f.* B   *g.* A

Exercise 14.2 Classroom Textbooks

1. False. Textbooks are generally written for nationwide consumption.
2. True. A teacher's edition provides everything contained in the student's edition, as well as instructional assistance.
3. True. The textbook-adoption process differs among states.
4. False. A thorough, dependable evaluation as to the worth of a textbook takes time and care.
5. content, organization, readability
6. workbooks, duplicated materials, newspapers

Chapter 15

Exercise 15.1 Management Approaches

1. False. Punishment relates to reactions to or consequences of misbehavior.
2. *a.* 3   *b.* 1   *c.* 2
3. True. Reality Therapy helps students take the responsibility for their actions.
4. *b, e, f*
5. *a, c, d, e*

Exercise 15.2 Control Techniques

1. False. Many factors—subtle and not so subtle—may be causing misbehavior.
2. True. Teachers who plan well usually contend with less classroom misbehavior.
3. True. Teachers should always remember that students have rights, values, and feelings.
4. *a, b, e*
5. False. It is generally best to start the year off as a firm teacher, to establish your credibility.
6. False. The use of rewards can be an effective way of curbing undesirable student behavior.
7. True. Students often learn behaviors by observing others.
8. True. Nonverbal teacher behaviors are effective techniques for dealing with both positive and negative student behaviors.

Chapter 16

Exercise 16.1 Educational Trends

1. social, political, educational, technological
2. True. The public appears to feel that schools are failing society.
3. teacher, student
4. True. Businesses and industries are encouraging educational change.
5. *b*
6. False. Professional organizations and staff development are important to all teachers.
7. True. Computers have become a critical component of effective classroom instruction.

Exercise 16.2 Education Reform

1. *A Nation At Risk*
2. *b, c, e, f*
3. National Teacher Exam (NTE)
4. False. Several states have a form of reciprocal certification agreement.

Appendix B

Laboratory Experiences:
Microteaching and Reflective Teaching

The primary purpose of teacher education is to prepare novice teachers for the classroom. Because teaching is such a highly complex series of acts, however, becoming a skillful teacher takes practice. Further, teacher preparation cannot be accomplished through the application of a formula or recipe. In short, teacher effectiveness is best developed through application-type experiences. In general, there are two ways such practice can be provided: laboratory and field-based experiences.

Laboratory experiences usually take place on campus, whereas field-based experiences generally take place in actual classrooms. Of course, field-based experiences would provide the most realistic experiences and, as such, would be more desirable. However, because actual secondary school classrooms are not readily available to most methods classes for practice purposes, application-type experiences are most commonly achieved through laboratory practice. Laboratory experiences come in two forms: microteaching and reflective teaching.

Essentially, microteaching and reflective teaching differ only in the complexity of the experience. While *microteaching* is concerned with the practice of a limited number of skills or behaviors, *reflective teaching* deals with the total teaching act.

Microteaching

Microteaching is a scaled-down sample of teaching in which a small group of four to six students are taught a 5- to 10-minute minilesson demonstrating one or more specific skills. In effect, microteaching provides a close simulation of actual classroom teaching for the purpose of practicing designated skills and behaviors.

Microteaching is often an integral component of methods classes in secondary school preparatory programs, whereby the various skills and behaviors addressed are practiced and demonstrated. Microteaching is a technique through which preservice teachers can home in on a particular aspect of teaching by placing it ''under the microscope'' for close examination. Each session focuses on a specific skill or behavior until a satisfactory level of mastery is demonstrated. Demonstration lessons usually are videotaped and critiqued by the teacher trainee and the instructor.

Microteaching simplifies the task of teaching by subdividing multifaceted teaching acts into simpler, less complex components. Because the teacher trainee is teaching a shorter, less complex lesson, he or she can better manage the lesson and focus it on a few major skills in the planning process. In addition, microteaching provides an opportunity for self-analysis and allows for constructive feedback from both the students being taught and an instructor. Videotaping the microteaching lesson offers a further advantage; because the tape can be replayed as many times as necessary, the viewer can focus on different aspects of a lesson with each viewing.

Microteaching does not just involve getting up in front of a small group and teaching. The experience must be thoughtfully planned. First, the skills or behaviors that will and can be practiced in the short time span must be selected with care. For example, the teacher trainee may want to work on effective questioning techniques; the appropriate application of reinforcement; the effective use of stimulus variation; the implementation of a specific teaching method (discussion, lecture, inquiry, discovery, exposition with interaction, etc.); or some combination of these skills or behaviors.

Second, a topic must be selected that will be appropriate for demonstrating the selected skills or behaviors. Not every topic is automatically appropriate for any teaching method. For example, time constraints dictate that the topic must be somewhat narrow—a single concept or subconcept that can be taught in a 5- to 10-minute time span. Therefore, the topic concept must be analyzed carefully in relation to the proposed method and procedure to be used as well as with regard to the allotted time.

Third, the teacher trainee should narrow the topic to a single concept or subconcept. Once the concept or subconcept has been determined, a limited number of objectives (perhaps only one) must be specified.

The Microteaching Preparation Form in this appendix can be used by the teacher trainee in developing a microteaching lesson. Remember to limit your teaching time to no more than 10 minutes.

Finally, a form must be developed that contains an appropriate set of criteria against which mastery of the desired skill(s) or behavior(s) will be judged. The Microteaching Evaluation Form and Microteaching Self-Analysis Form are examples of such evaluation forms and may be of some assistance in the design of similar evaluative instruments. The Microteaching Evaluation Form can be completed by the students taught and the instructor. The feedback obtained from the completed forms should be analyzed by the teacher trainee and the instructor with respect to mastery of the stated skill(s) or behavior(s). The Microteaching Self-Analysis Form should be completed by the teacher trainee, and perhaps the instructor, as a videotape of the microteaching session is replayed for analysis. Such an analysis will help in identifying specific teaching skills that need improvement.

Reflective Teaching

Reflective teaching was developed by Cruickshank and associates (1987) as a result of a desire to provide on-campus laboratory and clinical teaching practice in general secondary methods. Essentially, reflective teaching is a modified form of microteaching in that prospective teachers engage in the whole act of teaching; that is, they plan, teach, execute, and evaluate. Special emphasis is placed on a knowledge of whether the learners (peers) actually learned and how satisfied they were with the instruction. In effect, the potential teacher is called on to analyze and reflect on the teaching act itself.

Specifically, as conceived by Cruickshank and associates, reflective teaching has the following components and characteristics:

1. The total class is divided into groups of four to six students.

2. One student from each group is selected (designated) to teach the group.

3. Designated teachers teach toward *identical* instructional objectives using their own choice of teaching methods.

4. Designated teachers teach at the same time, either in nearby classrooms or in different parts of the same classroom, and are required to finish within the same period of time (usually 15 to 20 minutes).

5. Designated teachers focus on two things: learner achievement and learner satisfaction.

6. Learners (peers) are asked to be themselves and not to play the role of school-age students.

7. There must be a measurable product (evaluation) resulting from the teaching experience so that teaching and learning can be determined.

8. A learner satisfaction form is completed by the learners following the administration of the evaluation.

9. A large-group discussion follows the reflective teaching experience. That is, the total class reflects on and discusses the different teaching acts that took place.

10. The next teacher is selected (designated), and the cycle repeats.

The goal of reflective teaching is to teach and improve teaching skills through reflection on what was taught and how well it was taught. Each learner's achievement evaluation and lesson satisfaction is analyzed to elicit information relative to the effectiveness of the designated teacher. Reflection on this information is very instructive to the total class, because the students can compare the different methodological approaches and become aware that the effectiveness of the approach depends on the objective(s) and the teacher.

Because practice of the total teaching act is the ultimate goal of reflective teaching, students should be responsible for the development and presentation of a complete lesson. Thus, when planning for a reflective teaching session, the instructor should provide the instructional objective and, in most cases, a common evaluative instrument. However, the designated teachers should plan a total lesson using a form similar to the Lesson Plan Format guide in this appendix.

Feedback to the designated teachers is a major component in reflective teaching. It should be given as soon as possible after the teaching session, and it must be objective. If it is to be objective, an evaluation instrument employed should be based on identified effective teaching skills. An example of such an instrument is shown in the Teaching Evaluation Form. Feedback can be provided by having the instructor and learners complete and share the evaluative information with the designated teachers. Moreover, if the lesson can be videotaped, the designated teachers can complete an evaluation of their own teaching. Learners also should be asked to complete a Learner Satisfaction Form, such as the one that is depicted here. Feedback on lesson satisfaction can be used in addressing the areas that the learners found inappropriate in a lesson presentation.

Finally, grades are an important ingredient in any teacher-preparatory program. Thus, the Teaching Evaluation Form should be based on the program criteria for effective teaching. As such, the instructor's, learners', and designated teacher's self-evaluation of a teaching session can provide input for grades.

Microteaching Preparation Form

Microteacher: _____ Date: _____

Course title: _____

Use this form for preparation of your lesson. Prepare a copy for your instructor.

1. Concept to teach: _____
   _____

2. Skill(s) or behavior(s) to demonstrate: _____
   _____

3. Specific instructional objective(s): _____
   _____
   _____
   _____

4. Focusing activity: _____
   _____
   _____

5. Instructional procedure: _____
   _____
   _____
   _____
   _____

6. Closure: _____
   _____
   _____

7. Audiovisual materials and equipment needed: _____
   _____
   _____

8. Notes and comments: _____
   _____
   _____

Microteacher: _____ Date: _____

Subject: _____ Videotape number: _____

Rate the teacher trainee on each skill area. Code: 5 or 4, mastery of skill demonstrated; 3 or 2, some skill refinement needed; and 1 or 0, much skill refinement needed.

Organization of Lesson

5	4	3	2	1	0	Lesson preparation
5	4	3	2	1	0	Focusing activity
5	4	3	2	1	0	First skill/behavior _____
5	4	3	2	1	0	Second skill/behavior _____
5	4	3	2	1	0	Closure
5	4	3	2	1	0	Subject-matter knowledge

Comments: _____

_____

_____

Microteaching Self-Analysis Form[*]

Microteacher: _____   Date: _____

Concept taught: _____   Videotape number: _____

Replay the tape of your microteaching session as needed to collect data for the following items. Analyze the collected data, and draw conclusions with respect to the behavior addressed in each item.

1. **Teacher talk versus student talk.** Set up a small chart for tallying classroom talk.

   Teacher talk: _____
   Student talk: _____
   Silence or confusion: _____

   As you view your microteaching tape, mark a tally on the chart to represent who was talking approximately every three seconds. If no one was talking or if many people were talking simultaneously, then mark a tally in the category indicating silence or confusion. When you have finished, count the number of tallies in each category as well as the total number of occurrences of teacher talk and student talk combined. Use the following formulas to determine the percentage of teacher talk and student talk:

$$\text{Percentage of teacher talk} = \frac{\text{Tallies in teacher talk category}}{\text{Total of teacher talk + student talk}} \times 100$$

$$\text{Percentage of student talk} = \frac{\text{Tallies in student talk category}}{\text{Total of teacher talk + student talk}} \times 100$$

2. **Filler words.** Record the filler words or sounds ("okay," "you know," or "uh") and the number of times each was used. _____
   _____
   _____

3. **Questions.** Record the number of questions asked.

   Convergent: _____
   Divergent: _____

4. **Student names.** Record the number of times students are addressed by name.
   _____
   _____

5. **Pauses.** Record the number of times pauses are used to give students time to think.
   _____

6. **Reinforcement.** Record the number of times reinforcement is given.

   Verbal reinforcement: _____
   Nonverbal reinforcement: _____

7. **Sensory channels.** Record the number of times students are required to change sensory channels.
   _____
   _____

*Adapted from K. D. Moore. (1989). *Classroom teaching skills: A primer,* New York: Random House, pp. 225–226. Reprinted by permission.

Lesson Plan Format

Teacher: _____ Date: _____

Course title: _____

Topic: _____

Instructional objective(s): _____
_____
_____
_____

Focusing activity: _____
_____
_____

Content	Instructional Procedures
	a.
	b.
	c.
	d.
	e.
	f.

Closure: _____
_____
_____

Evaluation procedure: _____
_____
_____
_____

Instructional materials: _____
_____
_____

Notes and comments: _____
_____
_____
_____

Teaching Evaluation Form

Teacher: _____   Date: _____

Subject: _____   Videotape number: _____

Rate the teacher trainee on each skill area. Code: 5 or 4, mastery of skill demonstrated; 3 or 2, some skill refinement needed; and 1 or 0, much skill refinement needed.

Organization of Lesson

5	4	3	2	1	0	Lesson preparation
5	4	3	2	1	0	Focusing activity
5	4	3	2	1	0	Closure
5	4	3	2	1	0	Subject-matter knowledge

Comments: _____
_____
_____
_____

Lesson Presentation

5	4	3	2	1	0	Audience contact
5	4	3	2	1	0	Enthusiasm
5	4	3	2	1	0	Speech quality and delivery
5	4	3	2	1	0	Audience involvement
5	4	3	2	1	0	Verbal behaviors
5	4	3	2	1	0	Nonverbal behaviors
5	4	3	2	1	0	Use of questions and questioning techniques
5	4	3	2	1	0	Directions and pacing
5	4	3	2	1	0	Use of reinforcement
5	4	3	2	1	0	Incorporation of aids and materials

Comments: _____
_____
_____
_____

Learner Satisfaction Form

Teacher: _____ Date: _____

Subject: _____ Videotape number: _____

1. During the lesson, how satisfied were you as a learner? (Rate your satisfaction by placing an *X* on the following scale.)

    Very satisfied   Satisfied   Very unsatisfied

    ←————— · ————— · ————— · ————— · ————→

2. What would have increased your satisfaction? _____

    _____

    _____

    _____

    _____

    _____

    _____

    _____

    _____

    _____

GLOSSARY

A

Absolute grading standard: Student grades given relative to performance against established criteria—for example, 90% to 100%, A; 80% to 89%, B; 70% to 79%, C; and 60% to 69%, D.

Academic learning time: The time in class during which students are actively engaged in academic tasks that result in performance being at the 80 percent proficiency level or better.

Academies: Early American private or semiprivate secondary schools designed for preparing young people for business and life.

Accountability: Holding schools and teachers responsible for what is taught and what students learn.

Accreditation: Procedure for verifying school programs and course quality and uniformity.

Adolescence: The period beginning with the changes preceding the growth spurt and ending with achievement of adult status.

Advance organizer: An introductory statement, before instruction begins, that provides a structure for new information that is to be presented.

Affective domain: Learning domain in Bloom's Taxonomy concerned with values, attitudes, feelings, and emotions.

Allocated time: Time appropriated for students to engage in school activities such as classes, lunch, announcements, and so on.

Alternative certification: Process through which a person with a college degree, often in areas of critical teaching shortage, can obtain a teaching certificate and on-the-job training, without undergoing extensive prior teacher-preparation.

Anticipation guides: Before-reading strategy in which students react to a series of statements related to content of materials to be read. Also known as *reaction guides* or *prediction guides*.

Assertive discipline: A classroom management approach developed by Lee and Marlene Canter that stresses the need for and rights of teachers to communicate classroom needs and requirements in clear, firm, nonhostile terms, and that also stresses the rights of students to learn.

Assessment: Process of collecting a full range of information about students and classrooms for the purpose of making educational decisions.

Attitude: A mind-set toward a person, place, or thing.

B

Behavior: Actions that are observable and overt, and which must be seen and should be countable.

Behavioral learning theories: Theories of learning that emphasize changes in observable behavior or the way individuals act in particular situations.

Behavior modification: Shaping behavior by altering the consequences, outcomes, or rewards that follow the behavior.

Being need: The three higher-levels of Maslow's need hierarchy: intellectual achievement, aesthetic appreciation, and self-actualization.

Body language: Set of physical mannerisms that communicate and can be used to prompt students to stay attentive and on task—such as physical proximity, direct eye contact, body position, facial expressions, and tone of voice.

Boston Latin Grammar School: Forerunner to secondary school designed for preparing young men to attend college.

Brainstorming: An instructional technique in which small groups of students generate ideas, solutions, or comments relative to an assigned topic. All answers, no matter how wrong they may seem to the teacher or other students, are accepted as possibilities related to the assigned task.

Bulletin board: Display-media tool ranking among the least expensive yet most available for instructional communication.

Buzz group: An instructional technique in which a small work group is formed for a short duration to share opinions, viewpoints, or reactions.

C

Career education: Structured program through which students learn about occupational opportunities and about work.

Chalkboard: Display-media instructional tool that is possibly the most widely used media tool next to the textbook.

Checklist: A list of criteria or characteristics against which a performance or an end product is to be judged.

Classroom management: The process of organizing and conducting the business of the classroom relatively free of behavior problems.

Closure: Activity used for pulling a lesson together so concepts make sense and bringing it to a logical conclusion.

Cloze procedure: A reading diagnostic tool in which a student's ability to accurately identify and supply words that have been systematically deleted from a text passage is assessed.

Cognitive development: Changes in mental activity and thinking ability.

Cognitive domain: Learning domain in Bloom's Taxonomy that focuses on information, thinking, and reasoning ability.

Cognitive learning theories: Theories of learning that emphasize the unobservable mental processes that individuals use in learning and remembering information or skills.

Committee of Ten: Historic 1893 National Education Association committee that studied secondary education curriculum. The committee recommended that the high school curriculum stress mental discipline in the humanities, languages, and science.

Communication: The act by one or more persons of sending and receiving messages that are distorted by noise, have some effect, and provide some opportunity for feedback.

Competitive evaluation: Evaluation that forces students to compete with each other.

Computer: Electronic device that can store and manipulate information, as well as interact with user. Commonplace in many classrooms and in everyday life.

Computer-assisted instruction (CAI): The use of computers for presenting instructional information, asking questions, and interacting with students. Individualized instruction administered by a computer.

Computer literacy: A basic understanding of the general principles that underlie computer hardware, software, and the application of computer technology.

Computer-managed instruction (CMI): The use of computers for managing student records, diagnosing and prescribing instructional materials, monitoring student progress, and testing.

Content-area reading inventory (CARI): Means of assessing student reading level through materials actually used in a specific course.

Contingency contract: A grading system in which a formal written agreement between students and teacher is drawn up as to what students will do to receive a specified reward.

Continuous diagnosis: On-going collection of information on students' needs after instruction begins.

Convergent questions: Questions that allow for only a few right specific responses.

Cooperative learning: An instructional technique in which students of mixed abilities work together as a team on an assigned task. Interdependence and support for all members of the group is stressed.

Core curriculum: The common set of fundamental courses completed by all students.

Course planning: Broadest and most general type of instruction planning, usually divided into sequence of units of study.

Creative-generative level: Where an aggregate approach to course content is taken, based on analysis of student needs, society, and subject.

Creative thinking: Process of assembling information in developing whole new understanding of concept or idea. Four stages generally associated with creative thought are preparation, incubation, illumination, and verification.

Creativity: The capacity for producing imaginative, original products or ways of solving problems.

Criterion-referenced test: Testing in which interpretations are made by comparing a student's score against a predetermined standard.

Critical thinking: The ability to analyze complex situations critically using standards of objectivity and consistency, and to arrive at tentative conclusions.

Cumulative record: File that holds information collected on students during the school years.

Curriculum: The systematic plan of instruction for a school system. The learning, intended and unintended, that takes place under the sponsorship of the school.

D

Daily lesson plan: Detailed and specific plan detailing the objectives and class activities for a single day.

Dame school: An early form of primary instruction that focused on reading and writing for elite (boys and girls), often conducted in teacher's home.

Debate: An instructional technique in which two teams of two or three debaters competitively discuss topic issue.

Decision making: Thinking that asks students to choose the best response from several options.

Deductive thinking: Thinking that asks students to consider given generalizations and provide supporting data.

Deficiency need: The four lowest levels of Maslow's need hierarchy: survival, safety, belonging, and self-esteem.

Delinquency: Lawbreaking by those who are not considered adults.

Demonstration: An instructional method in which the teacher or some other designated individual stands before a class, shows something, and tells what is happening or what has happened, or asks students to discuss what has happened.

Desist approach: Method of classroom management that gives teacher full responsibility for regulating the classroom.

Development: Adaptive changes that occur in human beings (or animals) that begin with conception and continue through the entire life span.

Diagnostic evaluation: Evaluation administered prior to instruction to assess student's knowledge and abilities so that appropriate instruction can be provided.

Disabled: An inability to do something.

Discipline: Dealing with the prevention of classroom misbehavior as well as the reaction to or consequences of disruptive actions.

Discovery: An instructional method that focuses on intentional learning through supervised problem solving according to the scientific method. Students are encouraged to learn concepts and principles through their own exploration.

Discussion: An instructional method in which students exchange and share ideas relative to an assigned topic. Can take the form of either small-group or whole-class discussions.

Divergent questions: Questions that allow for many right responses.

Drill: The fixation of specific associations for automatic recall.

E

Empathic listening: Listening with feeling. An attempt to experience what a speaker is experiencing or feeling and responding to those feelings.

Empirical questions: Questions that require students to integrate or analyze remembered or given information and supply a single, correct, predictable answer.

Engaged time: The actual time individual students are actually engaged in purposeful classroom learning.

English High School: First American public high school, designed for teaching boys the knowledge needed to become merchants and mechanics.

Evaluation: The process of obtaining available information about students and using it to ascertain the degree of change in students' performance.

Evaluative questions: Questions that require that a judgment be made or a value be put on something.

Explicit curriculum: School learning experiences that are intentional.

Exploratory education: Schooling organized and structured to introduce students, on a limited basis, to a variety of specialized subjects.

Exposition teaching: Teaching method in which some authority—teacher, textbook, film, or microcomputer—presents information without overt interaction taking place between the authority and the students.

Exposition with interaction teaching: Authority-presented instruction followed by questioning that ascertains whether information has been comprehended.

Extracurriculum: School learning experiences that are elective extension of students' regular coursework (e.g., sports, clubs, band, chorus, and theater).

Extrinsic motivation: Motivation created by events or rewards outside the individual.

F

Factual questions: Questions that require the recall of information through the mental processes of recognition and rote memory.

Filmstrip: Series of related still pictures strung together on a length of 35-mm film to be shown in fixed sequence, one at a time.

Flat picture: An opaque, two-dimensional, still picture.

Focusing questions: Questions used to direct students' attention on a lesson or on the content of a lesson.

Formative evaluation: The use of evaluation information for supplying feedback to students before or during the learning process and for promoting learning.

Frustration level: Lowest reading level at which students are able to understand and where basic skills break down (i.e., students often are unable to pronounce many of the words and unable to comprehend the material satisfactorily).

Functionalist: Educators who believe school curriculum and teaching methodologies should serve society at large by preparing students to assume adult roles in that society.

G

Games: See **Simulations.**

General education: Education for all. Broad area of schooling that focuses on developing basic skills for success in society.

Goal: Broad statement of instructional intent, which describes general purpose of instruction.

Grade contract: A written agreement between student and teacher as to what students will do to earn a specific grade.

H

Halting time: A teacher's pause in talking, used for giving students time to think about presented materials and directions.

Handicapped: Possessing an impairment that limits one's activities.

Hearing: The transmission of eardrum vibration caused by sound impulses to the brain.

Heuristic approach: Active, reflective teaching methods that involve students in problem solving and comprise modes of discovery, inquiry (and Suchman inquiry), and simulations and games.

Hidden curriculum: School learning experiences, both positive and negative, that produce changes in students' attitudes, beliefs, and values, but are not part of the intentionally planned curriculum.

High school: See **Secondary school.**

I

I-messages: Teacher messages that clearly tell students how the teacher feels about problem situations and implicitly ask for corrected behavior.

Imitative-maintenance level: Where course content relies primarily on the textbook and routine activities.

Incentive system: Offering preferred activities or items for motivational purposes or for keeping students on task.

Independent level: Highest reading level at which students read fluently and with excellent comprehension.

Independent study: An instructional method in which students are involved in activities carried out with little or no guidance.

Individualized instruction: An instructional method in which instruction is tailored to interests, needs, and abilities of students.

Inductive thinking: Thinking that asks students to make generalizations based on knowledge of specific examples and details.

Informational objectives: Statement of instructional intent that is an abbreviation of instructional objective, with only the performance and product specified.

Information processing theory: Cognitive theory label for viewing learning in terms of sensory input, encoding, and retrieval systems.

Infusion approach: Method of teaching thinking skills where desired skill is used in conjunction with and incorporated into regular curriculum.

Initial diagnosis: See **Diagnostic evaluation.**

Inquiry: An instructional method that focuses on the flexible yet systematic process of problem-solving.

Inquiry demonstration: An instructional method in which students are asked only to observe in silence.

Instructional approach: Method of classroom management based on premise that well-planned and well-implemented instruction will prevent most classroom problems.

Instructional level: Highest reading level at which students can make progress in reading with instructional guidance.

Instructional objective: A narrow statement of learning intent comprising four components: the performance, a product, the conditions, and the criteria.

Instructional strategy: Primary ingredient, along with content, of well-planned lesson, consisting of two components: methodology and lesson procedure.

Instructional time: Amount of allocated time available for learning.

Interactive video: A video system linked to a computer system so individual can control images and sounds.

Intrinsic motivation: The stimulation of student learning that comes from activities that are rewarding in themselves.

J

Junior high schools: Schools designed to provide students in grades 7 to 8 or 9 with better preparation for high school. See **Secondary school.**

L

Latin grammar school: Schools that emphasized the study of Latin, literature, history, mathematics, music, and dialectics.

Law of effect: Principle within association theory that says individuals tend to accept and repeat satisfying experiences.

Learning: A relatively permanent change in an individual's capacity for performance as a result of experience or practice.

Lecture: Teacher presents information with no overt interaction with students.

Lecture recitation: Instructional technique in which the teacher makes a clear presentation, followed by student responses centered on the ideas that were presented by the teacher.

Lesson procedure: Sequence of steps designed to lead students to the acquisition of the desired learning.

Likert scale: Method of attitude assessment in which students respond to statements by indicating feelings according to a five-point scale ranging from "strongly agree" to "strongly disagree."

Limits: The accepted and nonaccepted actions in the classroom.

Listening: An active process of assigning meaning to what is heard, or the brain giving meaning to impulses transmitted from the eardrum to the brain. Barker defines four components of listening as hearing, attending, understanding, and remembering. Listening styles can be one-way, two-way, or empathetic.

Listening capacity: Reading level at which students can understand material that is read aloud.

M

Magnet schools: Schools that gear instruction to special themes (e.g., art, music, drama, etc.) or to students with particular curriculum interests (e.g., mathematics, sciences, language arts, etc.).

Mandated time: Total time available for all activities carried out in school.

Massachusetts Act of 1642: A law requiring each town to determine whether its young people could read and write.

Mastery curriculum: Learnings considered essential for all students to know (Glatthorn, 1987).

Mastery learning: A diagnostic-corrective-enrichment instructional model where students work on objectives until mastery is achieved. It is based on the assumption that every student is capable of achieving most of the course objectives if given the time and appropriate experiences.

Measurement: The assignment of numerical values to objects, events, performances, or products to indicate the degree to which they possess the characteristics being measured.

Mediative level: Where class content and structure derives not only from textbook, but extends beyond to draw from supplementary materials and issues.

Mental Operation system: Four-category question model, comprising factual, empirical, productive, and evaluative questions.

Mentoring: The assignment of consultant teachers to assist beginning teachers during their initial year of teaching.

Metaverbal component: The underlying or hidden message that cannot be directly attributed to the meaning of the words or how they are spoken.

Methodology: Planned patterned behaviors that are definite steps through which the teacher influences learning.

Microteaching: A technique of practicing teaching skills and processes in scaled-down and simulated situations.

Middle schools: Schools designed to meet unique needs of preadolescents, usually for grades 5 or 6 through 7 or 8.

Minimum competency testing: Exit tests designed to ascertain whether or not students have achieved basic levels of performance in basic skill areas—such as reading, writing, and computation—before they can graduate or continue to the next level.

Modeling: Person demonstrating or acting as one wants others to act and communicating examples of the values, ideas, and behaviors to be acquired by students.

Motion picture: Series of still pictures taken in rapid succession that give illusion of motion when projected.

Motivation: The influences of needs, desires, and drives on the intensity and direction of behaviors.

N

Nation At Risk: The first major national report calling for educational reform in the school curriculum, expectations, time, and teaching.

National Teacher Exam (NTE): An examination that covers communication skills, general knowledge, and professional knowledge. Currently required for teacher certification in many states.

Natural motive: An individual's internal desire. Many natural motives are believed to be innate.

Need: A deficiency or requirement in the individual or the absence of anything the person requires, or thinks he or she requires, for overall well-being.

Negative reinforcement: Strengthening the likelihood of a behavior or event by the removal of an unpleasant stimulus.

Noncompetitive evaluation: Evaluation that does not force students to compete with each other.

Nonverbal communication: Nonlinguistic communication, or the sending of messages without the use of words. Comprises facial language, body language (kinesics), use of the voice, and use of space, motion, and time.

Nonverbal reinforcement: The use of physical action as a positive consequence to strengthen behavior or event.

Normal curve: A bell-shaped distribution. Mathematical construct divided into equal segments that reflect the natural distribution of all sorts of things in nature.

Norm-referenced test: Test interpretation is made by comparing student's score with that of a norm group (a large representative sample) to obtain meaning.

O

Objective: The anticipated result or product of instruction. A clear and unambiguous statement of instructional intent.

Old Deluder Satan Act: Massachusetts act of 1647 stipulating that every town of 50 or more families pay someone to teach reading and writing.

Option guide: Study guide discussed before but completed during reading by students as part of active, decision-making process.

Oral reading assessment: Method of identifying student reading level in which teacher gauges comprehension through how students articulate responses to questions teacher has devised about short reading passage.

Overlapping: The ability to be engaged in or supervise several activities simultaneously.

P

Panel: An instructional technique in which five to eight students prepare and discuss a topic in front of class. Also known as *round tables*.

Percentage grading system: Percentage correct is recorded for each assignment, and an average is calculated to determine final grade.

Percentile score: Derived score on a distribution of scores below which a given percentage of raw scores fall.

Performance assessment: Assessment where students demonstrate the behaviors to be measured.

Personal development: Changes in the ways individuals view themselves.

Physical development: Physiological changes of the body and in motor skills.

PL 94–142: Federal law requiring provision of special education services to eligible students.

Point grading system: Student work is allocated points, and grades are assigned according to established grade range.

Portfolio: A systematic, organized collection of evidence (e.g., projects, written work, and video demonstrations of skills) that documents growth and development and that represents progress made toward reaching specified goals and objectives.

Positive reinforcement: Strengthening the likelihood of occurrence of a behavior or event by presenting a desired stimulus.

Practice: The repeating of specified tasks or skills for the purpose of improvement.

Prereading Plan (PreP): Langer's technique for assessing topic awareness before reading assignments by making and reflecting on associations with a particular topic and reformulating knowledge based on those associations.

Probing questions: Questions that follow a student response and require the student to think and respond more thoroughly than in the initial response.

Problem solving: An instructional technique that focuses on the intentional elimination of uncertainty or doubt through direct experiences and under supervision.

Productive questions: Broad, open-ended questions with many correct responses that require students to use their imagination, think creatively, and produce something unique.

Programmed textbooks (workbooks): The presentation of content information in a series of carefully planned sequential steps. Students can use the sequenced materials to teach themselves.

Progressives: Educators who believe school curricula and teaching methodologies should be student-centered and should relate to students' interests and needs.

Prompting questions: Questions that include the use of hints or clues to aid students in answering or in correcting an initial response.

Psychobiological development: Psychological consequences of biological changes.

Psychomotor domain: Learning domain concerned with muscular abilities and skills on a continuum ranging from the simple to the complex.

Psychosocial development: Erikson's eight stages of personal and social changes—due to cultural factors—marked by crises that must be resolved to progress successfully in life.

Punisher: Anything that is found unpleasant by individuals.

Punishment: The application of a negative stimulus or removal of a positive stimulus for inappropriate behavior.

Q

Qualified reinforcement: Differential reinforcement of acceptable parts of student actions or attempts.

Questionnaire: A list of written statements regarding attitudes, feelings, and opinions to which the reader must respond.

R

Rating scale: A scale of values, arranged in order of quality, describing someone or something being evaluated.

Reality Therapy: William Glasser's personality theory of therapy in which individuals are helped to become responsible and able to satisfy their needs in the real world.

Redirecting: The technique of asking different individuals to respond to a question in light of, or to add new insight to, the previous responses.

Reflective teaching: Teacher as an informed and thoughtful decision maker, who analyzes past experiences in planning and teaching and in promoting thinking about nature of teaching and learning.

Reinforcement: Theory that says the consequences of an action strengthen or weaken the likelihood of the behavior or event. Rewarding of desired actions.

Reinforcer: Anything that is found pleasurable by individuals.

Relative grading standard: Student's grades given relative to performance of other students. Grading on the curve.

Reliability: The extent to which individual responses are measured consistently. The coefficient of stability of scores.

Responsibility: The state of being accountable or answerable for one's actions. Ability to meet obligations or act without direct guidance.

Reward mechanism: A formal system of reinforcement.

Ripple effect: The spreading of behaviors from one individual to others through imitation. The "contagious" spreading of behavior.

Role-playing: An instructional technique designed to let students assume the role(s) of individuals in a recreation of an event or situation.

Round table: See **Panel.**

S

School choice: Policies in some districts that permit parents to choose the school that meets their individual needs.

Secondary school: Traditionally, any school that has students from the next grade following elementary or middle school and ending with or below grade 12. *Junior high schools* generally educate students from grades 7 through 8 or 9. *High schools* generally educate students from grades 9 or 10 through 12.

Self-discipline approach: Method of classroom management built on premise that students can be trusted to evaluate and change their actions so these behaviors are beneficial and appropriate to the self and to the class as a whole.

Self-fulfilling prophecy: A phenomenon in which believing that something will happen causes it to occur.

Semantic differential: Method of assessing degrees of attitudes, beliefs, and feelings—from very favorable to highly unfavorable—along a seven-point scale that links an adjective at one end to its opposite at the other end.

Separate approach: View suggested by Rueven Voyerstein that students need special, focused instruction on thinking skills.

Set induction: Something a teacher does at the outset of a lesson to get students' undivided attention, arouse their interest, and establish a conceptual framework.

Silent reading assessment: Method of identifying reading level in which comprehension is gauged through responses to written questions about selected passage. Can be applied to entire class at one time.

Simulations: Instructional techniques in which students are involved in models of artificial situations and/or events designed to provide no risk experiences for students. Also referred to as *games.*

Slides: Photographic film transparencies individually mounted for one-at-a-time projection.

Social development: Changes in the ways individuals relate to others.

Social learning theory: Developed by Albert Bandura, outgrowth of behavioral learning theory that emphasizes cues and internal mental processes.

Socratic method: An instructional method in which a questioning and interaction sequence is used to draw information out of students.

Staff development: Activities designed to increase the professional knowledge and practices of teachers.

Standard deviation: The extent to which scores are spread out around the mean.

Standardized test: A commercially developed test that samples behavior under uniform procedures.

Standard scores: A score based on the number of standard deviations an individual is from the mean.

Stimulus variation: Actions, behaviors, or behavior patterns designed to gain and maintain student attention during a lesson.

Strategy: The methodology and procedure of a lesson.

Student-centered curriculum: An activity curriculum that focuses on student needs, interests, and activities.

Student's edition: Student's course textbook, which includes preface, introduction, table of contents, sections (or units) divided into chapters, glossary, appendix, and index.

Subject-centered curriculum: School curriculum patterns wherein subjects are separated into distinct courses of study.

Suchman inquiry: The inquiry approach whereby students are presented and asked to explain discrepant events.

Summative evaluation: Evaluation completed after instruction to determine the extent of student learning.

T

Task group: An instructional technique in which a group of four to eight students is formed to solve a problem or complete a project.

Teacher Effectiveness Training (TET): Self-discipline approach to classroom management conceived by Thomas Gordon that stresses establishment of positive working relationships between teachers and students. Key is based on who owns the problem when one develops—teacher or student.

Teacher-made test: An evaluative instrument developed and scored by a teacher for classroom assessment.

Teacher's edition: Modified copy of student's edition, with accompanying manual that offers additional information and direction, and which may include pedagogical aids, answer keys, test questions, class activities, objectives and lesson plans, visual ideas, and evaluation tips.

Teacher-student planning: Participatory process that directly involves students in instructional planning.

Teacher testing: The requirement, usually legislatively mandated, that teachers pass a test prior to certification.

Teaching: The actions of someone who is trying to assist others to reach their fullest potential in all aspects of development.

Team planning: Coordination of teachers' instructional approaches among disciplines.

Telelecture: Lecture transmitted from central studio classroom to distant classroom.

Test: A task or series of tasks used to obtain systematic observations regarding ability, skill, knowledge, or performance.

Textbook adoption: Procedure for identifying and selecting school textbooks worthy for use in the classroom, which can begin at the state or local level.

Textbook recitation: An instructional method in which students are assigned content to read and study in a textbook and are then questioned on what has been read and studied.

Thinking: The act of withholding judgment in order to use past knowledge and experience in finding new information, concepts, or conclusions.

Three-level reading guide: Type of during-reading study guide that incorporates statements on selection's main points and statements related to content objectives to explore what author said, what author meant, and what students perceive of passage.

Time on task: See **Engaged time.**

Transfer: Ability to use classroom-acquired information outside the classroom or in different subjects.

Transparencies: Still projected material comprising images and words placed on clear acetate or plastic film.

U

Unit plan: Links goals and objectives, content, activities, resources and materials, and evaluation for particular unit of study for a course.

Usability: Suitability of a measurement device to collect desired data.

V

Validity: The ability of a test to measure what it purports to measure.

Verbal component: The actual words and meaning of a spoken message.

Verbal reinforcement: Presentation of positive comments as consequence to strengthen student behavior or event.

Vicarious motivation: Strengthening of behavior because of desire to receive consequences received by others who exhibit that behavior.

Videodisc: A platter resembling a phonograph record used for storing visual materials for presentation on a display screen.

Video programming (television): Broadcast video signals, such as commercial television programs, that are received and shown on a display unit.

Vocal component: The meaning attached to a spoken message, resulting from such variables as voice firmness, modulation, tone, tempo, pitch, and loudness.

Vouchers: A plan wherein credit for funds (*vouchers*) are allocated to students' parents, who then purchase education for their children in a school of their choice.

W

Wait-time: The time needed for students to consider their responses to questions. *Wait-time 1* is the initial time a teacher waits following a question before calling for the response. *Wait-time 2* is the total time a teacher waits for all students to respond to the same question or for students to respond to each other's responses to a question.

Weekly plan: Condensed version of week's daily lesson plans, written on short form provided by school.

Weighted grading system: Assignments are given a letter grade, and all grades are weighted in determining final grade.

Withitness: The ability of a teacher to be aware of what is going on in all parts of the classroom, and the ability to communicate this awareness.

BIBLIOGRAPHY

A

Adler, M. J. (1982). *The paideia proposal.* New York: Macmillan.

Alan Guttmacher Institute. (1989, April). Sex education in the schools: Policies and practice. *Family Planning Perspectives, 21* (No. 2), 52, 64.

Allen, D. W., Ryan, K. A., Bush, R. N., & Cooper, J. M. (1969). *Creating student involvement.* General Learning Corporation.

Allen, D. W., Ryan, K. A., Bush, R. N., & Cooper, J. M. (1969). *Questioning skills.* General Learning Corporation.

Alvermann, D. E., Moore, D. E., & Conley, M. W. (Eds.). (1987). *Research within reach, secondary school reading: A research guided response to concerns of reading educators.* Newark, DE: International Reading Association.

America 2000: An education strategy. (1991, April 24). *Education Week,* 24–25.

Anderson, R. C., Spiro, R. J., & Montague, W. E. (Eds.). (1977). *Schooling and the acquisition of knowledge.* Hillsdale, NJ: Erlbaum.

Anderson, V., & Hidi, S. (1989). Teaching students to summarize. *Educational Leadership, 46*(4), 26–28.

Armbruster, B. B., Anderson, T. H., & Ostertag, J. (1987). Does text structure/summarization instruction facilitate learning from expository text? *Reading Research Quarterly, 22,* 331–346. Newark, DE: International Reading Association.

Arons, A. B. (1988, April 9). What current research in teaching and learning says to the practicing teacher. Robert Karplus Lecture. *National Convention of the National Science Teacher Association,* St. Louis, MO.

Ashton, P. (1988). *Teaching higher-order thinking and content: An essential ingredient in teacher preparation.* Gainesville, FL: University of Florida.

Association for Supervision and Curriculum Development. (1985). *Developing minds: A resource book for teaching thinking.* Alexandria, VA: Author.

Association for Supervision and Curriculum Development. (1988). *Content of the curriculum: ASCD yearbook.* Alexandria, VA: Author.

Association for Supervision and Curriculum Development. (1990). *Teaching thinking skills* (Video). Alexandria, VA: Author.

Ausubel, D. P. (1963). *The psychology of meaningful verbal learning: An introduction to school learning.* New York: Grune & Stratton.

B

Baker, K. (1985). Research evidence of a school discipline problem. *Phi Delta Kappan, 66*(7), 482–488.

Bandura, A. (1969). Social-learning theory of identificatory process. In D. A. Goslin (Ed.), *Handbook of socialization theory and research.* Chicago: Rand McNally.

Barker, L. L. (1971). *Listening behavior.* Englewood Cliffs, NJ: Prentice Hall.

Bean, T. W., Singer, H., & Cowan, S. (1985). Analogical study guides: Improving comprehension in science. *Journal of Reading, 29,* 246–250.

Beane, J. A., Toepfer, C. F., Jr., & Alessi, S. J., Jr. (1986). *Curriculum planning and development.* Boston: Allyn & Bacon.

Becker, G. S. (1989, July 3). Tuning in to the needs of high school dropouts. *Business Week,* 18.

Beil, D. (1977, April). The emperor's new cloze. *Journal of Reading,* 601–604.

Bennett, W. J. (1987). *James Madison high school: A curriculum for American students.* Washington, DC: United States Department of Education.

Benson, P., Williams, D., & Johnson, A. (1987). *The quicksilver years: The hopes and fears of early adolescence.* San Francisco: Harper & Row.

Berger, E. H. (1991). *Parents as partners in education* (3rd ed.). New York: Merrill.

Berliner, D. (1987). Simple views of effective teaching and simple theory of classroom instruction. In D. Berliner & B. Rosenshire (Eds.), *Talks to teachers.* New York: Random House, 93–110.

Betts, E. A. (1946). *Foundations of reading instruction.* New York: American Book.

Beyer, B. K. (1984). Improving thinking skills: Practical approaches. *Phi Delta Kappan, 65,* 556–560.

Beyer, B. K. (1988). *Developing a thinking skills program.* Boston: Allyn & Bacon.

Blenkin, G. M., & Kelly, A. V. (1981). *The primary curriculum.* New York: Harper & Row.

Block, J. H., Efthim, H. E., & Burns, R. B. (1989). *Building effective mastery learning schools.* New York: Longman.

Bloom, B. S. (Ed.), Engelhart, M. D., Furst, E. J., Hill, W. H., & Krathwohl, D. R. (1956). *Taxonomy of educational objectives, Handbook I: Cognitive domain.* New York: David McKay.

Boyer, E. L. (1983). *High school.* New York: Harper & Row.

Brandt, R. S. (Ed.). (1988). Teaching thinking throughout the curriculum. *Educational Leadership, 45*(7), 3–85.

Brandt, R. (1989). On learning research: A conversation with Lauren Resnick. *Educational Leadership, 46*(4), 12–16.

Brawn, C. (1976). Teacher expectation: Socio-psychological dynamics. *Review of Educational Research, 46*(2), 185–212.

Brookfield, S. D. (1987). *Developing critical thinkers.* San Francisco: Jossey-Bass.

Brophy, J. (1981). Teacher praise: A functional analysis. *Review of Educational Research, 51*, 5–32.

Brophy, J. E., & Good, T. L. (1970). Teachers' communication of differential expectations for children's classroom performance: Some behavioral data. *Journal of Educational Psychology, 61*, 365–374.

Brown, J. W., Lewis, R. B., & Harcleroad, F. (1983). *AV instruction technology, media, and methods* (6th ed.). New York: McGraw-Hill.

Bruner, J. S. (1977). *The process of education.* Cambridge, MA: Harvard University Press.

Bullough, R. V., Sr. (1988). *Creating instructional materials* (3rd ed.). Columbus, OH: Merrill.

Burns, R. B. (1979). Mastery learning: Does it work? *Educational Leadership, 37*(2), 110–113.

C

Cabeceiras, J. (1972, Fall). Observed differences in teacher verbal behavior when using and not using the overhead projector. *AV Communication Review,* 271–280.

Callahan, J. F., & Clark, L. H. (1988). *Teaching in the middle and secondary schools: Planning for competence* (3rd ed.). New York: Macmillan.

Canter, L., & Canter, M. (1976). *Assertive discipline: A take-charge approach for today's educator.* Los Angeles: Canter & Associates.

Carnegie Task Force on Teaching as a Profession. (1986). *A nation prepared: Teachers for the twenty-first century.* New York: Carnegie Forum on Education and the Economy.

Cawelti, G. (1988, November). Middle schools a better match with early adolescent needs, ASCD survey finds. *ASCD Curriculum Update,* 1–12.

Charles, C. M. (1981). *Building classroom discipline.* New York: Longman.

Children's Defense Fund. (1989). *A vision of America's future.* Washington, DC: Children's Defense Fund.

Clabough, G. K., & Rozycki, E. G. (1990). *Understanding schools: The foundations of education.* New York: Harper & Row.

College Board. (1983). *Academic preparation for college.* New York: College Board.

Connors, N. A., & Irvin, J. L. (1989). Is "middle-schoolness" an indicator of excellence? *Middle School Journal, 20*(5), 12–14.

Cooper, H., & Good, T. L. (1983). *Pygmalion grows up.* New York: Longman.

Costa, A. L. (1984). Mediating the metacognitive. *Educational Leadership, 42*(3), 57–62.

Cruickshank, D. R. (1987). *Reflection teaching.* Reston, VA: Association of Teacher Educators.

D

Dale, E. (1969). *Audio visual methods in teaching.* New York: Holt, Rinehart, & Winston.

Davidson, N., & O'Leary, P. W. (1990). How cooperative learning can enhance mastery teaching. *Educational Leadership, 47*(5), 30–33.

Davies, G. M. (1976). *Objectives in curriculum design.* New York: McGraw-Hill.

DeVito, J. A. (1985). *Communication.* New York: Harper & Row.

Dillion, J. T. (1983). *Teaching and the art of questioning.* Bloomington, IN: Phi Delta Kappa Educational Foundation.

Dillion, J. (1987). *Classroom questions and discussions.* Norwood, NJ: Ablex.

Dobson, R., Dobson, J., & Kessinger, J. (1980). *Staff development: A humanistic approach.* Washington, DC: University Press of America.

Dreifurs, R., & Cassel, P. (1974). *Discipline without tears* (2nd ed.). New York: Hawthorn Books.

Dreifurs, R., Grunwald, B. B., & Pepper, F. C. (1982). *Maintaining sanity in the classroom* (2nd ed.). New York: Harper & Row.

Duke, L. L. (1990). *Teaching: An introduction.* New York: McGraw-Hill.

Duke, L. L., & Meckel, A. M. (1984). *Teacher's guide to classroom management.* New York: Random House.

E

Ebel, R. L., & Frisbie, D. A. (1991). *Essentials of educational measurement* (5th ed.). Englewood Cliffs, NJ: Prentice Hall.

Eggen, P. D., & Kauchak, D. P. (1988). *Strategies for teachers: Teaching content and thinking skills* (2nd ed.). Englewood Cliffs, NJ: Prentice Hall.

Eisenberg, A. M., & Smith, R. R., Jr. (1971). *Nonverbal communications.* Indianapolis, IN: Bobbs-Merrill.

Eisner, E. W. (1985). *The educational imagination: On the design and evaluation of school programs* (2nd ed.). New York: Macmillan.

Elkind, D. (1984). *All grown up and no place to go.* Reading, MA: Addison-Wesley.

Emmer, E. T., & Evertson, C. M. (1981). Synthesis of research on classroom management. *Educational Leadership 38*(4), 342–347.

Erickson, B., Huber, M., Bea, T., Smith, C., & McKenzie, V. (1987). Increasing critical reading in junior high classes. *Journal of Reading, 30*, 430–439.

Erikson, E. H. (1980). *Identity and life cycle* (2nd ed.). New York: Norton.

Estes, T. H., & Vaughan, J. L. (1973). Reading interest and comprehension: Implications. *Reading Teacher, 27*, 149–152.

Estes, T. H., & Vaughan, J. L. (1980). *Reading and learning in the content classroom.* Boston: Allyn & Bacon.

Evans, S. S., Evans, W. H., & Mercer, C. D. (1986). *Assessment for instruction.* Boston: Allyn & Bacon.

F

Fantini, M. D. (1986). *Regaining excellence in education.* Columbus, OH: Merrill.

Feuerstein, R. (1980). *Instrumental enrichment: An intervention program for cognitive modifiability.* Baltimore: University Park Press.

Finn, C. E. (1987). The two new agendas of education reform. *Independent School, 46*(2), 5–13.

Forrest-Pressley, D. L., MacKinnon, G. E., & Waller, T. G. (Eds.). (1985). *Metacognition, cognition, and human performance* (Vol. 1 & 2). Orlando, FL: Academic Press.

Friedman, P. G. (1986). *Listening processes: Attention, understanding, evaluation.* Washington, DC: National Education Association.

Fry, E. (1977). Fry's readability graph: Clarifications, validity, and extension to level 17. *Journal of Reading, 11,* 513–516.

Fulwiler, T. (1986). Journals across the disciplines. In E. K. Dishner, T. W. Bean, J. E. Readence, & D. W. Moore (Eds.), *Reading in the content areas: Improving classroom instruction* (2nd ed.). Dubuque, IA: Kendall/Hunt, 360–366.

G

Gage, N. L. (1985). *Hard gains in the soft sciences: The case of pedagogy.* Bloomington, IN: Center on Evaluation, Development, and Research.

Gage, N. L. (1990). Dealing with the dropout problem. *Phi Delta Kappan, 72*(4), 280–285.

Galloway, C. (1976). *Silent language in the classroom.* Bloomington, IN: Phi Delta Kappa Educational Foundation, Fastback 86.

Gallup, A. M., & Elam, S. M. (1988). The annual Gallup Poll of the public attitude toward the public schools. *Phi Delta Kappan, 70*(1), 33–46.

Galluzzo, G. R., Arends, R. I., & Ashburn, E. A. (1988). *Trends in teacher education as reported on the institutional questionnaire.* Paper presented at the meeting of the American Educational Research Association, New Orleans, LA. (ERIC Document Reproduction Service No. ED 294 870).

Gee, T. C., & Rakow, S. J. (1987). Content reading specialists evaluate teaching practices. *Journal of Reading, 31*(3), 234–237.

Gerlach, V. S., & Ely, R. P. (1980). *Teaching and media a systematic approach* (2nd ed.). Englewood Cliffs, NJ: Prentice Hall.

Gibran, K. (1989). *The prophet.* New York: Alfred A. Knopf.

Gilliland, H., (Ed.). (1988). *Teaching the Native American.* Dubuque, IA: Kendall/Hunt.

Gilstrap, R. L., & Martin, W. R. (1975). *Current strategies for teachers: A resource for personalizing education.* Pacific Palisades, CA: Goodyear.

Glasser, W. (1965). *Reality therapy: A new approach to psychiatry.* New York: Harper & Row.

Glasser, W. (1977). 10 steps to good discipline. *Today's Education, 66,* 61–63.

Glasser, W. (1986). *Control therapy in the classroom.* New York: Harper & Row.

Glatthorn, A. (1987). Cooperative professional development: Peer-centered options for teacher growth. *Educational Leadership, 44,* 31–35.

Goldman, L. (1984). Warning: The Socratic method can be dangerous. *Educational Leadership, 42*(1), 57–62.

Good, T. L., & Brophy, J. E. (1987). *Looking in classrooms* (4th ed.). New York: Harper & Row.

Goodall, H. L., Jr. (1983). *Human communication.* Dubuque, IA: Wm. C. Brown.

Goodlad, J. I. (1984). *A place called school: Prospects for the future.* New York: McGraw-Hill.

Gordon, T. (1974). *Teacher effectiveness training.* New York: David McKay.

Green, J. (1987). *The next wave. A synopsis of recent reform reports. Teaching in America: The possible renaissance.* Education Commission of the States. (ERIC Document Reproduction Service No. ED 305 358).

Greif, E. B., & Ulman, K. J. (1982). The psychological impact of menarche on early adolescent females: A review of the literature. *Child Development, 53,* 1413–1430.

Guilford, J. P. (1956). The structure of intellect. *Psychological Bulletin, 53,* 267–293.

H

Hall, E. T. (1959). *The silent language.* Greenwich, CT: Fawcett.

Hallahan, D. P., & Kauffmann, J. M. (1991). *Exceptional children* (5th ed.). Englewood Cliffs, NJ: Prentice Hall.

Haller, E. P., Child, D. A., & Walberg, H. J. (1988). Can comprehension be taught? A quantitative synthesis of "Metacognitive" studies. *Educational Researcher, 17*(9), 5–8.

Harris, A. J., & Sipay, E. R. (1990). *How to increase your reading ability* (9th ed.). New York: Longman.

Harrow, A. J. (1972). *Taxonomy of the psychomotor domain: A guide for developing behavior objectives.* New York: David McKay.

Heiman, M., & Slomianko, J. (1987). *Thinking skills instruction: Concepts and techniques.* Washington, DC: National Education Association.

Heinich, R., Molenda, M., & Russell, J. D. (1989). *Instructional media and the new technologies of instruction* (3rd ed.). New York: Macmillan.

Hennings, D. G. (1975). *Mastering classroom communications—What interaction analysis tells the teacher.* Pacific Palisades, CA: Goodyear.

Henson, K. T. (1981). *Secondary teaching methods.* Lexington, MA: D. C. Heath.

Henson, K. T. (1988). *Methods and strategies for teaching in secondary and middle schools.* New York: Longman.

Herber, H. (1978). Levels of comprehension. In *Teaching reading in the content areas.* Englewood Cliffs, NJ: Prentice Hall.

Hirsch, E. D., Jr. (1987). *Cultural literacy: What every American needs to know.* Boston: Houghton Mifflin.

Holmes Group. (1986). *Tomorrow's teachers: A report of the Holmes Group.* East Lansing, MI: Author.

Hunter, M. (1980). *Teach more—faster.* El Segundo, CA: TIP Publications.

Hurt, H. T., Scott, M. D., & McCroskey, J. C. (1978). *Communications in the classroom.* Menlo Park, CA: Addison-Wesley.

J

Jacobs, H. H. (Ed.). (1989). *Interdisciplinary curriculum: Design and implementation.* Alexandria, VA: Association for Supervision and Curriculum Development.

Jacobson, D., Eggen, P., & Kauchak, D. (1989). *Methods for teaching: A skills approach* (3rd ed.). Columbus, OH: Merrill.

Jewett, A. E., & Mullan, M. R. (1977). Movement process categories in physical education in teaching-learning. In *Curriculum design: Purposes and processes in physical education teaching-learning.* Washington, DC: American Alliance for Health, Physical Education, and Recreation.

Johnson, D. W., & Johnson, R. T. (1985). The internal dynamics of cooperative learning groups. In R. Slavin, S. Sharan, S. Kagan, C. Webb, & R. Schmuck (Eds.), *Learning to cooperate, cooperating to learn.* New York: Plenum, 103–124.

Johnson, D. W., Johnson, R. T., Holubec, E. J., & Roy, P. (1984). *Circles of learning: Cooperation in the classroom.* Alexandria, VA: Association of Supervision and Curriculum Development.

Johnson, J. A., Collins, H. W., Dupuis, V. L., & Johansen, J. H. (1988). *Introduction to the foundations of American education.* Boston: Allyn & Bacon.

Johnson, N. (1983). What do you do if you can't tell the whole story? The development of summarization skills. In K. E. Nelson (Ed.), *Children's language* (Vol. 4). Hillsdale, NJ: Erlbaum.

Johnston, L., Bachan, J. G., & O'Malley, P. M. (1990). *Monitoring the future study: Drug abuse among high-school seniors.* (Conducted for the National Institute on Drug Abuse). Ann Arbor: University of Michigan's Institute for Social Research.

Jones, B. F. (1986). Quality and equality through cognitive instruction. *Educational Leadership, 43*(7), 4–11.

Jones, B. F., Palinscar, A. S., Ogle, D. M., & Carr, E. (Eds.). (1987). *Strategic teaching and learning: Cognitive instruction in the content areas.* Alexandria, VA: Association of Supervision and Curriculum Development.

Jones, B. F., Pierce, J., & Hunter, B. (1989). Teaching students to construct graphic representations. *Educational Leadership, 46*(4), 20–25.

Jones, F. (1979). The gentle art of classroom discipline. *National Elementary Principal, 58,* 26–32.

K

Kagan, S. (1990). The structural approach to cooperative learning. *Educational Leadership, 47*(4), 12–15.

Kemp, J. E., & Dayton, D. K. (1985). *Planning & producing instructional media* (5th ed.). New York: Harper & Row.

Kibler, R. J., Barker, L. L., & Miles, D. T. (1970). *Behavioral objectives and instruction.* Boston: Allyn & Bacon.

Kindsvatter, R., Wilen, W., & Ishler, M. (1988). *Dynamics of effective teaching.* New York: Longman.

Klein, J. W. (1979). Designing a mastery learning program. *Educational Leadership, 37*(2), 144–147.

Knirk, F. G., & Gustafson, K. L. (1986). *Instructional technology a systematic approach to education.* New York: Holt, Rinehart & Winston.

Kolesnik, W. B. (1978). *Motivation: Understanding and influencing human behavior.* Boston: Allyn & Bacon.

Kounin, J. S. (1970). *Discipline and group management in classrooms.* New York: Holt, Rinehart & Winston.

Krathwohl, D. R., Bloom, B. S., & Masia, B. B. (1964). *Taxonomy of educational objectives, handbook II: Affective domain.* New York: David McKay.

Kryspin, W. J., & Feldhuysen, J. F. (1974). *Writing behavioral objectives.* Minneapolis: Burgess.

L

Langer, J. A. (1981). From theory to practice: A prereading plan. *Journal of Reading, 25*(2), 152–156.

Lillie, D. L., Hunnun, W. H., & Stuck, G. B. (1989). *Computers and effective instruction.* New York: Longman.

Lipman, M. (1988). *Philosophy goes to school.* Philadelphia: Temple University Press.

Lipman, M. (1988). Critical thinking—What can it be? *Educational Leadership, 46*(1), 38–43.

Livson, N., & Peskin, H. (1980). Perspectives on adolescence from longitudinal research. In J. Adelson (Ed.), *Handbook of adolescent psychology.* New York: Wiley.

Locatis, C. N., & Atkinson, F. D. (1984). *Media and technology for education and training.* Columbus, OH: Merrill.

Lorber, M. A., & Pierce, W. D. (1983). *Objectives, methods, and evaluation for secondary teaching* (2nd ed.). Englewood Cliffs, NJ: Prentice Hall.

Lyman, H. B. (1991). *Test scores & what they mean* (5th ed.). Englewood Cliffs, NJ: Prentice Hall.

M

Mager, R. F. (1984). *Preparing instructional objectives* (2nd ed.). Belmont, CA: David S. Lake.

Manning, G., & Manning, M. (1979). Meet Mrs. Ingle: A teacher who individualizes instruction. *Middle School Journal, 10*(1), 4–5.

Marzano, R. J., Brandt, R. S., Hughes, C. S., Jones, B. F., Presseisen, B. Z., Rankin, S. C., & Suhor, C. (1988). *Dimensions of thinking: A framework for curriculum instruction.* Alexandria, VA: Association of Supervision and Curriculum Development.

Maslow, A. H. (1970). *Motivation and personality* (2nd ed.). New York: Harper & Row.

McDaniel, T. R. (1984). Developing the skills of humanistic discipline. *Educational Leadership, 41*(8), 71–74.

Metropolitan Life Insurance Company. (1990). *The Metropolitan Life survey of the American teacher 1990.* New York.

Meyer, C. A. (1992). What's the difference between authentic and performance assessment? *Educational Leadership, 49*(8), 39–40.

Meyers, C. (1986). *Teaching students to think critically.* San Francisco: Jossey-Bass.

Miller, P. W. (1986). *Nonverbal communications.* Washington, DC: National Educational Association.

Montagu, A. (1977). The skin, touch, and human development. *Somatics, 3,* 3–8.

Moore, K. D. (1989). *Classroom teaching skills: A primer.* New York: Random House.

Moore, K. D. (1991). *Classroom teaching skills* (2nd ed.). New York: McGraw-Hill.

Murphy, K. R., & Davidshofer, C. O. (1991). *Psychological testing* (2nd ed.). Englewood Cliffs, NJ: Prentice Hall.

N

Naisbitt, J., & Aburdine, P. (1990). *Megatrends 2000.* New York: William Morrow.

Naisbitt, J., & Aburdine, P. (1990, March 16). The race is on to ready students for globalization. *The New York Times.* 85.

National Center for Education Statistics. (1990). *Digest of statistics 1989.* Washington, DC: United States Department of Education.

National Center for Health Statistics. (1992, May). *Health United States 1991.* Hyattsville, MD: U. S. Department of Health and Human Services.

National Commission on Excellence in Education. (1983). *A Nation At Risk: The Imperative for Educational Reform.* Washington, DC: U. S. Government Printing Office.

National Education Association, Commission on the Reorganization of Secondary Education. (1918). *Cardinal principles of secondary education.* (U. S. Bureau of Education, Bulletin No. 35 [Washington, DC: GPO]).

National Governors' Association. (1990). *Educating America: State strategies for achieving the national education goals.* Report of the Task Force on Education.

National Science Board Commission on Precollege Education in Mathematics, Science and Technology. (1983). *Educating Americans for the 21st Century.* Washington, DC: National Science Foundation.

Nelson, J. L., Palonsky, S. B., & Carlson, K. (1990). *Critical issues in education.* New York: McGraw-Hill.

Nichols, R. G., & Stevens, L. A. (1957). *Are you listening?* New York: McGraw-Hill.

Nickerson, R. (1985). Understanding understanding. *American Journal of Education, 93,* 201–239.

O

O'Leary, K. D., & O'Leary, S. (Eds.). (1977). *Classroom management: The successful use of behavior modification* (2nd ed.). Elmsford, NY: Pergamon.

Orlich, D. C., Harder, R. J., Callahan, R. C., Kauchak, D. P., Pendergrass, R. A., Keough, A. J., & Gibson, H. (1990). *Teaching strategies* (3rd ed.). Lexington, MA.: D. C. Heath.

Ornstein, A. C. (1990). *Strategies for effective teaching.* New York: Harper & Row.

P

Palinscar, A. S., & Brown, A. L. (1984). Reciprocal teaching of comprehension-fostering and comprehension-monitoring activities. *Cognition and Instruction, 2,* 115–175.

Palmatier, R. (1973). A notetaking system for learning. *Journal of Reading, 18,* 215–218.

Palmer, S. E. (1983, April 13). The art of lecturing: A few simple ideas can help teachers improve their skills. *The Chronicle of Higher Education,* 19–20.

Parkay, F. W., & Stanford, B. H. (1992). *Becoming a teacher* (2nd ed.). Boston: Allyn & Bacon.

Pearson, P. D. (1984). *Handbook of reading research.* New York: Longman.

Pearson, P. D., & Johnson, D. D. (1978). *Teaching reading comprehension.* New York: Holt, Rinehart & Winston.

Perkins, D. N. (1986). Thinking frames. *Educational Leadership, 43,* 4–10.

Perkins, D. N., Lochhead, J., & Bishop, J. C. (Eds.). (1987). *Thinking: The second international conference.* Hillsdale, NJ: Erlbaum.

Peterson, A., Richards, M., & Boxer, A. (1983). Puberty: Its measurement and its meaning. *Journal of Early Adolescence, 3,* 47–62.

Piaget, J. (1967). *Six psychological studies.* New York: Random House.

Pipho, C. (1986). States move reform closer to reality. *Phi Delta Kappan, 68*(4), K1–K8.

Presbie, R. J., & Brown, P. L. (1976). *Behavior modification.* Washington, DC: National Education Association.

Q

Quina, J., & Furlette, M. C. (1989). *Effective secondary teaching: Going beyond the bell curve.* New York: Harper & Row.

R

Raphael, T. E. (1984). Teaching learners about sources of information for answering comprehension questions. *Journal of Reading, 27,* 303–311.

Raths, L. E., Wassermann, S., Jonas, A., & Rothstein, A. (1986). *Teaching for thinking.* New York: Teachers College Press.

Raygor, A. L. (1977). The Raygor readability estimate: A quick and easy way to determine difficulty. In P. D. Pearson & J. Hansen (Eds.), *Reading, theory, research and practice.* Clemson, SC: National Reading Conference, 258–263.

Readence, J. E., Bean, T. W., & Baldwin, R. S. (1985). *Content area reading: An integrated approach* (2nd ed.). Dubuque, IA: Kendall/Hunt.

Readence, J. E., Bean, T. W., & Baldwin, R. S. (1989). *Content area reading: An integrated approach* (3rd ed.). Dubuque, IA: Kendall/Hunt.

Reed, A. J. S., & Bergemann, V. E. (1992). *In the classroom: An introduction to education.* Sluice Dock, Guilford, CT: The Dushkin Publishing Group, Inc.

Reid, E. R. (1980). Another approach to mastery learning. *Educational Leadership, 38*(2), 170–172.

Resnick, L. B. (1987). *Education and learning to think.* Washington, DC: National Academic Press.

Rich, J. M. (1992). *Foundations of Education.* New York: Macmillan.

Richardson, J. S., & Morgan, R. F. (1990). *Reading to learn in the content areas.* Belmont, CA: Wadsworth.

Rieck, B. J. (1977). How content teachers telegraph messages against reading. *Journal of Reading, 20,* 646–648.

Rowe, M. B. (1974a). Wait time and rewards as instructional variables, their influence on language, logic, and fate control: Part one, wait time. *Journal of Research in Science Teaching, 11*(2), 81–94.

Rowe, M. B. (1974b). Relation of wait time and rewards to the development of language, logic, and fate control: Part two, rewards. *Journal of Research in Science Teaching, 11*(4), 291– 308.

Rowe, M. B. (1978). Wait, wait, wait. *School Science and Mathematics, 78,* 207–216.

Rumelhart, D., & Ortony, A. (1977). The representation of knowledge in memory. In R. Anderson, R. Spurs, & W. Montague (Eds.), *Schooling and the acquisition of knowledge.* Hillsdale, NJ: Erlbaum.

S

Sadker, M. P., & Sadker, D. M. (1991). *Teachers, schools, and society* (2nd ed.). New York: McGraw-Hill.

Sadler, W. A., & Whimbey, A. (1985). A holistic approach to improving thinking skills. *Phi Delta Kappan, 67*(3), 199–203.

Sanders, N. M. (1966). *Classroom questions: What kinds?* New York: Harper & Row.

Sathrè, F. S., Olson, R. W., & Whitney, C. I. (1977). *Let's talk.* Glenview, IL: Scott, Foresman.

Sax, G. (1980). *Principles of educational and psychological measurement and evaluation* (2nd ed.). Belmont, CA: Wadsworth.

Schmuck, R. A., & Schmuck, P. A. (1988). *Group processes in the classroom* (5th ed.). Dubuque, IA: Wm. C. Brown.

Sears, J. T., Marshall, J. D., & Otis-Wilborn, A. (1988). *Teacher education policies and programs: Implementing reform proposals of the 1980s.* Research Triangle Park, NC. (ERIC Document Reproduction Service No. ED 296 985).

Self, J. (1987, Spring). The picture of writing to learn. In *Plain talk about learning and writing across the curriculum.* Virginia Department of Education.

Sex and schools. (1986, November 24). *Time,* 54–63.

Shostak, R. (1982). Lesson presentation skills. In J. M. Cooper, (Ed.), *Classroom teaching skills: A handbook* (2nd ed.). Lexington, MA: D. C. Heath.

Shulman, L. (1987). Knowledge and teaching: Foundations of the new reform. *Harvard Educational Review, 57,* 1–22.

Sikula, J. (1987). Commentary on reform: Implications for the education profession. *Teacher Education Quarterly, 14*(1), 52–59.

Silvernail, D. L. (1979). *Teaching styles as related to student achievement.* Washington, DC: National Education Association.

Simmons, R., Blythe, D., & McKinney, L. (1983). The social and psychological effects of puberty on white females. In J. Brooks-Gunn & A. Peterson (Eds.), *Girls at puberty: Biological and psychological perspectives.* New York: Plenum.

Simonson, M. R., & Volker, R. P. (1984). *Media planning and production.* Columbus, OH: Merrill.

Sizer, T. R. (1984). *Horace's compromise: The dilemma of the American high school.* Boston: Houghton Mifflin.

Skinner, B. F. (1968). *The technology of teaching.* New York: Appleton-Century-Crofts.

Skinner, B. F. (1971). *Beyond freedom and dignity.* New York: Alfred A. Knopf.

Snider, J., & Osgood, C. E. (Eds.). (1969). *Semantic differential technique: A sourcebook.* Chicago: Aldine.

Sokolove, S., Sadker, D., & Sadker, M. (1986). Interpersonal communication skills. In J. M. Cooper (Ed.), *Classroom teaching skills* (3rd ed.). Lexington, MA: D. C. Heath.

Spring, J. (1986). *The American school, 1642–1985.* New York: Longman.

Squires, D. A., Huitt, W. G., & Segars, J. K. (1981). Improving classrooms and schools: What's important. *Educational Leadership, 39*(3), 174–179.

Sternberg, R. J. (1987). A triarchic model for teaching intelligence. In D. N. Perkins, J. Lochhead, & J. C. Bishop (Eds.), *Thinking: The second international conference.* Hillsdale, NJ: Erlbaum.

Stewart, D. K. (1987). Materials on reform of teacher education in the ERIC database. *Journal of Teacher Education, 38*(3), 31–33.

Suchman, J. R. (1961). Inquiry training: Building skills for autonomous discovery. *Merrill-Palmer Quarterly of Behavior and Development, 7,* 147–169.

Suchman, J. R. (1966). *Inquiry development program in physical science.* Chicago: Science Research Associates.

T

Taba, H. (1962). *Curriculum development.* New York: Harcourt, Brace & World.

Tanner, D., & Tanner, L. N. (1980). *Curriculum development* (2nd ed.). New York: Macmillan.

TenBrink, T. D. (1986). Evaluation. In J. M. Cooper (Ed.), *Classroom teaching skills* (3rd ed.). Lexington, MA: D. C. Heath.

Torrance, E. P. (1983). *Creativity in the classroom.* Washington, DC: Library of Congress.

Towers, R. (1987). *How schools can help combat student drug and alcohol abuse.* Washington, DC: National Education Association.

Turnbull III, H. R. (1990). *Free appropriate public education* (3rd ed.). Denver, CO: Love publishing.

U

U. S. Department of Education. (1990, July). *National goals for education.* Washington, DC: Department of Education.

V

Vacca, R. T., & Vacca, J. L. (1986). *Content area reading* (2nd ed.). Boston: Little, Brown.

Vacca, R. T., & Vacca, J. L. (1989). *Content area reading* (3rd ed.). Glenview, IL: Scott, Foresman.

Voreacas, D. (1987, December 30). Tougher high school studies urged. *Los Angeles Times,* Part I, 4.

W

Walker, J. E., & Shea, T. M. (1980). *Behavior modification* (2nd ed.). St. Louis: Mosby.

Walsh, D., & Paul, R. (1988). *The goal of critical thinking: From educational ideal to educational reality.* Washington, DC: American Federation of Teachers.

Whimbey, A., & Whimbey, L. S. (1976). *Intelligence can be taught*. New York: Bantam Books.

Wilen, W. W. (1982). *Questioning skills for teachers*. Washington, DC: National Education Association.

Wiles, J., & Bondi, J. (1993). *The essential middle school*. New York: Macmillan.

Winograd, P., & Paris, S. G. (1988/1989). A cognitive and motivational agenda for reading instruction. *Educational Leadership, 46*(4), 30–36.

Wittich, W. A., & Schuller, C. F. (1973). *Instructional technology its nature and use* (5th ed.). New York: Harper & Row.

Wittich, W. A., & Schuller, C. F. (1979). *Instructional technology its nature and use* (6th ed.). New York: Harper & Row.

Wittrock, M. (1986). Students' thought processes. In M. Wittrock (Ed.), *Handbook of Research on Teaching* (3rd ed.). New York: Macmillan.

Wlodkowski, R. J. (1982). *Motivation*. National Education Association.

Wolvin, A. D., & Cookley, C. G. (1979). *Listening instruction*. Urbana, IL: ERIC Clearinghouse Reading and Communications Skills.

Woolfolk, A. E. (1987). *Educational psychology for teachers*. Englewood Cliffs, NJ: Prentice Hall.

Worsham, A. M., & Stockton, A. J. (1986). *A model for teaching thinking skills: The inclusion process*. Bloomington, IN: Phi Delta Kappa Educational Foundation.

Wulf, K. M., & Schane, B. (1984). *Curriculum design*. Glenview, IL: Scott, Foresman.

INDEX